The Work of Managers

Towards a Practice Theory of Management

Edited by
STEFAN TENGBLAD

OXFORD
UNIVERSITY PRESS

OXFORD
UNIVERSITY PRESS

Great Clarendon Street, Oxford OX2 6DP

Oxford University Press is a department of the University of Oxford.
It furthers the University's objective of excellence in research, scholarship,
and education by publishing worldwide in

Oxford New York

Auckland Cape Town Dar es Salaam Hong Kong Karachi
Kuala Lumpur Madrid Melbourne Mexico City Nairobi
New Delhi Shanghai Taipei Toronto

With offices in

Argentina Austria Brazil Chile Czech Republic France Greece
Guatemala Hungary Italy Japan Poland Portugal Singapore
South Korea Switzerland Thailand Turkey Ukraine Vietnam

Oxford is a registered trade mark of Oxford University Press
in the UK and in certain other countries

Published in the United States
by Oxford University Press Inc., New York

© Oxford University Press 2012

British Library Cataloguing in Publication Data

Data available

Library of Congress Cataloging in Publication Data

Data available

Typeset by SPI Publisher Services, Pondicherry, India
Printed in Great Britain
on acid-free paper by
MPG Books Group, Bodmin and King's Lynn

ISBN 978-0-19-963972-4

1 3 5 7 9 10 8 6 4 2

THE WORK OF MANAGERS

List of Figures

List of Tables

Notes on the Contributors

Johan Alvehus is University Lecturer at the Institution for Service Management, Lund University, Sweden. His research focuses on the management and organization of knowledge-intensive work, with a particular interest in professional work. His research is inspired by critical theory and post-structuralism.

Mats Alvesson works at the Department of Business Administration, Lund University, Sweden. His research addresses qualitative methodology, identity, critical management studies, and organizational culture. His most recent books are *Interpreting Interviews* (Sage, 2011) and *Metaphors We Lead By* (Routledge, 2011, with Andre Spicer).

Rebecka Arman, Ph.D., is a researcher/instructor of management and organization at the University of Gothenburg, Sweden. Her research focuses on managerial work activities, health care management, quantification practices, restructuring in corporations, intermediaries working to support restructuring, and ideologies and institutions in science-based practices. Her doctoral dissertation, *Fragmentation and Power* (University of Gothenburg, 2010), is a study of first- and second-line managers in health care.

Håvard Åsvoll has a postdoctoral position at the Norwegian University of Science and Technology, Department of Industrial Economics and Technology Management. His research focuses on the philosophy of management and qualitative research practice. He has published several articles on tacit knowledge in entrepreneurial management and professional practice.

Rob B. Briner is Professor of Organizational Psychology at the School of Management, University of Bath. His research focuses on the reciprocal links between work and various aspects of well-being such as moods and emotions. His other interests include the psychological contract at work, absence, ethnicity, work–nonwork relationships, and contextual performance. He is also involved with a number of evidence-based management initiatives.

Ethel Brundin is Professor in Entrepreneurship and Business Development at the Department of Entrepreneurship, Strategy, Organization and Leadership at Jönköping International Business School, Sweden. She is affiliated with the inter-disciplinary Center for Family Enterprise and Ownership. She is a visiting professor at the University of the Western Cape, South Africa, and a member of the European Leadership Council of STEP (Successful Transgenerational Entrepreneurship Practices). Her research interest is primarily micro processes in family businesses with a focus on the emotive side of entrepreneurship and strategic leadership. She has published in international journals and is the author of several book chapters.

Anna Cregård has a Ph.D. in public administration and is a lecturer at the School of Public Administration, the University of Gothenburg, Sweden. She has written several books and reports on leadership and organizational issues in the public sector, especially in municipal services and in health care. She also focuses on unconventional organizations/groups, for example, convents and religious communities.

Lotta Dellve is Associate Professor of Occupational Medicine at the University of Gothenburg, Sweden. Her research focuses on psychosocial working conditions, leadership and organizational conditions, and the importance of stress exposures and health outcomes for employees and managers. She has published more than thirty articles in international scientific journals and several book chapters on these topics.

Lars Engwall is Senior Professor of Business Administration at Uppsala University, Sweden. His research concerns bank management, the media, and universities as well as the production and diffusion of knowledge. He has published extensively in the management area. His most recent publications are *The University in the Market* (ed. with Denis Weaire, Portland Press, 2008) and *Reconfiguring Knowledge Production* (ed. with Richard Whitley and Jochen Gläser, Oxford University Press, 2010).

Henrik Florén has a Ph.D. from Chalmers University of Technology, Sweden, and is Assistant Professor of Industrial Management at Halmstad University, Sweden. His research interests mainly concern organizational change and renewal. This interest is currently expressed in research on management of the fuzzy front end, management of eco-innovations, and managerial behaviour in fast-growing firms. He has published in journals such as *IEEE Transactions on Engineering Management*, *International Journal of Entrepreneurial Behaviour & Research, Leadership and Organizational Development Journal*, and *Journal of Workplace Learning*.

Einar Häckner is Professor Emeritus of Business Administration at the Luleå University of Technology in Sweden and Visiting Professor at the Mid Sweden University. His research covers a broad range of business and management topics including accounting, management control, business strategy, information use, business performance, auditing, banking, and finance. He has many years of experience acquired in his former positions as a CFO, CEO, and Board Director in Swedish industry.

Ingalill Holmberg is Professor of Business Administration and Director of the Center for Advanced Studies in Leadership at the Stockholm School of Economics, Sweden. Her research covers the interface between leadership, identity, organizing, and managerial work, with a focus on the interplay between conceptions of leadership and management as an everyday practice. She is Associate Editor of *Leadership* and an editorial board member of the *International Journal of Action Research* and the *Scandinavian Journal of Management*. She is an advisor to public research organizations and the Swedish government on issues such as innovation and growth.

Leif Jonsson is Associate Professor at Linköping University, Sweden, where he is a researcher at the East Sweden Municipality Research Centre and the HELIX VINN Excellence Centre. His research interests are organizing, especially organizing municipality management.

Sten Jönsson is Professor Emeritus in Business Administration (with a focus on Scandinavian Management) at the School of Business, Economics and Law at the University of Gothenburg, Sweden. His research deals with organizational crises, local operational management, regulation of good practices in accounting, and integration of acquisitions across borders. He is currently leading a project on bank management in Sweden.

Tina L. Juillerat, Ph.D., MBA, is a senior managing consultant in the IBM Global Business Services Strategy and Transformation practice. Her research examines innovation, decision-making, organization and job design, including managerial work in complex and dynamic environments, and evidence-based management. She has published in the *Journal of Organizational Behavior* and the APA *Handbook of Industrial and Organizational Psychology*.

Gary Kokk is a research fellow at the Gothenburg Research Institute, School of Business, Economics and Law at the University of Gothenburg, Sweden. His research focuses on organization studies, including post-acquisition integration processes and the work practices of industry executives. He is currently studying the changing occupational practices of engineers and technicians in the Swedish production industry.

Carin Eriksson Lindvall is Associate Professor in the Department of Business Studies and Director of Leadership and Organizational Development at Uppsala University, Sweden. Her main research interests are leadership, change, and group development. She has published articles on emotions in change processes and leadership in knowledge-based firms. Her book, *Akademiskt ledarskap* (Almqvist & Wiksell International, 1997), deals with leadership in universities and the particular demands made on the department heads.

Leif Melin is Professor of Strategy and Organisation and founding Director of CeFEO, the Center for Family Enterprise and Ownership, at the Jönköping International Business School, Sweden. His research interests are strategizing and strategy-as-practice, especially ownership and leadership. He has published in international journals, including *Strategic Management Journal, Journal of Management Studies*, and *Strategic Organization*. He is co-author of *Strategy as Practice: Research Directions and Resources* (Cambridge University Press, 2007).

Henry Mintzberg is the Cleghorn Professor of Management Studies at the Desaultel Faculty of Management at McGill University in Montreal, Canada. He is a founding partner of CoachingOurselves.com. He is concerned with writing and research, especially about managerial work, strategy formation, and forms of organizing. He has collaborated with colleagues from Canada, England, France, India, Japan, China, and Brazil in developing new approaches to management education and development. He is the author of numerous books, including *Managers not MBAs* (Berrett-Koehler Publishers, Inc., 2004), *Tracking Strategies* (Oxford University Press, 2007), and *Managing* (Berrett-Koehler Publishers, Inc., 2009).

Frederick P. Morgeson is Professor of Management and the Valade Research Scholar at the Eli Broad College of Business at Michigan State University. He teaches, consults, and does research across the full spectrum of Human Resource

Management and Organizational Behavior topics, including leadership, work design, and personnel selection. His research has been published in numerous journal articles, book chapters, and books. He is editor of *Personnel Psychology*.

Anders Nilsson is Associate Professor of Accounting and Control at Luleå University of Technology, Sweden, and a Visiting Scholar and Member of CER (the Center for Research on Economic Relations) at Mid Sweden University. His research focuses on accounting and control in a broad sense. He has studied small- and medium-sized enterprises, large manufacturing firms, and firms in banking and auditing.

Michael G. Pratt is a Winston Center fellow and Professor of Organizational Studies and, by courtesy, Psychology, at Boston College. His research centres on how individuals relate to and connect with their work, occupations, professions, and organizations. His work has appeared in various outlets, including *Academy of Management Annual Review*, *Academy of Management Journal*, *Academy of Management Review*, *Organizational Research Methods*, and *Administrative Science Quarterly* (with Anat Rafaeli), and he is co-editor of *Artifacts and Organizations: Beyond Mere Symbolism* (Lawrence Erlbaum Associates, Inc., 2006).

Airi Rovio-Johansson is Professor at Gothenburg Research Institute, School of Business, Economics and Law at the University of Gothenburg, Sweden. Her main research topics are quality management, assurance and quality assessment of teaching, students' learning outcomes in higher education, organizational change processes, and discourse analysis. She has published articles in international journals and has contributed to several books on those topics. She is a co-author of *Essays in Supportive Peer Review* (Nova Science Publishers, 2008).

Rolf Solli is Professor of Management Studies at the University of Gothenburg, Sweden. His research focuses on processes of management, leadership, and accounting in public sector organizations. He has published more than fifteen books, including *Organizing Metropolitan Space and Discourse* (Liber, 2001, with Barbara Czarniawska) and *Constructing Leadership: Reflections on Film Heroes as Leaders* (Santérus Academic Press, 2006, with Björn Rombach).

Alexander Styhre is Professor and Chair of Organization Theory and Management, Department of Business Administration, School of Business, Economics and Law, University of Gothenburg, Sweden. His research interests include knowledge-intensive organizations and innovation work. His work has appeared in *Journal of Management Studies*, *Organization Studies*, *Human Relations*, *Organization*, and elsewhere. His most recent books are *Visual Culture in Organizations* (Routledge, 2010) and *Venturing into the Bioeconomy* (Palgrave, 2011, with Mats Sundgren).

Stefan Sveningsson is Associate Professor of Business Administration at the School of Economics and Management, Lund University, Sweden. His research interests include leadership, identity, and strategic and organizational change. He has published articles on leadership in several international journals including *Human Relations*, *Leadership Quarterly*, *Organization Studies*, *International Studies of Management*, and *Organization and Leadership*. His recent books include *Changing Organizational Culture* (Routledge, 2008, with M. Alvesson) and *Leadership* (Liber, 2010, with M. Alvesson).

Joakim Tell is Assistant Professor and Director of Studies in the Master's Programme, Innovation Management and Business Development, at the School of Business and Engineering at Halmstad University, Sweden. His research interests concern the development of different action technologies, such as learning networks, managerial behaviour in small enterprises, business simulations, and other leadership and learning issues.

Stefan Tengblad is Professor in Business Administration at the University of Skövde, Sweden. He has written several books and articles about leadership, managerial work, and employee relations. He has published in such journals as *Journal of Management Studies, Organization Studies, Journal of Business Ethics, Scandinavian Journal of Management*, and *Qualitative Research in Accounting & Management*.

Ellinor Tengelin is a doctoral student at the University of Gothenburg, Sweden, and a member of the research group Leadership and Health in the Department of Occupational and Environmental Medicine. Her research interests are health care managers' stress-related work approaches.

Mats Tyrstrup is Assistant Professor at the Center for Advanced Studies in Leadership at the Stockholm School of Economics, Sweden. His research interests are top and middle manager leadership, in particular, managerial leadership in professional services and inter-organizational collaboration. He is the author of *Sovereigns of Time – A Scandinavian View of Executive Work, Time and Leadership* (Studentlitteratur, 2005) and *On the Brink of Failure – The Art of Impromptu Action in Everyday Leadership* (Studentlitteratur, 2006).

Ola Edvin Vie is Associate Professor in Organization and Management, at the Department of Industrial Ecomomics and Technology Management, at the Norwegian University of Science and Technology (NTNU). His research interests are managerial work, leadership, and knowledge integration, which are themes pursued within the Centre for Sustainable Energy Studies (CenSES) at NTNU.

Mats Westerberg is Assistant Professor in Entrepreneurship at Luleå University of Technology, Sweden. His research interests mainly revolve around the role of CEO in SMEs and how networking and collaboration among SMEs is linked to entrepreneurial behaviour and performance. Other recent research interests include the role of entrepreneurship in the school system and effects of cooperation in the construction industry.

Ewa Wikström is Associate Professor in Business Administration at the School of Business, Economics and Law, Gothenburg University, Sweden. Her research focuses on managerial work, leadership, and collaboration in the public sector and in the health care organization. Her research interests include the intersections of organizing and communication. She has published in international journals including *International Journal of Public Sector Management, Journal of Health Organisation and Management*, and *Qualitative Research in Organizations and Management*.

Part I

Framework

1

Overcoming the rationalistic fallacy in management research

Stefan Tengblad

According to the economics professor Deirdre McCloskey (1998), only two important European novels since 1848 have portrayed businesspersons sympathetically. One is Thomas Mann's *Buddenbrooks* (1902) and the other is David Lodge's *Nice Work* (1988). Lodge's novel is especially interesting here since it concerns the adventures of a female university lecturer (Robyn Penrose) as she shadows the managing director (Victor Wilcox) of a struggling foundry factory. By having a main character use the shadowing technique, Lodge presents the reader with a close-up look at managerial work and the people who manage.

Lodge's fictional description of the managing director in question is very realistic; it is, sadly, a description many well-known management and leadership scholars ought to envy. Unfortunately, much of the research in management and leadership is not primarily driven by the wish to develop such empirically grounded understandings but rather to present theoretical assumptions and methodological preferences. Most such management theories are developed in order to improve management practices rationalistically.

At the beginning of the novel, Lodge gives us an insight into the work and life of the manager in his description of Wilcox's unsuccessful attempt to get some sleep before his alarm clock rings:

> Worries streak towards him like an enemy spaceship in one of Gary's [his son] video games. He flinches, dodges, zaps them with instant solutions, but the assault is endless: the Avco account, the Rawlinson account, the price of pig-iron, the value of the pound, the competition from Foundrax, the incompetence of his Marketing Director, the persistent breakdowns of the core blowers, the vandalizing of the toilets in the fettling shop, the pressure from his divisional boss, the last month's account, the quarterly forecast, the annual review.... (Lodge, 1988: 3)

In this description of a sleepless managerial night, Lodge gives us clues as to why the systematic and classical approaches to management are better in theory than in practice. Managerial work means dealing with many complex and interrelated issues at the same time. And much of the manager's work requires dealing with human relationships and emotions. In the novel, Wilcox is often frustrated, but he remains controlled and polite, even when he has to work with people he dislikes.

Nice Work splendidly describes the communication difficulties between a scientist who believes in absolute values and abstract thinking and a seasoned manager who has learned from experience that there are many more problems and ideas to consider in managing than scientific reasoning can grasp. The novel's message is that the activity of analytical contemplation may not be particularly useful in the work of managing, which may be compared to juggling hot potatoes.

Nevertheless, the common expectation among scientists, the public, and even managers themselves is that managers should be enlightened, deliberate, rational, and always in full control. Theoretically, the general belief is that the muddling-through manager, who deals sequentially and reactively with problems as they arise, suffers from a professional pathology. However, for at least sixty years, this idealized image of good management as an applied science has sharply conflicted with the gloomy reality of actual management practice. As the following comments indicate, the real work of managers has never been the centre of attention in management research and education:

> The work of managing directors in large firms] is so varied and so hard to grasp. It is also different from many other kinds of intellectual work in that it is more a practical art than an applied science. (Carlson, 1951: 109)

> Only managers who can deal with uncertainty, with ambiguity, and with battles that are never won but only fought well can hope to succeed. (Sayles, 1964: 259)

> ... the manager, particularly at senior levels, is overburdened with work. With the increasing complexity of modern organizations and their problems, he is destined to become more so. He is driven to brevity, fragmentation, and superficiality in his tasks, yet he cannot easily delegate them because of the nature of his information. (Mintzberg, 1973: 173)

> While the ideal functions of administrative systems are clear, the work itself is carried out in an environment that is complex, dynamic, and ambiguous. There are no procedures, no technologies, and no blueprints that ensure success; nor are there clear and certain connections between the actions managers take and their effects. Managers make decisions and provide guidance to organizations in a world that permits only partial understanding, where even learning by doing is limited because of ambiguous feedback. (Hannaway, 1989: 2)

> ... Managerial competence or effectiveness is indeed a subtle, multi-faceted and context-bound thing. It does not just involve skills and attitudes, but encompasses knowledge – even if that knowledge is 'stored' in the form of intuitions and is manifested in what Donald Schön calls reflection-in-action, whereby managers draw on repertoires of cumulatively developed organisational knowledge, which they transform in the context of some unique situation. (Watson, 1994/2001: 222–3)

Despite such observations, which over the years have described a quite different reality of managerial work than the management literature presents, the dream of sequential and deliberate managerial control flourishes in management books, scientific research, and management education. The authors of the chapters in this book do not necessarily reject the idea that managerial work should be well-ordered and controllable, but they recognize the limitations of such a prescription. They suggest an alternative approach to managerial work that is better adapted to the complex and changing environments that today's managers typically face. In this book, with our new contributions and our references to previous studies (some disturbingly neglected), we refer to this approach as the practice perspective on management. According to this perspective, the most real and important aspects of management are how management is performed in everyday work practices by countless numbers of managers all over the world, working in various kinds of companies and organizations.

The practice perspective applied in this book basically sees management as work practices conducted by managers in their everyday work (cf. Barley and Kunda 2001). This perspective uses the behaviour and activities of successful, experienced, and skilful managers as the primary data for theorizing about good management. Managerial work is seen as a craft that requires experience, skill, and artistry. Instead of evaluating management techniques according to their internal logic and systematic qualities, the practice perspective is interested in how widespread certain management practices are, how they are performed in everyday work, and what the outcomes are. Viewing management as work practices often shifts the attention from formal management techniques to rules-of-thumb and behavioural patterns.

Management theorists have almost never considered management a craft that requires artistic managerial traits. Instead, they have defined, simplified, and routinized the work practices of managers (in the spirit of Frederick Taylor and the scientific management tradition) into subsets of activities and functions. Many researchers have divided managerial work into small, separate tasks (as in manual industrial work) and have created models using sequential charts and decision trees. The first obvious problem with this approach is that the resulting work instructions are complex, detailed, and contradictory. A second problem is that such models are seldom useful and often are not even useable because of the many unanticipated events that usually occur. To exemplify the point about the poor correspondence between management theory and practice, I quote a frustrated manager from the book *Real Managers*:

> We all went through the B-schools when we were young and the professors had all the answers on the blackboards, computer printouts, and reading assignments. Everything was so clean and precise. The problems in the accounting and quantitative courses always had logical answers. Even the principles of management and policy courses had structure and form, citing the five functions a manager performs or the three steps of strategic planning. The same is true of the management development programs I have attended over the years. The trainer has all the answers to my problems – one, two, three. But I'm here to tell you it really isn't like that. My day consists of running from one meeting to the next, fielding questions from my internal staff and outsiders, trying to respond to telephone messages, trying to smooth over an argument between a couple of people, and keeping my ever higher in-basket from toppling down on top of me. In fact, I feel guilty that I'm not doing the things that the management educators, trainers, and the things I read say I *should* be doing. When I come out of one of these sessions, or after reading the latest management treatise, I'm eager to do it. Then the first phone call from an irate customer, or a new project with a rush deadline, falls on me, and I'm back in the same old rut. (Luthans et al., 1988: 27–8)

Based on the findings in this book and other studies, my claim is that the limitations of rational-normative models of management are generally valid. Also, in places where one expects to find strongholds of rational-normative management (e.g. project management in industrial settings), work practices are very different from how they are typically described (i.e. with an emphasis on formal planning, clear goals, and sophisticated step-by-step control techniques). Kaulio (2008: 344), who has investigated project management work using the critical incident method, describes project managers' constant and urgent need to focus on human issues, to reshape their projects in terms of emerging circumstances, to defend and promote their projects in a politicized milieu, as well as to survive in a very demanding work environment:

> Project leaders, living their lives in multi-project organisations, hold similarities with a middle-mafia boss who, not only executes specific tasks (i.e. projects), but who also must ensure the group's cohesion and stability while protecting it and its territory (i.e. scope and resources) from competing gangs. The leadership challenge is: to stay alive (cases of burnout were identified in the empirical part of the study); to please stakeholders and co-suppliers (i.e. clients, steering committees, and consultants); to keep motivation high in the group; and, to initiate action.

It is time to look at managers, such as those above, as competent practitioners. We should see their adaptive and responsive behaviour in coping daily with the intense demands, complexity, and uncertainty of managing as functional rather than dysfunctional.

THE PURPOSE OF THE BOOK

Originally, the main purpose of this book was to disseminate the results from a rather large number of studies of managerial work behaviour conducted in Sweden and Norway in the last decade. Many of these studies followed in the spirit of the Swedish Professor, Sune Carlson, who published the first systematic study of administrative managers in his book, *Executive Behaviour* (see Chapters 2 and 12). The launching of the book project coincided with the centennial anniversary of Sune Carlson's birth. Two symposia were held in 2009 in his memory: one in Uppsala, Sweden, where Sune Carlson was a professor and lived the second half of his life, and one in Chicago, at the Academy of Management meeting (see Chapter 17).

A second purpose was to commemorate the sixtieth anniversary of *Executive Behaviour*, which was published in 1951. Carlson viewed managerial work as an art that would gradually transform into an applied science. Sixty years later, we still claim that managerial work is more an art than an applied science. While we agree that the study of management lends itself to scientific analysis, good managerial practices also develop rather independently from management science. Although new concepts are continuously implemented in managerial practices, with experience such concepts may be interpreted differently that originally intended or may even be rejected altogether.

As we worked on the book, its purpose broadened. The book remains a tribute to Sune Carlson and his work, but now it has additional goals. Our first new goal is to provide rich and contemporary descriptions of managerial work in different settings. Second, we hope to establish a theoretical foundation about managerial work where actual work practices are recognized as privileged sources for obtaining scientific knowledge about managing. Our intention is not to criticize managers for having underdeveloped management practices that do not fit the theoretical models, but rather to criticize such models for not being sufficiently based in effective managerial practices. If scientific management knowledge is really superior to knowledge gained in practical managerial work, why don't management professors lead our most successful companies and organizations? And why do university professors in management so seldom and/or so unsuccessfully use the models they were taught when they are given managerial responsibilities?

We acknowledge that students of management may be inclined towards analytical and conceptual models – their creation and analysis. Knowledge of such models may give researchers, as well as managers, the illusion that they have command of the latest management methods and the fate of the organization. Such models can also provide a valuable conceptual understanding of management and identify the areas that current management practices do not pay sufficient attention to. However, the good manager also needs improvisational skills and stress-coping tools that are not acquired in classrooms or by reading textbooks. These are skills and tools the analytical and conceptual models cannot provide.

In short, there is an urgent need to establish a strong research tradition based in the realities of managerial work – for example, the realities of information and work overload, complexity, uncertainty, performance pressure, surprises, unintended consequences, and irreconcilable expectations, to say nothing of the emotional demands of work. Such a research direction is a significant departure from mainstream management theory that we look at next.

THE THEORETICAL–ANALYTICAL APPROACH IN MANAGEMENT THEORY

It is not possible here to detail all the reasons for the popularity of the theoretical–analytical approach in management theory. In the following sections, we explain three important reasons.

Management as a low-prestige occupation

Nowadays, well-paid managers (including highly overpaid managers) have a certain social prestige. A huge industry even exists just to train managers and managerial candidates, not only in how to manage but also in how to play the role of the manager. It may be hard to understand, or even remember, that this situation was very different when management was first studied scientifically in the first half of the twentieth century. In that era, salaried managers were considered stewards or even helpers for the owners/entrepreneurs who had positions with high social prestige. Industrial managers typically had fairly humble origins and were often self-made – like Victor Wilcox in *Nice Work*. Industrial management was a very curious career choice for a person from the upper and wealthier classes. Thus, when university scholars first began to study industrial managers their research work was considered 'studying down'. (Sune Carlson's study of the Swedish business elite was an exception.) To avoid the stigma of studying a low-prestige occupation, management theorists applied scientific reasoning in an effort to raise the academic status of their research.

Theorists' need for theoretical inspiration from science

Unlike other professions, such as in medicine, law, and government, originally there were no professional training institutions for managers that could bridge the gap between the professional and the scientific/education communities. Thus there was no way that good professional practice could influence these other communities. Instead of studying skilled professionals, management scientists sought respectability for their own emerging discipline in academia by applying a deductive methodology based on applied mathematics, modelling, computer science, and analytical philosophy. The logic of Newtonian physics influenced the development of theories about market equilibrium, international trade, and production. The reality is that very few of these methods and theories are used in management practice. The theories on, and experience with, complexity, paradoxes, and change may offer a more realistic understanding of what managers really do.

In looking at the 'messiness' of actual management practices, many management theorists have concluded that radical reforms, using systematic management techniques, are needed. The rapid expansion of the computer sciences, beginning in the 1960s, has led to the hope that the retrieval, storage, and analysis of large quantities of information will be useful in creating a new logic of managerial work. To date, this hope is unfulfilled.

The publication industry's fragmentation and orthodoxy

The most extreme versions of formalized management techniques, such as long-range planning, systematic decision-making, and mathematic modelling, lost popularity in the 1970s. However, it has been difficult to find a viable alternative to this so-called strong paradigm of management. Journal editors and reviewers, who have made their careers in the old paradigm, are reluctant to approve articles that do not advance or refine established theoretical perspectives and methodological conventions. Indeed, the article format is better suited for the highly formalized version of management theory. It is less well suited for the presentation of management practices that are context-dependent, complex, processual, and/or holistic.

In addition, the publication industry has become increasingly fragmented. While there are journals for computerized decision-making systems, budgeting models, stress management, international purchasing, and numerous other sub-disciplines, prestigious management journals do not focus on management as a multifaceted craft (perhaps with the exception of the *Journal of Management Studies*). In the current academic system that requires researchers to publish in these journals, the chances of having an article accepted increase if authors follow established research perspectives and make only small advances in the sub-disciplines. This pressure to publish strengthens the orthodox view of management theory and practice.

AN ALTERNATIVE THEORETICAL FRAMEWORK FOR MANAGEMENT

Each chapter in this anthology has a somewhat different theoretical framework. Therefore, here I present only the book's theoretical themes that conceptualize an alternative meta-understanding of managerial work that all chapters rely on, explicitly or implicitly (see also Chapter 18).

In sum, the argument here is that much of the static and linear reasoning in management science should be replaced (or at least supplemented) with theories based on studies of experienced managers' work behaviour. There are no stable equilibriums or precise forecasts in the world of management. In complex and changing systems, where many actions have unintended consequences, it is not possible to determine outcomes in advance. For this reason, there is a problem with the strong institutionalization of concepts such as strategy, decision-making, and leadership (with their bias towards calculated control). Of course, managers strive to be leaders who make absolute (as well as optimal) decisions aimed at achieving carefully defined goals. The image of managers in temporary control, constantly reinterpreting, readjusting, and renegotiating goals and decisions, is somewhat unappealing, but it is a realistic image. The advantage of a reformulated management theory is that it can substantially narrow the gap between normative management theory and management practice at work.

Management as a social practice (1)

An important, perhaps obvious, theme in this book is that management essentially is a human artefact, or more precisely, a social practice. The study of management should therefore be ontologically different from the study of phenomena in the natural sciences in which human intervention is less apparent. Human artefacts are often diverse and mutable. While we find regularities in human behaviour, and sometimes their causes, natural laws only partially determine human behaviour. This means, in large degree, that time, context, and actor strategies influence scientific results in management in the same way they do in the social sciences such as sociology and anthropology.

Management practices, which are socially constructed, change over time as new knowledge, technology, and understandings emerge (cf. Berger and Luckmann, 1966). Giddens' concept (1987) of double hermeneutics, which can be used to highlight the difference between studying human and non-human actors, is relevant in this discussion. In the theory of double hermeneutics, interpretations move in both directions in various spheres of social practice. Thus managers can learn from the work of management scientists (and vice versa). Birds do not learn about ornithology or flying techniques from books, but managers can learn about their own occupation from reading management books. Such learning can change and even refute previously hard-won 'scientific facts'.

Complex and unpredictable human/social systems (2)

While most quantitative management research is still based on linear assumptions derived from Newtonian physics, human systems are typically emergent and evolving. Various concepts have been used to describe human systems: non-linearity (Styhre, 2002), emergence (Bergmann Licthenstein, 2000), dissipative structures (Prigogine, 1997), and complexity (Pagels, 1988; Roetzheim, 2007; Uhl-Bien et al., 2007).

Complexity theory, which is an expanding field in both the natural and the social sciences, has developed as a response to the inability of traditional scientific perspectives to deal with and understand systems that are interrelated, dynamically evolving, and highly unpredictable. Complexity has been defined as the transition region between stability and chaos (Pagels, 1988; Roetzheim, 2007). Management as a field practice is probably characterized more by stability than chaos (even if managing sometimes is very chaotic); however, managerial stability is not so strong that one can describe it in terms of a static and simple order. The exception is the ordered management system that may exist in highly bureaucratic settings where following the rules takes priority over following managerial directions, and where organizations are typically unresponsive to external stimuli. Except in perhaps extremely stable environments, management as a highly ordered activity should be seen more as pathologic than ideal.

Multiple perspectives on the complexity of human/social systems (3)

Gareth Morgan (1986) argues there is no best way to understand organizations. He advises us that we will better understand organizations if we look at them as many things at the same time (for instance, as production systems, cultures, power and career structures, societal institutions, and organisms). This advice applies to managerial behaviour as well. Instead of searching for the 'stable truth', one should look for better representations, more penetrating insights, and deeper/ richer understandings. Recurrent action patterns, and perhaps also their causes, should be treated as scientific evidence, not as natural laws. There are always exceptions to the rules.

The complexity of human systems is often so extensive that we can only partially understand them. The world economy is an example of an extremely large and complex human system that is shaped by countless exchanges of money, goods, services, technologies, and knowledge; by a vast number of factors such as currency rates, money supply, ownership of financial assets, wars, political upheavals; and by numerous institutions such as governmental and transnational entities, NGOs, lobbying organizations, and elite networks. Organizational life and control is another complex human system where environmental disturbances force responses of very different kinds – from following rules passively to risking innovative initiatives. Such responses, which are emergent and interactive, influence the responses of others. Examples are complaints by employees and counter-moves by competitors (Uhl-Bien et al., 2007).

Complexity theory has also attracted the interest of physicists and other natural scientists who recognize the limitations of linear systems theory (Wolfram, 1984, 1985). Because of this growing realization of the complexity in both human and non-human systems, there has been a call for multidisciplinary research. According to the political scientist, Elinor Ostrom (2009 Nobel Laureate in Economic Sciences), it is necessary to combine at least three to five disciplines if we are to find answers to important environmental questions (Eriksson and Lundgren, 2010). It is possible that social scientists and natural scientists can cooperate on issues related to global climate, ecosystems, and transportation. And just as Newtonian physics is now out-of-date in the modern natural sciences, in management science there are also invalid research theories and methods.

Professional excellence – adapting to unique contexts (4)

In addition to their ambition to transform management into an applied science based on facts and rational procedures, many researchers have generally assumed that the most skilled managers follow the most complex rules and models, as in a sophisticated computer algorithm. Much effort has been invested in the fields of management cognition and management knowledge in an attempt to explain these complex rules and models that are said to influence advanced managerial behaviour.

However, Hubert and Stuart Dreyfus (1986), who have studied how professionals at different stages of competences – novices to experts – solve problems, found that skilled actors and experts rely less on rule-following. Less experienced people rely more on rational models to guide their actions while experienced experts use experiential-based intuition and context awareness in solving problems. Furthermore, experts do not divide their problem-solving activity into the separate phases of problem definition, evaluation of action alternatives and outcomes, and so on. Flyvbjerg summarizes the expert level of competence in the Dreyfus and Dreyfus model as follows:

> Finally, experts' behavior is intuitive, holistic, and synchronic, understood in the way that a given situation releases a picture of problem, goal, plan, decision, and action in one instant and with no division into phases. This is the level of true human expertise. Experts are characterized by a flowing, effortless performance, unhindered by analytical deliberations. (Flyvbjerg, 2001: 21)

The Dreyfus and Dreyfus model is similar to Donald Schön's conception (1983) of reflective practitioners who base their actions on experience and intuition and are sensitive to specific contexts. To describe such sensitivity, Schön uses the splendid concept 'conversation with the situation'. Such reflective practitioners are more oriented towards what works than towards what scientists think is best conceptually.

Perhaps the most severe drawback of the rational analytical approach to management stems from its inability to generate innovative solutions. Technological breakthroughs are to a great extent based on 'silly ideas', serendipities, or 'flashes from heaven'. Creativity does not flourish in environments where personal relationships, emotions, experiments, and playfulness are suppressed. The main implication of this idea is that great respect should be shown for managers' creative expertise in their responses to challenging work demands. Managers often acquire this expertise through hard-won experience and not by the study of the rational and scientific models.

Research as a reflective practice (5)

Research is a reflective process where the interpretations and inductions from empirical facts normally do not follow in a logical progression. An experienced researcher also converses with the situation and knows the importance of sensitivity to it. There is no guarantee that acting rationally will lead to objective and valid conclusions; instead, there is a significant risk that the rational approach may generate self-fulfilling results where researchers impose their assumptions on the empirical material.

Sensitivity to managerial work as a social practice also implies an openness to using inductive and social-constructivist research approaches, for instance, ethnographic and observational methods (Czarniawska, 2007). The researcher should not assume that informants are guided by explicit rules nor expect to acquire a complete understanding of actions, situations, and behaviours simply by posing a number of well-conceived interview questions.

There are various research approaches that are designed to study management from the non-traditional perspective. One interesting approach, used to co-construct a reality, is for researchers and their informants to engage in conversations. When such conversations are successful, they lead to joint learning – knowledge that is new to both the researcher and the informant (Kreiner and Mouritsen, 2005). Other methods that are suitable are interactive methods such as action research (cf. Gustavsen, 1992) and the use of practitioners as co-researchers (Häckner, 2005). Yet other approaches, which recognize that the empirical world is complex, ambiguous, and multifaceted, collect different versions about an investigated phenomenon using a polyphonic approach (Czarniawska, 1992) or focus on phenomena that are particular, concrete, and holistic (Flyvbjerg, 2001).

These reflective approaches for studying managerial practices do not agree with the standard approaches presented in traditional texts on research methods. Experienced researchers use such books sparingly and never as cook books in their research design. Research novices and advanced beginners may refer to them, but experienced researchers find them too limiting in the rigidity of their prescriptive rules. Methods books are generally aimed at master's and doctoral students but rarely at professors. *Making Social Science Matter* (Flyvbjerg, 2001) and *The Art of Science* (Tengblad et al., 2005) are exceptions. In both these books,

Table 1.1 Theoretical themes and researcher advice

Theoretical themes	Advice for researchers
1. Management as a social practice	Use a different ontology and methodology than mainstream positivism/natural sciences research.
2. Complex and unpredictable human/ social systems	Be attentive to the ambiguous, emergent, and unexpected. Use insights from complexity theory.
3. Multiple perspectives on the complexity of human/social systems	Apply multiple and holistic perspectives.
4. Professional excellence – adapting to unique contexts	Use expert knowledge way to understand complex social practices; be attentive to the improvisational character of expert knowledge.
5. Research as a reflective practice	Be open to the practitioners' lifeworlds and engage them in interactions.

experienced researchers reflect on their studies of management in practice and make recommendations for innovative research that is not bound by inflexible rules.

This book's five theoretical themes and advice to researchers are summarized in Table 1.1.

THE CULTURAL AND ECONOMIC SETTING OF THIS BOOK

Although the contexts for the chapters are quite varied, with few exceptions they reflect the same national context. One study was conducted in Norway; all other studies were conducted in Sweden. The other chapters are descriptive, methodological, or theoretical. In a sense this cultural homogeneity is a limitation since the focus necessarily excludes the rich variety of managerial practices found worldwide. However, in a book such as this we cannot examine differences in management practices in various countries, for example, in Egypt, South Korea, Chile, Hungary, Canada, or Indonesia, to name only a few settings where comparisons to Swedish–Norwegian management practices would be of interest. Every nation or a business case is unique; yet, in various degrees, each is similar to other nation and business cases. Therefore, each case should be treated as relevant but not as universal.

In order not to focus on what can be seen as the idiosyncrasies of the managerial culture in Sweden (and Norway), the authors in this book focus on aspects of managerial work that are not specifically context-bound. In the Conclusion (Chapter 18), the results from our studies are compared to previous studies of managerial work made in other countries at other times. By taking this approach, the attempt is to show that much of the form and content managerial work practice is little influenced by specific context. Many managerial habits, practices, behaviours, problems, and solutions, which arise from complexity, uncertainty, and urgency, are doubtless of universal relevance.

We also find there are definite advantages to our research context. First, within the Scandinavian culture, we are able to compare managerial practices in different sectors and at the different hierarchical levels that exist in those sectors. Second, as much as anywhere, and perhaps more so, organizations in Scandinavia (both in the private and public sectors) are uncommonly accessible and supportive of researchers. The fieldwork tradition (e.g. observations, case studies, shadowing, and interviews) is very strong in Scandinavian management research. Furthermore, such research is relatively generously supported by private and public grants. Such support of research innovation probably explains why Scandinavian research has had the good fortune to be able to focus on the 'irrational' aspects of management (i.e. managerial behaviour outside prescriptive management theory and its assumption that management should be seen as deliberate choices). In the last four decades, Mats Alvesson, Nils Brunsson, Barbara Czarniawska, Bent Flyvbjerg, Bo Hedberg, Sten Jönsson, Kristian Kreiner, Rolf A. Lundin, Jan Mouritsen, Johan P. Olsen, Kjell A. Røvik, Kerstin Sahlin, Guje Sevon, and Sven-Erik Sjöstrand, just to name a few prominent scholars, have published notable examples of such research.

The Scandinavian tradition of management research includes the view of strategy work as mythmaking (Jönsson and Lundin, 1977), 'garbage can' processes of decision-making (Cohen et al., 1972), and the concept of 'the irrational organization' (Brunsson, 1985). The concepts explored in these studies acknowledge the limits of bounded rationality and recognize that talk, decisions, and actions in organizations often are decoupled and scattered over time and space (Brunsson, 1989; March and Olsen, 1989; Brunson and Olsen, 1993), and that decision-making can be seen as a ritual (cf. Olsen, 1970).

In a similar vein, Mats Alvesson and Barbara Czarniawska have used cultural and anthropological perspectives in their studies of organizational behaviour. Alvesson has written extensively about organizational symbolism, ideology, and power (Alvesson, 1991; Alvesson and Berg, 1992; Alvesson, 1996); the limitations of the conventional understanding of leadership (Alvesson and Sveningsson, 2003); and formalized control systems (Alvesson and Kärreman, 2004) (see Chapter 4). Barbara Czarniawska has written numerous books and articles on a 'narrative approach to organization studies' (Czarniawska, 1997, 1998). In an examination of the main themes of this book (complexity, paradoxality, and unpredictability), she criticizes the inability of formal rationality as a way to understand organizational life and behaviour (Czarniawska, 1992).

Advocates of systematic management practices may be surprised that two such relatively prosperous and developed countries as Sweden and Norway have been at the forefront in the study of 'irrational' management practices. Norway, on a per capita basis, is one of the richest countries in the world. In the last fifteen years, Sweden has experienced a very high productivity growth rate compared to most developed countries, including Japan and the United States, and is usually listed among the top five or ten countries in the world in various global rankings (competitiveness, sustainability, innovation, life quality, human development, etc.). In the years 2010 and 2011, with its balanced national budget, Sweden had the best fiscal performance and the highest growth rate among all the EU member states. Given the relative economic success of Sweden and Norway and the related high living standard of their citizens, a strong argument can be made in favour of Scandinavian management practices. It is this management style that these chapters examine as they develop practice-oriented theories of management. While the work of managers may be performed in different ways, the work described here is a relatively successful variant.

While this book relies to a significant extent on the Nordic management research tradition, it also relies on the work of scholars outside this admittedly small region, for instance, research by Chris Argyris, Stephen Barley, Tom Burns, Melville Dalton, Anthony Giddens, Colin Hales, Linda Hill, Anthony Hopwood, Rosabeth Kanter, John Kotter, Gideon Kunda, Charles Lindblom, Fred Luthans, James March, Diedre McCloskey, Robert Merton, John Meyer, Henry Mintzberg, Gareth Morgan, Mirko Noordegraaf, Donald Schön, W. Richard Scott, Philip Selznick, David Silverman, Herbert Simon, Linda Smircich, Rosemary Stewart, Tony Watson, and Karl Weick. Successful research efforts require international cooperation and exchange of ideas.

Book structure

The book contains eighteen chapters, divided into six parts according to themes and topics. There is a brief summary of the chapters at the beginning of each part.

In Part One, this chapter, and Chapter 2 summarize key findings in previous research about managerial work. Part Two (Chapters 3, 4, and 5) presents studies that discuss leadership from a practice perspective based on the everyday work of managers. The research in these chapters is based on ethnographic studies, management training sessions, and video-recordings of executive management meetings. Part Three (Chapters 6, 7, and 8) presents studies of different kinds of operational managers – managers in health care, research and development, and construction. Part Four (Chapters 9, 10, 11, and 12) presents studies about administrative managers – managers in universities and municipalities and CEOs in private companies. Part Five (Chapters 13, 14, and 15) presents studies about managerial work in small companies where the managers are the owners/entrepreneurs. Part Six (Chapters 16, 17, and 18) has two methodology chapters – a chapter about the shadowing technique and a chapter by several management scholars about the possibilities of narrowing the theory and practice gap. Chapter 18 is the Conclusion chapter that argues for building a foundation for a new practice-based theory of management. The book's empirical chapters are summarized in Table 1.2.

Table 1.2 Empirical chapters and methods used to study managers

Types of managers studied	Main method(s)	Chapter
Part 2: Middle and senior managers in private industry		
Middle managers from a telecommunication company	Self-reporting of typical work, feedback discussions	3
Middle managers from knowledge-intensive firms	Interviews, observations	4
Executive group meetings in an high-tech firm	Video recordings of meetings, feedback discussions	5
Part 3: Operational managers		
First- and second-line health care managers	Observations, pulse and stress measurements	6
Construction site managers	Interviews	7
First line R and D managers	Observations, interviews	8
Part 4: Administrative managers		
Senior municipal managers	Interviews, questionnaires	9
Municipal directors	Diaries, observations, interviews	10
University managers	Interviews, questionnaires	11
CEOs in private companies	Observations, diaries	12
Part 5: Managers in small business		
Entrepreneurs in fast-growing entrepreneurial companies	Observations, interviews	13
Entrepreneurs in small companies	Observations, interviews	14
Family business managers	Interviews	15

REFERENCES

Alvesson, M. (1991). Organizational symbolism and ideology. *Journal of Management Studies*, 28(3): 207–25.

——(1996). *Communication, Power and Organization*. Berlin/New York: de Gruyter.

——Berg, P. O. (1992). *Corporate Culture and Organizational Symbolism*. Berlin/New York: de Gruyter.

——Kärreman, D. (2004). Interfaces of control. Technocratic and social control in a global management consultancy firm. *Accounting, Organizations and Society*, 29: 423–44.

——Sveningsson, S. (2003). Good visions, bad micro-management and ugly ambiguity. *Organization Studies*, 24(6): 961–88.

Barley, S. R. and Kunda, G. (2001). Bring work back in. *Organization Science*, 12(1): 76–95.

Berger, P. and Luckmann, T. (1966). *The Social Construction of Reality*. Garden City, NY: Anchor Books.

Bergmann Licthenstein, B. M. (2000). Emergence as a process of self-organizing – New assumptions and insights from the study of non-linear dynamic systems. *Journal of Organizational Change Management*, 13(6): 526–44.

Brunsson, N. (1985). *The Irrational Organization: Irrationality as Basis for Organizational Action and Change*. Chichester: Wiley.

——(1989). *The Organization of Hypocrisy: Talk, Decisions and Actions in Organizations*. Chichester: Wiley.

——Olsen, J. P. (1993). *The Reforming Organization.* London: Routledge.

Cohen, Michael D., March, James G., and Olsen, Johan P. (1972). A garbage can model of organizational choice. *Administrative Science Quarterly*, 17(1): 1–25.

Czarniawska, B. (1992). *Exploring Complex Organizations.* Newbury Park, CA: Sage.

——(1997). *Narrating the Organization.* Chicago: University of Chicago Press.

——(1998). *A Narrative Approach to Organization Studies.* Thousand Oaks, CA: Sage.

——(2007). *Shadowing and Other Techniques for Doing Fieldwork in Modern Societies.* Malmö, Sweden: Liber.

Dreyfus, H. and Dreyfus, S. (1986). *Mind over Machine. The Power of Human Intuition and Expertise in the Era of the Computer.* New York: Free Press.

Eriksson, A. and Lundgren, E. (2010). Scientists need to cross disciplines. *GU Journalen*, 2 April: 19.

Flyvbjerg, B. (2001). *Making Social Science Matter.* Cambridge: Cambridge University Press.

Giddens, A. (1987). *Social Theory and Modern Sociology.* Cambridge: Polity Press.

Gustavsen, B. (1992). *Dialogue and Development.* Assen/Maastricht: Van Gorcum.

Häckner, E. (2005). Interventionist case research with actors as 'co-researchers'. In: S. Tengblad, B. Czarniawska, and R. Solli (Eds.), *The Art of Science*. Malmo, Sweden: Liber and Copenhagen Business Press.

Jönsson, S. and Lundin, R. A. (1977). Myths and wishful thinking as management tools. *Studies in the Management Sciences*, 5: 157–70.

Kaulio, M. A. (2008). Project leadership in multi-project settings: Findings from a critical incident study. *International Journal of Project Management*, 26: 338–47.

Kreiner, K. and Mouritsen, J. (2005). The analytical interview. In S. Tengblad, B. Czarniawska, and R. Solli (Eds.), *The Art of Science*. Malmo, Sweden: Liber and Copenhagen Business Press.

Lodge, D. (1988). *Nice Work.* London: Martin Secker & Warburg.

March, J. G. and Olsen, J. P. (1989). *Rediscovering Institutions: The Organizational Basis of Politics.* New York: Free Press.

McCloskey, D. N. (1998). Bourgeois virtue and the history of P and S. *The Journal of Economic History*, 58: 2.

Morgan, G. (1986). *Images of Organization.* London: Sage.

Olsen, J. (1970). Local budgeting: Decision making or a ritual act. *Scandinavian Political Studies*, 5: 85–118.

Pagels, H. (1988). *The Dreams of Reason. The Computer and the Rise of the Sciences of Complexity.* New York: Bantam Books.

Prigogine, I. (1997). *The End of Certainty.* New York: The Free Press.

Roetzheim, W. (2007). *Why Things Are. How Complexity Theory Answers Life's Toughest Questions.* Jamul, CA: Level 4 Press.

Schön, D. (1983). *The Reflective Practitioner.* New York: Basic Books.

Styhre, A. (2002). Non-linear change in organizations. *Leadership & Organization Development Journal*, 23(6): 343–51.

Tengblad, S., Czarniawska, B., and Solli, R. (2005). *The Art of Science.* Malmo, Sweden: Liber and Copenhagen Business Press.

Uhl-Bien, M., Marion, R., and McKelvey, B. (2007). Complexity leadership theory. *The Leadership Quarterly*, 18: 298–318.

Wolfram, S. (1984). Cellular automata as models of complexity? *Nature*, 311: 419–24.

——(1985). Undecidability and intractability in theoretical physics. *Physical Review Letters*, 45: 735–8.

2

Management in practice: Overview of classic studies on managerial work

Stefan Tengblad and Ola Edvin Vie

INTRODUCTION

The aim of the chapter is twofold: first, to give the reader an overview of what has been achieved in Management and Work Behaviour (MWB) research in the last sixty years; and second, to support this book's empirical and theoretical contribution by identifying linkages between previous studies and our own studies. We have for this purpose reviewed twenty-one significant studies, covering a time span of sixty years and various settings.

The chapter consists of four sections: *Early studies* (1951–69), *Mature studies* (1970–89), *Recent studies* (1990–), and *Discussion*. We chose the three time periods to show how the essential features of MWB research have developed chronologically – from the pioneering studies in the first period, to the second period of significant synthesis, and to the third period dominated by replications, extensions, and new theoretical insights.

In each of the first three sections, we review various influential studies in terms of their scope, context, theoretical framing, methods, and important results. Our criterion for selecting these studies is our definition of 'important results': results that we, as researchers in the field, think are valuable; results that subsequent research has judged significant; and results well suited for comparison to the research and theoretical discussion of this book. The fourth section, the *Discussion*, addresses the issues we found worthy of further analysis.

The comprehensive studies of managerial behaviour originate in the United States (eleven), Great Britain (six), Sweden (two), the Netherlands (one), and Germany (one). Sixteen of the lead authors are men and five are women (see Table 2.1).

Bon appétit!

Table 2.1 Studies of managerial behaviour

Early studies (1951–69)

1. The pioneering study: *Executive Behaviour*, Carlson (1951/91)
2. First study of middle management work: Burns (1954, 1957)
3. Classic studies of foremen and supervisors: Guest (1956), Jasinski (1956), Walker et al. (1956)
4. Pathologies in supervisory work: Wirdenius (1958, 1961)
5. Exploring unofficial aspects of managerial work: *Men Who Manage*, Dalton (1959)
6. Describing systemic influences on managerial behaviour: *Managerial Behavior*, Sayles (1964)
7. Revisiting UK middle managers: *The Work Activities of Middle Managers*, Horne and Lupton (1965)
8. Examining the variation within managerial work: *Managers and Their Jobs*, Stewart (1967/88)

Mature studies (1970–89)

9. Synthesizing the nature of managerial work: *The Nature of Managerial Work*, Mintzberg (1973)
10. (Gendered) structures that stifle managers' work: *Men and Women of the Corporation*, Kanter (1977)
11. The opportunist manager: *The General Managers*, Kotter (1982a)
12. What choices do managers have? *Choices for the Manager*, Stewart (1982)
13. What characterizes successful and effective managers? *Real Managers*, Luthans et al. (1988)
14. The moral mazes of managerial work: *Moral Mazes*, Jackall (1988)
15. Managers managing in an administrative system: *Managers Managing*, Hannaway (1989)

Recent studies (1990–)

16. Learning to become a manager: *Becoming a Manager*, Hill (1992)
17. Managers in search of themselves: *In Search of Management*, Watson (1994/2001)
18. Public managers amidst ambiguity: Noordegraaf (2000a, 2000b)
19. Post-bureaucratic managers? Hales and Tamangani (1996), Hales (1999, 2002, 2005), Hales and Mustapha (2000)
20. Revisiting the nature of managerial work: *Managing*, Mintzberg (2009)
21. Stability and change in top managerial work: *The Nature of Executive Work*, Matthaei (2010)

EARLY STUDIES (1951–69)

Because of his pioneering study, *Executive Behaviour*, Sune Carlson (1951/91) is generally honoured as the founder of the managerial work approach in research. After Carlson's study, a number of other researchers conducted work activity studies in which they measured managers' time allocation using either the diary method (Burns, 1957; Dubin and Spray, 1964; Horne and Lupton, 1965; Stewart, 1967/88), activity sampling (Kelly, 1964), or direct observation (Guest, 1956; Jasinski, 1956). This group of studies have created the enduring image of managerial work as work characterized by numerous contacts, task fragmentation, and constant interruptions. Although not as frequently commented upon by readers, these studies also pointed to the importance of managers' lateral relationships with other managers and to the variation in managerial positions (Stewart, 1967/88).

Following a different trajectory, researchers in the industrial sociology and the human relations movements conducted ethnographic studies of managers at work. Walker et al. (1956) studied the foreman's role on an automobile assembly line; Dalton (1959) examined the informal and ambiguous position of middle managers; and Sayles (1964) looked at middle managers as participants in the complex and interdependent process of workflow.

The disparity between management theory and management behaviour in these studies is striking. In this respect, we find some interesting similarities between these early studies and more recent management studies. Today, when we are less convinced that a manager should work systematically from goal setting to performance to results, and after several decades of management education and training efforts designed to replace reactive and fragmented work patterns, we see that much of managerial behaviour has not changed since the 1950s and 1960s. We also see that these early studies treated several management behaviour topics that were less frequently discussed then but are quite commonly discussed today – for example, power, informal behaviour, unofficial behaviour, managers' emotions, and decision-making and strategy as emerging processes.

The pioneering study (1)

In the year 2011, sixty years have passed since Sune Carlson, a Swedish Professor of Business Administration, published *Executive Behaviour* (Carlson, 1951/91). In his book, Carlson described his extensive investigation of the work behaviour of ten managing directors (CEOs) of what were then prominent Swedish companies.[1] During a four-week study, the directors each kept a diary of their daily work behaviour that detailed where and when they worked and with what and with whom they worked. Each director's secretary kept a record of the director's incoming and outgoing mail and telephone calls.

Carlson worked in close cooperation with these directors who thought that the information and insights gained from such administrative research would help them work more efficiently. Such was the practical aim of the research project although Carlson also made anthropological interpretations of the directors' work behaviour.

Carlson's study resulted in several important findings. One finding relates to what he described as 'administrative pathologies' – conditions that cause a managing director to act inefficiently and unproductively (1951/91: 68–71). For example, the diary complex refers to the pathology where the director only performs the tasks that are scheduled on his calendar. In performing these tasks, which often reflect other people's interests and priorities, the director most often does not have enough time to address the tasks he thinks are more important. Another finding is the high degree of fragmentation in the director's workday that means there is little time for planning, thinking, and reflecting. Carlson also recognized that the directors in his study were inclined towards wishful thinking about 'right now' situations that they described as atypical and exceptionally challenging. Their hope was that the present chaotic situation would somehow, in the near future, become more stable and controllable. Carlson also found, to his surprise, that these ten directors seldom wrote letters and rarely met customers and suppliers. A significant finding in the study, but largely neglected in later research, was the importance of office layout and other physical arrangements for determining whom the CEOs met and how often.

Executive Behaviour describes managerial work as hectic, fragmented, complex, often disorganized, and steered more by work habits and the logic-of events than by reflective and deliberate planning. Carlson concluded that executive behaviour should be studied in context, taking both the social and physical environments into consideration. The proper focus of such study should be the executives' interests, goals, and attitudes. However, Carlson's preoccupation was with administrative techniques that support systematic methods of planning and decision-making. His study revealed his conviction that the largely inductive and reactive ways of working he observed were the result of a low level of managerial professionalism rather than the result of the difficulty of using rational management techniques in these chaotic post-war years.

Carlson wrote that at the beginning of his research, he imagined chief executives as orchestra conductors, but at the end of the research in some ways he saw them as puppets in a marionette theatre. Despite what he had seen, there is no doubt Carlson preferred the orchestra conductor image. Many of his followers have agreed that managerial practices should be reformed when they have observed executives who are unable to control events through foresight and resolute pursuit of priorities.

First study of middle management work (2)

Tom Burns was one of the first researchers to follow-up on Carlson's work. Burns made two diary studies in Great Britain in the mid-1950s (1954, 1957). His 1954 article was based on a pilot study of four middle managers – a factory department manager and his three subordinate managers. For the study, the four managers estimated the time they spent on ten work activities (e.g. sales, personnel, production difficulties, etc.). Then, over a five-week period, they recorded actual time spent in these various activities including where and with whom they interacted. In 1957, Burns published a larger study of seventy-six senior and middle managers from eight firms. In the second study, using a methodology similar to that used in the earlier study, the managers recorded how they spent their time for periods of three, four, or five weeks.

A number of interesting findings emerged from Burns' two studies. First, Burns saw that the managers spent a high proportion of their time in conversation, mostly in lateral communications with a small group of managers. They spent relatively little time with their immediate subordinates (Burns, 1957). Second, Burns observed differences in how managers communicated depending on whether their firms faced high or low degrees of change. In stable firms, following a vertical line more closely, more communications were written than spoken. According to Burns: 'Generally speaking, the faster the rate of change, the more time is spent by managers in talking with each other' (1957: 51). Burns later developed this idea with G. M. Stalker as the contingency perspective on the management of innovation (Burns and Stalker, 1961). It should be noted that one of the characteristics of the organic system they describe is its informal and friendly code of conduct. Their view of the organization as a system of personal relationships rather than a hierarchy of authority is an early hint of the more emotional aspects of organizational life that later studies have addressed. Third,

Burns also noticed several discrepancies in the managers' records of their activities. One-third of the time managers described the same meeting differently. For example, middle managers often interpreted communications as information or advice that senior managers had intended as instructions or decisions. The managers also overestimated the amount of time they spent on production and underestimated the amount of time they spent on personnel, suggesting they were unaware of the extent of their involvement in 'human relationships'.

Burns' findings led to his early and influential work on the micro-politics of organizations. In a 1955 article, Burns noted that an individual's political behaviour leads to group formation of coalitions, cliques, and cabals. In a 1961 article, Burns pointed out that when people work in relationships where cooperation is required to achieve common organizational goals, there is intense rivalry for organizational positions and rewards.

Classic studies of foremen and supervisors (3)

Research in industrial sociology in the 1950s produced a number of publications about managers, in particular foremen and supervisors. Notable among this research was the work of C. R. Walker, R. H. Guest, and A. N. Turner. Following their classic study of automobile workers, *The Man on the Assembly Line* (Walker and Guest, 1952), Walker and Guest undertook a research project on supervisory work funded by the Institute of Human Relations at Yale University. The major publication from this research was *The Foreman on the Assembly Line* (Walker et al., 1956) that was based on interviews with fifty-five foremen at a manufacturing company, supplemented with observations. The interview excerpts illustrated how the foremen saw their relationships with others in the factory. While the book focuses on the development of personal relationships, not surprisingly it also addresses issues of staffing, quality in production, and handling of emergencies. A remarkable finding is that the foreman takes the role of a 'shock absorber' that absorbs, but does not transmit, work pressure.

Both Guest (1956) and Jasinski (1956) reported the results of their minute-by-minute, full-day observations of fifty-six foremen. Guest researched the average time foremen spent on work topics and in work places. He also examined the extent and nature of the foremen's contacts with others. He described the foremen's work as a hectic round of activities, with each activity lasting on average only 48 seconds. In particular, he highlighted the foremen's lack of idle time, the constant interruptions in their work, the great variety of their contacts, and the many different and coincident problems. Taking a different approach, Jasinski examined the relationships between the foremen and people outside their work groups. The foremen were involved in both horizontal line relationships and diagonal relationships with employees not directly in their line of reporting. On average, these foremen spent half their contact time with people outside their work groups; those foremen rated most effective by supervisory foremen and other superintendents spent most of their contact time with these outside work groups.

Pathologies in supervisory work (4)

H. Wirdenius (1958, 1961) made an early study of eighty-two foremen and supervisors in five industries in Sweden, primarily the construction and textile production sectors. The supervisors' time usage was recorded through observation and self-reporting of activities at regular bell rings. This study generally confirms Walker et al.'s results (1956) that supervisory work is multifaceted and very fragmented.

Wirdenius' study can also be seen as an interesting continuation of Carlson's study of administrative pathologies in executive work, although at the opposite end of the managerial hierarchy. His study revealed there was a large variance between what the supervisors were expected to do and what they actually did. A large proportion of their time was spent in routine clerical work and in unproductive activities such as purely personal matters, travel between machines in different production areas, and just waiting. In the textile companies, no less than 16 per cent of their time was spent in walking the long distances between the machines.

Wirdenius' special interest was how supervisors handled the personnel activities of recruitment, introduction, training, and work safety that were supposed to be central work tasks. He found that such activities took only a very small part of supervisors' work time (2–5 per cent) even though they spent a lot of time on work matters in brief contacts with employees. The supervisors worked even less with activities related to the development of new work methods and to the implementation of cost reductions. Instead, almost all their work time was spent responding to immediate problems and making certain that production processes flowed as well as possible given the constant disturbances and the disparities between planned and actual activities.

Exploring unofficial aspects of managerial work (5)

The most extensive account of the unofficial and informal aspects of managerial work in these years was Melville Dalton's *Men Who Manage* (1959). Dalton's contribution is especially noteworthy because it was written in a time when management research mainly concerned the rational and formal aspects of work. Using his formal staff positions at two US companies (Milo Fractionating Center and Fruhling Works), Dalton applied a covert research approach to collect data on four firms in the same Midwestern US city. He conducted formal and informal interviews, kept a work diary, made participant observations, and attended social events outside work.

Dalton's research offers a detailed empirical description of the unofficial side of managerial work. In the book, he describes the power struggles between management cliques as they compete for resources and trade information and favours, the strained collaboration between line and staff, the informal rewards system, and the active reinterpretation, negotiation, and implementation of company policies at the local level. His description of the unofficial influences that affect promotions and careers is of particular interest – managers' ethnicity, religion, club memberships (e.g. the yacht club and the Masons), and political affiliations. Thus, managers' private lives merge with this highly complex 'web of commitments' and 'workable arrangements' at work. In short, Dalton paints a picture of managers caught up in a whirl of ambiguity, complexity, and conflict; to make sense of this confusion, they engage in unofficial and informal activities outside the normal boundaries of their formal positions. In many respects, the book presents a timeless description of the interplay between managers' private lives and their work lives.

Describing systemic influences on managerial behaviour (6)

Leonard Sayles, who studied at MIT with Karl Lewin and disciples, used this training in writing *Managerial Behavior* (1964). Although the book lacks methodological descriptions and considerations, it contains many novel and important insights. (The methodology commentary is limited to noting that the author interviewed and made anthropological observations of seventy-five lower and middle managers in a large American corporation.) Sayles, arguing against the traditional view of the management role, convincingly located managerial work within the numerous and simultaneous organizational processes stating that the 'individual manager does not have a clearly bounded job with neatly defined authorities and responsibilities . . . he is [instead] placed in the middle of a system of relationships' (1964: 27). Since a manager is responsible for maintaining workflow, each manager's activities affect all surrounding groups. Managers depend on the people in these groups even as they recognize that each person may also pursue individual interests. Because of this dependency, managers' lateral relationships with other managers are their most important relationships. Through a categorization of such lateral relationships, Sayles' analysis of this relatively unknown territory reveals managers' mutual interdependencies and their accompanying frustrations. The manager, according to Sayles, does not operate in a static system; rather, the manager is forced to seek 'a dynamic type of stability, making adjustments and readjustments to both internally generated and externally imposed pressures . . . to maintain a moving equilibrium' (1964: 163).

Sayles' view of management as fundamentally an interpersonal and interactive process has several implications. First, planning and decision-making are not exclusively managerial activities, performed in isolation; they are elements of a social process likely influenced and shaped by interaction with many others in the organization. Second, the organization is bound together by a web of interpersonal relationships rather than by rules, standards, and procedures. (Interestingly, Sayles suggests there is a bias against such 'soft' aspects of management since he notes that the technical aspects of managerial work are emphasized more than the interpersonal aspects.) Third, since the organization's guiding policies are always imperfect, managers have the latitude to act in their own interests. According to Sayles, 'Only managers who can deal with uncertainty, with ambiguity, and with battles that are never won but only fought well can hope to succeed' (1964: 259).

Revisiting UK middle managers (7)

J. H. Horne and T. Lupton (1965) conducted a one-week study of sixty-six British middle managers at ten companies using a specially designed form for the managers to record their activities. For each activity, the managers noted its type, duration, location, contacts, purpose, and functional area. One form was used to record the episodes where the primary purpose and contacts were the same. Horne and Lupton supplemented this data with 'daily diaries' and 'communication records' maintained by secretaries and assistants. They summarized the conclusions of their study as follows:

> Managers talk most of the time, and mostly face-to-face. They seem not to be overwhelmed with paper or formal meetings. They swop information and advice and instructions, mostly through informal face-to-face contact in their own offices. Middle management does not seem, on this showing, to require the exercise of remarkable powers to analyse, weigh alternatives, and decide. Rather, it calls for the ability to shape and utilize the person-to-person channels of communication, to influence, to persuade, to facilitate. (Horne and Lupton, 1965: 32)

Horne and Lupton's study highlights two important aspects of managerial work. First, managers spend most of their time exchanging information. Throughout the workday, managers give, receive, and ask for information in both informal and formal meetings as they seek, offer, or compare explanations. Second, middle managerial work is more about influencing others through one-to-one communication than it is about deciding on objectives, policies, and plans. All in all, managers are more concerned with day-to-day problems than with long-term goals.

Examining the variation within managerial work (8)

Probably the most ambitious study in MWB research in this period is Rosemary Stewart's *Managers and Their Jobs* (1967, revised in 1988).[2] In her book, Stewart charted the work activities during a four-week period for 160 managers who were employed in a broad range of management positions. Using her large sample of more than 40,000 work activities, Stewart compared various manager types and also examined the differences among managers in similar positions. She concluded that because of the large variation among management positions, it is misleading to talk about these positions in general terms without acknowledging this variation. For example, she noted that general managers spend only 7 per cent of their time on paper work compared to 84 per cent for chief accountants. Using a computer factor analysis, Stewart identified the following five categories of managers:

- *The Emissaries* (field sales managers and public figures who travel extensively)
- *The Writers* (backroom specialists and head office specialist-advisers with relatively low levels of work fragmentation)

- *The Discussers* (a diverse group of managers whose recorded activity times are close to the average time distributions)
- *The Trouble-shooters* (managers who spend the highest proportion of work in – often fragmented – encounters with subordinates)
- *The Committee-men* (managers with a high level of intra-organizational horizontal contacts)

Stewart's second important discovery was that the large variance among managers with similar positions raises the possibility of choice. She developed this idea in her 1982 book, *Choices for the Manager*, discussed in the next section.

Like Sune Carlson, Stewart reported on the problem of high fragmentation in managerial work that is disruptive to the time required for thinking and setting priorities. She used a grasshopper image to describe managers who hop from one problem to another as 'a perpetual excuse for postponing considerations of the long-term ones' (Stewart, 1967/88: 111).

Summary of the Early Studies (1951–69)

Much of the MWB research from the 1950s and 1960s in Britain, Sweden, and the United States can still inform current research. In the studies from those years, management is described as a complex social practice, primarily conducted face-to-face, and influenced significantly by political and personal factors. Managerial work is often multifaceted and fragmented, leaving managers little time to spend on formal planning and decision-making. Plans are constantly revised as managers transform them into action.

MATURE STUDIES (1970–89)

These years were the golden era in MWB research (see Stewart, 2008) when many of the most well-known studies were written. These studies contributed to the theoretical advance in the field with their many original findings that later studies developed. Henry Mintzberg, for example, became increasingly critical in the 1970s of the planning-oriented approach that dominated mainstream management science and strategy. Owing to his observations of executive work, the influential concept of emergent strategy developed as a response to the failures of long-range planning and highly structured management techniques.

In addition to Mintzberg's observational study (1973) of five chief executives performed in combination with a sweeping literature review and an extensive theory discussion, other important research from these years includes Kotter's study (1982a) of fifteen senior managers and Stewart's useful conceptualization (1976, 1982) of demands, constraints, and choices. Kotter's and Mintzberg's studies, popularized by publication in the *Harvard Business Review*, are frequently cited (Mintzberg, 1975; Kotter, 1982b).

In addition to these classic MWB studies, a number of other studies in this period highlight important aspects of the political, symbolic, ethical, and gender dimensions of managerial work (Kanter, 1977; Jackall, 1988; Luthans et al., 1988; Hannaway, 1989).

Synthesizing the nature of managerial work (9)

Mintzberg's *The Nature of Managerial Work* (1973), based on his 1968 doctoral thesis, was his first study to receive widespread attention. Interestingly, his book does not include the idea, advanced in his thesis, of strategic decision-making as an emerging process. Nevertheless, among the book's important contributions are its authoritative summary of earlier research, its synthesis of the nature of managerial work in thirteen propositions, its model of ten managerial roles, its discussion of how managerial work can be developed through systematic work analysis and programming, and its observational study of five chief executives. While the ten managerial roles probably have received the most attention, our interest is with his other contributions. We are especially interested in his synthesis of the nature of managerial work, perhaps best summarized by these four characteristics of managerial work:

1. Much work at an unrelenting pace
2. Activities characterized by brevity, variety, and fragmentation
3. Preference for live action
4. Attraction to the verbal media

Mintzberg's book belongs to the management science tradition that asserts that traditional management practices should be replaced by work practices developed by management scientists. Like many of his predecessors (e.g. Carlson and Stewart), Mintzberg regarded executives' behaviour as dysfunctional. Mintzberg attributed this dysfunctional behaviour to their preoccupation with current problems and their constant involvement in meetings. As a result, executives are trapped in vicious circles of ever-increasing work pressure. Mintzberg claimed that 'a science of managing will require that managerial programs be identified, that the contents of the programs be specified, that they be linked together into a simulation of managerial work, and that specific programs be systematically analyzed and improved (reprogrammed) by the management scientist' (1973: 161).

In general, the task of programming managerial work has proven too complex for widespread adoption in practice. However, today many managers in large, global organizations, working with computerized systems, are required to use programmed models, for example, systems for Human Resource Management (HR Transformation). Additionally, many managers work with programmed, bureaucratic procedures in budgeting and financial reporting. Yet many managerial tasks are still unstructured. Rational models for decision-making, communications, etc. have not gained popularity with managers and, when adopted, are seldom used as intended. The complexity, variation, and uncertainty of managerial tasks (e.g. negotiations, personnel issues, decisions, and evaluations) pose a significant challenge to programming managerial work.

In *The Nature of Managerial Work*, Mintzberg recognized this problem and pointed to the necessity of making highly adaptable plans that take uncertain events and unpredictable timing into consideration. (However, such planning is easier said than done!) As noted above, in later years, Mintzberg became a fierce critic of the overly scientific perspective on management. Despite the fact that some aspects of his book now seem out-of-date, in general it is still a brilliant and relevant synthesis of managerial work. Its description of the essence of managerial work – activities characterized by brevity, variety, fragmentation, with an orientation towards live action and verbal media – is perfectly contemporary.

(Gendered) structures that stifle managers' work (10)

Men and Women of the Corporation by Rosabeth Moss Kanter (1977) is a classic in the field of gender and organization. Kanter's important contribution to MWB research is her discussion of the gender dimension in bureaucratic structures that influence the work of both male and female managers. The inspiration for her research was her work as researcher and consultant in a Quality of Work Life programme at a Fortune 500 company – in the study, called the Industrial Supply Corporation (Indsco).

Kanter's book also contains an interesting analysis of the ideology behind managerialism and the bureaucratic corporation as well as the enormous work inequities such an ideology produces. Kanter borrowed an idea from Reinhard Bendix and Michel Crozier that argues that managers, in order to legitimize the centrality of their roles in organizations, claim they act rationally in their quest for logical and efficient solutions to problems. Successful managers, the argument goes, are therefore the individuals who can control their emotions. Since women are stereotyped as too emotional, they are excluded from managerial positions; they lack the masculine quality of rationality. Kanter found that the few female managers at Indsco were mere tokens. Such women managers were generally assigned stereotypical roles, such as 'the mother', 'the seductress', 'the pet', and 'the iron maiden'.

Kanter described Indsco as socially a very conformist organization. Managers tried to conform to both explicit and implicit behavioural norms in an uncertain environment. This conformity was a self-perpetuating process that Kanter referred to as 'homosexual reproduction' (1977: 48). Kanter described the either/or career game for managers at Indsco – managers either advance or perish. The 'kiss of death' for a manager was being labelled 'not promotable' because then both supporters and followers fell away. Since actual work performance was so difficult to measure, the decisive factor for promotion was social acceptability. Thus, Indsco managers engaged in organizational politics – they networked, they built relationships, they manoeuvred, and they monitored the behind-the-scenes action.

In addition, Kanter found Indsco managers' workloads demanding and their work complex. Their most time-consuming activity was communication in one form or another – mail, telegrams, telephone calls, meetings, and field visits. Working to the limits of human capacity signalled their loyalty to the corporation and to those higher in the management hierarchy. Kanter concluded, however, that no matter how much managers work, there were always unfinished tasks: managerial jobs are so designed (1977: 65).

Men and Women of the Corporation paints a gloomy picture of US corporate life in the mid-1970s. One can wonder what connection there might have been between stifling corporate structures that forced managers to play the social acceptability game and the competitive challenges to the US economy at the time. Perhaps it was this kind of bureaucratic dysfunction that motivated the widespread restructuring efforts of the 1980s (increased customer orientation, downsizing, outsourcing, the creation of internal markets, and the beginnings of cultural change programmes). But that's another story.

The opportunist manager (11)

Before becoming a 'management guru', John P. Kotter published *The General Managers* (1982a). In this book, Kotter used multi-method research to examine the general manager position. In his study of fifteen general managers at nine major US companies, he used documents on each manager's position, the company and the industry, interviews with the managers and their key subordinates, appointment books, background and occupational interest questionnaires, and two shadowing observations, each two to three days in length. In his reliance on Whyte's methodology (1943/93), Kotter supported the value of field research while admitting that such research cannot be performed in a 'clean way that fits traditional notions of "science"' (1982a: 152). In addition, Kotter included financial indicators that rated the general managers' performance combined with appraisals from peers, subordinates, and superiors.

The major findings in Kotter's book concern the concepts of 'agenda' and 'network' that he and Paul Lawrence first developed in a study of American mayors (Kotter and Lawrence, 1974). Using these concepts, Kotter (1982a) emphasized managerial choice and argued that managers have greater opportunities to influence their work by establishing agendas and by building and utilizing personal networks to implement those agendas. These agendas require access to large amounts of information that can be gathered quickly, while networks require interaction, preferably informal contact, with numerous people, both inside and outside the corporation. Kotter also argued that differences in performance are related to the manager's ability to excel in taking advantage of these agendas and networks.

In his study, Kotter confirmed that little of managerial behaviour can be described as 'planning' or 'organizing' of separate activities. Furthermore, he explained that chaotic conversations may in fact be highly effective: '... the agendas and network allowed all the GMs to engage in short and disjointed conversations that were often extremely efficient' (1982a: 89). Because of the inevitable ambiguity and uncertainty in the general manager's job, managerial decisions emerge from social processes rather than from rational and calculative analysis of data. Kotter is also one of the few researchers to note that joking, kidding, and talking about non-work issues are an integral part of managerial conversations. Such small talk, Kotter argued, is important for creating and maintaining networks. Perhaps his most important finding, however, is that fragmented interactions in problem-solving situations are not necessarily inefficient ways of working: they may even be effective in implementing long-term agendas. Kotter's achievement is his breakaway from the management science paradigm with its rigid emphasis on working systematically (i.e. deductively, deliberatively, logically, and sequentially).

What choices do managers have? (12)

The studies reviewed so far in this section (except Kotter's) emphasize that managers lack control over work processes due to environmental pressures and/ or structural job features. Rosemary Stewart and colleagues, however, pursued another research stream. In the 1970s, they studied the differences in work behaviour among managers in similar positions. They also conducted related studies, which Stewart summarized in *Choices for the Manager* (1982). The empirical data for the book are impressive – over 200 interviews and several months of observations. The main study consists of interviews with forty-one district administrators in the British National Health Services (NHS) (between three and seven hours each) and eleven observations of district administrator work (three to five days each). The basis for selection of the administrators related to the study's purpose: whether the number of beds, geographic location, and the proximity of professional teaching institutions affected their work in some systematic way.

The main contribution of Stewart's study is her model for choice. In her study, the choice is between demands (what NHS district administrators have to do) and constraints (what they cannot do). This analysis of choice in managerial work shows that while these administrators had opportunities to make choices, largely they did not exercise them. The explanation is that the administrators were either unaware of their choice opportunities or they were more comfortable with not making choices. Stewart's book concludes with a chapter of exercises for managers designed to help them become more aware of their opportunities for choice. Issues such as power, conflicts, legitimacy, emotions, and symbolic actions are not highlighted in Stewart's book, but a sentence in the methods appendix has caught our attention. Here she writes that they had gathered data on the district managers 'satisfactions and frustrations of the job and their feelings' (Stewart, 1982: 131). We definitely wanted to find out more about these feelings.

What characterizes successful and effective managers? (13)

One of the most ambitious studies from these years is *Real Managers* (1988) by Fred Luthans and his research team at the University of Nebraska. The team's goal was to examine the differences, if any, in the work activities of successful managers (those on fast track career paths) and effective managers (those whose perfor-mance was rated as superior) compared to the work activities of the managers in the study's general sample. Based on 440 hours of observations and 165 inter-views, the team developed a four-activity model with twelve descriptive categories. In the next step, trained observers recorded the activities of 248 managers on some eighty occasions during a two-week period. The following time distributions for all managers resulted from more than 20,000 observations:

- *Traditional management* (32 per cent – planning, decision-making, controlling)
- *Routine communications* (29 per cent – exchanging information, handling paperwork)
- *Human Resource Management* (20 per cent – motivating, disciplining, managing conflict, staffing, training/development)
- *Networking* (19 per cent – interacting with outsiders, socializing/politicking)

What did the successful managers do? Did they plan, decide, and control more than the effective managers? The answer is no. The successful managers spent far less time on traditional management activities than other managers. Their major activity was networking, especially in socializing/politicking activities. Such social network skills were the elements most crucial to their career success.

Luthans and colleagues also found that managers identified as effective spent much less time on traditional management activities. Decision-making, of the twelve categories studied, had the weakest relationship with effectiveness. Effective managers generally worked more with routine communications and Human Resource Management. One may ask whether management education really teaches managers how to be effective and successful? A conclusion from this study is that management education, at least, should concentrate more on communication and handling relationship practices than on planning, decision-making, and controlling.

The moral mazes of managerial work (14)

Robert Jackall's *Moral Mazes* (1988), consistent with Dalton's theme (1959) that managers adapt to their social environment, offered numerous examples of the moral and political dimensions of managerial work. The core data in Jackall's book came from 143 intensive, semi-structured interviews with managers at various levels in four US companies. (Thirty-six companies refused to participate in the research.) Extensive participant and nonparticipant observations, in both formal and informal settings, complemented the interview data.

Jackall's book highlighted the ethical ambiguity inherent in the management position. According to Alvesson (2004), ambiguity means there are several plausible interpretations of the same event or data, which, in contrast to uncertainty, cannot be clarified by more facts. Jackall described how managers, in this fluid state of context, often experience dissonance between their personal values and the demands of the corporation. Despite this conflict, corporate pressure causes widespread compliance with 'what the guy above you wants from you' (Jackall, 1988: 6). Compliance means acquiescence with superiors as well as with corporate rules and procedures. Since the corporation is an intricate matrix of individuals and rival groups, all seeking advantages and advancements, survival depends on the ability to live with the ambiguity of this moral maze.

In this rather pessimistic account of corporate life, Jackall observed that managers continually express excitement about their work even as they hide their anxieties. Although they constantly worry about making mistakes and being blamed for others' mistakes, they feel the pressure to appear cheerful and in total control, whatever the situation. Combined with the vague criteria of their performance evaluations, the unpredictability of their everyday work makes managers insecure. Thus, Jackall's study illustrated the inevitable conflict between the organization's normative demands, or at least the superior's demands, and the manager's personal needs and values. This conflict can also be seen as the struggle to shape the managers' perceptions of their experiences.

Jackall (1988) found an interesting connection between managers' long work hours and their social bonding in management teams. Managerial work in general (working late at night, in particular) appears to contain a rather large social and ritualistic element. Managers discuss amusing or provocative newspaper/journal articles with each other, chat informally together, casually take opinion polls, and pop in and out of offices with cartoons and jokes. Managers who do not work long hours and engage in this endless round of face-to-face encounters are in grave danger of being 'sidelined'. Jackall also argued that managers have to surrender or set aside their personal morals when they enter the corporate world if they aim for a meteoric career. However, in a subsequent study investigating similar themes, Watson (1994/2001: 210) claimed that the majority of managers in his study 'would be incapable of acting as amoral and unfeeling agents of remote financial interests'. The opposing conclusions of the two studies suggest the need for continued research into the variety and commonality of managerial work ethics.

Managers managing in an administrative system (15)

In *Managers Managing* (1989), Jane Hannaway described the workings of an administrative system based on a study of fifty-two managers in a central office of a US school district. In the study, she used a random signalling method that required the managers to record their activities on a standard form whenever they heard a random beep. There were 29,640 activities recorded, for an average of 570 activities per manager. The study emphasized the effects of uncertainty on managerial work, in particular related to initiating actions and searching for correct behaviour. Hannaway convincingly demonstrated that the effect of uncertainty differs at various levels of management. In addition, she also demonstrated that the managers' perception of task importance, based on the extent of their task involvement, depends on the source of the task. The managers thought tasks given them by their superiors, budget tasks, and tasks related to large meetings were more important than other tasks. This finding reveals the more symbolic aspects of managerial work that include the key activities of display and impression management.

Hannaway's book also highlighted several political aspects of managerial work. First, she noted the tendency of administrative systems to expand over time when managers create work for other managers to justify their own positions and when administrative work involves significant interaction with others. Second, using rather novel explanations, she described why managerial work is informal and reactive. Managers use informal, oral communications not only to ensure the message has been sent but also to avoid possibly inculpatory documentation. Responding reactively to the demands of others allows managers to define problems and take appropriate action. In this way, managers reduce the uncertainty associated with acting in ambiguous situations based on their own priorities. Third, she explained why managers so often are caught off guard. Upper management problems are often more associated with local levels than with the organization as a whole. Such problems are exacerbated when lower level managers are reluctant to consult their superiors about matters they feel uncertain about, probably for fear of seeming incompetent.

Summary of the Mature studies (1970–89)

The books by Mintzberg, Stewart, and Kotter reflect an increasing maturity in the MWB literature. It is interesting to note that while a fairly large consensus had developed about the practice of managerial work, dissent was growing on how managerial work practice, using new theoretical models and new insights, should develop. Mintzberg addressed the central role of the management scientist, Stewart focused on self-reflective management education, and Kotter took the radical view that management researchers could learn about managerial work from skilled practitioners.

In addition, several other studies in this period highlight the importance of the political dimension of managerial work vis-à-vis promotions (Luthans et al., 1988), ethical issues (Jackall, 1988), the legitimacy seeking behaviour of managers in administrative systems (Hannaway, 1989), and hierarchy and gender issues (Kanter, 1977). These studies describe managerial work as a quest for legitimacy where managers make a pretence of acting rationally even as they informally build networks, create alliances, and gossip about colleagues in order to deal with the harsh pressure, ambiguity, and uncertainty of their everyday work.

RECENT STUDIES (1990–)

The most recent MWB studies increasingly emphasize the emotional, political, and symbolic aspects of managerial work. In this section, we review Linda Hill's in-depth study of newly appointed managers, Tony J. Watson's skilful ethnography study of management culture, a series of articles by Colin Hales and colleagues on the potential effect of post-bureaucratic management practices, and Mirko Noordegraaf's illuminating study of public managers. We also review Henry Mintzberg's recent book that reports on observations of twenty-nine managers in many different settings and Emilio Matthaei's new study of German top executives.

These recent studies continue the focus of previous studies on work behaviour. In this regard, the research reveals the timeless character of managerial work. These studies are our best accounts of the uncertainty and ambiguity in management. They also describe how this managerial environment affects managers and how managers respond.

Learning to become a manager (16)

Linda Hill's *Becoming a Manager* (1992) examines how new managers master the challenge of becoming management practitioners. Her study is based on a number of in-depth interviews with and observations of nineteen first-year managers in the United States who were employed in financial services and computer industries.

Hill's research describes the emotional side of management – the consequences of dealing with irreconcilable expectations, constant interruptions, and the incessant needs of subordinates. The managers in her study find it difficult to cope with subordinates unlike themselves, with subordinates they do not like, or with subordinates who perform badly. (For instance, one manager stated that while he wanted to club a problem subordinate to death, of course he had to stay calm.) These managers say their work is generally very stressful, and yet they are expected to contain their emotions. A manager must suppress negative feelings, cope with isolation and loneliness, and handle the responsibility for good economic performance without showing any sign of frustration, anger, or anxiety. On some occasions, managers are expected to display emotions but only if such displays will strengthen morale and camaraderie. As one manager reports, despite the emotional drain, controlling one's feelings is an integral part of managerial work:

> A lot of days, I'm here early and out late. Still I accomplish nothing that I was supposed to accomplish. I have so many interruptions and have to keep shifting my priorities. By the end of the day I feel drained, with nothing to show for all my work. (Hill, 1992: 192)

Another valuable contribution of Hill's study is her description of the symbolic aspects of managerial work. The managers in her study were expected to act towards superiors and subordinates in accordance with corporate values by being respectful and fair. Any special recognition or benefit given to a subordinate would quickly arouse jealousy. One manager explained (Hill, 1992: 113): 'Even my most insignificant decisions can have an impact on the atmosphere around here'.

Hill is critical of traditional management education with its focus on formal knowledge and analytical skills. The manager requires a mental transformation in order to learn to think, feel, and value as a manager. Such a transformation, Hill argues, cannot be achieved through management courses. Hill concludes that the most profound learning occurs in on-the-job-training where jobholders learn from their experiences – successes, failures, confused situations, and insights. It is in on-the-job-training that managers learn to cope with complexity, ambiguity, fragmentation, emotional stress, conflict, and the importance of handling the symbolic aspects of management.

Managers in search of themselves (17)

The most well-known managerial book in recent years is Tony J. Watson's *In Search of Management* (1994/2001). Watson was a participant observer for a year at ZTC Ryland Company in the United Kingdom (later identified at GEC Plessey Telecomunications) where he worked to develop a schema for identifying and expressing management competencies. He chose this company because its management had been involved in numerous change initiatives in line with the zeitgeist of the 1980s and 1990s and because the company had an explicitly stated corporate culture that included elements of total quality management, performance-related compensation, teamwork, and personal development. His study is an ethnographic account of the everyday thinking and attitudes of the company's managers, supported by his academic scholarship and interests. In the book, Watson discusses a number of interesting themes that he develops using long and detailed conversational excerpts from interviews with managers. The result is an intriguing and revealing study of how middle managers in a British manufacturing company talk about their experiences at work, struggle with conflicting expectations, and try to define their own roles as managers.

Watson's study is guided by a view of management as a strategic exchange between managers and other people (inside and outside the company) with the aim of ensuring the long-term survival of the company. Watson builds on this idea by extending it to the more general view that human action is shaped to some degree by individuals and groups because of their need to cope with environmental challenges. Individuals act strategically as they try to shape circumstances to their own advantage. This perspective fits well with Watson's view of culture as a man-made system of meaning and morality that can help people construct their identities.

The major contribution of Watson's book is its depiction of the chaos, uncertainties, ambiguity, and contradictions that surround managers. Concepts like 'strategy' and 'culture' are presented as important empirical artefacts and rhetorical devices. More than any other research on managerial work practices – most of which describes such practices as stable and somewhat isolated from top management influence – Watson shows that top management exerts its influence through change programmes, mission statements, and corporate policies. However, as 'Dr. Watson' reveals, such influence seems only to create unanticipated effects in the paradoxical, complex, and ambiguous world of middle management.

Watson's book is particularly illuminating in its accounts of managers' emotions, especially their disillusion and cynicism when the organizational discourse about empowerment is replaced with a more traditionally hierarchical approach. In listening to the managers, we sense their insecurity, doubts, and anguish when personal values conflict with company goals. Watson pursued these ideas in a later book, co-authored with Pauline Harris (Watson and Harris, 1999), and reached conclusions similar to Hill's (1992). Both of Watson's books portray managers as human beings who struggle to turn fashionable management ideas into practice even as they try to manage a company, other managers, and, not least, themselves.

Public managers amidst ambiguity (18)

Mirko Noordegraaf's research (2000a, 2000b), based on one week of shadowing observations of twelve high-level, Dutch public managers in action, is among the

largest of the recent MWB studies. His study is an interesting combination of
MWB research linked with the 'garbage can' theory of decision-making in public
administration (Cohen et al., 1972; March and Olsen, 1976, 1989) and sharpened
by a Weickean sense-making perspective (Weick, 1995). Noordegraaf's research
has received more attention in the field of public management than in the broader
management behaviour field. His work is of particular interest since it touches on
the institutionalization of the symbolic aspects of management with its focus on
text production, lines of communication, and status hierarchy.

In exploring what public managers do, Noordegraaf points out that their main
task is the management of issue streams. Amidst political struggles, they ensure
that written and spoken texts flow upward to the political level. Noordegraaf's
analysis is guided by the three concepts of actor attendance, actor attention, and
issue attention. Actor attendance describes how public managers' work is meet-
ings-driven and papers-driven: rules dictate when, where, and how meetings are
held; reading, writing, and discussing papers are the reasons for interaction with
colleagues. Political triggers and cues direct their attention, leading to the production of texts with specific deadlines and to meetings they can influence. Issues
that catch their attention are those with institutional foundations that can be
identified and labelled. Public managers are capable of initiating and supporting
these issue streams by altering the form and content of meetings. Such issues,
which are associated with a textual structure, responsible officials, and meetings,
are found in plans, policy papers, or budgets, each with its own procedures. By
controlling and allocating information through texts and meetings, public managers, as professional sense-makers, can influence issues. In short, they know how
to change the rules of the game by playing by the rules.

Post-bureaucratic managers? (19)

In his in-depth, critical reviews of managerial work, Colin Hales is a major
voice in the continuing discussion on the stable vs. the changeable nature of
managerial work (Hales, 1986, 1999, 2002, 2005). In the last decade, the concept of
post-bureaucracy has framed this discussion. One topic in the discussion is the
post-bureaucratic organization that, compared to the traditional, bureaucratic
organization, has more network control, more flexibility, more freedom from
rules, more coordination based on dialogue and trust, more self-organized units,
and more decentralized decision-making (Daft and Lewin, 1993; Heckscher, 1994;
Grey and Garsten, 2001). Associated with this notion of the post-bureaucratic
organization is the claim that radical changes are needed in managerial work
(Drucker, 1988; Zuboff, 1988; Kanter, 1989; Peters, 1989). According to this claim,
managers should be less preoccupied with bureaucratic control and routine
administration and more engaged in the empowerment of their subordinates
through support, consultation, and inspiration.

Hales has written extensively about post-bureaucratic managerial work for
middle managers, both in the United Kingdom and abroad. In one study (Hales
and Tamangani, 1996), he and a colleague researched the retail and hotel sectors
in Zimbabwe where they interviewed five senior managers, four unit managers,
and fifteen to twenty other unit members at four organizations. In this study, they

made a detailed record of the work activities of two unit managers (a week each) in each organization and conducted activity sampling for at least two managers at each organization. In another study, Hales and Mustapha (2000), using a case study design similar to the one used in the Zimbabwe study, studied management at four organizations in the electronics and textile manufacturing sectors in Malaysia. Both studies reveal the prevalence of traditional managerial roles and behaviours. Hales and Mustapha observes only small steps taken towards the post-bureaucratic ideal.

As he had proposed in an earlier article (Hales, 1986), Hales finds the managerial role perspective quite a promising lens for the study of managerial work. In his study of two UK public sector organizations, Hales (2002) collected data on managerial work from in-depth interviews with middle managers and subordinates, supplemented by document reading and two one-week observations. In his comparison between centralized and more decentralized organizations, Hales concludes that middle managers are granted more formal autonomy in the decentralized organizations. However, each middle manager is nevertheless held accountable for the unit's performance. The evidence from this study also reveals that despite the empowerment rhetoric, hierarchical reporting relationships persist, although in a different, less directly regulated form. Because the managers are held personally responsible, there is little likelihood that employees will be treated as independent partners or that close monitoring of performance will be abandoned. According to Hales, this new way of organizing is not post-bureaucratic but rather 'bureaucracy-lite: all the strength of bureaucracy control with only half the hierarchical calories' (2002: 64).

Revisiting the nature of managerial work (20)

Henry Mintzberg's most recent book, *Managing* (2009), is in part a sequel to his *The Nature of Managerial Work* (1973). *Managing* is an updated synthesis of previous studies of managerial work, combined with new empirical material, in this case, twenty-nine managers observed for one day each. The managers are quite varied – for example, the CEO of Canada's largest bank, hospital head nurses, refugee camp managers, and entrepreneurs. The book presents only eight accounts, but all twenty-nine accounts are available from the publisher as a downloadable pdf file.[3]

Using these observations as his support, Mintzberg takes a very critical view of organizational research that highlights the role of leadership to the extent that the importance of other aspects of managerial work is diminished. He believes the view of the manager/leader as a visionary and a goal-setter is too simplistic and biased. Such a view produces a distorted image, both in theory and in practice, of super-heroic and self-aggrandizing managers (leaders). Mintzberg is also critical of the popular distinction between management and leadership, which he says is easy to make conceptually but much harder to make practically.

Mintzberg also acknowledges the highly complex, fragmented, hectic, and often chaotic nature of management. Thus, he presents a multifaceted and integrated model of management that, in a rather complex way, avoids the either/or reasoning that is typical of popular management textbooks. According to Mintzberg, a manager has the generalist's ability to think, communicate, lead, and execute, and yet is also knowledgeable about the fine-grained operational affairs in the organization. He proposes an interactive view of leadership, based on the interdependence of managers and subordinates, in which a good manager strives to create a genuine sense of community – in his term, a 'communityship'.

Mintzberg presents his conception of the required competences of good managers, which reveal the complexity of the managerial role:

- *Personal Competencies*: Managing oneself (reflecting, managing time, prioritizing, and agenda setting).
- *Interpersonal Competencies*: Leading individuals and groups, and building organizational culture (selecting, mentoring/coaching, inspiring, team-building, and resolving conflicts). Administering and linking the organization/unit (allocating resources and delegating).
- *Informational Competencies*: Communicating verbally and non-verbally, and analysing information (listening, presenting, seeing, sensing, information gathering, evaluating, modelling, and disseminating).
- *Actional Competencies*: Designing and mobilizing (planning, visioning, fire-fighting, negotiating, politicking, and managing change).

In addition, Mintzberg's *Managing* argues for a new theoretical understanding of managing/management, namely as 'a practice, learned primarily through experience, and rooted in context' (2009: 9). Management practice, according to Mintzberg, develops from three major human spheres: Art (the imaginative, creative, and insightful), Science (analysis and systematic evidence), and Craft (experience and practical learning). Management at its best is insightful, engaging, and mindful; at its worst, it is disconnected from reality, de-spiriting, and disorganized. Mintzberg concludes that while no manager can master all aspects of management, it is sufficient that the manager avoids a bias towards one aspect as well as avoid narcissism and self-aggrandizement.

Stability and change in top managerial work (21)

We conclude this section on important studies of managerial work with a recent study by Emilio Matthaei, *The Nature of Executive Work* (2010), which was his doctoral thesis at the Leipzig Graduate School of Management. For his thesis, Matthaei studied the time allocation of twelve top executives employed by large corporations. He made a detailed examination of each executive's calendar (over four weeks) and also interviewed the executives about their work. In total, he studied more than 3,000 hours of work.

The results confirmed to a large extent findings from previous studies, especially the recent developments in top managerial work described by Tengblad (2002, see also Chapter 12 in this book). Matthaei found that the work life of these executives was hectic and demanding. On average, they worked 65.5 hours a week. Unlike most supervisors and middle managers, the executives did not divide their work into small activities and brief encounters. Most of their work was conducted in rather lengthy meetings, with many participants, outside their offices. They also travelled a great deal. In addition, they used e-mail extensively for routine communications and held personal meetings for dealing with complex matters and for building relationships.

An important finding in the study is the influence of new communication technology (not least, BlackBerries) on the executives' work life. Due to strong competitive pressure, executives must always be ready to respond quickly to questions and requests. Even on weekends and in their free time, they make themselves available. The border between their work and private lives is increasingly blurred.

A particular strength of the study is its large number of illuminating quotations from the interviews, some of which follow. Two of the most significant ideas that emerge are the role of unforeseen events in executives' work and the increasing complexity of their work that requires them to seek advice and exchange information in a thoughtful way. Matthaei writes:

> Everybody needs to bring flexibility to his job. Internal meetings take place during a flexible time window, and of course, also on the weekend, because those are the hours where it is less likely that something unforeseen will happen. (p. 229)

> Via video conferencing or any other form of virtual exchange, you can usually only do daily business tasks. When it comes to important matters, it is required that one can look into the eyes of the other. I think this physical closeness is simply necessary, and I believe that this will not change. (p. 130)

> Things that I have to deal with are so complex that you can only in rare cases find somebody who can give you an advice. I must always seek several expert opinions and then form a big picture. (p. 169)

WHAT DO WE KNOW OF MANAGERIAL WORK? A SYNTHESIS OF PREVIOUS RESEARCH

What can we learn from these studies of managerial work conducted in the last sixty years? The answer is, of course, a great deal. As much as, if not more than, other disciplines and sub-disciplines in management research, these studies, which are generally sensitive to context and setting, offer very detailed, convincing, and representative accounts of managerial work and behaviour. Therefore their empirical findings and theoretical conclusions are of value for more specialized research in management science.

However, we see little evidence that MWB research is particularly influential in other areas of management studies, except perhaps in such areas as Organizational Behaviour and Organization and Management Theory. In fact, in some areas such as Managerial Cognition, Business Strategy, and Decision-Making there seems to be a systematic neglect of MWB research. Nevertheless, we ask: How can you study management without taking an interest in what managers do? The increasing complexity of managerial work affects managers' work behaviour; it should definitely affect our entire discipline. If not, our discipline is better described as philosophical, ideological, or even theological instead of as scientific.

Summarizing the main results of MWB research

The studies reviewed in this chapter present a general picture of managers who spend little time dealing with systematic approaches to planning and decision-making; instead, most of their time is spent discussing issues and exchanging information in personal meetings, often in response to unanticipated problems. These findings are applicable to all managerial levels, time periods, business cultures, and organizational contexts. Repeatedly, the explanations offered are the extreme job pressure, the great complexity and variety of managerial work tasks, and the disturbing occurrence of unexpected events.

Gradually, authors have acknowledged that the obvious disparity between classic management theory and observed managerial practices is not necessarily due to poorly developed management practices. Rather, the emerging conclusion is that there are also deficiencies in rational management theory. The implication of this conclusion is not that managers should ignore such classic activities as planning, decision-making, organizing, and controlling, but that they should conduct these activities in ways rather unrelated to textbook descriptions. Frequently, these activities have a strong symbolic and political character. Since managers cannot function without legitimacy and power, it is natural that they are concerned with achieving both.

The reviewed studies also display the incremental or processual character of many managerial work activities. Decision-making and strategic planning are often such spontaneous activities that the use of these terms to describe managerial work is somewhat misleading.

Furthermore, it appears that too little focus is given to the informal and emotional aspects of management, such as the influence of social relationships and other arenas not typically associated with management. In the Nordic countries, these arenas are often sailing, golf, sports, cultural events, and, probably most important, hunting. Managers can learn the secrets of management in hunting lodges as much as in conference venues. This is true especially for those managers who are able to distinguish between rather impractical, formal management theory and more hands-on, practical tricks-of-the-trade as well as profound and experienced-based wisdom.

We can, moreover, learn from these studies that managers spend between two-thirds and four-fifths of their time communicating with other people (Hales, 1986: 98). Since human relationships are fundamentally emotional, it is impossible to separate completely the individual from the profession. Thus, when managers interact with their colleagues, they have to deal with their own emotions as well with others' emotions. However, many newly promoted managers are surprised to learn that this requirement is a vital aspect of managerial work (Hill, 1992; Watson and Harris, 1999). This is something seldom taught in management education.

To summarize, the following behavioural patterns are firmly rooted in empirical evidence about managerial work practices, in almost all settings and times:

- Managerial work is generally very demanding with intense time pressures and heavy workloads.
- Managerial work is varied, complex, and often conducted in a rather fragmented manner (especially close to the 'ground level').

- Work outcomes in managerial work are often uncertain and difficult to measure because of the frequent open-endedness of such work.
- Managers mostly work through verbal interactions in different kinds of meetings with subordinates, colleagues, superiors, and outsiders.
- Because of environmental pressures and ambiguity, managerial work is often more about 'looking good' than 'doing right' since many activities are of a symbolic character. The most successful managers master the informal, symbolic, and emotional aspects of managerial work as well as the formal administrative procedures.
- Managers, despite being trained to work deliberately and systematically according to 'textbook models', typically work much more intuitively and inductively. They often need to prioritize on the spot between several on-going tasks and problems, relying heavily on their own work experience and on imitation.
- Rational management models may help managers work in a more structured way, but these models are often poorly adapted to practical work situations.

The theoretical contribution of managerial work research

A frequent charge against MWB research is that it is atheoretical. This is a false criticism. While the MWB research stream challenges the validity of the purely theoretical approaches that attempt to build theories resting on single assumptions of cause and effect, it claims only that management science is too complex and ambiguous to be explained by simple prescriptions and formulas. Nevertheless, despite its resistance to overly formalistic and rationalistic approaches to management science, MWB research has made several important theoretical contributions.

- *Contingency theory.* To a large degree, the study of managerial behaviour by Tom Burns, Rosemary Stewart, among others, made other researchers sensitive to the importance of technological and structural factors in organization theory. It is nowadays essentially taken for granted that size, technology, governance structure, and gender should be considered as potentially important contextual factors in research design work.
- *Emergent strategy/processual perspectives of management.* This view of management, which challenges the sequential thinking idea in management research, particularly as developed by Henry Mintzberg, has had a profound effect on the conventional understanding of management.
- *The notion of general management.* John Kotter's was one of the first researchers to introduce this concept in management research. The general management perspective is now dominant in research about leadership and Human Resource Management as well as in organizational practice.

There is yet a fourth potential contribution from the MWB research. This is the practice theory of management that pulls together the recurrent and enduring findings of previous studies in a holistic conception of management as a complex and multifaceted practice, conducted in a hectic pace in ambiguous settings where outcomes are often uncertain. This chapter and the book as a whole strive to advance that theory.

NOTES

1. For an overview and discussion of the study's background, context, theoretical framing, and methods, see Tengblad (2003).
2. We refer to the revised 1988 edition since our overriding purpose in this chapter is to review research contributions rather than to adhere to a strict chronology of its development.
3. See http://www.pearsoned.co.uk/highereducation/resources/mintzbergmanaging/

REFERENCES

Alvesson, M. (2004). *Knowledge Work and Knowledge-Intensive Firms.* Oxford: Oxford University Press.

Burns, T. (1954). The directions of activity and communication in a departmental executive group: A quantitative study in a British engineering factory with a self-recording technique. *Human Relations,* 7(1): 73–97.

—— (1957). Management in action. *Operational Research Quarterly,* 8(2): 45–60.

—— (1961). Micropolitics: Mechanisms of institutional change. *Administrative Science Quarterly,* 6(3): 257–81.

—— Stalker, G. M. (1961). *The Management of Innovation.* London: Tavistock Publications.

Carlson, S. (1951/91). *Executive Behaviour.* Reprinted with contributions by Henry Mintzberg and Rosemary Stewart. Uppsala, Sweden: Studia Oeconomiae Negotiorum.

Cohen, M. D., March, J. G., and Olsen, J. P. (1972). A garbage can model of organizational choice. *Administrative Science Quarterly,* 17(1): 1–25.

Daft, R. L. and Lewin, A. Y. (1993). Where are the theories for the 'new' organizational forms? An editorial essay. *Organization Science,* 4(4): i–vi.

Dalton, M. (1959). *Men who Manage: Fusions of Feeling and Theory in Administration.* New York: John Wiley.

Drucker, P. F. (1988). The coming of the new organization. *Harvard Business Review,* 66(1): 45–53.

Dubin, R. and Spray, S. L. (1964). Executive behavior and interaction. *Industrial Relations,* 3: 99–108.

Grey, C. and Garsten, C. (2001). Trust, control and post-bureaucracy. *Organization Studies,* 22(2): 229–50.

Guest, R. H. (1956). Of time and the foreman. *Personnel,* 32(6): 478–86.

Hales, C. (1986). What do managers do? A critical review of the evidence. *Journal of Management Studies,* 23(1): 88–115.

—— (1999). Leading horses to water? The impact of decentralization of managerial behaviour. *Journal of Management Studies,* 36(6): 831–51.

—— (2002). 'Bureaucracy-lite' and continuities in managerial work. *British Journal of Management,* 13(1): 51–66.

—— (2005). Rooted in supervision, branching into management: Continuity and change in the role of the first-line manager. *Journal of Management Studies,* 42(3): 471–506.

—— Mustapha, N. (2000). Commonalities and variations in managerial work: A study of middle managers in Malaysia. *Asia Pacific Journal of Human Resources,* 38(1): 1–25.

—— Tamangani, Z. (1996). An investigation of the relationship between organizational structure, managerial role expectations and managers' work activities. *Journal of Management Studies,* 33(6): 731–56.

Hannaway, J. (1989). *Managers Managing: The Workings of an Administrative System.* New York: Oxford University Press.

Heckscher, C. (1994). Defining the post-bureaucratic type. In C. Heckscher and A. Donnellon (Eds.), *The Post-bureaucratic Organization: New Perspectives on Organizational Change* (pp. 14–62). Thousand Oaks, CA: Sage.

Hill, L. A. (1992). *Becoming a Manager: Mastery of a New Identity*. Boston: Harvard Business School Press.

Horne, J. H. and Lupton, T. (1965). The work activities of 'middle' managers – An exploratory study. *Journal of Management Studies*, 2(1): 14–33.

Jackall, R. (1988). *Moral Mazes: The World of Corporate Managers*. New York: Oxford University Press.

Jasinski, F. J. (1956). Foremen relationships outside the work group. *Personnel*, 33: 130–6.

Kanter, R. M. (1977). *Men and Women of the Corporation*. New York: Basic Books.

——(1989). The new managerial work. *Harvard Business Review*, 67(6): 85–92.

Kelly, J. (1964). The study of executive behaviour by activity sampling. *Human Relations*, 17(3): 277–87.

Kotter, J. P. (1982a). *The General Managers*. New York: The Free Press.

——(1982b). What leaders really do. *Harvard Business Review*, 60(3): 156–67.

——Lawrence, P. R. (1974). *Mayors in Action: Five Approaches to Urban Governance: Five Approaches to Urban Governance*. New York: Wiley.

Luthans, F., Hodgetts, R. M., and Rosenkrantz, S. A. (1988). *Real Managers*. Cambridge, MA: Ballinger.

March, J. G. and Olsen, J. P. (1976). *Ambiguity and Choice in Organizations*. Bergen, Norway: Universitetsforlaget.

————(1989). *Rediscovering Institutions: The Organizational Basis of Politics*. New York: Free Press.

Matthaei, E. (2010). *The Nature of Executive Work*. Wiesbaden, Germany: Gabler.

Mintzberg, H. (1968). *The Manager at Work – Determining his Activities, Roles and Programs by Structured Observation*. Cambridge, MA: Massachusetts Institute of Technology.

——(1973). *The Nature of Managerial Work*. New York: Harper & Row, Publishers.

——(1975). The manager's job: Folklore and fact. *Harvard Business Review*, 53(4): 49–61.

——(2009). *Managing*. San Francisco, CA: Berrett-Koehler Publishers.

Noordegraaf, M. (2000a). *Attention! Work and Behavior of Public Managers Amidst Ambiguity*. Delft: Eburon.

——(2000b). Professional sense-makers: Managerial competencies amidst ambiguity. *The International Journal of Public Sector Management*, 13(4): 319–32.

Peters, T. J. (1989). *Thriving on Chaos*. London: Pan.

Sayles, L. R. (1964). *Managerial Behavior: Administration in Complex Organisations*. New York: McGraw-Hill.

Stewart, R. (1967/88). *Managers and Their Jobs: A Study of the Similarities and Differences in the Ways Managers Spend Their Time* (2nd ed.). Basingstoke: The Macmillan Press.

——(1976). *Contrasts in Management*. Maidenhead: McGraw-Hill Book Company.

——(1982). *Choices for the Manager*. Englewood Cliffs, NJ: Prentice-Hall.

——(2008). A tougher world: Managerial work and behaviour. In S. Dopson, M. J. Earl, and P. Snow (Eds.), *Mapping the Management Journey: Practice, Theory, and Context* (pp. 49–62). New York: Oxford University Press.

Tengblad, S. (2002). Time and space in managerial work. *Scandinavian Journal of Management*, 18(4): 543–65.

——(2003). Classic, but not seminal: Revisiting the pioneering study of managerial work. *Scandinavian Journal of Management*, 19(1): 85–101.

Walker, C. R. and Guest, R. H. (1952). *The Man on the Assembly Line*. Cambridge, MA: Harvard University Press.

Walker, C. R. and Guest, R. H. Turner, A. N. (1956). *The Foreman on the Assembly Line.* Cambridge, MA: Harvard University Press.

Watson, T. J. (1994/2001). *In Search of Management: Culture, Chaos and Control in Managerial Work* (Rev. ed.). London: Thomson Learning.

—— Harris, P. (1999). *The Emergent Manager.* London: Sage.

Weick, K. E. (1995). *Sensemaking in Organizations.* Thousand Oaks, CA: Sage Publications.

Whyte, W. F. (1943/93). *Street Corner Society. The Social Structure of an Italian Slum* (4th ed.). Chicago, IL: University of Chicago Press.

Wirdenius, H. (1958). *Supervisors at Work.* Stockholm: The Swedish Council for Personnel Administration.

——(1961). *Förmän i arbete.* Stockholm: The Swedish Council for Personnel Administration.

Zuboff, S. (1988). *In the Age of the Smart Machine: The Future of Work and Power.* New York: Basic Books.

Part II

A practice perspective on leadership and managerial work

The three chapters of Part Two discuss managerial work and leadership in a general sense from the book's practice perspective and establish an empirical foundation for the book's theoretical framework. These chapters are based on numerous observations, interviews, video recordings, and discussions with industrial managers at senior- and middle-management levels, and provide solid evidence for their claims.

CHAPTER 3. MANAGERIAL LEADERSHIP AS EVENT-DRIVEN IMPROVISATION

Ingalill Holmberg and Mats Tyrstrup describe their study of the events that sixty-two managers at a telecom company think typify managerial leadership. The authors' in-depth analysis of such events reveals that leadership is mainly about 'facilitating work processes that are interrupted by unforeseen events in ambiguous circumstances'. To a considerable extent, everyday leadership is reactive and driven by urgent demands. The work outcomes are often unexpected. An important implication of this study is that improvising skills are normally more essential than planning and forecasting skills in helping managers cope with urgent job demands.

CHAPTER 4. MANAGERIAL LEADERSHIP: IDENTITIES, PROCESSES, AND INTERACTIONS

Stefan Sveningsson, Johan Alvehus, and Mats Alvesson discuss three perspectives of leadership: the heroic, the post-heroic, and the mundane. Their main message is that if we want to understand leadership as an empirical phenomenon of work practices, we need to base our understanding in ordinary managers' work (i.e. the work of jobholders who have leadership responsibilities). In order to understand leadership as a work practice, more theories grounded in the actual behaviour of leaders are needed. Such research contrasts with the theoretical and ideological ideas that researchers and other societal actors have about how leaders should behave. The authors claim that aligning leadership research with studies of managerial work is a good beginning.

CHAPTER 5. MULTI-FRAMING AS A TOOL IN TOP MANAGEMENT TEAMS

Gary Kokk, Sten Jönsson, and Airi Rovio-Johansson study management as a collective action in a very intense and longitudinal investigation of a senior management group. The authors use video recording and follow-up discussions in their research. The chapter provides an illustration of how corporate strategies emerge in collective sense-making and sense-giving discussions. In such discussions, the managers not only cope with complexity and uncertainty but also align the organization towards the emerging objectives of the management group. This view of management as a collective performance also reveals how various managerial competences and knowledge are used in managerial work settings.

3

Managerial leadership as event-driven improvisation[1]

Ingalill Holmberg and Mats Tyrstrup

INTRODUCTION

The HR manager of the Swedish international telecom company, TECO, opened the internal workshop on leadership with the following question: 'How do ideals and ideas on leadership shape the work of managers?' She also welcomed us, two researchers from the Stockholm School of Economics, who had been invited to give a short lecture on leadership and leadership ideals from the academic point of view. It was a sunny day in September, and the group consisted of about fifteen people from the HR department.

We spent an exciting day discussing the expectations that people generally have of managers, and more specifically their expectations based on the assumption that managers are leaders. By afternoon it was obvious to everyone that the normative models of leadership were of limited use in understanding and explaining the role of leadership in everyday managerial work. With no clear answers in the group, we summarized the meeting with a simple question: 'What does leadership mean to managers whose everyday work takes place in relatively ordinary circumstances?' This question became the starting point for a four-year, collaborative project on everyday leadership at TECO.

This chapter examines leadership in practice through an investigation of how sixty-two TECO managers (including project leaders), competing in a cutting-edge environment, perceive and describe the characteristics of everyday leadership. Based on the common notion of fragmentation in managerial work, as well as the unfortunate lack of understanding of how managerial work relates to the overall work processes of the organization, the chapter addresses the integrated job of managing (e.g. see Mintzberg, 1994; Hales, 1999).

With its focus on the more or less objective facts of managerial work and their causal, situational factors, the research on managerial work systematically neglects the connection between individuals' actions and their understanding of organizational activities (Noordegraaf and Stewart, 2000). Therefore, studies are needed that place everyday work, the creation of meaning, and sense-making (creation of meaning) processes at centre stage (Weick, 1979/67, 1995; Alvesson, 1989; Weick and Sutcliffe, 2006; Sandberg and Targama, 2007). We used sixty-two narratives ('live cases'), roughly classified according to a simple process model – a situation we call 'Well then – What now?' – to examine leadership activities in everyday work. Using this situation model as a point of departure, we present and discuss three mini-cases in this chapter. Our research revealed a sense-making process consisting of three sets of activities – the need for interpretations, constant adjustments, and formulations of temporary solutions. We propose that everyday leadership, as an event-driven activity rather than an intention-driven activity, requires improvisation and the ability to tune in. The chapter concludes with a discussion of some practical implications of the research.

MANAGERIAL WORK AND LEADERSHIP

Since the literature on managerial work and leadership is extensive, a theoretical framing focus is needed for more explicit study of these topics in everyday settings. A seminal and well-known study of managerial work, particularly of managers' activity patterns, from the early 1950s revealed that managers have a heavy workload with many issues to attend to. In addition, this study revealed that the time spent on each of these issues was less than ten minutes (Carlson, 1951).

Carlson's pioneering work in the field has been validated by almost every later study of managerial work where the focus is on activity patterns and work content (e.g. Burns, 1957; Mintzberg, 1973; Stewart, 1976, 1982; Kotter, 1982; Hales, 1986; Holmberg, 1986; Tyrstrup, 1993; Tengblad, 2002, 2003, 2006).[2] The main conclusion of these studies, including Carlson's, is that managerial work is highly fragmented, and managers would be better off if they managed their time so that they could devote more time to strategic thinking. In one of the most quoted sections from his study, Carlson describes his assumption that the managing director is an orchestra conductor who can and should supervise both operations and the organization at the same time. Although this image starkly contrasts with his findings, that is, the manager as a puppet, controlled by people 'pulling the strings', the conductor image of the strategic manager has endured among both managers and academics (Yukl, 1989; Collins, 2001a, 2001b; House et al., 2007).

Although most studies that take the management behavioural approach have argued against detached conceptualizations – for example, Gulick and Urwick's famous POSDCORB (planning, organizing, staffing, directing, coordinating, reporting, and budgeting) (1987/37) – the fragmentation of managerial work remains a major concern. While challenging the depiction of management as the rational, reflective, systematic accomplishment of predetermined objectives, the understanding of the highly reactive work pattern of managers is still in dispute. Snyder and Glueck (1980) claimed that the methods used in studies of managerial work themselves produced what looked like fragmentation. They argued that managerial tasks, such as problem solving, often consist of several, sometimes seemingly disparate, activities, which may seem 'fragmented' if aims and purposes are not related to each other on an overall level. Tengblad (2006), in his replication of Mintzberg's 1973 study of managerial work, concludes that measuring the amount of time spent on activities, as opposed to measuring the frequency of activities, provides a different view of the fragmented pattern of managerial work. Thus, the appreciation of the fragmentation of work as a problem may be due to a lack of understanding of how managerial work relates to the overall working processes of organizations (Hales, 1986). Mintzberg (1994: 11) expresses a similar idea in his argument that researchers have been 'so intent on breaking the job into pieces that we never came to grips with the whole thing. It is time, therefore, to consider the integrated job of managing'. Noordegraaf and Stewart (2000) also support this conclusion with their claim that the majority of research studies try to understand the more or less objective facts of managerial work and the causally determined situational factors. With a few exceptions (e.g. Watson, 1994, 1996), the study of processes and sense-making, and thus the creation of meaning related to organizational activity, is severely neglected.

Evidently there seems to be a growing understanding among leading scholars, who have researched managerial work for decades, that for a deeper understanding of the role of managerial work and leadership, studies are needed that more explicitly take everyday work, the process-perspective, and 'sense-making' as points of departure.

In his explicit focus on the interplay between individuals' actions and how they reach understandings in organizations, Weick (1979, 1995) has convincingly shown that individuals act first and understand the significance of their actions afterwards. Based on this research, Weick also claimed that in an organized context there is a constant need for interpretation and sense-making. Since actions precede their interpretation, the time-perspective is crucial in understanding how things are done in organizations and, thus, in understanding how managerial leadership functions in everyday settings. Even though the sense-making processes tend to filter away information that does not fit in or contribute to the process of making sense of problems, situations, or events (Knorr Cetina, 1981), the output of sense-making processes is by no means self-evident: actors create their environment and the environment creates the actors (Weick, 1995; see also Berger and Luckmann, 1966; Giddens, 1984).

Returning to Carlson's pioneering work, there is no reason to believe that today's managers work less hard than in previous years or that the number of issues they attend to has diminished. On the contrary, recent studies show that the intensity of work is increasing, the mode of work is now based on coordination of activities in both time and space, and there is a constant need for change and adjustment (Mintzberg and Westley, 2001; Tengblad, 2006). However, in recent decades, the focus on managerial work has been replaced by studies emphasizing the leadership dimension. In contrast to managerial work, leadership is defined as the ability to present compelling visions and goals that are grounded in a company's value system (Bass, 1985; Conger, 1989; Yukl, 1989; Bryman, 1992; Conger and Kanungo, 1998; Holmberg and Åkerblom, 2001).

When scholars distinguish leadership from managerial work in the fragmentation of day-to-day work, they imply a certain sense of timing – partly reflecting the different tasks that should be completed and partly reflecting who is responsible for them (Zaleznik, 1977; Kotter, 1990). Expressed differently, the concept of leadership is closely connected to a perception of the ordering of things that is quite different from Weick's ideas on sense-making and action: in the present, certain people (the leaders) take actions that have consequences for the future because others (the followers) perform activities as a consequence of these actions.

Thus, leadership becomes a question of relationships between activities that occur today and those that are expected to occur in the future. This view of managers as strategic actors with a mission clearly places the manager at the centre stage of the sense-making processes (Selznick, 1957; Bass, 1985; Bennis and Nanus, 1985; Nanus, 1992; Collins, 2001a, 2001b; House et al., 2007). Based on our studies of everyday work and leadership, we argue that there is a far more complicated interplay between current activities, historical events, expectations, and the perceived need to exercise leadership.

METHODOLOGY

How do you capture people's everyday experiences? How do you understand leadership in such a context? How do you study the events and developments that are important in and for individuals' everyday tasks? Such questions are not easily answered. In the preparation for our study, we decided to address these questions with the TECO managers in a relatively simple and straightforward way. Therefore, we asked them to briefly describe an example of leadership by writing one or two pages about an event or a situation that they associated with leadership. Our only requirement was that the event or situation should be a personal experience.

The study described in this chapter is one of several studies undertaken jointly with the TECO Group in Sweden. The main goal of these studies was to collect live cases of everyday leadership (i.e. leadership events or situations that the TECO managers consider everyday phenomena). In total, sixty-two managers participated in the study – twenty-eight managers submitted written live cases, and thirty-four managers presented their cases verbally. All cases were documented and analysed at workshops that took place during the years 2001–3. The managers in the study were middle managers or project leaders. There were more than two organization layers between most of these managers and TECO's top management group. With a few exceptions, these managers, who had other managers reporting to them, had operational leadership responsibilities, including human resources responsibilites. It is important to note that a middle manager in a company such as TECO can be responsible for a substantial budget and a considerable number of co-workers. These responsibilities are comparable to those required of managing directors of medium-sized companies.

TECO as an international telecom company operates in an extremely competitive environment where product development and innovation are crucial for survival and success. Our study of everyday leadership was conducted during the years when TECO was engaged in a huge downsizing programme. Due to heavy investments in the late 1990s, combined with an aggressive expansion strategy, TECO suffered serious difficulties when the IT and telecom markets collapsed in 2000–1. In the struggle to avoid bankruptcy, the company's top management group, headed by the CEO, launched a series of tough cost-cutting programmes in combination with the adoption of outsourcing programmes, including the formation of a joint venture mobile telephone company. In 2003, the TECO Group had recovered from the severe crisis and was once again a competitive global player. However, these rather extreme circumstances raised the question of whether the results of this particular study could be generalized to other organizations and other contextual settings. We will return to this issue at the end of this section.

Methodologically, the study is a structured interpretation process conducted jointly by those individuals providing the research data (i.e. the TECO middle managers and project leaders) and the project researchers. It is worth mentioning that our studies were not quantitative in nature and had no quantitative ambitions. Our research design is based on a qualitative approach where the analysis emphasizes identification of 'typical' cases and themes. Our main purpose was to reveal interesting and, from a managerial point of view, relevant aspects of leadership in an everyday context.

Different ways of structuring the material were developed during the workshops where we analysed and discussed the leadership narratives. While some workshops were an integrated part of a senior management training programme, other workshops took place because the participants asked for a follow-up session. Using the narratives as points of departure, the workshops were designed to identify relevant themes. Plenary sessions (with ten to fifteen participants and six full-day seminars) were combined with small group work (approximately five participants per group). By alternating between small group discussions and plenary sessions, the process of joint analysis and interpretation moved from the individual cases towards more generalized concepts and models that portray the perception of leadership in an everyday context.

INTRODUCTION OF A PROCESS PERSPECTIVE

In analysing and discussing the managers' cases, two questions immediately arose in the plenary sessions: (*a*) What were the narratives about? and (*b*) What were the narratives not about? It was also evident that time was an active ingredient in the managers' narratives about their leadership experiences (see Czarniawska, 1998). Although the first question was quite difficult to answer precisely, more so than the second question, our general conclusion was that most cases were concerned with some type of 'critical incident'. Since we gave no instructions to the managers on either the content or the form of their cases of everyday leadership, the concept of 'critical incident' is a research result rather than part of the research design.

In order to identify and classify the everyday aspects of leadership, a simple process model was introduced. It was obvious that a process model was requried since all cases had a beginning and an end, and leadership in an everyday context was usually framed as a kind of intervention in an on-going series of events. Yet another aspect of time reflected in the cases was the common agreement that many activities are performed working against the clock or working according to a very tight schedule (i.e. the calendar). Time was also significant in understanding leadership action in that a decision that appeared very logical one day might seem completely absurd a few days later. For example, information, events, etc. may suddenly pop up that affect how the situation appears to all involved.

INTRODUCTION

Opportunities	vs.	Problems

PROCESS

Smooth	vs.	Difficult

OUTCOME

According to plan	vs.	Other than planned

Figure 3.1 Classification scheme for leadership narratives from a process perspective

Hence, we started to discuss what most of the TECO managers acknowledged as a common point of departure for thinking about leadership and leadership conditions. Quite early in the discussion, opportunities vs. problems and intentional vs. chance outcomes were mentioned. Our next step was to characterize the leadership process as either smooth or difficult, depending on the conditions where leadership was required. A smooth process implied there was a reasonably high degree of predictability concerning efforts made and measures taken; such predictability was not a characteristic of a difficult process. Finally, we classified the outcomes by comparing them to what had been the managers' initial intentions. The outcome was either 'According to plan' or 'Other than planned'. See Figure 3.1 for a schematic structure of this classfication of the outcomes.

We used this classification scheme to discuss the managers' cases individually. In the first step, we asked the managers to classify their cases according to the classification scheme. The results were the following: 36 per cent of the live cases began with an 'opportunity' of some kind, which means that 64 per cent of the cases had a perceived 'problem' as a beginning. In terms of whether the process was smooth or difficult, 25 per cent of the cases were described as fairly 'smooth' and 75 per cent were described as 'difficult'. In terms of outcomes, 54 per cent of the cases were classified as 'according to plan' and 46 per cent were classified as 'other than planned'. Interestingly, however, most cases classified as 'other than planned' were not, in themselves, judged as failures.

From a theoretical point of view, the interpretative scheme specifies eight different models or possible courses of events. However, the narratives clearly indicated that three models – the Textbook Version, the Heroic Story, and the Well then – What now? scenario – were more relevant than the others as far as how the managers think about their leadership in an everyday context. According to most managers in this study, these three models reflect the tension between controlling and managing events as opposed to finding oneself trapped by circumstances.

Next, we discuss the context of the study, followed by a detailed presentation of the three models.

CONTEXT OF THE STUDY – POSSIBLE LIMITATIONS

Because our study was conducted during a period of severe economic crisis at TECO, we asked ourselves whether the managers' narratives were significantly influenced by these economic conditions. In some instances, the managers were very engaged in dealing with the crisis. Many managers, however, described events that had occurred a few years before the crisis. A few managers described events and situations that occurred during the crisis but were neither influenced by the crisis nor involved in the efforts to resolve it. The implication, supported by our findings, is that managerial leadership in an everyday setting seems to develop as more or less intensive 'crisis management'. However, since the study was not explicitly designed to examine such variations, the impact of 'crisis' calls for a more systematic approach to this particular issue. The argument could, of course, be raised regarding the environmental context (i.e. the highly innovative and rapidly changing world of the telecom industry). Since contextual factors clearly play an important role in the practice of everyday leadership at TECO, further study of these factors is needed.

The Textbook Version

We arrived at the first model by beginning in the left column in Figure 3.1 – the sequence of opportunities–smooth–according to plan. We call this model the Textbook Version. The starting point is that there are opportunities that can be exploited. The model is positive and expectant and suggests that something new must be created, built, or developed. It is certainly about change. There is a design for a process and a plan that not only includes the different stages and the activities that must be carried out but also includes a chronological time schedule. The plan is put into action and, through the foresight that characterizes good leadership, is realized without too many disturbing elements. Thus, the matter concludes with the realization of the original purpose and the fulfillment of the plan's intentions. Everything has occurred just as intended.

   This is leadership in its full glory. What was just an idea of the future has been realized in accordance with the original intentions. It can be said that the majority of what we usually call management literature deals with how this smooth process will be effected. There are numerous models that claim to describe the factors and phases that help to realize this sequence of the opportunities–smooth–according to plan pattern (see e.g. Kotter, 1990; Collins, 2001*a*). Yet the Textbook Version of leadership was not typical among the leadership cases we studied at TECO. Only 10 per cent of the cases followed this model of leadership.

The Heroic Story

We identified the second model by combining a problem with a cross between smooth and difficult, while still allowing the whole process to end according to plan. This course of events, as outlined in Figure 3.1, thus ranged diagonally from the upper right corner to the lower left corner. This sequence was managers' favourite narrative – the story of heroic feats. Approximately 20 per cent of the cases of this study were close to this heroic model of leadership.

Many managers tend to describe their efforts according to this model. They begin with a challenging problem (which, by the way, is much bigger than initially expected). A process follows that includes many difficult turns. Knotty problems arise, and at times everything looks bleak – very bleak indeed. But the competent manager has a basic agenda consisting of a number of stages to follow and steps to take. In hindsight, it can be claimed that the whole process has gone according to plan and a successful conclusion has been reached.

There are many stories of chief executives, managers, project leaders, etc. who have had significant triumphs in turning adversity into success and problems into solutions (Carlzon, 2008/1985; Welch, 2005). For these managers, the questions of what should be done and how it should be done are obvious at an early stage. Those who claim such leadership skills believe they know what things will be like at a certain period of time and whether things will actually turn out as planned. Knowing today what should be done tomorrow in order to reach the desired results – plan, implementation, outcome – is presented as an essential factor of leadership. Although such early-stage analysis is considered the hallmark of good leadership, it is, however, far from clear that such insight corresponds to leadership in practice.

Well then – What now?

We identified the third model through a description of a problem situation such as the following. You find yourself in a problematic situation, working hard and wrestling with the issues as they appear, only to find you are constantly trying to grasp the situation. It is not at all certain how you got where you are or what the situation means. It is extremely difficult to assess how the situation fits with the intentions articulated a few days, a week, or a month ago. It is hard to tell what has been completed, what is still going on, or what is yet to be accomplished. People are constantly at your throat, asking for different instructions or directions. People higher up in the hierarchy, those lower down, and even those at the same level want information and reports that give the results of decisions taken and activities performed. One event seems to give rise to another according to a logic that is anything but obvious. As a manager, you are tired and need a break to go through your papers, e-mails, the heaps of files, and the phone messages in order to sort out your thoughts and feelings. In Figure 3.1, this model corresponds to the sequence indicated in the right column – problem–difficult–other than planned.

The managers of this study identified this model as the most typical one in their everyday work. This leadership model accounted for approximately 50 per cent of the live cases. To describe this familiar situation confronting managers, we labelled the model: 'Well then – What now?' In this chapter we focus on this third model by an analysis of three of the cases in our research.

Table of Contents

THREE CASES OF LEADERSHIP

Our purpose in selecting these three cases is not to illustrate either good or bad leadership. Rather, our intention is to present examples of issues and situations that arise in the everyday work of managers – including other people's expectations as far as the exercise of management and leadership. We have given fictitious names to the managers and other actors in these three cases.

Collaboration problems in John's unit

John was responsible for what was then a recently established system management unit. In addition to the staff he 'inherited' from another unit, there were a number of new appointments to his unit. John described one inherited staff member, Bengt, as a person of 'considerable competence' but who had difficulties 'fitting' into the organizational set up. Bengt was a member of staff who did not 'produce any results'. The situation gradually became untenable as more people began to talk about Bengt in similar terms, as if mirroring John's opinion.

From the start, John tried to give Bengt 'open and autonomous tasks as that is what he insisted upon and nobody else really wanted to work with him'. When Bengt worked with anyone else, the result was his 'rushing angrily from the meeting' or stopping 'all work by arguing and protesting'. John also gradually began to regard Bengt as increasingly 'sloppy' in his work that was often 'inaccurate and couldn't be used'. The situation was an uncomfortable one for all concerned.

After a while, John's manager requested a meeting with John to ask if he could do anything to help with regard to Bengt. This meeting led John to have a 'serious talk' with Bengt. The help he had been offered was, in fact, either Bengt's transfer or dismissal. Finding a solution was essential, John and his manager nonetheless agreed that they should wait a little longer before making any decision. John wanted to try to solve the problem in other ways – at least for a while longer.

In talking to Bengt, John explained that the situation 'was serious' and that he 'wanted to help him', but that he found the present situation 'unacceptable'. There was, however, as John said, 'no great change even though Bengt's conduct became somewhat calmer and less disruptive'.

'More out of desperation than thinking it might help', John said he began to give Bengt 'limited and in my view boring tasks of documentation and general information gathering' in connection with a report for the unit. John said, 'This was completely the opposite of what Bengt said he wanted to do, and I was concerned that he would argue too much'. As it turned out, it was a very successful solution. As a result, Bengt found it easier to work with others in the unit, and John saw that Bengt was 'happier and, above all, has started to produce results'. To conclude, John could say that he and Bengt 'had reviewed the salary scales today and agreed that while the previous year's results had not been very good, the situation had now changed'. Bengt himself said he was 'on board' again. The future was looking brighter.

Peter and a solid resistance to change

At the end of the 1990s, a TECO unit was created to coordinate purchases and the internal flow of components for a certain product. Production was distributed among a number of different units around the world. Responsibility for purchasing and logistics had previously been decentralized within these production units.

Peter worked in this newly created unit. As far as the production set up is concerned, he said that the supply of components had previously been rather haphazard and had 'damaged the whole product area'. Therefore, Peter and his staff were supposed to develop systems and routines for the purchase and distribution of components to those units responsible for production. The new unit was also supposed to deal with questions on the life cycle of the products supplied. This task meant dealing with new as well as older components, in both small and large quantities, depending on whether the components were intended for newly developed products, for more mature products, or for obsolete products. Peter said that 'because the R&D units had not had sole responsibility for the supply of these products before, they were not interested in how supply functioned in volume, so we had to deal with the problems ourselves as best we could'.

After a number of planning meetings, Peter and his staff decided that the right approach would be to 'work themselves into the different research and development projects in three different places in Europe'. They would start with Research and Development (R&D) in order to develop routines that would lead to an efficient work flow.

Peter and his staff began visiting these three units with the intention of establishing an efficient and cooperative production supply system. It was also intended that some suppliers might participate by developing smooth routines and methods that would also be used with external parties. However, Peter and his staff returned home having achieved little. On their visits they had encountered an atmosphere of surprise. This was discussed with people individually and in the group to try to determine what the others might be thinking and experiencing. The decision to create a purchasing unit had been taken at quite a high level in the organization. What was really going on?

Eventually, people in Peter's unit saw a pattern of obvious resistance to cooperation by all three research units. After spending a lot of time trying to understand why collaboration was so difficult since they could identify no particular provocation, Peter and his staff concluded that the problem might be solved if the people in the purchasing and R&D units could get 'to know each other better'. They set to work again, thinking that time would solve the problem, although time had become a problem in itself. At this stage, some of the time-tabled deadlines for the development of the new activity had already passed without the planned results being achieved.

Peter and his staff then revisited the three European sites. However, this time, they had fewer ambitious expectations about the future activities of the new unit. Their priority was to understand how the work in these units was organized and what the units' staffs thought about the issues of supply and flow. By taking this approach, it was thought that relationships would develop, knowledge would increase, and a platform would be created for working on routines and work methods for the joint supply of components.

Despite this renewed effort, Peter and his staff still did not have very many opportunities to accomplish their objective. As the weeks passed, the feeling of not getting anywhere increased in the new purchasing unit. Time was now critical. Yet they were scratching their heads over a problem that later was shown to be quite trivial. Peter learned that there had previously been quite severe downsizing in the R&D units. He realized there was a fear that the new purchasing unit would take over both the work and the decision-making. To some extent, this fear was justified.

The signs of difficulties were numerous. 'We could barely agree on anything', Peter said, pointing out that they 'weren't given any information about the projects'. The suppliers were excluded from a large part of the work. He continued: 'Agreements that we made as a result of numerous and long discussions' were never carried out. Indeed, this was still the situation when Peter told his story.

Development work around Lisa and her group

Lisa was a project leader for a group that worked with the development of production concepts and production processes. In her narrative, she described how 'after a hectic period of construction and production preparation' everything was set to move to a second phase where the purpose was to prepare a new product for serial production. It was then realized that '85% of the products' that had been tested didn't meet the 'performance requirements'. When this fact became known, the management group that had overall responsibility for the new product and Lisa's team began to blame each other.

According to Lisa, the product developers had difficulty in 'accepting that the product suddenly didn't work' and concluded that it must have something to do with mistakes in the testing. She said that people on the project side claimed 'the product's construction was unstable and not sufficiently developed'. Therefore, they could not initiate preparations for serial production. In her narrative, Lisa explained that it was only after some weeks of dispute that these opinions crystallized and were expressed at a crisis meeting. She also said that 'during the same evening', she had been contacted by her superior who asked her 'to explain it to him', as he had also been faced with 'difficult questions' from the individual with overall responsibility for the product. While this individual maintained he had received information from Lisa's superior, Lisa did not think this claim agreed with what she and her superior 'had been discussing earlier that same afternoon'.

There was clearly a crisis of confidence between the two units as a result of the many different messages received about the problems and their possible solutions. These conflicting messages originated in part from Lisa and her unit and in part from Lisa's superior.

Lisa's staff also wondered what on earth was going on. They thought that a lot of different information was being circulated, leading to the spread of rumours. Lisa discussed the situation with her staff and tried, as she said, 'to pep them up a bit'. But the confusion continued, both in Lisa's group and in the development work. No one really knew what to do. Most people chose to wait and see whether the situation would become any clearer.

A few days later Lisa, her superior, and the product manager decided to draw up a troubleshooting list, headed as 'problems', without specifying any kind of design or test fault. They would go through the list to see what could be done in each case, partly by changing the product design and partly by looking at the manufacturing process. This was how the work would be structured, and alternatives for how they might go forward would be identified. As Lisa summarizes the affair: 'The final solution was, as usual, a mix of reconstruction and improved production with closer controls'. She notes that during this period, much of her time was spent supporting and encouraging her staff and getting them to work 'together with those who complained that we were careless and not interested in the new product' and how it should be produced.

ANALYSIS

As noted above, we selected these three narratives to exemplify the issues and situations that characterize the everyday work of managers. We see these issues and situations as typical elements in what is perceived as managerial work that also includes other people's expectations about their management skills and leadership abilities.

There is a noteworty, and typical, commonality in these narratives – things do not always turn out as expected. Either something unexpected happens, or what was expected to happen does not. What is obvious is that in many situations, everyday work is event-driven. At first one person, then many persons, and finally everyone in a situation experiences a sense of confusion about what is going on, what needs to be done, who should perform the required tasks, and who should take responsibility. If the situation does not improve, the expectations for action are targeted at the manager in charge. In general, the process that follows requires three managerial measures: interpretation, adjustments/choices, and solution formulations. The first measure is to interpret the situation in order to identify what has happened and to formulate some kind of explanation. The second measure, resulting from the interpretation, is to decide among a number of adjustments and choices. The interpretation points in a certain direction. Acting in accordance with this interpretation may solve a number of problems but at the same time may create others. The third measure is to find a solution, on the spur-of-the-moment, that can be implemented immediately to get things going.

The need for interpretation

An important and very central feature of everyday leadership, according to our study, is to contribute to the interpretation process in which one or more people attempt to understand what has happened and/or to understand why what had been expected has not occurred.

The Peter narrative is an example of a situation in which the expected did not happen. Peter and his staff were concerned with one particular question: Why didn't the R&D units want to cooperate in solving an important problem in the product area? The expectation was there would be a collaborative approach to the problem, but the units refused to cooperate. The John and Lisa narratives are examples of situations where events that were neither planned nor foreseen occurred. Lisa said she was constantly surprised by new information about the activities related to her group; this new information led her to re-evaluate her perception of what was going on. John said that he really tried to accommodate Bengt by giving him acceptable tasks, but was obliged to intervene on numerous occasions when Bengt rubbed his colleagues the wrong way. Bengt's actions led John to wonder what he could do to help Bengt work more flexibly and cooperatively in the unit.

In each case, the manager had to interpret what had already happened in order to formulate what the next step should be. What was the significance of what had or hadn't happened? How might these events and non-events be best explained, and what are their implications? While these are questions managers ask themselves when expectations are not realized, they are not the questions that managers need to actively plan for or explicitly think about. Such events and non-events occur spontaneously and require managers to understand what is happening at the time (Weick, 1979/67, 1995). Of course, managers manage such situations with varying degrees of sucess, especially when many people are involved. A certain awareness of the situation, however, increases every manager's ability to actively contribute to, as well as influence, such processes (Gioia and Chittipedi, 1991; see also Styhre, this book, Chapter 7, and Kokk et al., this book, Chapter 5). Based on our live cases, it can be said that a significant part of everyday leadership is concerned with interpretative processes.

Constant adjustments and choices

One aspect of these interpretive processes is that they tend to generate several possible scenarios. As a situation continues, the possibilities for a number of adjustments or different alternatives become apparent although the best path is far from obvious. The best path may mean adjustments are needed that allow more time to communicate, to search for a satisfactory solution, or to consider who needs to be involved. Choosing the best path may even involve balancing ethical, practical, and economic considerations or balancing short- and long-term goals. These are only a few examples of factors that the TECO managers highlighted in this context.

The situation is made more difficult by the fact that such decisions are never static. Often what seemed right and was a priority one day may seem completely wrong in the light of new experience and information. This was particularly apparent in Peter's narrative. When the decision to change was first announced,

Peter decided on the necessary tasks. As time passed, and the whole picture of the change problem became clearer, the lack of urgency also became more evident.

John tried to achieve a balance between behaving humanely towards a staff member and meeting his responsibility for efficient production in his unit. If Bengt's behaviour had not changed, how long would it have been before the transfer or dismissal that John's boss had suggested became a necessity? If tolerance of the disruptive behaviour of one individual damages the working environment for other staff in a unit, how much damage can be tolerated?

Perhaps it may be said that in the world of everyday work, it is difficult for a manager to formulate solutions that cannot be misinterpreted in the local context. Consistent with previous studies on managerial work (Carlson, 1951; Mintzberg, 1973; Kotter, 1982; Tengblad, 2002, 2003) that suggest most leadership, to some extent, is shaped by a series of disruptive and fragmented events, we agree that generally leadership requires 'muddling through' (Lindblom, 1959). This actually means paying sequential attention to events and problems (Simon, 1947; Cyert and March, 1963). Certain problems and questions are solved while others must quite simply be left to fortune – at least temporarily.

Momentary solutions

The need for everyday leadership emerges constantly since there are always events that require immediate management action. Much leadership is thus about finding the right solutions for the problems of the particular moment and making sure that the most important and urgent problems are solved so that the work may continue. In Lisa's narrative, in particular, this sense of urgency was notoriously present and very important.

Many TECO managers talked about the need to adapt their leadership style to the situation. Where the situation is ever-changing, they constantly search for solutions that typically require them to make adjustments or new choices, both in their ways of working and in their priorities. Sometimes it is necessary to change direction – perhaps even permanently. Often the timing of activities has to be recalculated to meet a changed schedule. Many people are involved – staff, peers, superiors – when these adjustments and choices are required. In different ways, these people have to be involved, informed, and allowed to express their opinions. The managers in our study argued that plenty of time has to be allowed for discussions and explanations. In addition, as it becomes clearer, the motivation for the present policy might be explained. But then something else happens. It may only be a matter of days or weeks, sometimes only a matter of hours and minutes, before new circumstances arise and turn the entire situation in a different and unexpected direction. This development requires finding new solutions for the moment. Some scholars refer to this search for new solutions as a form of 'tinkering' (Knorr Cetina, 1981; Clarke and Fujimura, 1992). Tinkering involves a kind of 'indexical' (local or situational) logic and a fair amount of opportunism – using what is at hand to resolve situations and to solve problems (see also Styhre, this book, Chapter 7).

Swedish Agency for Innovation. I moreover thank Ola Edvin Vie and Rebecka Arman for their effort as co-authors and coordinators of several chapters in the book and Marcia Halvorsen for language editing. My thanks finally go to all the studied managers, to Sten Jönsson for introducing me to this research field, and to David Musson and his very professional and helpful colleagues at the Oxford University Press. Thank you all!

Stefan Tengblad
Skövde and Gothenburg

Preface

Editing a book with more than thirty authors is a challenging task. Thanks to the responsible collaboration by all the authors, to say nothing of their impressive research competence, my task was greatly simplified. In my opinion, this book is a unique collection of high quality studies on managerial work.

As the book progressed, I noted the many similarities between editorship and the managerial work that the book's authors describe. First, uncertainty was a constant. Will the invited authors join the project? Will they deliver their chapters on schedule? Will their contributions be high quality? Will a respected publisher accept the manuscript?

Second, there is complexity. It was a challenge to unify the book's goals and themes and to write the introduction and conclusion chapters that would do justice to the individual contributions.

Third, there is the dynamic process of planning, rescheduling, and making adjustments and innovations. An anthology editor begins with a formal plan that appeals to the invited authors, but as the project evolves, it is constantly necessary to improvise and innovate. However, a project to edit a research book that does not include an important degree of learning is not worth undertaking. And anything more than 10–15 per cent of the total work effort spent on planning instead of execution is procrastination.

Fourth, and perhaps most important, an editor must establish and maintain good relationships with the book's contributors in the same way that managers need to develop good relationship with their peers. Many promising book projects have failed because of poor rapport between editor and contributor(s). It is my hope that the process of editing this book has strengthened my professional, as well as personal, relationships with the chapter authors.

The fifth and last similarity between managerial and editorial work is the pride of having completed a challenging project. Successful editorial work, like successful managerial work, is fun and rewarding!

Despite the complexity, uncertainty, and pressure of assembling a book on innovative management research, the editor of such a book, like the managers these chapters describe, can contribute to better organizations and societies. For both editors and managers, the key is to remain energetic, curious, optimistic, adaptive, and communicative.

For practical reasons, I am hesitant to undertake such a book project again as sole editor in the near future. Nevertheless, I will always remember my positive experience of finalizing this book. Therefore, I thank all the authors for their chapters, as well as their support. I especially thank Lars Engwall and Carin Eriksson Lindvall for their valuable assistance in the work of launching this book project and for their efforts as hosts for a book workshop and a Symposium in memory of Sune Carlson held in Gustavianum, Uppsala, in August 2009.

I also want to acknowledge the financial support for this book project from the Jan Wallander and Tom Hedelius Research Foundation, and from Vinnova; the

To Professor *Sune Carlson*
and all his followers
who have studied management
as work practices

DISCUSSION

In summary, if it is unclear what a number of people are doing, if people's demands and expectations seem conflicting, and if the person who provides input to the team seems confused, there will be uncertainties. Resolution of those uncertainties will take the highest priority in the manager's schedule. That is the lesson of these three narratives – at least for managers in similar circumstances. They have to direct their energy towards trying to bring order to what has become unclear or chaotic. Only then are people prepared to get on with their own work. It is thus quite clear that everyday leadership is concerned with situations that call for an answer to the question 'Well then – What now?'

Two management ideas appear to overshadow all others in the consideration of everyday leadership. The first idea is that the manager is pressured to interpret the problem situation. The manager has to understand the situation, as well as what has led to it. What are the implications of the situation for the working group, the unit, the project, the company, and the future? The second idea concerns the importance of the manager's ability to take impromptu action, to act in the here and now, and, at least, to identify the next step in the process. These ideas are very closely connected. If, for example, the interpretation of a situation is that a 'task is much more difficult than we first imagined', the manager may have to take different action than if the interpretation is that it is necessary 'to find out what is going on'. What needs to be done in any situation depends on its particular interpretation.

Thus, according to the managers in this study, the major difficulty in handling their everyday context is that 'you have to draw the map while orienteering'. Clearly, the map has to be redrawn – over and over again. Next, we will elaborate on this seemingly simple idea.

Sense-making and the ability to take impromptu action

Keeping the map metaphor in mind, it is time to return to our two questions that guide the analysis of these leadership narratives: (*a*) What were the narratives about? and (*b*) What were the narratives not about? In our analysis of the three cases, we found two particularly interesting themes. The first theme, which relates to the managers' understanding of leadership in the everyday setting, highlights the following points: managers deal with events, past and present; new events constantly require new framings for and interpretations of upcoming situations; there is a continual need for adjustments; and the solutions available to managers are often momentary and temporal. In sum, our analysis reveals a pattern where managers' ability to contribute to intepretations of situations coincides with their ability to take more or less improvised actions (Mintzberg, 2009).

When asked about their jobs, experienced managers, especially CEOs, reveal quite a similar work pattern. This is a pattern where good and bad luck, chance and opportunity, and even lack of foresight can either play into their hands or turn everything upside down, creating chaos and confusion (Burns, 1982; Burns et al., 1985; Noordegraaf, 2000; Tyrstrup, 2005, 2006).

However, these experiences have not yet changed the more general perception of what is considered effective leadership – rather, the opposite is true. The ability to eliminate or fend off the elements of surprise and chance and to take the steps necessary to avoid being at the mercy of luck is the skill we most associate with leadership. A good leader turns situations into constructive challenges and smooth processes by which expected outcomes are realized. Stating this point more strongly, the ability to deal with challenging incidents and situations is the primary characteristic of a competent and skillful leader (Bryman, 1992; Mintzberg, 1994; Conger and Kanungo, 1998; Bass and Steidlmeier, 1999; House et al., 2007).

The second theme relates to what most narratives in our study left out. We did not find the image of the strategic and inspirational leader who takes planned action through well-organized teams and a series of developmental activities in the everyday setting. However, this does not mean that this leadership model lacks relevance. Our analysis only shows that everyday work in highly innovative and rapidly changing environments requires other processes and quite different managerial skills.

Our aim in collecting leadership examples through narratives was to test our assumption that the experiences of individuals are crucial in understanding leadership as a practice. Another important assumption, built into the research process, was our belief in the group's ability to present narratives of common interest. We recognized that the managers had a clear understanding of their leadership role – as far as leadership is concerned, each was familiar with the Textbook Version and each had a slight preference for the Hero Story. How, then, do we explain that their narratives dealt with good and bad luck, chance, coincidences, and unpredictable events as well as sometimes favourable outcomes, sometimes unfavourable outcomes? In the group setting, the managers saw that their individual experiences, which reflected their everyday work environment, were not exceptional. There was a pattern in the various narratives that could not be explained by bad management. Unexpected events occur again and again, usually resulting in some degree of uncertainty and confusion. Yesterday's well-prepared plan of action may be completely useless or irrelevant today or tomorrow. Hence, the managers acknowledged that everyday leadership requires a significant amount of framing, interpretation, and action – all of which must take place more or less simultaneously. Although these narratives had a micro-setting, in a sense they captured the fundamental conclusion that leadership is most needed in crisis management situations. The narratives also showed that in such crisis management situations, processes are typically not smooth and outcomes are usually unexpected.

Event-driven vs. intention-driven leadership

Leadership is usually depicted as setting goals, formulating strategies, providing guidelines, and incorporating values (Yukl, 1989). Leadership means setting suitable tasks for co-workers followed by careful supervision or even coaching in the performance of those tasks. Paradoxically, this view of leadership places the managers both at the centre of events as well as at a certain distance from the action. Concepts such as 'causing' and 'all-embracing' may summarize and describe this general understanding of leadership.

The argument that managerial leadership, and even excellent leadership, is event-driven may be hard to accept. As noted above, leadership is generally framed differently: leadership is generally thought to mean initiating actions rather than dealing with unforeseen or unplanned events (Yukl, 1989; Holmberg and Tyrstrup, 2002; Tyrstrup, 2005). The event-driven action that characterizes leadership in the everyday context, however, places leadership in the wake of events. Leadership is exercised, and, according to this logic, must be exercised, step-by-step, often using hindsight. This also means that 'intervention' and 'strong temporary focus' are two concepts that should be explored further in order to fully understand the leadership practice of everyday work.

CONCLUSIONS

In this study, we conclude that the most distinctive characteristic of everyday leadership is the strong focus on processes. A second important characteristic is that leadership, to a considerable extent, is event-driven. Everyday leadership is triggered by unexpected occurences and develops as a reaction to some urgent situation. Since leadership takes the form of an intervention, there are strong implications for the exercise of leadership. For instance, everyday leadership seems to involve a high degree of more or less direct leadership, quite often described in terms of firm actions. The idea that leadership is based on interpretation and a necesssity for action can be explained by events such as those that disrupt regular work and place the leader at centre stage.

However, this conclusion does not disregard the notion that everyday leadership consists of mundane and sometimes even trivial acts (e.g. Alvesson and Sveningsson, 2003a). In many instances, it can certainly be argued that leaders largely spend their time doing what other people in the organization do: they talk, they listen, they joke, and they chat (see Sveningsson et al., this book, Chapter 4). We conclude merely that when managers and leaders believe leadership is needed, another mindset is triggered that is more closely related to what is sometimes referred to as crisis management.

However, by framing everyday interaction as leadership, we may, of course, boost leaders' identity and their self-esteem, thereby sustaining their privileged positions as central actors in organizations (Alvesson and Sveningsson, 2003b). In acknowledging that leadership may also take the form of processes, where the contributing actors are not just the formal managers, our study aims at understanding what constitutes everyday leadership from the point of view of the managers. When reality has to be (re)created on an everyday basis, the role of the manager becomes more focussed on sense-making and intepretation (Weick, 1979/67, 1996; Smirchich and Morgan, 1982; Sandberg and Targama, 2007). In settings characterized by knowledge-intensive work, such as managerial work in the telecom industry, the need for sense-making and interpretation seems even more crucial (Watson, 1994). Then this need becomes a strategic issue.

PRACTICAL IMPLICATIONS

Our findings imply a rather different view of managerial leadership than managers usually describe, scholars propose, or management education promotes. In this section, we discuss four possible implications that we believe have considerable importance for managers, their co-workers, and others involved in management issues. We discuss these implications in the following areas: (*a*) organizational settings and procedures, (*b*) attitudes of managers, (*c*) selection of managers, and (*d*) management training.

Organizational settings and procedures

Our findings suggest careful scrutiny is needed of organizational problems and tasks that are subject to planning rather than of those requiring more improvisational action. In our opinion, most organizations rely heavily on the assumption that uncertainty related to problem situations can best be reduced by analysis and planning – that is to say, by knowledge before action. Such procedures are, of course, also part of the authorization of actions and, thus, an aspect of organizational hierarchies. However, besides being extremely time-consuming and administratively demanding, analysis and planning are also costly. Thus, the effectiveness of such procedures has to be examined from time to time and perhaps also from situation to situation. Are we really dealing with a planning problem and, if so, to what extent can it be solved by pre-planned actions? That seems to be the valid question in reviewing the effectiveness of many procedures that organizations use as the main tools to authorize their actions.

Attitudes of managers

Our findings relate to the attitudes of managers towards their work and towards others' work. Managers in general are somewhat frustrated by the lack of control of the work processes that constitute much everyday work in organizations. However, having come to terms with this situation, they may look at the advantages of problems and tasks by taking a step-by-step approach that continuously integrates efforts and various coordination strategies. For example, how should a team working on a particular task, or perhaps many tasks, keep each other informed so as to promote sense-making? When are meetings the most effective way to coordinate actions? When can the team rely on mobile phone conversations and e-mail correspondence to clarify problems and proposed solutions? These are the kinds of questions managers need to ask themselves, other managers, and co-workers.

Selection of managers

There is a concern about whether head hunters, HR departments, and senior managers select managers who are best equipped to work in a context requiring improvised actions. Our findings imply the hiring of managers may involve selecting managers who are prepared to give up unilateral control and instead to rely on the creativity inspired by improvised actions. Perhaps the methods currently used to select managers lack the dimension of entrepreneurial skills that our findings suggest are necessary; those methods may exaggerate the importance of skills that are required in the more formal exercise of managerial leadership. Nevertheless, while many managers are skilled improvisers – a necessary competence in managing everyday work – they may not be the best people available. For example, what seems to be important, based on our findings, is the manager's ability to cope with organizational stress and ambiguity. Do we have such managers or do we have managers who perhaps even contribute to the stress and ambiguity because they are unable to handle the intensity of everyday work in organizations?

Management training

Finally, our findings imply an adjustment is needed in the training and development of managers. How do managers improve their decision-making skills if they lack the time to reflect on them and even, in most circumstances, have insufficient information about situations? How do managers improve their ability to deal with misunderstandings and conflicts unfolding in the wake of constant adjustments and endless changes in working scenarios and situational interpretations? What competencies are necessary to cope with a set of different issues that occur almost simultaneously and involve many co-workers with their unique personalities? Although there have been many advances in management education in recent decades, we still do not fully understand how to prepare managers, especially newer ones, for the kind of managerial leadership that does not rely on 'knowing everything before doing anything'. This is the major challenge that our study raises. How do we prepare managers so that they can, jointly with other managers and co-workers, answer the simple but very important question: Well then – What now?

NOTES

1. This chapter is a modified version of the article 'Well then – What now? An everyday approach to managerial leadership', *Leadership*, 2010, 6(4): 353–72.
2. For more comrehensive reviews, see Hales (1986, 1999) and Stewart (1989).

REFERENCES

Alvesson, M. (1989). *Ledning av kunskapsföretag: Exemplet Enator.* Stockholm: Norstedt.
——Sveningsson, S. (2003a). *Managers Doing Leadership: The Extra-ordinarization of the Mundane.* Lund: Working paper series.
———(2003b). *Managing Managerial Identities: Organizational Fragmentation, Discourse and Identity Struggle.* Lund: Working paper series.

Bass, B. (1985). *Leadership and Performance Beyond Expectations.* New York: Free Press.
——Steidlmeier, P. (1999). Ethics, character, and authentic transformational leadership behavior. *Leadership Quarterly,* 10: 181–217.
Bennis, W. and Nanus, B. (1985). *Leaders: The Strategies for Taking Charge.* New York: Harper & Row.
Berger, P. and Luckmann, T. (1966). *The Social Construction of Reality.* London: Penguin Books.
Bryman, A. (1992). *Charisma and Leadership in Organizations.* London: Sage Publications.
Burns, T. (1957). Management in action. *Operational Research Quarterly,* 8(2): 45–60.
——(1982). *Power, Conflict and Exchange in Social Life: An Actor-oriented Systems Theory of the Structuring and Dialectics of Social Systems.* Uppsala: Uppsala Universitet.
——Baumgartner, T., and Deville, P. (1985). *Man, Decisions, Society.* New York: Gordon and Breach Science Publishers.
Carlson, S. (1951). *Executive Behaviour.* Stockholm: Strömbergs.
Carlzon, J. (2008/1985). *Riv Pyramiderna!* Stockholm: Natur & Kultur.
Clarke, A. E. and Fujimura, J. H. (1992). What tools? Which jobs? Why right? In A. E. Clarke and J. H. Fujimura (Eds.), *The Right Tools for the Job. At Work in Twentieth-Century Life Sciences* (pp. 3–45). Princeton, NJ: Princeton University Press.
Collins, J. (2001a). *Good to Great: Why Some Companies Make the Leap and Others Don't.* London: Random House Business.
——(2001b). Level 5 leadership: The triumph of humility and fierce resolve. *Harvard Business Review,* 79(1): 67–76.
Conger, J. (1989). *The Charismatic Leader: Behind the Mystique of Exceptional Leadership.* San Fransisco: Jossey-Bass.
——Kanungo, R. N. (1998). *Charismatic Leadership in Organizations.* Thousand Oaks, CA: Sage.
Cyert, E. M. and March, J. G. (1963). *A Behavioural Theory of the Firm.* Englewood Cliffs, NJ: Prentice-Hall.
Czarniawska, B. (1998). *A Narrative Approach to Organization Studies.* London: Sage.
Giddens, A. (1984). *The Constitution of Society: Outline of the Theory of Structuration.* Berkeley: University of California Press.
Gioia, D. A. and Chittipedi, K. (1991). Sensemaking and sensegiving in strategic change initiation. *Strategic Management Journal,* 12: 433–48.
Gulick, L. and Urwick, L. (1987/37). *Papers on the Science of Administration.* New York: Garland.
Hales, C. (1986). What do managers do? A critical review of the evidence. *Journal of Management Studies,* 23: 88–115.
——(1999). Why do managers do what they do? Reconciling evidence and theory in accounts of managerial work. *British Journal of Management,* 10: 335.
Holmberg, I. (1986). *Företagsledares mandat.* Lund: Studentlitteratur.
——Åkerblom, S. (2001). The production of outstanding leadership – An analysis of leadership images in the Swedish media. *Scandinavian Journal of Management,* 17: 67–85.
——Tyrstrup, M. (2002). Ledarskapets olika skepnader. In A. Danielsson and I. Holmberg (Eds.), *Ledarskapets olika skepnader: Exemplet.* Hallandsås, Lund: Studentlitteratur.
House, R. J., Hanages, P. J., Javidan, M., Dorfman, P. W., and Gupta, V. (Eds.) (2007). *Culture, Leadership and Organization – The GLOBE Study of 62 Societies.* Thousands Oaks, CA: Sage Publications.
Knorr Cetina, K. D. (1981). *The Manufacture of Knowledge: An Essay on the Constructivist and Contextual Nature of Science.* Oxford: Pergamon Press.
Kotter, J. (1982). *The General Manager.* New York: Free Press.

Weick, K. and Sutcliffe, K. M. (2006). Mindfulness and the quality of organizational attention. *Organization Science*, 17(4): 514-24.

Welch, J. (2005). *Winning*. New York: Harper Collins Publishers.

Yukl, G. (1989). Managerial leadership: A review of theory and research. *Journal of Management*, 15: 251-90.

Zaleznik, A. (1977). Managers and leaders: Are they different? *Harvard Business Review*, (May-June): 67-78.

4

Managerial leadership: Identities, processes, and interactions

Stefan Sveningsson, Johan Alvehus, and Mats Alvesson

INTRODUCTION

Contemporary discussion on managerial leadership covers a broad terrain indeed. There seem to be no limits concerning managers' responsibility for influencing (and improving) their followers' well-being, values, attitudes towards change, job satisfaction, and work performance. We expect managers to practice leadership by formulating visions, initiating change, and motivating followers. It is popular to regard manager-leaders as people who initiate transformation in a convincing manner, partly by using their charismatic talents and partly by communicating their compelling future visions (Rost, 1993; Conger and Kanungo, 1998). There is often a heroic glow in these portraits of charismatic and visionary leaders who, because of their extraordinary leadership traits, are routinely credited with successful organizational outcomes, turnarounds, mergers, and acquisitions.

There is, however, an increasing interest in recognizing more everyday managerial actions – talking, listening, and informally walking around – as expressions of leadership. These are the actions of the more moderate but nevertheless determined manager who takes a participative leadership approach – sometimes labelled post-heroic – by listening to and communicating with followers. Although not as publicly acclaimed as their more celebrated colleagues, such leaders are nevertheless framed as the everyday heroes upon whom the fate of organizations depends (Badaracco, 2002).

While some post-heroic forms of leadership describe a kind of quiet heroism – for example, references to the leader's professionalism and exercise of an iron will – other forms describe a different ideal than the leader who controls the fate of the organization. The 'true' post-hero is more involved in working with specific issues and relationships, improving followers' working conditions, and supporting, rather than driving, their accomplishments. A key idea in this understanding of the leader is that there are limits to leaders' superiority over their followers.

Both the heroic and post-heroic approaches to leadership have contributed to a surge in the leader and leadership discussion in the last two decades. This possibly exaggerated focus on leaders may have created a market for such views of leadership and even perhaps a tolerance for problematic lines of thinking. A significant problem in leadership theory is its rather strong ideological under-tone that suggests leaders and leadership are to be celebrated. And when the ideological value of a theory is high, it is easier to escape criticism of rather crude and un-nuanced reflections related to that theory. Following this, a significant question concerns what happens when people try to work with the popular (and theoretical) ideas on leadership in practice.

In this chapter, we examine some effects resulting from contemporary notions of leadership by listening to how managers position themselves as leaders. We investigate how the widely celebrated models and ideas about leadership operate in organizations. Our objective, beyond merely showing that the relationship between popular ideas and managerial practice is tenuous, is to discuss a version of leadership that is an integral part of everyday interpersonal interaction. Hence, besides presenting a critical discussion of some leadership literature, our ambition is also to present a version of leadership that is processual and relational.

ON LEADERSHIP STUDIES

Researchers have used a variety of approaches – trait, style, situation, transforma-tive/heroic, and post-heroic – to study leadership (Yukl, 1989). For a long time, the results from studies of the classic trait orientation were disappointing since the conclusion was that successful leaders were not much different from other mortals. There is, however, a renewal of the trait approach in transformative leadership research – sometimes it is claimed that some leaders have it within themselves to act as transformative characters because of their superior talents, morality, and will. Advocates of this claim (e.g. Bass and Steidlmeier, 1999) say such leaders are 'authentic' transformational leaders. Other researchers place more emphasis on the style of leaders while still others draw attention to the characteristics of the relationship between leader and follower. Some researchers are even inclined to disregard specific and separate identities, such as leader and follower, in order to emphasize the relationship between them (Uhl-Bien, 2006). Some researchers argue for the importance of the situation in order to frame leadership as processes of influence. For example, it is claimed that policemen, in acute situations, want a more direct, instrumental leadership style (Bryman et al., 1996), while people involved in more research-intensive activities favour a more indirect, supportive leadership style (Trevelyan, 2001). Yet another approach regards leadership as matter of the management of meaning and sense-making. Here the idea is that leaders frame the reality of others by influencing the ways people define and understand situations and orient themselves at work (Smircich and Morgan, 1982; Sandberg and Targama, 2007). This almost endless number of approaches, foci, and general assumptions about 'leadership' is still growing.

In spite of (or because of) the many attempts to define leadership, there is still no agreed-upon definition of the phenomenon. Yukl (1989: 253) argues that 'the numerous definitions of leadership that have been proposed appear to have little else in common' other than their common referral to an influence process.

The claim that leadership is a form of influence process makes general sense, but it does not really say a great deal specifically since influence can mean almost anything, from threatening people to cajoling them. For some researchers, leadership refers to the processes of influencing organized group activities in specific directions (Barker, 1997), while for others leadership is a sense-making activity that entails symbolic actions and processes that generate meaning (Bryman, 1996). Perhaps we should cease talking about leadership and refer to 'influencing work' instead. Antonakis et al. (2004: 5) comment on the influence process in leadership:

> Most leadership scholars would agree, in principle, that leadership can be defined as the nature of the influencing process – and its resultant outcomes – that occurs between a leader and followers and how this influencing process is explained by the leader's dispositional characteristics and behaviours, follower perceptions and attributions of the leader, and the context in which the influencing process occurs.

However, it is questionable how much research has actually dealt with the influence process empirically. The questionnaire-research studies can hardly be said to examine leadership in accordance with Antonakis et al.'s definition. It is also doubtful whether interview-studies can address leadership processes and situations. If we agree that leadership should refer to change, as many definitions commonly suggest, it is even more obvious that the number of leadership studies is limited. If we add other reasonable criteria, such as the execution of leadership in a real organization, additional studies are excluded. Consequently, there is a lack of in-depth studies of leadership that acknowledge social and cultural organizational complexities.

Since the early 1980s, qualitative research has accounted for about 15 per cent of the research on leadership (Bryman, 2004). Of these studies, few are oriented towards observation (Conger, 1998); instead, they focus narrowly on a detailed analysis of specific instances of verbal interactions with little attention paid to their meaning and context outside the studied conversations. Thus, there are very few studies of leadership as defined by Antonakis et al. In comparison with the study of managerial work in managerial research, leadership studies seem much weaker in terms of understanding their research subject. While leadership researchers often devise types and styles of leadership – portraying managers/ leaders as having one coherent style – managerial work researchers often point to diversity and fragmentation of managerial styles. One may imagine that this difference is partly due to the more ideological nature of leadership research and partly due to the deeper and more realistic studies conducted in the observation-based managerial work tradition.

In contrast to many conventional approaches to leadership, we suggest that the study of leadership requires careful consideration of the social context in which leadership processes take place. Leadership does not simply mean that when a leader acts, followers respond mechanically. Rather, leadership is a complex social process in which the interpretations of what is said and done are crucial. Assumptions, values, and norms on a variety of levels – societal, organizational, and group – frame and guide both expectations and evaluations of what is considered 'good' leadership.

In the research reported on in this chapter, we take this proposition seriously by listening to and observing people as they talk about, experience, and possibly practice leadership. We next present a short review of two concepts of leadership: transformative/heroic and post-heroic.

Transformative and post-heroic leadership

Leaders who exhibit transformative/heroic leadership styles rely heavily on their personal talents. While they often lead from a position of authority, such leaders use overt, although non-coercive, strategic, and visionary tactics such as empowering and caring for others in order to influence followers' feelings and thinking (e.g. Kotter, 1990; Sashkin, 2004). Increasingly, such leaders are distinguished from managers as those people who can initiate and facilitate change (Barker, 1997; Carroll and Levy, 2008). Given its appeal, it is not surprising that people like to identify with this idea of 'leadership' – such people include many academics who may think that the study of such leadership is more rewarding and interesting than the study of managerial or supervisory work.

In contrast, some of the literature suggests that leadership is related to collaborative action distributed among individuals in organizations (Badaracco, 2002). This concept of leadership, in its emphasis on the relational and processual aspects, proposes that most people in an organization are involved in the exercise of leadership. This post-heroic approach to leadership takes a more progressive, participatory, and shared view of leadership (Huey, 1994). By decoupling leadership from its transformative connotations, the post-heroic approach encourages more humanistic and democratic workplace relationships. Leadership is here tied to everyday and mundane acts but may nevertheless be significant for the commitment and engagement of employees. Managers' actions of informally walking around and communicating with their subordinates, for example, are presumed to have a positive influence on work climate and may even facilitate creativity (Mintzberg, 1998). It can be argued that, in many ways, leaders largely spend their time doing what other people in the organization do – they talk, listen, joke, and chat. However, when they act like other people, the impact is much more powerful.

By framing leadership as matter of listening and chatting, managers may exhibit social competence, progressiveness, and humanism. These everyday actions can also, of course, be interpreted as symbolic tricks managers use to sustain their leader identity and self-esteem, particularly in certain contexts, such as knowledge-intensive settings where managerial authority and privileged positions are habitually undermined (Alvesson and Sveningsson, 2003*b*). The post-heroic approach to leadership thus suggests that seemingly everyday and ordinary managerial actions are (potentially) of great significance. Such leadership actions may inspire motivation, create a sense of direction, and, more importantly, confirm identity.

The terms, heroic and post-heroic, are vague when used to summarize general views on leadership. Each points to specific aspects of popular thinking about leadership: the celebration of, and reaction to, the effects of extraordinary leaders. The heroic label draws attention to a strong tendency to exaggerate and idealize managers and to make far too much of the unusual, a tendency that the mass media supports with its publicizing of well-known cases. Post-heroic, as a description, warns us of this exaggeration and, to some extent, suggests an alternative view of leadership. However, the problem with the term 'post-heroic' is that it is a response to the overemphasis of the term, heroic. As realistic accounts of most managers' leadership efforts generally do not correspond to the heroic ideal, the term post-heroic necessarily covers a very broad terrain that may say rather little about leadership.

Both approaches have had an impact on how we look at leadership in contemporary organizations, in part no doubt because of the heroic element that they explore differently. While each approach has relevance for most organizations, both are particularly relevant for professional organizations and knowledge-intensive work environments. In organizations that employ mostly highly qualified professionals, the leader's role is often that of the visionary strategist, operations facilitator, and organization spokesperson. However, whether this role actually corresponds to the reality in organizations is another matter. Therefore, it is of value to investigate how managers relate to these approaches and to match experiences of leadership with some of the popular ideas.

In the next section, we turn to what happens when these ideas about leadership meet the organizational reality and to how managers interpret and work with these ideas in contemporary organizations.

LEADERSHIP IN PRACTICE

In our research projects the ambition is to embrace a more open approach to leadership and to acknowledge the presence of inconsistencies, fragmentation, and ambiguity (see e.g. Alvesson and Sveningsson, 2003*a*, 2003*b*, 2003*c*; Sveningsson and Larsson, 2006; Alvesson, 2010).

Method

Our studies are mainly based on interviews with mid-level and senior managers. Some of these studies are more ambitious than others and also involve observations and interviews with subordinates. These studies gave us in-depth knowledge of the organizations and furthered our understanding of the relevance of leadership for managerial work in settings dominated by professionals and knowledge workers.

The interviews were mainly loosely structured as our interest was in hearing the personal experiences of the interviewees so that we could obtain indications of meanings and learn about their views on leadership (Silverman, 1993). We explicitly raised the subject of leadership in the interviews by asking managers to speak unreservedly about their work as managers. We asked what they thought of management, how they manage, and if leadership has any particular relevance in their managerial work.

Our observations took place at formal and informal manager and employee gatherings where management and leadership issues were discussed. We were closely involved in many management and leadership discussions through our participation in a variety of managerial decision groups where managers often struggled with trying to make sense of their roles as leaders. We followed up on themes raised in the observations in subsequent interviews.

In this chapter, we partly regard leadership as expressions of meaning. Talk of leadership is treated as a clue to understanding how people make sense of what they do and how they view themselves in relation to other organizational actors and situations. We used these observations to examine leadership as a possible practice in terms of the processes of interpersonal influence.

Transformative leadership – identity work

In the transformative leadership approach, which managers frequently related to in our interviews, the managers talk about the attractive world of strategies and visions for change. This is contrasted with management, by which we refer to activities aimed at monitoring, controlling, and securing stability – activities that are not so attractive.

We saw this difference very clearly in our study of R&D managers in a global, pharmaceutical company. These managers expressed strong beliefs about the exercise of leadership (in contrast to the exercise of management). The words they used most frequently were visions, strategy, development, values, and culture. However, when we asked them to describe in more detail what they actually did, they did not stick to these words so emphatically. Referring to leadership, a senior middle manager said: 'It is about the larger picture, the strategic questions rather than the operative'. Yet, when asked to explain his strategic leadership, he described it as 'revenue budgeting and project budgeting, study leave and other operational issues, whether the department should have an internal webpage'. He commented further: 'I experience it as very frustrating that we talk about these issues to the extent that we do'.

Another manager described leadership as follows: 'A common understanding, a common vision, and a common purpose. Leadership is about creating a common vision and what values we should work towards and also how we live that vision'. Asked to clarify his meaning, the manager spoke about operational issues: 'I involve myself a lot in the technical aspects of the work'.

These statements suggest that managers frequently talk of and identify with transformative leadership – 'I'm a leader exercising leadership' – but less often actually exercise such leadership. Managers in large companies are often caught between two forces: leadership talk that celebrates work in terms of visions, values, and strategies, and the practical constraints and administrative work demands that often take priority over transformative leadership behaviour. Despite its popularity among managers, generally only a rather small fraction of the work in organizations involves the creation of strategies and visions. Since the many routine administrative tasks require constant management, managers usually prioritize such demands.

Although they constantly have to manage such everyday administrative work, many managers still try to present an image of themselves as visionary and strategic leaders. However, it can be difficult in the long term to maintain this self-image when one's time is primarily spent on administrative work. In the worst situation, this split managerial role can make managers frustrated and cynical as well as undermine their self-confidence. As suggested by Sveningsson and Larsson (2006), managers' leadership claims may occasionally be so inconsistent with reality that their self-images as leaders may be regarded as fantasy. One case study (Alvesson and Sveningsson, 2008) of a cultural change project in a firm indicated that its managers had great difficulty in working with values and meanings. Senior managers had no real success in inspiring mid-level managers to take the initiative. Furthermore, the mid-level managers treated instructions to address values in workshops with subordinates as 'tick-off-activities' ('that's done, now on to something else') rather than as work that could increase understandings and practices.

This suggests that transformative leadership has a limited impact on organizational practice. As observed by Parry and Bryman (2006), transformative leadership is seldom witnessed in qualitative research where the researcher searches for a deeper and richer understanding of a subject. It is also uncertain whether questionnaires really tell us much about whether managers are transformative (Alvesson, 1996). It is clear that heroic conceptions, such as transformational leadership, play other roles than that of informing leadership practice (e.g. offering material for identity work and legitimation). The very idea of visionary and strategic leadership may be interpreted as identity work that enhances the self-esteem of those attracted to transformative leadership. Such a leadership conception may appeal to managers when they try to define who they are – or fantasize about who they would like to be – in ideological ways that are more attractive than everyday organizational realities. In addition, managers may claim they are transformative leaders in order to establish managerial legitimacy in the context of a workforce that celebrates the post-bureaucratic idea of worker independence that is a bit intolerant of managerial interference.

Post-heroic leadership – the magic of small talk and listening

Since much of managerial work requires the manager to deal with subordinates as persons, a more psychological leadership approach may have appeal. This approach fits nicely into the popular theoretical conception of post-heroic leadership that emphasizes distributed influence, horizontal relationships, etc. For example, researchers studying this type of leadership write about the leader as a therapist (Western, 2008) or the mutual dependence of leader and follower (Fletcher and Käufer, 2003).

Here, we emphasize collective leadership efforts that relate to processual approaches to leadership where leadership emerges as a result of mutual, interpersonal interaction (Andersson and Tengblad, 2008). However, it is common that the leader orientation remains at the centre even if we talk of leadership as a collective process. Post-heroic is often closely tied to what is demanded by managers in order to sustain development. It is frequently said that managers should act as facilitators in order to make employees more independent. We also often hear that managers should lead by listening to employees and by making small talk with them during their daily activities since employees in contemporary organizations are thought to demand personal recognition from their managers. Therefore, some managers are inclined to act as buddies to their subordinates in order to increase the subordinates' self-esteem (Sveningsson and Blom, 2010). In such leadership, managers' ordinary and everyday gestures towards employees may increase employee commitment to the organization and engagement in the work. In fact, many managers in one R&D organization that we studied said that a very significant element in their leadership approach was listening to and chatting with employees. There is a magical element in this type of leadership where the magician leader produces extraordinary results through the performance of simple, everyday actions. Many researchers as well as practicing managers believe in the effectiveness of such leadership (Alvesson and Sveningsson, 2003c).

Some R&D managers we refer to in this section are the same managers we referred to in the previous section on the transformative/heroic leadership approach. Whereas in the previous section these managers described leadership in terms of vision and strategy, although without being able to demonstrate such leadership in practice, in this section we reveal how they describe other aspects of leadership. They still discuss leadership in traditional management terms (as in the previous section), but they also describe leadership as consisting of rather ordinary and routine activities.

One manager described leadership as follows: 'Everyone can make suggestions . . . everyone else is listening to that person. This in order to make them feel that they are included and have mutual responsibility for the work. You have to listen to others; otherwise you are not a team'. Another manager said that leadership is a question of 'listening to everyone's view in all situations, showing respect for everyone's opinion and then making a decision'. Some managers said listening provides a sound basis for team spirit and increases respect for employees. Other managers talked about listening as a way of making people feel appreciated, included, and visible.

While these post-heroically flavoured expressions sound fine in principle, they are not unproblematic. We found it difficult to determine whether listening and chatting had a substantial effect on subordinates since the managers lacked insight into the results of these actions. They seemed to think that the very act of listening, chatting, and/or giving the appearance of listening and chatting was sufficient for good leadership. The managers suggested that such communications have a special value, both for themselves and for their subordinates. They believe that in the exercise of such leadership, there is almost a magical transformation as ordinary acts achieve extraordinary results.

It is not our suggestion that listening and making small talk are unnecessary or unimportant management acts. However, we propose that managers have a tendency to exaggerate their influence as they fantasize about the results such acts can produce. We actually know very little about whether such listening/chatting has a positive, long-lasting impact on employees or whether it merely produces a temporarily beneficial effect.

Like the transformative/heroic leadership approach, the post-heroic approach may also relate to leader identity. Managers who talk about leadership in terms of listening and chatting may be using a symbolically and morally laden language

—— (1990). *Force for Change: How Leadership Differs from Management.* New York: Free Press.

Lindblom, C. E. (1959). 'The science of "muddling through".' *Public Administrative Review*, 19: 79–88.

Mintzberg, H. (1973). *The Nature of Managerial Work.* New York: Harper & Row Publisher.

—— (1994). 'Rounding out the manager's job.' *Sloan Management Review*, 36(1) (Fall): 11–26.

—— (2009). *Managing.* San Francisco, CA: Berrett-Koehler Publishers.

Wesley, F. (2001). 'Decision making: It's not what you think.' *MIT Sloan Management Review*, 42(3): 89–93. ABI/INFORM Global.

Nanus, B. (1992). *Visionary Leadership: Creating a Compelling Sense of Direction for Your Organization.* San Francisco, CA: Jossey-Bass.

Noordegraaf, M. (2000). 'Professional sense-makers: Managerial competencies amidst ambiguity.' *The International Journal of Public Sector Management*, 13(4): 319–32.

Stewart, R. (2000). 'Managerial behaviour research in private and public sectors: Distinctiveness, disputes and directions.' *Journal of Management Studies*, 37(2): 427–43.

Sandberg, J. and Targama, A. (2007). *Managing Understanding in Organizations.* London: Sage.

Selznick, P. (1957). *Leadership in Administration: A Sociological Interpretation.* New York: Harper & Row.

Simon, H. (1947). *Administrative Behavior: A Study of Decision-Making Processes in Administrative Organization.* New York: Macmillan.

Smircich, L. and Morgan, G. (1982). 'Leadership: The management of meaning.' *Journal of Applied Behavioural Science*, 18: 257–73.

Snyder, N. and Glueck, W. (1980). 'How managers plan – The analysis of managers' activities. *Long Range Planning*, 13: 70–6.

Stewart, R. (1976). *Contrasts in Management.* Maidenhead, Berkshire: McGraw-Hill.

—— (1982). *Choices for the Manager.* Maidenhead, Berkshire: McGraw-Hill.

—— (1989). 'Studies of managerial jobs and behavior: The ways forward. *Journal of Management Studies*, 26(1): 1–10.

Tengblad, S. (2002). 'Time and space in managerial work. *Scandinavian Journal of Management*, 18: 543–65.

—— (2003). 'Classic, but not seminal: Revisiting the pioneering study of managerial work.' *Scandinavian Journal of Management*, 19(1): 85–101.

—— (2006). 'Is there a 'New Managerial Work'? A comparison with Henry Mintzberg's classic study 30 years later. *Journal of Management Studies*, 43(7): 1437–61.

Tyrstrup, M. (1993). *Företagsledares arbete – En longitudinell studie av arbetet i en föetagsledning.* Stockholm: EFI.

—— (2005). *Sovereigns of Time: A Scandinavian View of Executive Work. Time and Leadership.* Lund: Studentlitteratur.

—— (2006). *On the Brink of Failure: The Art of Impromptu Action in Everyday Leadership.* Lund: Studentlitteratur.

Watson, T. J. (1994). *In Search of Management: Culture, Chaos and Control in Managerial Work.* London: Routledge.

—— (1996). 'How do managers think? Identity, morality and pragmatism in managerial theory and practice. *Management Learning*, 3, 323–41.

Weick, K. (1979/67). *The Social Psychology of Organizing.* Readings, MA: Addison Wesley.

—— (1995). *Sensemaking in Organizations.* Thousand Oaks, CA: Sage.

—— (1996). 'Prepare your organization to fight fires. *Harvard Business Review*, 74: 143–8.

to boost their self-esteem and establish their managerial identity. In this way, managers can reclaim some of the legitimacy and authority that is often lost in knowledge-intensive settings. They can compensate for this loss by presenting themselves as socially skilled and interested in the well-being of the employees. There is a strong moral component in this attitude: managers appear as really good and virtuous people – friendly, attentive, and people-oriented. Thus, many managers in knowledge-intensive settings seem to compensate for not knowing what their subordinates actually do by being open and honest with them. Such employee concern becomes an identity pillar and a way to accomplish something that appears like leadership (Alvesson, 2010).

This leadership style, in which managers take a therapeutic attitude towards their subordinates, is becoming more popular in sectors dominated by professionals or by employees who traditionally are used to more autonomy. Consulting and education are examples of such sectors. Problems may arise with such leadership, however, when an exaggerated view of the importance of managers leads to an overemphasis on their presence and to the risk that unhealthy dependency relationships will develop. In particular, such problems may result when professional employees associate their self-esteem with the everyday managerial actions we have described.

Does leadership 'exist'?

Given that leadership primarily constitutes material for leader identity and symbolic manoeuvring, we may ask ourselves whether leadership actually refers to a distinct set of ideas and practices, as most definitions of leadership assume. Of course, in a minimalist sense, leadership exists – there is no shortage of studies and theories about it and no shortage of verbal claims that it is practiced. We live in an age of leadership discourse. Yet to what extent does leadership 'exist' in other senses? For example, it is problematic to think of leadership as a distinct group of behaviours or as a distinct idea and set of meanings that guide managerial work towards some substantial result that affects people's thinking and actions. Is it possible to argue that leadership as a more coherent phenomenon – whether we refer to style, approach, or role – perhaps does not commonly 'exist' in organizations?

The study of managers claiming to practice strategy and vision leadership, referred to above, does not seem to maintain a coherent view and practice of their presumed 'leadership'. It is also questionable whether chatting/listening by managers has a significant effect on subordinates' attitudes and performance.

When we look more carefully at interviews about leadership in our studies, we find it is very common that managers exhibit uncertainty, inconsistency, and ambiguity in how they view leadership (Alvesson and Sveningsson, 2003c). One manager seemed somewhat confused about what was necessary for good leadership. The manager moved confusingly between a view of leadership that emphasized the team as most important, on the one hand, and a view that emphasized key individuals as most important, on the other. This manager finally described leadership as a matter of trying to limit his own influence and letting others decide, a kind of *laissez faire* approach. Another manager talked about leadership as 'leading and developing people' so that they could develop individually; at the same time he talked about leadership as the allocation of 'creativity and talent to the most likely projects' rather than the development of new talents. He also said the role of the leader was to 'create a common orientation', 'harness energy', 'coach people', and 'lead people'. He emphasized 'allocating the best scientists to best projects' and said that 'managers are there to make sure that the creativity is there'. There is a lack of specificity in these comments about what a manager actually does. His ideas on leadership veer in many directions.

What does this tell us about leadership? Of course, one may assume that leadership always exists. As a very generous category, it includes most managerial actions. 'Leadership' can, perhaps, be everything and nothing. Some authors argue that it is fruitless to try to find an essential meaning of leadership. Instead they suggest that we should look at how people use the term (Kelly, 2008).

Alternatively, 'leadership' may be used to understand situations, relationships, or people under certain conditions. We think it makes sense to talk about leadership as a somewhat intentional process of influence exerted in more important organizational issues, even if this process is not immediately evident or relevant to those involved (or acknowledged by them). Leadership should not be referred to as just any kind of influence but rather as more specific efforts and outcomes of influence, such as issues of a general kind of organizational influence on how individuals think, feel, and act in relation to overall organizational objectives. We also think it makes more sense to see leadership as a matter of at least modest coherence rather than as contradictory behaviour where a gap exists between the ideal and practice. Therefore, it is questionable whether the empirical examples this chapter reports on can be characterized as examples of leadership and thus whether we can say that leadership actually exists as a coherent process of influence.

Despite the recent focus on leadership by the media, popular management articles, and academic textbooks, we still believe it is fairly rare to find a coherent idea about the phenomenon that guides managers in organizations. Since leadership may actually be a rather rare phenomenon, perhaps we should be cautious about attributing leadership to complex organizational processes.

UNDERSTANDING LEADERSHIP – PROCESSES, RELATIONSHIPS, AND ACTIONS

Much of the heroic and post-heroic literature on leadership supports the mystification of leadership – either by associating leadership with vague, transformative ideas that are disconnected from any plausible practice or by depicting the leader as the ultimate magician in control of others' well-being. As suggested previously, this does not mean that the concept of leadership is irrelevant for understanding organizational processes, relationships, and actions. It is necessary, however, to demystify this view of leadership.

Although some researchers study followers in depth (e.g. Harter, 2006) or even focus exclusively on them (e.g. Meindl, 1995), most pay only lip service to them (e.g. Fairhurst, 2001). In the latter group, researchers see followers as managerial tools rather than as active individuals in the interaction. An alternative view is that the way people react to another person's action depends on how they interpret and value it. Do followers interpret management behaviour as authoritarian or powerful? Participatory or incompetent? The same behaviour can be interpreted very differently depending on the specific social and cultural circumstances. Following this, more than one person contributes to the view of reality that is developed in a group or organization. The social interaction and the relationship are central (Uhl-Bien, 2006). For example, if the response to a manager's requests is silence (resistance), the effect will be different than if the response is acknowledgement (acceptance, approval).

Leadership – viewed not merely as the discourse found in management literature, ceremonial talk, or interview responses, but rather as a part of organizational practice – is thus a genuine social phenomenon. The exercise of leadership in splendid isolation is meaningless. Leadership by definition exists between people; therefore, it is an expression of a mutual relationship. The central importance of mutuality for leadership may be regarded as obvious, but if one looks at mutuality closely, the implications for understanding leadership are significant (Alvesson and Ydén, 2000). Relationships do not automatically follow the prescriptions of laws, titles and organizational schemes, and the role of leader does not emerge specifically from the formal structure of positions. Leadership does not emanate a priori because someone in the organization is assigned the leadership role. Therefore, the attempt to identify people as either leaders or followers is often a superficial and fruitless task. According to Shamir (2007), the individuals, who are co-makers of the leadership relationships that evolve, connect and define one another, mutually and relationally. Individuals become leaders when one or several people accept the importance of their directions/ideas and are influenced by them. The leader who is influenced by someone else's conceptions and interpretations is being led. The leader then becomes a follower.

The salience and scope of a particular leader–follower relationship is contingent upon the characteristics of the interaction between the leader and the follower. At one end of the spectrum, we find self-governing people with little need for leadership; at the other end, we find people who require and/or demand stronger leader involvement. In the latter situation, the follower can initiate and co-construct the relationship with the leader.

It is a broadly shared view that leadership involves influencing people's thinking and feelings. Zaleznik (1977: 71) describes leaders' influence as a 'change atmosphere [that] evokes images and expectations and determines certain aspirations and objectives . . . the net result of this influence is changing how people think about what is desirable, possible and necessary'. In this understanding, leaders may exert more influence beyond that which is related to the formal position of manager (although leadership can hardly be seen as unaffected by formal position). Formal managerial influence involves trying to accomplish things through traditional activities such as structural arrangements, planning, and control (without worrying too much about what people think and feel).

In contrast, leadership involves trying to accomplish (significant) things through influencing people's ideas and feelings.

   If we regard leadership as a process where some leaders exercise significant influence over followers – thus contributing to the shared definition of reality within a group – it is possible that the leadership position may shift depending on the dynamics of the interpersonal interaction. Individuals who are the driving forces behind a specific definition of reality may exercise leadership even if they hold a subordinate position. Based on this understanding, we may view leadership as consisting of actions performed in specific situations that are not necessarily acknowledged as leadership (by those involved in the processes). In the context of managerial leadership – the main focus of this chapter – it is leadership strongly supported by the formal position (and the legitimacy to exercise the associated authority) that is central. However, this concept should be considered in relationship to other influencing processes, including informal leadership that may either supplement or undermine managerial leadership.

Leadership action and interaction – an illustration

George is the newly appointed manager of a software development team at a global, high-tech company that primarily employs software engineers engaged in advanced development of software solutions for high-tech consumer products. George, who describes himself as 'a leader', has clear ideas about leadership; his managerial identity is very much that of a leader. He is also very eager to exercise his leadership responsibilities that include creating group identity, promoting team feeling, and developing people. In his view, his leadership is based on his respect for the engineers' expertise. George states:

> And I very much base my leadership on showing respect for those who are really doing the tasks. I don't have any tendency to point and direct. Instead, I build my leadership on confidence, respect, and a very open dialogue with all co-workers, with no hidden agenda.

George spends a good part of his time working with the group, for example, in team activities such as workshops and meetings. He believes such activities foster the group's coherence, commitment, and identity. George describes how he thinks the group sees him:

> Open and very inviting. I tell them about my private situation and I say what I can and cannot do. I hope they have understood that.

Yet George also believes that the engineers doubt the value of many of these identity-enhancing activities. He states:

> But then, my group is really deep, technically, and it is a fact that they do not reflect on their manager as others do.

He also believes it is difficult to engage in discussions with his subordinates on the subject of group identity. George attributes this reluctance to the nature of their work that makes them sceptical, even dismissive, of his leadership ambitions to create group identity and to promote teamwork. Does this response mean that

George's wish to be a leader is just an ambition, wishful thinking, or even a fantasy? Given his current position, actions, and relationships, George may be a 'leader-wannabe' rather than a recognized leader since his subordinates do not confirm his leadership role and do not behave as 'followers'.

We argue, however, that the situation is not so clear-cut. Even though George senses the engineers' lack of interest in his ambitions to create a group identity and to develop group competence, his leadership efforts are not entirely unproductive or unsuccessful (or rejected). The following two scenarios that describe George's interactions with subordinates may illustrate this.

> The first scenario concerns Justin who has constructed a database for managing some problems that sometimes appear in a specific area of the software. George suggests to Justin that the database is perhaps unnecessary since another employee, David, has built a similar database for other parts of the application. Justin disagrees and says that this software is quite different from the other software; his database should be freestanding. But George maintains that this could lead to a situation where all distinct parts become separate, 'because we can say that about all parts', indicating there is a risk of fragmentation if they pursue Justin's orientation. Following that, Justin agrees: indeed, the different parts of the software are distinct. They talk a bit about the technical solution for integrating the databases, and Justin agrees to spend some time trying to find a solution for this problem.
>
> In the second scenario, George and Mickey discuss some data compression graphs. They talk about how these graphs depict efficiency in performance that they can show to other organizational levels and departments, mainly product management. Mickey shows George some performance graphs while admitting that a charge may be made that every graph used to display efficiency is just a well-chosen example. George then asks if these graphs can be used for comparison with competitors as a way of communicating and integrating with other organizational levels. George wonders if there are any performance standards they can use. According to Mickey, there are none. Since it is important to show the performance efficiency to others, they decide to wait until Elaine (the product manager) makes more explicit demands about what they want to show. Following this discussion on the graphs, George and Mickey talk about Mickey's workload that includes heavy involvement in the Greenland Project. George asks how he can help Mickey with this responsibility. As it is evident that Mickey's replacement in the project lacks some competence, it is difficult for Mickey to leave the project. George listens to Mickey, takes notes on the project's required competencies, and promises to try to do something about the situation.

In both scenarios, George engages in minor, everyday management. Although he admits he lacks competence in the technical aspects of the work of the engineers, he willingly involves himself in these rather everyday work problems that his subordinates raise with him.

However, George's involvement can also be seen as efforts to exercise leadership (with some positive effect). In the database discussion, George tries to create team spirit and foster integration of work tasks in an effort to promote cooperation in the team (something commonly seen as constitutive of group identity). In the performance efficiency exchange, George works on creating space and legitimacy for the team in the organization so that both the team and the entire organization recognize the team's contribution to the firm (thereby also strengthening group identity). These scenarios suggest interpersonal influence aims at enforcing an idea of what is desirable and achievable. Based on this, George can be seen as exercising leadership by trying to create team spirit, although in a more mundane way than he usually describes leadership.

However, George does not acknowledge he is engaged in leadership. For example, he explicitly denies that the leadership role applies to him when he says that there is no value in making observations (i.e. in studying his leadership) of the interaction between him and his subordinates. Although these two scenarios demonstrate his leadership, he claims such exchanges with his subordinates are not leadership since he talks of leadership as consisting of extraordinary actions, such as providing shared visions (see Conger and Kanungo, 1998). Although he has possibly accomplished something extraordinary in these mundane acts, such as contributing to team feeling and group identity, George prefers to stick with framing leadership in accordance with the heroic ideal.

The heroic ideas of leadership generally mean a leader performs extraordinary acts that lead to significant results that are recognized beyond the everyday world of the organization. In the absence of feedback from his subordinates that he acted in accordance with those ideas, George doubts his leader identity. However, in our examination of George's interpersonal influence, as reflected in the two scenarios, we identify clear elements of leadership. His leadership, unlike the mostly symbolic acts of heroic leadership, is not insignificant. By influencing others' ideas and actions, his interpersonal exchanges with subordinates may even enhance his leadership authority.

There are, however, problems with identifying such mundane acts as leadership. If George were to recognize everyday interaction as leadership (potentially, extraordinary leadership), his self-esteem might increase and his leadership identity might strengthen. Yet, as discussed above, such a leadership description may increase the tendency to identify all managerial actions as important and special (even non-managerial actions). One result of labelling everyday interaction as leadership might be the increased, and non-productive, interference by managers in the work of the people they manage. In addition, when managers are singled out as the key to everyday work success, managerialism in areas that traditionally promote self-governance is encouraged. While George's subordinates are not proponents of managerialism ('leaderism'), in many groups a strong managerial focus may unnecessarily strengthen asymmetrical relationships and co-worker dependency.

Despite the likelihood of such problems, in combination with more post-heroic notions of leadership, we propose that the more mundane managerial acts are elements of good leadership in contemporary organizations. In the concluding section, we reflect on that possibility.

CONCLUSIONS

There are a variety of concepts, theories, models, and approaches aimed at understanding leadership in organizations. While a great deal is known about leadership, we are not entirely convinced the subject has been fully explored. We believe that the entire field relies too heavily on certain assumptions about the leader-driven nature of organizations and about the ideological commitments to the leader-as-hero (or, at least, the extraordinary individual) who performs fantastic deeds. This overemphasis on the leader characterizes most current leadership literature. In particular, researchers and practitioners endorse two broad approaches to leadership: the heroic and the post-heroic. These approaches to leadership – or rather, the umbrella concepts that cover a wide set of views, ideas, and vocabularies – have gained wide acceptance in how managers talk about themselves as leaders.

Upon close examination, however, it appears that these assumptions about leadership are somewhat, even highly, decoupled from what managers actually do in organizations. To some extent, one may actually ask whether leadership really exists in the way it is normally presented in much of the literature. Rather than engaging in leadership (as they themselves describe), managers are more often involved with traditional administrative and operational tasks. In such tasks, their concern is with keeping the organizational machinery running as smoothly as possible. This concern does not leave them much time for vision-building and/or strategic planning. We think that these more mundane activities, which may sometimes cause others to think more generally about what needs to be done, may be regarded as leadership. We make this statement in recognition that managers themselves may be disinclined to see leadership in this way because of the less dramatic and self-aggrandizing nature of such activities.

In order to capture and understand this more mundane form of managerial leadership, we think combining theory with a careful attention to actual leadership experiences may be an ideal research approach. Based on the discussion above about the significance of processes, relationships, and actions, we think that such an understanding should address the following four topics:

1. The presumed leader's actions
2. The social, relational dynamic between leaders and followers
3. The organization's cultural and social contexts that set the stage for the interaction and relationships
4. The interpretations of a leader's actions (and those of others that affect the relationship)

We also support a more 'realistic' view of management leadership that challenges the contemporary dominance of heroic and post-heroic leadership ideas. We believe it is essential to view 'mundane managerial leadership' as instrumental in getting the work done in organizations. This viewpoint contrasts with the idea that leadership is disconnected from the 'core' aspects of work by its more or less exclusive focus on visions or personnel issues (e.g. subordinate empowerment). We think that 'mundane managerial leadership', while less impressive as a description of leadership, is a more realistic and typical description of what managerial leadership is in practice. We summarize some elements of comparison in Table 4.1.

Our goal in this chapter is not to offer the final word on leadership. As our commentary illustrates, leadership is complicated and problematic. Even precise leadership definitions and self-confident claims about its nature in theory and practice present ambiguities and paradoxes. However, we think more attention

Table 4.1 Positions on leadership

	Heroic leadership (transformative)	*Post-heroic leadership*	*Mundane managerial leadership*
Key activities of leaders	Creating vision, transforming values, and fostering commitment towards a common purpose	Personal relationships where socializing, motivating, and encouraging others to step forward create a shared leadership	Influencing expectations, meaning, and values about what is desirable and necessary to accomplish related to everyday work
Empirical focus	The leader performs extraordinary acts associated with visions and values, thus producing a strong effect on followers	The leading–following interaction	Managing everyday problems, talking and listening, taking care of routine work, and 'nagging'
Conceptual focus	The traits, styles, and charismatic behaviour of the leader	Leaders as therapists, coaches, and facilitators	Leadership connected to managerial work Interpersonal relations and interactions
Attentiveness to leader/ manager	Strong leader centricity	Moderate leader/manager centricity	Low leader/moderate manager centricity

should be paid to leadership issues and processes in work contexts (not just the issues of intentions and value claims). Leadership, as a research subject, could relate much more to the managerial work tradition.

REFERENCES

Alvesson, M. (1996). Leadership studies: From procedure and abstraction to reflexivity and situation. *The Leadership Quarterly*, 7(4): 455–85.

—— (2010). The leader as saint. In M. Alvesson and A. Spicer (Eds.), *Understanding Leadership in the Real World*. London: Routledge.

—— Sveningsson, S. (2003a). The great disappearance act: Difficulties in doing 'leadership'. *The Leadership Quarterly*, 14: 359–81.

—— —— (2003b). The good visions, the bad micro-management and the ugly ambiguity: Contradictions of (non-)leadership in a knowledge-intensive company. *Organization Studies*, 24(6): 961–88.

—— —— (2003c). Managers doing leadership: The extra-ordinarization of the mundane. *Human Relations*, 15: 1–25.

—— —— (2008). *Changing Organizational Culture. Cultural Change Work in Progress*. London: Routledge.

—— Ydén, K. (2000). Ledarskap som verklighetsdefinition, relation och process. In K. Ydén (Ed.), *IT, organiserande och ledarskap*. Stockholm: Försvarshögskolan.

Andersson, T. and Tengblad, S. (2008). The responsible worker. Expectations of and responses on responsibility at work. Paper presented at the 26th International Labour Process Conference, Dublin, Ireland, 18–20 March 2008.

Antonakis, J., Cianciolo, A. T., and Sternberg, R. J. (Eds.) (2004). *Introduction. The Nature of Leadership*. Thousand Oaks, CA: Sage.

Badaracco, J. (2002). *Leading Quietly*. Boston: Harvard Business School Press.

Barker, R. (1997). How can we train leaders if we don't know what leadership is? *Human Relations*, 50(4): 343–62.

Bass, B. M. and Steidlmeier, P. (1999). Ethics, character, and authentic transformational leadership behavior. *The Leadership Quarterly*, 10: 181–217.

Bryman, A. (1996). Leadership in organizations. In S. Clegg, C. Hardy, and W. Nord (Eds.), *Handbook of Organization Studies*. London: Sage.

——(2004). Qualitative research on leadership: A critical but appreciative review. *The Leadership Quarterly*, 15: 729–69.

——Stephens, M., and Campo, C. (1996). The importance of context: Qualitative research and the study of leadership. *The Leadership Quarterly*, 7(3): 353–70.

Carroll, B. and Levy, L. (2008). Defaulting to management: Leadership defined by what it is not. *Organization*, 15(1): 75–96.

Conger, J. A. (1998). The necessary art of persuasion: The language of leadership is misunderstood, underutilized – and more essential than ever. *Harvard Business Review*, May–June, 76(3): 84–95.

——Kanungo, R. N. (1998). *Charismatic Leadership in Organizations*. Thousand Oaks, CA: Sage.

Fairhurst, G. (2001). Dualisms in leadership research. In F. Jablin et al. (Eds.), *Handbook of Organizational Communication*. Thousand Oaks, CA: Sage.

Fletcher, J. K. and Käufer, K. (2003). Shared leadership: Paradoxes and possibility. In C.I Pearce and J. A. Conger (Eds.), *Shared Leadership: Reforming the Hows and Whys of Leadership* (pp. 21–47). Thousand Oaks, CA: Sage.

Harter, N. (2006). *Clearings in the Forest: On the Study of Leadership*. West Lafayette, IN: Purdue University Press.

Huey, J. (1994). The new post-heroic leadership. *Fortune*, 21: 24–8.

Kelly, S. (2008). Leadership: A categorical mistake? *Human Relations*, 61, 763–82.

Kotter, J. (1990). *Force for Change: How Leadership Differs from Management*. New York: Free Press.

Meindl, J. (1995). The romance of leadership as a follower-centric theory: A social constructionist approach. *The Leadership Quarterly*, 6: 329–41.

Mintzberg, H. (1998). Covert leadership: Notes on managing professionals. *Harvard Business Review*, November–December: 140–7.

Palmer, I. and Hardy, C (2000). *Thinking about Management*. London: Sage.

Parry, K. and Bryman, A. (2006). Leadership in organizations. In S. Clegg, C. Hardy, and W. Nord (Eds.), *Handbook of Organization Studies* (pp. 447–68). London: Sage.

Rost, J. C. (1993). *Leadership for the Twenty-First Century*. Westport, CT: Praeger.

Sandberg, J. and Targama, A. (2007). *Managing Understanding in Organizations*. Thousand Oaks, CA: Sage.

Sashkin, M. (2004). Transformational leadership approaches. In J. Antonakis et al. (Eds.), *The Nature of Leadership*. Thousand Oaks, CA: Sage,

Shamir, B. (2007). From passive recipients to active co-producers: Followers' role in the leadership process. In B. Shamir, R. Pillai, M. Bligh, and M. Uhl-Bien (Eds.), *Follower-centered Perspectives on Leadership. A Tribute to the Memory of James R. Meindl*. Greenwich, CT: Information Age Publishing.

Silverman, D. (1993). *Interpreting Qualitative Data*. London: Sage.

Smircich, L. and Morgan, G. (1982). Leadership: The management of meaning. *Journal of Applied Behavioural Science*, 18: 257–73.

Sveningsson, S. and Blom, M. (2010). Leaders as buddies: Leadership as making people feel good. In M. Alvesson and A. Spicer (Eds.), *Understanding Leadership in the Real World*. London: Routledge.

——Larsson, M. (2006). Fantasies of leadership: Identity work. *Leadership*, 2(2): 203–24.

Trevelyan, R. (2001). The paradox of autonomy: A case of academic research scientists. *Human Relations*, 54: 495–525.

Uhl-Bien, M. (2006). Relational leadership theory: Exploring the social processes of leadership and organizing. *The Leadership Quarterly*, 17(6), 654–76.

Western, S. (2008). *Leadership: A Critical Text*. Thousand Oaks, CA: Sage.

Yukl, G. (1989). Managerial leadership: A review of theory and research. *Journal of Management*, 15: 215–89.

Zaleznik, A. (1977). Managers and leaders: Are they different? *Harvard Business Review*, May–June: 67–8.

5

Multi-framing as a tool in top management teams

Gary Kokk, Sten Jönsson, and Airi Rovio-Johansson

INTRODUCTION

Scholars have long recognized the need for more close-up and longitudinal studies of corporate elites, such as senior managers, executive officers, boards of directors, top management teams, and executive boards, but the difficulty of obtaining first-hand data (interviews will not suffice) remains a major obstacle (e.g. Pettigrew, 1992; Finkelstein and Hambrick, 1996; Clarke, 1998; Samra-Fredericks, 2000, 2003). Much of the work of these individuals and groups takes place behind the doors of conference rooms and offices, which, in combination with their social power, insulates them from outside scrutiny (Kunda, 1992). As a result, there are very few close-up, empirical studies of executive levels, especially ethnographically informed studies (Morrill, 1995). In this chapter, we address that scarcity by analysing the work practice of a top management team in a Swedish-based multinational industrial company.

Our point of departure is the observation that much of the work done in the top management meetings we have attended (more about this in the next section) was case-specific and non-routine. Issues that require a response from the group may arise from, for example, novelty of conditions or conflicts of intra-organizational jurisdiction. Many years ago, in his classic book, *The Functions of the Executive*, Chester Barnard (1946) suggested calling such cases appellate cases. It is, he wrote, exactly the function of the executive or executive team 'to raise and decide those issues which no one else is in a position to raise effectively' (ibid.: 191). It is the typical uniqueness, the aspect of novelty, of appellate cases that usually gets in the way of fitting them into existing organizational workflows. Instead, such cases are elevated to the upper echelons of the organization. We spotlight one such case in which the strategic potential of an opportunity, in combination with the uniqueness and unknowability of the evolving situation, made it impossible to incorporate the required decision-making into the ordinary work processes elsewhere in the organization. The issue had to be resolved at the executive level before being resubmitted to other parts of the organization.

In complex and novel situations, managers reduce dimensionality and improve preparedness for action by sense-making and sense-giving (Gioia and Chittipeddi,

1991). Weick (1995) points out that we make history account-able by narrating what we perceive as the relevant aspects of past events. This is sense-making: sorting out the facts (as we see them) and giving them relevance and meaning. When we face possible futures there is the added problem that the relevant facts are not yet there. To bring them forth into an emerging prospect, we need to insert our own agency and invite the commitment and help of other team members. This is sense-giving: influencing the meaning construction of others towards a redefinition of organizational reality (Gioia and Chittipeddi, 1991). Sense-giving is thus ultimately concerned with inserting action – one's own and that of others – in order to bring about a possible and jointly desired future.

When participating in sense-making and sense-giving, team members are required to signal commitment to common action as well as contribute rational analysis of possible cause-and-effect chains. Complexity will render general goals, such as return on investment, impotent as criteria since few reliable facts are available to make prospects calculable. We usually understand the complexity of a managerial situation as stemming from multidimensionality, limited knowledge, the presence of risk, and uncertainty as to the outcomes of action. It is the 'real world' conditions that are seen as the generator of complexity rather than the process of deliberation itself. It is often assumed that the decision-making process of a management team gradually, step by step, reduces the dimensions of the situation to an expected cash flow that can be discounted to a net present value. We claim that the process of common deliberation itself is complex, by virtue of its use of multi-framing as a social tool to involve different competences and perspectives in the assessment of the situation. The typical non-linear flow of the process gives team members opportunities to discover holes (gaps) in the discourse where their contributions may fit, and where they can apply their specific expertise and related judgement in relevant dimensions. It thus gives them the chance to see how and where their support is called for as well as to signal their support (loyalty) to the project.

The different perspectives (frames) that are introduced in a discussion may, however, also pose a risk. Centripetal forces may cause disintegration of the management team instead of uniting it around a common mission. Therefore, membership work is a vital element of the multi-framing process. The individual must do two things to achieve membership confirmation (Munro, 1996): (a) establish and maintain identity in the team and (b) produce contributions to the team that are aligned with the emerging team mission. These actions include designing solutions to common problems that are likely to work in the world. Consequently, competence in some technical sense is a prerequisite for membership. In fact, the composition of the team may well have been designed to accommodate different competences while avoiding too much overlap. It is common knowledge that diversity in a team generates creativity in problem solving. So how do team members communicate and cooperate in solving complex problems related to future organizational action? That is the main question we address in this chapter.

According to Goffman (1981), the concept of 'frame' is used as a tool in conversation to recontextualize a situation. Tannen (1993) explains that frames can be understood as structures of expectations based on past experience, without which no utterance can be interpreted. As many perspectives are evoked, multi-framing is the result. The sequence of frames in a discussion will be somewhat disordered, depending on the attention given and action taken by team members in the unfolding discussion. Frames will have been stacked on each other in a seemingly random fashion, mixing rational aspects with deontic ones. There will be loops and reiterations and, hopefully, at some point members will feel ready to assume responsibility for setting an organizational project – with all its provisional assumptions about the action of relevant others – in motion.

Since team members (normally) cannot question, in any detail, factual statements of professional judgement in colleagues' fields of expertise, their interaction must be based in trust. Consequently, it is essential for each member to invest in building and maintaining an identity as a trustworthy team member. In an industrial and engineering environment, it means demonstrating keen functional judgement ('Will it work?') as well as avoiding demonstrations of incompetence by interfering in discussions where one cannot productively contribute. Constructive suggestions or pertinent facts that others do not have access to should be inserted in such a way that other team members can integrate them in a collective and pragmatic redefinition of organizational and industrial reality. In preparing for future action, the team members can act concertedly towards realization of a common prospect, not worked out in all its details but, as displayed in the case we look at in following pages, making enough sense for members to commit themselves with a 'resounding yes'.

METHOD AND RESEARCH DATA

Our field data were collected through a close-up study of a group of senior managers in a business unit of a Swedish-based multinational company (identified as the Company). Our research presence at the Company spanned a period of more than three years, during which we became acquainted with the industrial, corporate, and social settings surrounding the case and episode selected for analysis. Our fieldwork culminated in the observation and audiovisual recording of (*a*) a series of eleven consecutive half-day executive team meetings and (*b*) an overlapping series of sixteen project meetings with project-participation ranging from first-line shop floor management to executive management levels. We recorded 125 hours of managerial work practice over the course of thirteen months. We also engaged in numerous informal conversations, conducted seventy semi-structured interviews, and collected various PowerPoint presentations and a number of other Company documents.

We used audiovisual recording to focus on how members make frames visible and learnable to the team and on how members orient themselves towards the practical accomplishment of understanding each other in meetings. Methodological research literature often argues that audiovisual recording reduces the risk that analytical considerations 'arise as artefacts of intuitive idiosyncrasy, selective attention or recollection, or experimental design' (Heritage and Atkinson, 1984: 4). The use and value of audiovisual recording is well documented in various theoretical and methodological perspectives (Lomax and Casey, 1998; Atkinson, 2007; Pink, 2007; Bryman, 2008). One of its strengths is the permanency of the data that permits observation and analysis of entire episodes or minutiae, repeatedly, independent of the time when observations and recordings are made (Jordan and Henderson, 1995).

We chose to look closely at a half-hour episode in a top management team meeting in 2002. Whittington (2006) notes that a large part of the managerial work of strategizing and executing strategy takes place in the form of episodes or sequences of episodes. Such episodes are important not just for initiating strategic change but also for confirming and reinforcing strategy, which provides an organization with stability and direction (Hendry and Seidl, 2003). The episode we selected occurs as a scheduled point on the meeting agenda and therefore has a clear beginning and end. In transcribed form (in Swedish), the discussion amounts to 630 lines. Due to its length, we selected two brief sequences (in total, less than four minutes) to illustrate our claims. The English translation, although not strictly literal, tries to capture the meaning of the Swedish utterances as closely as possible.

The organization and industrial setting

The Company is a supplier/producer of highly engineered, mechanical components to a handful of multinational customers in the market for industrial machinery. Our fieldwork took place at one of the Company's five business units (hereafter identified as the BU), with 2,200 employees. At the time of our field work, the General Manager (GM) of the BU, who is also one of the Company's Senior Vice Presidents, meets with his immediate executive team (of Vice Presidents) semi-weekly in half-day meetings. In addition to the GM and his secretary, the group consists of three division heads (hereafter identified as Division 1, Division 2, and Division 3) and five functional managers (hereafter identified by their functional areas of responsibility) representing Quality, HRM, Finance, Marketing, and Operational Development.

The prevailing production principle at the Company is 'make-to-print': production according to specifications and drawings furnished by its customers. The Company is thus in a vulnerable position as it is squeezed between, on one side, the relentless price pressure from its customers, and, on the other, a host of challenging new industry entrants with production concentrated in low-cost countries. It had become clear to the Company as early as the mid-1990s that producing its customers' designs was no longer a viable strategy. To secure its long-term survival, the Company needed to add more value to its products. A product specialization strategy was formed with the goal of integrating backwards in the value chain by taking responsibility for (a) product development of selected components and (b) the integration of larger modules of components. Consequently, insourcing product development work from their customers became a strategic objective. The technology department in the BU was gradually expanded to take on the new challenge. However, executing the strategy proved to be much more difficult than reaching consensus on the strategic direction.

In 2002, when we arrived at the BU, its management team was trying to respond to the increasing price pressure in the industry. First, many improvement projects with the common aim of increasing productivity (and thus competitiveness) were launched. These projects included reviewing and improving production flows, shortening lead times, making improvements in supply chain management, and increasing the levels of mechanization. Second, and at least equally important, the BU managers were trying to breathe life into the product and production specialization strategy. It is a step on this latter strategic path that we examine in the following section.

THE EPISODE

A mid-level manager in the Technology Department at the BU (identified here as Tech) is invited to an executive team meeting to report on the efforts to achieve Centre of Excellence (CoE) status in product development and production stages for an important group of components, vis-à-vis (as a first step) their largest customer. Eleven people are present: the ten BU team members and Tech. Tech takes the floor, standing at the head of the conference table in the Company's spacious boardroom. GM's secretary sits to his right, followed by GM and Division 1, a vacant chair, HRM, and Quality. On the opposite side, the order is Marketing followed by Division 2, Division 3, Finance, and Operational Development.

Tech's introduction takes the first seven minutes. He uses overhead transparencies to clarify his points. He is interrupted only by some brief questions. The background is that their largest customer (identified here as the Customer) is in the midst of developing an advanced industrial machine in close cooperation with a partner company (a company that is normally one of the Customer's competitors). Their joint project is running far behind schedule due to persistent technical problems with a component group that is the Customer's responsibility. These problems have implications for other parts of the machine, and may, in practice, bring the entire development project to a standstill.

The vision of becoming a CoE builds on the idea that the Company has developed a technology that (*a*) will solve the functional problem encountered by the Customer and (*b*) is considerably cheaper, both in production and maintenance, than the unsuccessful alternatives that the Customer has already tried. The solution is ready in terms of a generic technology, but it has not yet been applied in operative use. The design of the component is still in the early conceptual phase, and the Company has little prior experience in running product development projects of this type.

At the beginning of the episode, the group members are unevenly informed about the topic, and their professional backgrounds and knowledge bases are heterogeneous. GM, with twenty-five years in the Company, is one of the initiators of the strategic repositioning efforts. He is familiar with the general outline of the efforts to reach CoE status, but he is less informed about the nitty-gritty technical complexities involved. Marketing, who has a broad and deep industrial, technical, and product competence after fifteen years in various Company roles, is in a similar position. With GM, Marketing is a driving force behind the vision of developing the BU into a CoE for selected component groups. They invited Tech to the meeting. Division 1, with fifteen years of industry experience, heads a unit that will be directly influenced by whatever decision is taken. If the venture is successful, his division will produce the components. Division 2, a veteran with forty years of industry experience, has not been previously involved in the CoE discussions, but he is well acquainted with the Customer and has good personal ties with its key people. Division 3 heads a smaller R&D-oriented division that is not directly influenced by the CoE discussions. However, he is an experienced engineer familiar with managing product development projects. The other four managers are more or less unacquainted with the project.

Seven minutes into Tech's introduction of the topic, sparked by a question by GM (addressing Tech), some group members begin taking an active part in making sense of the situation. As they raise various issues and aspects that may be relevant, the discussion meanders between, on one side, technical, product-related issues on a fairly detailed level and, on the other, efforts to understand what is happening (or about to happen) in other parts of the industry.

Sequence 1

The first sequence we look at is a three-minute clip beginning fifteen minutes into the episode. The discussants are GM, Marketing, and Division 2. The group has just discussed the far-reaching responsibilities that come with the much-desired CoE status and the consequences for the Customer in terms of outsourcing the critical areas of competence. That is the catalyst that provokes a question by Division 2. (The line numbering refers to the location of the sequence in the original Swedish transcript.)

Transcription symbols used in the two sequences:

[anonymous]: words altered for confidentiality or privacy reasons
((added information)): information added by the transcriber
(.) pause less than one second
(3) pause of three seconds
emphasis spoken with emphasis

---

287 Division 2:	Do we know that [the Customer) wants this? (.) ((Looks at
288	Tech and then turns towards GM)) Give away the competence
289	(.) or give it up.
290	(1.5)
291 GM:	Yes [a name] said that he (1.0) was aware of these discussions
292	and and (.) I don't remember his exact words. He (1.0) he
293	supported and (.) backed it up. Uuh [Marketing] can you
294 Marketing:	Yes-yes ((clears his throat)) I think they are interested (2.0),
295	very much so. (1.5) Then again, we may ask ourselves what
296	the reason is for that interest.
297 Division 2:	Right (.) 'cause now they have reached a point (.) where [one
298	component] is at [a competitor]. The odd thing is that, (.) as a
299	consequence of [the competitor] specializing in [one

300		component type] (1.0) and then if we get [two other
301		components], (1.0) soon they must start asking what the hell
302		they are going to do themselves.
303	GM:	But that's
304	Division 2:	Ok, that's *their* problem, ((laughs)) but to me it seems a bit
305		odd.
306		(2.0)
307	Marketing:	I think that [the Customer] (2.0) struggles with an overall
308		complex of problems. (1.0) Will they (1.0) or are they (.)
309		going to, in the future, develop and make new big [machines]
310		to [a specific market niche]? (1.0) I think that (1.5) at present
311		the main bet is that they will not do that but instead they will
312		focus on (1.0) smaller [machines] for [another market niche].
313		(1.5) In case they would succeed in finding a partnership
314		structure that spreads the risk, then it is possible that their
315		attitude changes. Especially if they get a new leadership and
316		such things, since the present one seem focused (1.0) on
317		maximizing profits.
318		(1.0)
319	Division 2:	mm [three words inaudible; talks simultaneously with
320		Marketing]
321	Marketing:	If they get a sensible structure in place then maybe they will
322		change that basic stance. Because I think that [the product
323		development project under discussion] is an isolated (.) case of
324		cooperation between [the Customer] and [the Customer's
325		partner].
326	GM:	But what you are saying then ((points at Marketing and then at
327		the screen)) is that it's adventurous but being [a cooperative
328		project between the Customer and its partner]
329	Marketing:	Yes.
330	GM:	makes it less adventurous.
331:	Marketing:	Yes, it is adventurous but if we succeed then I think we have a
332		great
333	GM:	Yes.
334	Marketing:	marketing value towards
335	GM:	Yes.
336	Marketing:	other potential customers.
337		(4.0)

Division 2 has listened quietly for six minutes before re-entering the discussion at line 287. His question, which is primarily addressed to GM and Marketing, touches upon a central issue: the Customer's reasons for interest in what the Company offers. The Company must convince the Customer that this is the best course for their mutual long-term benefit. Based on the joint confirmation by GM and Marketing that the Customer has provisionally indicated its interest, Division 2 adds an explanation to his seemingly silly question, ending with 'soon they must start asking what the hell they are going to do themselves'. He cannot fully understand the logic behind the Customer's interest.

Marketing's comments that begin at line 307 set the scene for much of the discussion in the remaining thirteen minutes of the episode. His framing of the situation responds both to Division 2's feeling that the Customer's assumed intentions are odd and to his own rhetorical question 'we may ask ourselves what the reason is for that interest?' With phrases like 'I think', 'the main bet is', and 'it is possible', Marketing signals the unknowability of the situation and the uncertainty surrounding the entire CoE project.

Marketing makes at least four arguments, all of which require some background knowledge from the other meeting participants. First, the Customer 'struggles with an overall complex of problems', which basically means the Customer is experiencing financial difficulties. The issue is how the Customer will address these difficulties. Marketing's more or less informed guess is that, after the completion of this machine project, the Customer will decide to concentrate its limited resources on product niches where it has been more successful in recent years.

Marketing's second point is that, in the short term, that scenario is strengthened by the fact that the Customer's CEO is about to retire (line 315). His recent actions show that he is focusing on short-term financial window dressing. Some of his closest executives will probably leave with him, but it is still unclear when this change of leadership will occur. A scenario with a new and more long-term-oriented leadership team could improve the Company's chances to 'get in'.

Marketing's third point is that this is a one-time cooperation between the two partners (lines 323–325). The problems experienced in the current machine project increase the likelihood of this project being an isolated case of cooperation between the two companies who are normally fierce competitors.

Finally, Marketing's fourth point is that the Customer is looking for new partners (lines 313 and 321). If the Customer is able to build a partnership structure that reduces the financial pressure on them, then it may decide to stay in this market niche (perhaps even with the current leadership). Consequently, it is important that the Company becomes involved in the sense-making process among key people at the Customer in order to make them realize the feasibility and joint benefits of the venture. In the short term, the Customer's repeated and expensive failures to solve the technical problem may give the Company the opportunity to introduce its technical solution for the new machine. Ultimately, however, the Customer must trust the Company's capability as a key actor in a long-term partnership structure. As Marketing points out, if they are successful with this specific component then they can better market themselves to other potential customers. On the other hand, it is an adventurous undertaking. If the Customer relies on the Company for a solution, a failure to provide the expected solution could ruin the Company's chances to 'get in' for a long time and perhaps even jeopardize the Company's survival.

Sequence 2

After twenty-four minutes the discussion gradually, over the course of a few turns, moves towards decision-making, or rather, formalizing decisions (leading to Sequence 2). Tech has two main objectives at the meeting. The first is to get a 'go-ahead' from the group to approach the Customer with a concrete offer of cooperation, which will hopefully later deepen into a full business partnership. The second objective is to get the group's approval for the funding of a conceptual design study of initially one component (estimated to cost 4 million Swedish crowns). The design study will provide information about (*a*) some critical functional requirements of the component, (*b*) the component's fit with other parts of the machine, and (*c*) production cost. These three pieces of information are essential for the dialogue with the Customer.

While the tone of the discussion is optimistic, this sequence also includes a late challenge to the viability of the enterprise. The challenge comes when the R&D-oriented Division 3, who has been fairly passive in the discussion, questions whether it is possible to accomplish the ambitious objective. The sequence is a brief, less than a minute, excerpt from minutes 27–28 of the episode.

548 GM:	((Looks at Tech)) Yes, it's (.) We have (.) we have nothing to
549	ask for ((turns his head towards Division 1)).
550 Division 1:	No, we have to take it.
551 GM:	Yes (.) No it's pretty clear, isn't it? Is anyone of a different
552	opinion? ((looks around the table)).
553	(1.5)
554 Division 2:	No. If we want in.
555 GM:	That reminds me ((points at Marketing)) How much is it [the
556	Customer] owes us on [another machine]? Do you remember?
557	((Looks at Marketing))
558 Marketing:	As far as I recall it's three million dollars ((Marketing turns in
559	his chair, GM is nodding))
560	(1.0)
561 GM:	Right. ((looks at Tech)) That's good. ((snickering))
562 Tech:	Yes, it's a lot of money. Well (.) so I (.) can't hear a no here
563	but it (.) Do we all agree that this ((points at the screen)) is a
564	terrific step?
565 GM:	No, you hear a (.) *resounding* yes.
566 Tech:	Yeah ((laughs)) right.
567 GM:	Yes, or what do you say? ((GM looks around the table. Tech
568	laughs)) Damn it! This is ((slowly pounding the back of the
569	empty chair next to him with his fist)).
570 Division 3:	Sounds like a great opportunity ((looks at GM)).
571 GM:	Yes
572 Division 3:	But really, what is the time frame? Because it's a huge
573	responsibility too. Design responsibility for several
574	components that we don't have today.

575 Tech: What (.) [the Customer] has started to talk
576 Division 3:   ((breaks in)) Is it two three years or what?
577 Tech: What [the Customer] starts talking about
578 GM: ((breaks in)) Hell no! It's now. It's (.) [the name of a machine]
579   starts here and now.

In this sequence, GM's opening comment responds to a few prior remarks on how to allocate the cost of the design study (the 4 million Swedish crowns). The question (line 555–556) about the sum that the Customer owes them (the 3 million dollars) seems incidental. The issue refers to an on-going contractual dispute in connection with the manufacture of components for another industrial machine. GM may view the unsettled money issue as an argument in the upcoming talks with the Customer.

Tech does not view the turn (at lines 548–554) as a clear go-ahead decision, leading him to ask for a clarification. With the subsequent 'resounding yes' (line 565), GM interprets what he feels is the consensus of the group, but he is also to some extent imposing his (and Marketing's?) view as the consensus. He concludes, emphasizing, in a symbolic way, the 'resounding yes' by slowly pounding his fist on the back of the empty chair beside him (lines 568–569). Yet, while doing so, he also seeks confirmation from the group. In their brief comments, Division 1 (line 550) and Division 2 (line 554) confirm the consensus. Without saying so explicitly, both of them refer to the strategic objective of integrating the Company upstream in the value chain (Division 2's 'If we want in' especially makes this point). That may be a reason for the two division heads' apparent lack of enthusiasm at this point in the discussion. The decision does not initiate strategic change but confirms the Company's current strategy. Therefore, for them, a 'no go' decision would be hard to imagine.

Division 3, however, is not fully committed. He intervenes (line 570) by challenging GM's optimism. His late entry is triggered, or forced, by two factors. The first is GM's questions, '... isn't it? Is anyone of a different opinion?' (line 551) and, 'or what do you say?' (line 567). The second factor is the brief but supportive consensual statements by the other division heads (lines 550 and 554). As one of three division heads, it is appropriate for Division 3 to voice his opinion, too. He softens his criticism by pointing out what a great opportunity this is, or sounds as if it is (line 570). However, his subsequent questioning of the feasibility of the project stems from his knowledge that unforeseen problems often arise in product and technology development. Tech attempts to respond twice (lines 575 and 577), but he is interrupted both times, first by Division 3 and then by GM. It signifies that Division 3 is not addressing Tech but GM. GM responds by pointing out that it is 'here and now'. Some additional explaining (after the sequence) by GM, Division 2, and Tech settles that the 'now' only refers to one component, not the several components suggested by Division 3 (line 573–574). When the timing of the different components is somewhat clearer, Division 3 accepts the decision with a brief 'OK'. He has made his point. Addressing Tech, GM finalizes the go-ahead decision: 'We all agree that this is the way to go.'

While Tech collects his papers and prepares to leave, the group spends a couple of minutes on practical matters, such as, for example, which documents concerning this point should be attached to the minutes of the meeting. The professional tension and focused effort that characterized the prior discussion have decreased. Four group members (Quality, HRM, Finance, and Operational Development) were more or less silent throughout the half-hour episode. Now some of them make half-joking comments appropriate to the upbeat atmosphere. As Tech closes the door behind him, GM turns to the next item on the agenda: 'OK, next'.

DISCUSSION

This chapter addresses the work practice of a management team that is trying (*a*) to outline a market opportunity that has been identified and provisionally delineated in other organizational settings and (*b*) to decide how to continue. The group discussion and ensuing decision set the scene for a range of subsequent actions by several group members, including Tech. These actions include disseminating the prospect to internal and external stakeholders. When a go-ahead decision is reached, a crucial task is to get the Customer involved in making and, not the least, giving sense to the vision of a long-term partnership.

The multitude of frames that are applied to the case is the prime mover in the group's collective process of managing the future of the BU and the Company. However, the novelty of the evolving industrial situation combined with the diversity of perspectives that are applied may also create instability in group members' ways of understanding the emerging prospect. The managers may thus need to apply additional frames, until a provisional point of saturation is reached where the group members feel ready to commit themselves to future action.

During the social process of revising (or re-visualizing) organizational identity in the industrial network, the discussion also powerfully affects how managers produce their own membership status and identity in the management team (Maitlis, 2005). Division 2 undoubtedly confirms his identity as a knowledgeable manager. Marketing confirms his role as an important team member by, for example, his analysis of the Customer's situation. For Division 3, the outcome is more uncertain. His remark, made late in the discussion, about the strain on resources (should they be successful in persuading the Customer to outsource product development) shows that the 'resounding yes' was somewhat premature. Division 3 is not yet quite ready with his own sense-making. His framing of the situation introduces the risk of failure. In a way, his framing thus responds to the comment (in Sequence 1) about the project being adventurous (implying an element of danger), which, however, Marketing quickly reframes as an opportunity (lines 331–336). In order to strengthen his membership position in the team, Division 3 could, for example, have inserted his remark in the pause at the end of Sequence 1 instead of challenging GM's cheerful 'resounding yes'. Some members sit quietly because they have no contribution to make based on their specific professional perspectives. Notably, Finance does not see enough structure for her expertise to have any bearing yet. She might have disturbed the process by asking questions about finance while not gaining (or losing) much in standing created by her silence. The upbeat atmosphere in the group after GM has finally concluded (after Sequence 2) addressing, primarily Tech, that 'we all agree that this is the way to go' seems to feed on a mixture of the possibilities that success would bring and the sheer adventure of setting a daring initiative in motion.

If the management team had made a different valuation of the individual members' contributions, the outcome might have been a 'no go' decision. That would have altered the alignment of statements in the discussion. Division 3's warning about the strain on resources would have gained significance (and Finance or HRM might have found reason to get involved in the discussion, too). We may conclude that the 'go-ahead' decision crowns the contributions of members in the sense that facts and value statements that turn out to support the outcome will confirm or improve the membership status of speakers (given the team mission). In general, those who are quiet will not lose status (i.e. if the topic of discussion lies outside their area of competence and outside their jurisdiction). Those who speak against may recover lost status by indicating later (i.e. if the future shows that their criticism was justified) that they, despite having doubts about the feasibility of the enterprise, were persuaded by the arguments (loyal opposition).

CONCLUSIONS

A general conclusion from this case is that the process of sense-making and sense-giving seems to be very robust given a lack of facts and given the uncertainty about available facts. The team members do not know what the different actors in their environment will do. Still they construct a prospect that they believe 'will work' (at least well enough to justify a 'go-ahead' decision). The process may be robust given the uncertainty in facts, but it is very sensitive to group members' criticisms or expressions of doubt. We should note that decisions like this one are almost always taken unanimously. This is supported by Moscovici and Doise's findings (1994) on group polarization and by Brunsson's study (1976) of decisions in the development of products that are new to an organization. In this sense, the discussion in the episode is a mobilization of bias (for action). It is therefore reasonable to assume that teamwork and especially membership work play important roles in overcoming uncertainty. The integration of arguments from trusted members (in a complex situation) into a collective project narrative of some form carries over to a more 'normal' execution state.

There are methodological implications in this case for the researcher. The audiovisual recording allows the researcher to analyse the discourse as it unfolds, registering how frames are activated and how they guide the exchange for a while. A particular frame will bring some members to the front while silencing others. The researcher may note that frames overlap at times as members speak past each other. Speaking out of order for an extended period, after the focus of the conversation has shifted to another frame, may signal incompetence, but it may also be a way of introducing a new frame.

The important aspect here is that the use of multiple frames enhances the effectiveness of conversations, and skilful framing increases a group's ability to manage complexity. A well-composed team (with trust in, and care for, other members) may have established practices that can be analysed as institutional communication, exhibiting what Sacks (1992: 40) calls 'inference rich'-ness (by using multiple framing). The problem for the researcher then is that the management solution or project that is taking shape will appear in the 'undertext'. Team members continuously draw strategic implications as well as practical ones as deliberation progresses. They have possible and emerging solutions in mind as they make their contributions. A researcher who has spent some time in the organization, observing organizational members at work, will have a much better chance of seeing what is at stake than the complete outsider. The researcher is also at an advantage in judging what is the appropriate action in the situation at hand and in discovering competent frame shifts as well as missteps. And, with audiovisual recording, there is always the possibility to rewind, replay, and discuss what is going on with colleagues – applying multiple framing in the analysis, as it were.

Our case study illustrates a kind of strategic work in top management (or project) teams that is often neglected in conventional management research because of its unique character as well as the difficulty in obtaining direct research access to the meetings (including permission to record the interaction) where the work is done. The managerial work on such *appellate cases* (Barnard, 1946) may be difficult to study, but it is very common in top management teams as well as in project management (Jönsson, 2004). Besides the defining *uniqueness*, such cases are characterized by a *lack of facts* and that available 'facts' are fraught with *uncertainty*. There may also be a lack of applicable judgement criteria. The work done under such circumstances can be seen as a type of *design-work*, where a project inside a scenario (called a *prospect*) is hammered out. The tools for that design-work are the competences of participating members and a skilful *shifting between frames* that such competences presuppose. We have called such shifting that makes use of members' different expertise '*multi-framing*'. To counteract the risk that the divergent perspectives that are applied in such work generate centripetal forces that may cause disintegration of the team, membership work should be present at all times. In *membership work*, a member (or prospective member) simultaneously (*a*) displays an identity in action (e.g. as an expert in some relevant area) and (*b*) contributes by aligning suggestions with the common, emerging mission (or policy statement). Such demonstrations of competence and good will provide *team-confidence*, which makes the process tolerant of uncertainty. The decision (in our case, the 'go-ahead' decision) that comes from such a collective process of management should not be regarded as a set of coordinated steps towards a fixed goal (a plan), but as an act of strategizing that sets the project in motion in a certain direction (e.g. Samra-Fredericks, 2003). The prospect thus serves as a general guide that is continuously revised as organizational members continue their work in future episodes with various strategic significance.

With the benefit of hindsight, we can see that the managerial work in this episode constituted a small but necessary step in the progress towards a strategic and commercial breakthrough that took place some five years later. In 2007, a series of press releases announced the project success. A first announcement stated that the Customer had awarded the Company an important and prestigious

'Best Supplier Award'. A second press release announced that the Customer had decided to use the Company's design-solution in their machines. Some months later the Company proudly stated that it was the industry leader in the development and production of this type of high-tech component. The Company had finally reached its goal of becoming a CoE for this component group, although that specific term was no longer used.

REFERENCES

Atkinson, P. (2007). *Handbook of Ethnography.* London: Sage.

Barnard, C. (1946). *The Functions of the Executive.* Cambridge, MA: Harvard University Press.

Brunsson, N. (1976). *Propensity to Change.* Göteborg: BAS.

Bryman, A. (2008). *Social Research Methods.* Oxford: Oxford University Press.

Clarke, T. (1998). Research on corporate governance. *Corporate Governance: An International Review,* 6(1): 57–66.

Finkelstein, S. and Hambrick, C. (1996). *Strategic Leadership – Top Executives and Their Effects on Organizations.* Minneapolis/St. Paul: West Publishing Co.

Gioia, D. A. and Chittipeddi, K. (1991). Sensemaking and sensegiving in strategic change initiation. *Strategic Management Journal,* 12: 433–48.

Goffman, E. (1981). *Forms of Talk.* Oxford: Blackwell.

Hendry, J. and Seidl, D. (2003). The structure and significance of strategic episodes: Social systems theory and the routine practices of strategic change. *Journal of Management Studies,* 4(1): 175–96.

Heritage, J. and Atkinson, J. M. (1984). Introduction. In J. M. Atkinson and J. Heritage (Eds.), *Structures of Social Actions: Studies in Conversational Analysis* (pp. 1–15). Cambridge, MA: Cambridge University Press.

Jönsson, S. (2004). *Product Development – Work for Premium Values.* Malmö: Liber.

Jordan, B. and Henderson, A. (1995). Interaction analysis: Foundations and practice. *The Journal of Learning Sciences,* 4(1): 39–103.

Kunda, G. (1992). *Engineering Culture: Control and Commitment in a High-Tech Corporation.* Philadelphia: Temple University Press.

Lomax, H. and Casey, N. (1998). Recording social life: Reflexivity and video methodology. *Sociological Research Online,* 3(2): 1–9.

Maitlis, S. (2005). The social process of organizational sensemaking. *Academy of Management Journal,* 48(1): 21–49.

Morrill, C. (1995). *The Executive Way: Conflict Management in Corporations.* Chicago: The University of Chicago Press.

Moscovici, S. and Doise, W. (1994). *Conflict and Consensus – A General Theory of Collective Decisions.* London: Sage Publications.

Munro, R. (1996). Alignment and identity work: The study of accounts and accountability. In R. Munro and J. Mouritsen (Eds.), *Accountability, Power, Ethos & the Technologies of Management.* London: Thompson.

Pettigrew, A. M. (1992). On studying managerial elites. *Strategic Management Journal,* 13: 163–82.

Pink, S. (2007). *Doing Visual Ethnography: Images, Media and Representations in Research.* London: Sage.

Sacks, H. (1992). *Lectures on Conversation* (Vol. 1). Cambridge, MA: Blackwell Publishers.

Samra-Fredericks, D. (2000). Doing 'Boards-in-Action' research – An ethnographic approach for the capture and analysis of directors' and senior managers' interactive routines. *Corporate Governance: An International Review,* 8(3): 244–57.

—— (2003). Strategizing as lived experience and strategists' everyday efforts to shape strategic direction. *Journal of Management Studies*, 40(1): 141–74.

Tannen, D. (1993). 'What's in a frame? Surface evidence for underlying expectations'. In D. Tannen (Ed.), *Framing in Discourse*. New York: Oxford University Press.

Weick, K. E. (1995). *Sensemaking in Organizations*. Thousand Oaks, CA: Sage Publications.

Whittington, R. (2006). Completing the practice turn in strategy research. *Organization Studies*, 27(5): 613–34.

Part III

Operational managerial work

The three chapters of Part Three present studies from different managerial work settings: health care, construction, and research and development (R&D). The managers in these chapters are close to daily operations and front-line personnel. Their fragmented work involves complex problem solving and high work pressure. Only a small part of their work involves decision-making. While these studies largely confirm the results of previous studies of operational managers, one chapter emphasizes the importance of technical problem solving and work planning (construction site management), and two chapters emphasize the importance of interpersonal relations and the preoccupation with administrative tasks (health care management and R&D management).

CHAPTER 6. WORK ACTIVITIES AND STRESS AMONG MANAGERS IN HEALTH CARE

Rebecka Arman, Ewa Wikström, Ellinor Tengelin, and Lotta Dellve describe the daily hassles and stress in the work of ten first-line and second-line health care managers. While these health care managers can rely on rather independent health care providers, they also have to cope with administrative burdens and leadership responsibilities. The study shows that health care managers also struggle to gain legitimacy among the health care professionals who often have little respect for managerial work tasks. The health care managers therefore have to build legitimacy by engaging in extensive and time-consuming communication activities.

CHAPTER 7. LEADERSHIP AS MUDDLING THROUGH: SITE MANAGERS IN THE CONSTRUCTION INDUSTRY

Alexander Styhre studies the work behaviour of site managers in the construction industry using Charles Lindblom's classic concept (1959) of 'muddling through'. These site managers do not have to compromise and use covert tactics as extensively as Lindblom's political administrators. However, like those

administrators, they have to deal with complexity, stress, and various disturbances. Muddling through is a way of coping with the work challenges when
formal planning has lost its relevance. In this perspective, a 'muddling through'
manager with various administrative, relational, and ill-specified work tasks can
do excellent work. By contrast, the manager who assumes the role of the rational
manager or heroic leader could well be following a recipe for disaster.

CHAPTER 8. R&D MANAGERS LEADING
KNOWLEDGE WORKERS WITH CARE

Ola Edvin Vie presents a study of four managers at research and development
units. His study was designed as a replication of Henry Mintzberg's classic study
(1973) of five chief executives. While Vie's study supports many of Mintzberg's
findings, it also identifies a managerial behaviour that is more internally oriented,
more informal, more open to consensus, and more relational. An important
contribution of the study is its recognition of the work activities that relate to
the concept of care, particularly the care of subordinates. The R&D managers in
the study consider their personnel responsibilities the most emotionally stressful
and difficult part of their work.

6

Work activities and stress among managers in health care

Rebecka Arman, Ewa Wikström, Ellinor Tengelin,
and Lotta Dellve

INTRODUCTION

Kerstin, a health care manager, arrives at the office at 7:30 am before the administrative staff and medical secretaries who work in the same corridor. As she hangs her jacket in the closet, her beeper and cell phone signal simultaneously. She recognizes the number on her beeper as that of the physician who was on call during the night. She then reads the text message on her cell phone that is from her supervisor who asks for a meeting at 9:00 am. It is the supervisor's first day at work after a week's vacation abroad. Kerstin guesses that her supervisor wants to find out what has happened in the department while she was gone. She calls her manager to say the 9:00 time is fine with her. 'No, it has been pretty uneventful,' she replies in answer to a question. 'Yes, there were some articles in the press about the waiting times for emergency operations at the hospital. OK, see you soon.'

After the phone call, Kerstin mumbles to herself: 'I wonder if I will get the things done today that I planned.' There are piles of papers on her desk, organized in several rows, waiting to be attended to. She then turns her attention to the five wards where she is the second line manager. There is an urgent matter about the number of free beds on the wards. There has been a nightmare of overflow in the last few days. She, as well as her subordinate managers and the physicians she manages, wonder how long the situation will last and how they should handle it. She logs on to her computer and looks at the screen: 'It looks a bit better today, but it is so stupid that you can't trust the computer system!' At 7:45 she calls the physician in charge to find out what the situation is on the wards so that she can begin to deal with it before the meeting with her supervisor and colleagues from the other specialties in her department.

In recent decades as the number of health care managers (HCMs) has grown, the number of such managers who report job stress has also grown. This study, in the tradition of managerial work studies on activities and time-use (Tengblad, 2006), was undertaken in an effort to understand how HCMs manage their time in performing their various activities and what the consequences of this time management are, including the nature and causes of such stress. Our focus in this chapter is the lower level HCM.

Researchers have promoted time management as a particularly important workplace tool that may be useful in increasing the efficiency of managers, including HCMs (Perlow, 1999; Marquis and Houston, 2006). Studies of time-use focus on the number, flow, duration, and sequencing of different activities during the workday. The goal of such studies is to understand the content and organization of an individual's work. Some studies of time point to professional, organizational, and cultural (societal) norms and mechanisms of control that influence the conscious and less conscious self-regulation of work behaviour and time-use. These norms and mechanisms of control are part of managerial communication that is a large part of everyday managerial work (e.g. Mintzberg, 1973; Kotter, 1982; Hannaway, 1989; Tengblad, 2006).

Time can also be seen as an ontologically central construct that is seldom made explicit in the organizational literature. Instead, time is often considered merely as a boundary condition that enables or limits work activities (Pina e Cunha, 2004). However, a few studies of workers' experiences and interpretations of time have revealed important knowledge, for example, on the effect on freedom, collaboration, and work-time flexibility (Perlow, 1999; Evans et al., 2004).

In our previous studies, we found that HCMs have difficulty managing their time as they try to practice 'good' and 'sustainable' leadership. For instance, Wikström and Dellve (2009) report on interviews with HCMs who describe themselves as torn between administrative, personnel, and strategic duties. Such managers experience ethical stress and face legitimacy dilemmas that are related to these conflicts in time allocation. As Östergren and Sahlin-Andersson (1998: 13) conclude, their dual position as both a health care professional and a manager means dealing with 'different worlds' (see also Öfverström, 2008). The combination is not always easy since HCMs' clinical competence may be valued more highly than their financial management competence. On the other hand, when HCMs lack economic management expertise, they may feel vulnerable in their managerial role (Llewellyn, 2001).

Several problems arise as a result of HCMs' communication with others at work and their handling of stress-related problems among themselves and the employees they manage (Skagert et al., 2008; Dellve and Wikström, 2009; Wikström and Dellve, 2009). In addition, when managers leave their positions and when organizations recruit new managers, there are problems in the continuity of the organization. However, studies of these problems have been based primarily on accounts elicited during interviews. Previous research has shown that what managers say they do and what they do are two different things (Mintzberg, 1973). Hence, an observation-based study would give us a better understanding of the activities and micro events in the managers' everyday managerial work. Our purpose also included acquiring knowledge about sustainability as related to the managers' time-use in this type of work and organization. Sustainability in this study, which integrates health and organizational perspectives, means both the individual's ability to stay healthy while working as a manager and the organizational consequences of the individual's sustained time allocation patterns in the workplace. Set against this background of problems, the aim of this study is to further investigate HCMs' work activities, time-use patterns, and stress.

Specifically, this chapter addresses the following questions:

1. How do HCMs handle everyday stressors, and hassles, particularly the fragmentation of work activities?
2. How are HCMs' patterns of communication constituted through legitimacy practices?
3. What are the consequences of HCMs' patterns for handling work fragmentation and legitimacy practices?

To answer these questions, we collected qualitative and quantitative data on HCMs' routine, daily activities, and stress. This data provided us with evidence of problems in their time allocation. We created a body of rich empirical data through shadowing, semi-structured observations, and interviews. We also used a stress questionnaire with the HCMs and periodically measured their heart rates. In using these research methods, we hoped to acquire new knowledge of structural, environmental, and individual constraints in the workplace as well as a better understanding of agency and organizational capabilities or opportunities. The goal was to learn how these combined forces interact in the everyday micro practice of HCMs.

It is clear that HCMs work in a complex context. They are both the managers of other health care professionals like themselves and the organizational representatives to the general public and to their political overseers. The research reported on in this chapter, using examples and discussing consequences, shows that their work is not only a matter of situational adaptation or adjustment but also of active participation in negotiations between competing and integrating logics.

The chapter begins with comments on health care managerial work and stress as described in our and others' studies, followed by a brief summary of the relevant theories used. The setting of the research is presented next. The main results of the research are discussed in terms of a theoretical framework and are summarized in the chapter's conclusions. The research methodology is presented in the Appendix.

MANAGERIAL WORK AND SOURCES OF STRESS IN HEALTH CARE

Competing logics and legitimacy processes in health care management

Earlier studies argue that managerial work in health care organizations has specific characteristics (see e.g. Ferlie et al., 1996; Llewellyn, 2001; Kitchener, 2002). The claim is also made that the management and organization of professionals demand the use of a different logic than is typical, for example, in many bureaucracies (see e.g. Larson, 1977; Freidson, 1994). This claim is applicable to the management of health care professionals. Mintzberg (2002: 205), who studied how HCMs manage from *within* and at the centre of the organization instead of from above, concluded: 'A management that does not see itself on top can engage the professional in improving operations that they themselves appreciate'. He described lower and middle management in health care as the 'inner management'. In a study of hospital managers, Braithwaite (2004: 255) stated:

'Partnership rather than instruction appears more appropriate for professional-managerial relationships, given the networks of stakeholder complexity'.

Other studies, taking a somewhat different perspective, discuss the existence of power struggles embedded in the relationships among the administrative, managerial, and professional domains. Various researchers describe the tensions and conflicts between occupational groups and top administrative management (Degeling and Carr, 2004; Dellve and Wikström, 2009). This research emphasizes that economic directives seldom agree with medical priorities. As a result of the complex meetings between representatives from health care professions and managers at different levels, a new discourse has arisen where the clinical and administrative ways of thinking combine to create a new and unique way of thinking and acting as a manager. HCMs must handle the overlapping of regulating systems that belong to 'different worlds', for example, that of the professional and that of the management system (Östergren and Sahlin-Andersson, 1998: 13; Öfverström, 2008). Reed (1996) stated that the roles of professionals would therefore change as they perform managerial work. Ferlie et al. (1996) called this changed role a hybrid of the professional–manager roles. Doolin (2002) showed how health care professions manoeuvre in the organization by using clinical discourse, on the one hand, and a combined managerial and financial discourse, on the other. Llewellyn (2001) used the metaphor of the 'two-way window' for the dual managerial role of clinical professionals. The task of HCMs, then, is to use this new discourse and management style as they manage the overlap of these two regulating systems.

Thus, compound identities, conflicting loyalties, and opposing professional–administrative interests may shape a HCM's range of influence. HCMs may use various strategies to retain their legitimacy (such as the use of professional, clinical skills and the creation of a strong occupational identity) or to develop legitimacy in their role as administrative leaders. An alternative strategy is to adapt the two identities to suit the particular setting (Dellve and Wikström, 2009). Managers themselves describe the different logics associated with the two identities: (*a*) an administrative logic avoids being drowned with administrative issues and details, (*b*) an 'employeeship' logic supports employees and develops the partnership with managers, and (*c*) a strategic logic creates space for strategic work such as long-term planning. Effective managerial work means tuning in and tuning out the various logics, depending on the task (Wikström and Dellve, 2009).

Wikström and Dellve's interview study (2009) examined the two managerial work models that meet these contemporary demands in health care organizations. The first model is managerial work that separates the different logics; the second model is managerial work that integrates the different logics. In the 'separating model', complexity and dilemmas are defined as tensions and contradictions between the various logics, previously described by Kouzes and Mico (1979) as tensions between various domains. Furthermore, the various logics are perceived as different realities. In the 'integrating model', complexity and dilemmas are defined as concurrent where managers work to meet various logics in order to solve tasks. In the discourse about change, leadership, and performance, there is support for an overlap of the models with greater emphasis on the concurrent model (see also Tengblad, 2006).

Giddens' (1984/6) structuration theory and organizational communication theory are both useful in understanding how the complexities of communication patterns of managerial work are handled. These theoretical perspectives point to the importance of communication in signifying and to the process of interpretation, as well as to the consequences communication has on the interests in the organization including the use of power mechanisms and legitimacy. According to Giddens, communication and interpretation (signification) are, on the one hand, connected to power and control (domination) and, on the other hand, are related to legitimacy and acceptance (legitimation). Signification is produced through interpretive schemes. Scholars in organizational communication describe how these interpretive schemes function through the referencing of 'texts' that compete in the social world. By their usage, the texts are constantly reproduced, negotiated, and thus strengthened or weakened, and sometimes even changed (Deetz, 1995).

In health care organizations, the struggle to maintain and repair societal legitimacy seems constant and pervasive. Giddens (1984/6) says such legitimacy is created by both norms and sanctions. According to Suchman (1995: 575), legitimacy is a generalized perception or assumption that certain actions are desirable, proper, or appropriate within some socially constructed system of norms, values, beliefs, and definitions. Previous studies of health care have shown that in these kinds of professional organizations there are competing or complementing systems of norms governing legitimacy. In his discussion, Suchman identified three interrelated types of legitimacy: pragmatic, moral, and cognitive. Power (2007) described risk management as another type of legitimation work in which people try to manage uncertainty in order to prevent loss of reputation among the general public. In the Swedish health care context, the strong public actors include the patients, the politicians, the National Board of Health and Welfare (NBHW), the unions, and the relevant professional organizations.

Another useful concept for understanding how complexities in managerial work are handled is the concept of 'boundaries'. Many different boundaries are constructed in health care organizations in order to demarcate how and what people do, with whom and for what reasons, and whether in competition or in collaboration with other people and groups (Wikström, 2008). Previously, Kerosou (2006) showed how boundaries in health care reflect traces of past activities while at the same time establish 'border zones' where development, learning, and change are located. In a study of other types of organizations using the concept of boundaries, Hernes (2004) illustrated the types of processes involved (physical, social, and mental) and the consequences of boundaries (ordering, distinction, and threshold). Other studies have shown how boundaries in the work-life balance can be shifted so that organizational life and culture colonize the lives, emotions, and identities of the organizations' members (Kunda, 1992/2006; Hochschild, 1997). However, such colonization may meet resistance when boundaries are equally constructed through alterity, that is, by defining the individual's differences when compared to other people or groups (Wikström, 2008). In short, boundaries are constantly negotiated through the processes of legitimacy, signification, and domination.

Daily hassles and stress in health care managers' work

Increasingly, psychosocial stress is an occupational health concern due to the complex interactions between individuals and their work context. These challenges that health care workers encounter in their daily work, and the stress, hassles, or support they experience as a result, are typical of their psychosocial work conditions that depend on the relationship between the individual and the organization/environment. People experience stress if the balance between their interior resources and the demands of a situation is disturbed. Then physiological stress response systems activate in order to maintain a biological balance. However, if it is prolonged, constant activation of stress responses means there is a physiological overload that wears out the physiological systems, making individuals even more susceptible to stress and increasing their risk of a stress-related disorder (McEwen, 2005). Two common theoretical mechanism models explain psychosocial stress in health care – Karasek and Theorell's demand–control–support model (1990) (i.e. high work-life demands combined with low control and low social support) and Siegrist and Theorell's effort–reward imbalance model (2006) (i.e. a perceived imbalance between personal efforts and rewards).

Research reveals that HCMs often work under extreme pressure with high demands but with lower decision latitude and limited space for acting (Pousette, 2001; Skagert et al., 2008). Their somewhat undefined managerial role, which is complicated by the existence of various, conflicting interests, may add to the stress-related pressure (Maslach et al., 2001; Pousette, 2001). Additionally, HCMs, as leaders, must be readily available to offer assistance and support to other employees in order to sustain the health of health care workers (Theorell et al., 2001; Dellve et al., 2007; Nyberg et al., 2009). One longitudinal study demonstrated that managerial behaviour and employee well-being are linked in a feedback loop over time (van Dierendonck et al., 2004).

The challenge in handling stress is also a matter of taking time for recovery. Since each managerial logic may require boundless time and attention, a manager needs to prioritize, delegate, and set boundaries in order to limit the amount of mental and practical overtime work. As managers are expected to be available during all working hours (and sometimes even after working hours), it is likely that the boundaries between working and private spheres are perceived as *flexible* and *permeable*. Flexibility in working hours has the potential to blur the boundaries between different life spheres; all time is then potential working time (Allvin et al., 2006; MacEachen et al., 2008). Strategies to delimit work and gain recovery time are then essential. Because of its potential effect on health-related sustainability, boundary-setting for the HCMs thus becomes a complex issue in which they exert at least some control over when, where, and how to perform their managerial work. Some researchers have argued that the vague boundaries between work and home are not necessarily detrimental to health as long as individual preferences for the boundary-setting fit the actual working conditions (Edwards and Rothbard, 1999; Kreiner, 2006; Bryson, et al., 2007; Kreiner et al., 2009). However, other researchers have observed stress responses due to spillover factors from the work to the private sphere, especially among women (e.g. Frankenhaeuser et al., 1989). According to McEwen (1998), unless time for recovery is taken, everyday stressful work means a risk of long-term detrimental health effects. Handling boundaries in managerial work thus means segregating or integrating work logics and life spheres in ways that are sustainable for the individual.

A complexity in the study of health care managerial work is that HCMs manage professionals with health care responsibilities. Earlier studies seem to emphasize either a partnership or a conflict between the managerial and professional systems. In both scenarios, the typical elements in health care managerial work – negotiation, fragmentation, or integration – may cause workplace stress for HCMs. This chapter suggests relationships between work complexity and work-related stress. In addition, the chapter describes approaches used to handle the central conflicts of boundary negotiation.

THE SETTING OF THE STUDY

We studied ten HCMs (first-line and second-line managers) working in different health care areas in the Western Region of Sweden (see the Appendix for details of our methodology). This regional government body manages all public health care in the community that has 17 hospitals, 134 primary care health centres, and 45,000 employees. In Swedish health care, first- and second-line managers have at least some direct contact with the operative level of care production. First-line managers are typically in charge of a unit such as a ward, an outpatient clinic, or a primary health care centre. Second-line managers direct several units and first-line managers. Often second-line managers have a simultaneous first-line managerial function related to certain professional groups (e.g. physicians). Nurses in Sweden may hold either first- or second-line positions while physicians commonly hold second-line positions. In psychiatric care, psychologists and social workers are common as managers.

The health care employer in this study selected nine 'basic criteria' that were directed to all managers. The expectations and qualities sought in managers are, in the following order: a willingness to lead (and understand what leadership involves); clarity/directness; a holistic view; the ability to build relationships; team-orientation, structure, analytical abilities; confidence-inspiring; and determination (decision oriented). It may initially seem surprising that the first criterion is a 'willingness to lead'. Yet Öfverström's study (2008) of physicians in management revealed that many physicians say they have entered this work somewhat reluctantly or circumstantially. Several criteria are connected to time-use. For example, 'structured' means delivering on time and informing others when time frames are changed, and 'determined' involves making sure that tasks are completed 'at a high activity level', according to the official document (VGREG, 2009).

DAILY HASSLES OF FRAGMENTATION
AND COMMUNICATION

This chapter focuses on the research's main results concerning the work of HCMs. These results relate to how managers generally used their time and specifically how they used their time when stress was observed. The focus is on the people they met with, their work content, and their resistance to or acceptance of their workload. These findings are presented thematically in the following order. First, we describe HCMs' general patterns of time-use and the activities that give rise to fragmentation and daily hassles. In this description, we also present qualitative results on how the HCMs handle fragmentation through boundary negotiations. Second, we describe the HCMs' patterns of communication including their contacts. We conclude with a brief presentation of managerial legitimation practices used in HCMs' communications.

General patterns of activities and stress

On average, the ten HCMs in this study engaged in seven activities per hour (a range of 3–14) and sixty-three activities per day (a range of 25–111). The first-line managers had twice the number of activities that second-line managers had (an average of 8 activities/hour compared to 4 activities/hour). The HCMs' average working day was nine hours (a range of 8–11 hours).[1] The *average* activity lasted ten minutes (a range of averages from 5 to 21 minutes). A representative example of work activities, coded according to purpose, for one first-line hospital ward manager follows in Table 6.1. The time frame is slightly more than one hour. This example typifies the data we collected in our observations, some of the categories we used, and the types of interruptions common in the managers' work.

The observations show that the managers use both separating and integrating strategies in combining different logics in their work. A simple example of a concurrent strategy appears in the first managerial activity. In thanking an employee for her work, the manager concurrently maintains a good manager–employee relationship, encourages shared responsibility for covering shifts (employeeship), and demonstrates administrative efficiency in simultaneously reminding the employee of the extra night shifts scheduled. This activity also reflects a long-term strategic logic since staffing nights in this particular ward is a key issue in the quality of care. It has important consequences for the care of post-operative patients, and thus affects other units such as surgery.

In the example shown in Table 6.1, unscheduled meetings are the main cause of interruptions in the manager's work. Our research shows that other people often initiated such interruptions. Most of the managers answer to many employees who may contact them at almost any time since the managers even take their telephones to meetings. In the interviews, the managers said they think it is important that they are always available; we observed this as a characteristic approach. However, the frequent interruptions, particularly when the managers needed to concentrate on demanding tasks, were related to the stress experienced.

A common dilemma concerning stress was the managers' lack of time and space to reflect between activities. This also includes time for strategic work where

Table 6.1 Representative example of work activities

Time	Activity and notes	Purpose
06:47	*Unplanned meeting with an employee in the hallway*: Thanks the employee for working the night shift and for agreeing to cover two additional shifts.	Social
06:48	*Desk work alone in her office*: Starts the computer and unpacks her bag.	Admin
06:51	*Tour to the nurses' station and around the ward*: Checks with the staff who worked the night shift, looks at the computerized schedule, checks the number of patients and empty beds on the ward, and asks a nurse to come to her office when she gets a chance during the day.	Scheduling
07:04	*Desk work alone in her office*: Checks the statistics on the number of patients on the ward, goes through several computer 'network' programmes to check for messages, assembles documents for a meeting, and checks and approves recent computerized work time reports from the staff.	Admin
07:12	*Unscheduled meeting with an employee in her office*: The nurse spoken to earlier enters to ask if it is ok to talk now. The manager informs her about her new salary (a raise).	Gives information
07:17	*Unscheduled meeting with an employee at the nurses' station*: Looks for a nurse to see if there are any extra patients on the ward. Informs the nurse that the neighbouring ward has four extra patients beyond their official capacity.	Gets information
07:30	*Desk work alone in her office*: Reads some e-mails and prints minutes from a meeting.	Admin
08:00	*Unscheduled meeting with manager from a neighbouring ward*: The manager comes to her office. They discuss and review information about the hospital's new organization. Then they talk about a summons from the NBHW concerning an investigation of the care of a patient who died on the ward. They also discuss an assistant manager's health and several other employees. The discussion is interrupted when the next activity begins (a phone call), so the other manager leaves.	Review

more time is needed for consideration (Tengelin et al., in press). In this study, the managers' use of time to a large extent consists of many brief activities lasting less than nine minutes (75 per cent of their activities, with a range of 60–86 per cent). However, these brief activities on average represent only a small part of their work time (25 per cent, with a range of 6–42 per cent) (Arman et al., 2009).

On average, the level of 'fragmentation', as measured by the number of activities, among the ten managers was higher compared to other managers in similar studies (Mintzberg, 1973; Kurke and Aldrich, 1983; Florén, 2005; Tengblad, 2006). The managers' time was divided among administration, secondary work, informational work, decision-making, requests and solicitations, some transportation, breaks, socializing, and set-up time. Table 6.2 presents the details of the fragmentation of work activity according to purpose. Informational activities, secondary (clinical and scheduling) together with administration, take most of the managers' time. Some managers are also active in direct patient care. Even the managers who are not involved directly in patient care often had substantial indirect

Table 6.2 Main purpose of activities

	Total time			Meetings
	Proportion of time (%)	Range (%)	*Hours per week	Proportion of time (%'s rounded)
Total administration	16	7–26	7.5	4
Clinical/non-managerial work	10		4.3	1
Scheduling	6		2.7	4
Ceremony**	1		0.5	1
External board work	1		0.3	1
Total secondary	18	2–42	7.8	9
Observational tours	1		0.5	2
Receiving information	5		2.2	8
Giving information	3		1.5	4
Review	24		111	49
Total informational	33	14–47	15.3	64
Strategy (important decision-making)	5		2.4	8
Negotiation (and other decisions)	1		0.6	2
Total decision-making	6	0–31	3.0	11
Requests and solicitations	2		1.1	3
Manager requests	4		1.6	3
Total requests and solicitations	6	4–9	2.7	6
Transportation	2		0.7	0
Breaks	6		2.9	0
Socializing	7		3.2	5
Set-up time	2	0–9	1.0	0
Interaction with observer	3		1.4	0
Unable to categorize	1		0.3	1
Other activities	21		9.5	6
Total	100		45.8	100

* This calculation is based on the average hours worked per day times the five days of the week.
** In our study, 'ceremony' includes contacts with the media.

involvement. There was some evidence that the managers found patient care work both interesting and necessary to meet the competing logics in their work.

Individual variation in time-use was observed. This was an expected result given the variation in the sample of participating managers (see 'Methodology' description in the Appendix). The amount of 'clinical work' varied between none and a third of their work time. This variation, combined with the ceremonial work of one manager during one week of observation, explains the large variance in 'total secondary' work. The variance in 'total decision-making' is explained by the fact that two managers spent many hours in strategy meetings, working on long-term planning, by the fact that two managers spent time negotiating salaries, and by the fact that other managers spent no time on such matters during the observations.

The first-line managers in hospital wards with 24-hour patient care spent much of their time in unscheduled meetings with their employees while first-line managers in outpatient settings on average did more clinical work. In general,

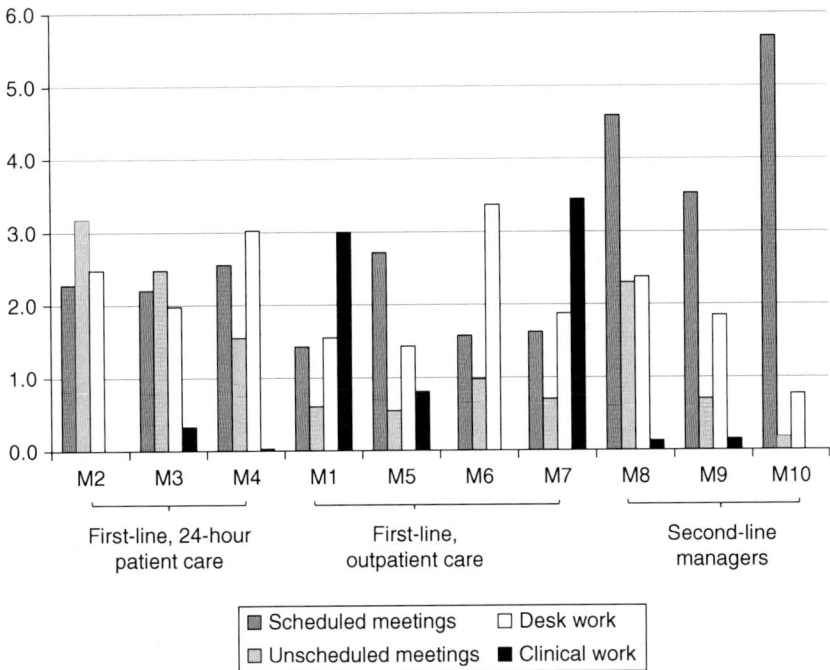

Figure 6.1 Examples of individual variation for a select set of activities (average number of hours/day)

the time spent on administrative deskwork was sizeable, among the first-line managers in particular. Since second-line managers on average had more as well as longer planned meetings, they had fewer activities during a typical day (see Figure 6.1). Thus, the fragmentation of work time and work content was considerable, as studies have shown for managers in other settings. However, since most managers in the study did not travel much, space fragmentation was low (Tengblad, 2006; Arman et al., 2009).

The analysis of the measurements of the managers' self-reported stress and energy levels showed that most managers in the study rated their stress lower than health care workers in non-managerial positions and also lower than other HCMs in a previous study (Hultberg et al., 2009). We identified three stress and energy patterns: (*a*) a natural wakefulness cycle with no heightened levels of stress (i.e. high energy at the beginning of the day and lower in the evening); (*b*) arousal patterns (i.e. heightened stress activity with synchronized increases in energy levels, often seen before and during the start of their own activities and important meetings); and (*c*) patterns of increased stress with no or decreased mobilization of energy.

We related biophysical measures of stress in the managers to the following circumstances: (*a*) interrupted when they needed to focus on a challenging task (e.g. by frequent, unplanned, and/or inconvenient meetings); and (*b*) personally affected (e.g. by conflict-loaded or ineffective meetings or by private dilemmas). We measured low heart rates when the managers had time to themselves and could work on administrative tasks without interruption. We observed the absence of stress in comfortable situations, for example, during clinical work and in interactions with co-workers. One manager had heightened indications of stress during a long meeting that she thought frustrating and inefficient. However, another manager seemed to recover during longer, planned meetings. The challenging work tasks related to stress when interrupted were those that demanded a longer time to handle (e.g. sudden problems with the budget process or with schedules due to sick leave).

Boundary approaches in a context of fragmented time

All the managers said their work was potentially boundless because of the long working hours and the spillover of work into their private lives. A central concern about their leadership, with an effect on both legitimacy and sustainability, was their approach to *time-giving* to others and to the *interruptions* from others (colleagues and patients). How they handled this seemed to be related to their view of good leadership. Sometimes they used reactive rather than active strategies since time-giving and interruptions could mean a lack of control over their time-use. Maintaining the expected availability and flexibility, while still staying in control, meant using different approaches (Tengelin et al., in press). In these approaches, the managers defined boundaries based on relationships, situations, or calendar-time. However, in using these approaches, they rarely questioned or challenged the boundlessness of their work.

One approach identified was the approach managers used when responding reactively to the needs of others. Specifically, they practiced very flexible boundary-setting as a result of the enquiries and interruptions during formal work hours. Allowing relationships to set the boundaries made flexible boundaries necessary. The managers could also allow some permeability, for example, when colleagues called them at home. In addition, managers often took work home so they could work in peace. Although some managers said they felt guilty about working too much, most managers felt it was natural that the needs and expectations of others set the boundaries. This attitude may be because of their inexperience as leaders and their doubts about their responsibilities. They may also have been influenced by altruistic ideals about giving people care that made them feel they had to be constantly available. This attitude may also influence this kind of relational boundary-setting. One manager stated: 'The work must take the time it takes'.

Another way to approach time-giving and interruptions was to accept them as part of the conditions of managerial work practice. The managers referred to their boundless workload as self-chosen. They also defended their weak boundaries by stressing their own controlling and negotiating abilities and accepted that the boundaries between work and other life spheres were very often open to influence from events in the work sphere. Thus, they said they did mental work and practical preparations at home in the early mornings and late evenings or on weekends. Interestingly, the managers did not seem to feel any stress or work dissatisfaction because of their boundless work conditions. In fact, the organizational attempts to limit the long work hours could be experienced as more stressful since such limitations might decrease the managers' control and autonomy. What distinguished the accepting approach from the reactive approach was that the managers were aware that they were using it. Reactively responding to the needs of others was certainly not a voiced strategy. Accepting the managerial work conditions, on the other hand, was described as an active reflection upon the working conditions.

Some managers had more restrictive rationales for their boundary-setting for time-giving and interruptions. For example, these managers constantly re-evaluated each situation for a situational adequate time-use. Their presence in the work activities on the ward allowed their boundaries to be defined, depending on the situations rather than on the relationships. Continuous observation and reflection of what was best in each situation kept them updated and guided their choices and actions. In this way, they set boundaries by making continuous trade-offs in their work. This approach seemed to promote balance for these managers as they carried out several activities per hour without feeling stressed. In evaluating each situation individually, they could set priorities, for example, in giving time to an employee or completing the day's administrative work. Hence, by paying attention to situations, they could evaluate the work tasks and thus delimit them.

Finally, in taking a time-focused approach to handling time-giving and interruptions, the managers delimited their work by using a well-planned calendar. This approach was characterized by a high degree of time-control through constant boundary-setting and a focus on the day's planned time-use. Using time-control in this way required managers to be self-confident and experienced leaders. One strategy to decrease the fragmentation caused by interruptions was to set aside time to answer employees' questions or to address unexpected events.

The managers' contacts

Our study showed that most of the managers' time was spent with their own employees (on average, 44 per cent, ranging between 24 and 71 per cent) (Arman et al., 2009). Most of this time was for informational communication activities (on average, 64 per cent) of which review of information was the most common (on average, 49 per cent). The type of information varied, but mostly related to administrative and employeeship work. An interesting finding concerned the managers' proximity to daily supervision of the many employees combined with a distance from their own superiors in the formal hierarchy. The managers spent very little time alone with their superiors. This finding of the distance between managerial levels in health care is supported by the data from the observed second-line managers. The second-line managers, on average, spent 3 per cent of their working time with their subordinate managers in one-on-one meetings. All the managers spent more time with their peers and co-managers (on average, 32 per cent, ranging between 17 and 51 per cent). Internal comparisons between first- and second-line managers in the study showed that second-line managers, on average, spent more time in collaboration groups (i.e. meeting with people from other departments and/or organizations). They also had less time alone and spent less time with their employees alone, implying that they were less available (see Figure 6.2).

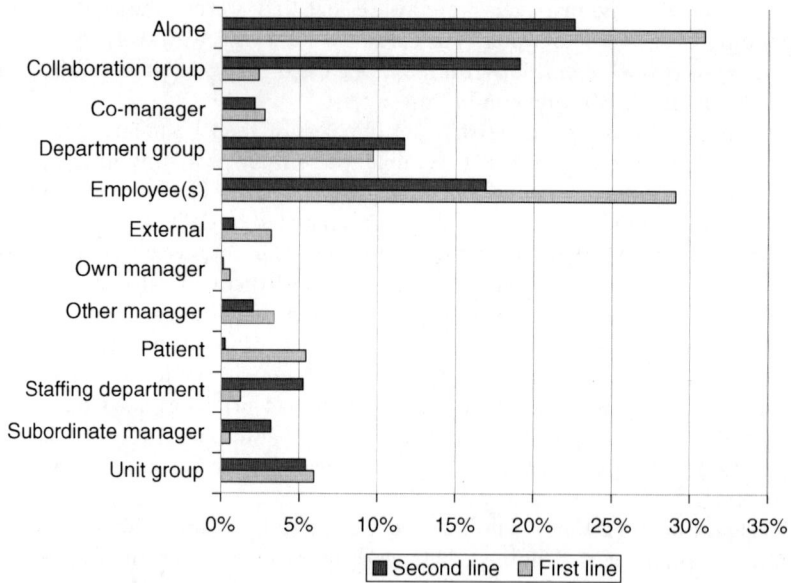

Figure 6.2 Comparison of contact patterns, first- and second-line managers (average percentage of time, the smallest categories excluded)

Managers most often met their superiors in department groups, which are management groups of several managers from different units. The staffing departments have experts who deal with various administrative tasks, for example, HR, Quality, and Finance. Some managers paired with a co-manager in their unit. Meetings with representatives from other organizations were rare (see 'External'). First-line managers had regular group meetings for all or some sections of the employees in the unit. 'Other manager' is a category for one-on-one meetings, informal meetings with other managers, and meetings with managers outside the managers' departments.

Handling uncertainties and risks

Finally, the analysis of the managers' communications showed how they used their time to deal with future risks and to maintain the appearance of having procedures that protect against such risks. They performed this legitimation work both for themselves and for the organization's various stakeholders and the general public. We noted an example of such work when the media contacted a second-line manager about the waiting times for patients in the unit. (The story in the Introduction to this chapter is an example of the importance of media reports to top management.) We also observed three managers who worked with systematic organizational analyses of extraordinary care events where there were problems. One manager supported a nurse under investigation by the NBHW following a patient complaint, and several other managers managed direct patient complaints made in the mandatory system in the organization. Such legitimation work was sometimes combined. At other times, it conflicted with the traditional ways of establishing legitimacy from caring for patients and employees or working to advance the interests of the organization (e.g. professional groups, top management, and the administrative system). In these situations, there were higher or added risks of stress because the degree of responsibility was uncertain. This uncertainty related to the managers' prolonged exposure to increased heart rates.

DISCUSSION

The findings of the study reveal the complex situation of first- and second-line managerial work in health care. Here, we discuss the rich empirical data resulting from our observation methods and interviews in relation to the research questions. The section concludes with a discussion of the theoretical and practical implications of our research.

Handling fragmentation and interruptions through negotiating boundaries

The first research question concerns how managers handle their everyday stressors and hassles, given the fragmentation of their work activities. The results from our empirical observations show that the managers handle the various degrees of daily hassles due to the heavy workloads, fragmentation, and interruptions by negotiating their boundaries as they work to increase or sustain their influence. They negotiate boundaries to demarcate their workload. At the same time they engage in multiple processes involving legitimation of themselves and their organization. One consequence of these daily hassles and the strategies chosen to handle them is the managers' lack of one-on-one communication with their own managers.

The fact of managerial work in this setting of brief activities may be a factor in the managers' experience of daily fragmentation and hassles. However, such brief activities usually take only a small part of their total work time. The time-use patterns of the managers in the study often accommodate organizational demands and institutional norms. We suggest that the individual variations are a result of both personal patterns of interpreting and negotiating the available options as well as contextual norms such as group and organization cultures. Variations also relate to the perception of time and change, which also suggests that the subcultures differ within different work groups and units (see also Perlow, 1999). The setting and type of care delivery influence how the managers preschedule their time while their positions seem to determine how much time remains for administrative and unscheduled meetings. Second-line managers and managers working in outpatient settings more often follow a cyclical time-use pattern of recurring, planned meetings. This implies a perception of an 'even' flow of time and the structuring of planned situations. In 24-hour care settings, the time-use seems more linear and action oriented, with time scheduled for solving sudden 'events' and anticipating problems in the near future (Pina e Cunha, 2004).

One of the most common causes of stress among HCMs is the strain related to the tensions resulting from the need to prioritize tasks (Eklöf et al., 2010). The managers' strategies and choice of various managerial work models for meeting complexities that stem from the coexistence of the different logics have consequences. Managers who separate the various logics often complain about fragmentation and insufficient time for strategic work because so much of their time is spent on administration and in meetings with employees. The classic managerial work research has often described this dilemma for managers in their everyday work (Carlson, 1951; Stewart, 1967, 1996; Mintzberg, 1973, 1991; Tengblad, 2002, 2003). Moreover, Wikström and Dellve (2009) have observed and described integrating work models with more concurrent solutions of tasks. In this study, a harmonious combination or hybridization of the different logics was not always negotiated. Instead, a hierarchy leading to the (temporary) dominance of one logic over other logics was created. An example was when the external legitimation work, such as handling media and external reporting, was given more importance than both employeeship and other administrative and strategic duties (see also Arman et al., forthcoming).

The boundless conditions of managerial practice demand concrete boundaries of time and space. However, the degree of individual awareness and control of time-use and boundary-setting varies. The managers in this study often had more options to control their time than they actually used. In theory, they could turn off the phone, close the office door, and prioritize and complete the day's work in order to leave on time. Yet few managers used such strategies and some were even unaware of them. The demand made by superiors, employees, and patients that the managers be constantly available was considered a general requirement of good managerial practice. The managers, rather than questioning these boundless demands, accepted them and felt ashamed when they failed to meet them. We find it relevant to question whether the possible organizational effectiveness gained was at the expense of the managers' health.

More intense communications between these managers and their superiors might lead to reduced workloads and improved prioritization of work tasks. In this study, the managers spent less than 1 per cent of their time in one-on-one meetings with their own manager. Their additional contact with their managers was largely in brief telephone calls, short e-mail exchanges, or in group meetings. The second-line managers only spent 3 per cent of their time in one-on-one meetings with their subordinate managers. In studies of industrial managers (e.g. Kurke and Aldrich, 1983; Tengblad, 2006), the time averages were between 9 and 14 per cent. Hence, supervisors gave these managers little individual direction or support in their work, in particular with the problems encountered in dealing with the conflicting logics they experienced. This communication pattern between the managers and their supervisors had consequences for the managerial communication flow and top-down implementation of ideas and conduct as well as upward implications for decisions taken (Milliken et al., 2003; Tourish and Robson, 2006; Skagert et al., 2008). The managers stated they had serious difficulties in communicating with upper management about practical problems and about their stress level. As a consequence, the managers received little support in these areas. They discussed successes rather than failures in order to present an image of control.

Other studies have also shown that there are few arenas for this kind of communication and thus few opportunities to gain support from superiors (Skagert et al., 2008; Tengelin et al., 2011).

Building legitimacy through communication

Our second research question asked how managers' patterns of communication are constituted through legitimacy practices. Our research shows that the time these managers spent with employees agrees with Holmblad Brunsson's (2007) and Czarniawska's (2008) findings that state the core of managerial work is to 'handle people' and to help employees work as professionals. Our findings show that the managers in higher positions often spend a large proportion of their time attending group meetings, leaving little time for one-on-one meetings with their subordinate managers. The consequence is a system that fosters self-governance and autonomous leadership where managers learn to interpret signals from superiors and to work in groups and teams. In previous interview studies, managers indicated that they protected both superiors and employees by filtering sensitive information upwards and downwards. Leaders may thus act as 'shock absorbers' who structure tasks and stabilize the staffing situation in order to maintain trust and legitimacy throughout the formal hierarchy (Skagert et al., 2008).

From a stress perspective, the more serious dilemmas or situations of 'ethical stress' are experienced when there is a conflict between organizational and individual norms for achieving influence and participating in decision processes regarding allocation of resources (Dellve and Wikström, 2009). Central conflicting values are described as either focusing frames and 'doing things in the right way' (*procedural norms*) or testing boundaries and 'doing the right things' (*consequential norms*) (Dellve and Wikström, 2009). The competing logics of the medical professions and administrative management that the managers take part in, described above, illustrate some of this complexity. Competing texts carry different 'interests' and charges, creating complexity in the communication (Deetz, 1995). The managers' communication patterns are one indication of such interests that were voiced.

Initially in our study we categorized clinical work as 'non-managerial', following Mintzberg's terminology and logic (1973: 249) where this label applies to 'specialized work in [the] organization'. However, this simple, dualistic view is not supported by our analysis of how clinical work in health care is used for legitimation purposes. Many HCMs in this study expressed the need to encompass the strategies and norm systems involved in focusing on professional *and* strategic work. In addition, we perceived that the work of employeeship was important in accordance with several logics. Sometimes it was experienced as an inner conflict to balance the different logics (Dellve and Wikström, 2006). In the conflict among the three different logics that govern HCMs' work, the managers described a model that focuses on working with strategy and encourages employees to take an active part (Dellve and Wikström, 2009). Based on our observations of the time the managers spent on strategic work activities (e.g. preparing or making long-term decisions), only two managers in our study clearly favoured this strategy. These two managers spent more than 10 per cent of their time with these types of activities (compared to the average in Table 6.1).

Our observations of managers complicated as well as developed our understanding of the dilemma involved in negotiating among the different logics. Our findings can be understood using concepts of the creation of legitimacy, a process called 'legitimation' (Giddens, 1984/6). In our previous interview studies, managers have been shown to vary in their choice of sources for legitimation (Dellve and Wikström, 2009). The *first* kind of legitimacy for the managers in health care relates to their possession and maintenance of professional health care skills. In the current research, we saw communication with reference to patient care and concern for employees as an activity related to Suchman's moral legitimacy (1995). Such communication rests on judgements about whether or not activities promote social welfare.

Our research shows that managers in health care require a *second* kind of legitimacy, one not solely based on professional aptitude and skill in meeting the core operative needs of the organization. This second legitimacy is administrative legitimacy, which is related to the management system in the organization. Such legitimacy, using Suchman's terminology (1995), may be described as pragmatic because it seems to rest on a self-interested social exchange. Managerial activities are judged according to how they benefit the evaluators (in this case, the organization's management system). Administrative efficiency and control, for example, staying within budget, is mainly in the immediate interests of those who govern the organization.

Our research reveals a *third* kind of legitimacy that the managers in health care use in their everyday activities. This legitimacy relates to organizational legitimacy in society at large. We suggest that this legitimation practice relates to Suchman's cognitive type (1995) because it attempts to create comprehensiveness where alternatives are perceived as unthinkable. The managers' communication in our study shows traces of a legitimation process characterized by risk management, creating the appearance of comprehensive transparency and accountability that do not permit of any alternatives (see also Arman et al., forthcoming).

Communication for legitimation purposes in this context is a recurring negotiation between the three different types of legitimacy. This had consequences for the boundary-setting in the managers' work. The differences between the kinds of legitimacy are sometimes contradictory, with the result that communication work becomes a balancing act. The managers say that the time spent communicating is vague and difficult to justify (Dellve and Wikström, 2006).

Implications of the study

Our third research question concerns the consequences of the HCMs' methods of dealing with fragmentation and establishing their legitimacy practices. Our findings show there are two main challenges in managerial work in health care related to stress and 'sustainability': handling fragmentation and interruptions by negotiating boundaries and several types of legitimation activities. These findings have implications for both theory and practice.

A *theoretical implication* consists of the combinations of concepts describing what Giddens (1984/6) calls types of legitimation. We combine Giddens's (1984/6) and Suchman's (1995) concepts to show the connection between the types of legitimation practices in managerial work activities. In managerial communication, we found new relationships between the concepts through connecting daily activities to macro-structures and cultures affecting the organizational system. We observed the use of competing and integrating moral, pragmatic, and cognitive texts in the legitimation processes. Managerial activities and communication have meanings that are interpreted and constantly negotiated in the social world of human interaction, in organizational life, as well as in society at large. In this sense, observed activities can be 'read' as a 'text' in the same way that interviews and spoken accounts are. These texts can be contradictory, dominant, and varied (Deetz, 1995; Czarniawska, 2004).

The study of legitimation practices also shows the *empirical contributions* of the processes of power and control (domination) exercised and which issues are signified and seen as part of the agenda (Giddens, 1984/6). The third type of legitimacy practice traced in this study, reputation and risk management, could be interpreted as counterproductive. It involves maintaining oneself in organizational everyday life and has little to do with development or even the operative core work. From this perspective, such legitimacy practice is passive and reactive work. However, an alternative interpretation may be that the work is a stabilizing and continuity-creating activity that the managers specialize in. Our study thus supports Power's ideal (2007) of managerial work as creating 'blame free zones' for the other employees. Loose coupling protects the work in the organization if the managers take responsibility for dealing with the uncertainty (Power, 2007; Czarniawska, 2008).

To decrease stress and to support a balanced working situation for the individual manager, we suggest more effort should be placed on organizational support structures. Such effort involves a focus on increasing communication, on improving individual insight and coping strategies, as well as on clarifying decision processes, assignments, responsibilities, and goals. Holmblad Brunsson (2007) thinks that the ideals, models, and norms that are taught run the risk of laying unfair responsibility on the individual managers. Hales (1999) suggests that management should be seen as a team, whereas Hannaway (1989) thinks management can be described as an administrative system. Supporting communication activities to increase sustainable boundary-setting can be done through regular manager-to-manager meetings in which everyday challenges are discussed and prioritized. Also, when there is a lack of guiding principles, a forum for collegial reflection and discussion can be supportive for collective boundary-setting (Tengelin et al., 2011).

Our research programme included feedback to managers in groups, pointing to the *practical implications* of the complexities of their work. We found that the mirroring of activities and stress was evaluated positively and supported the learning and handling of dilemmas. We found the observation method is useful and believe it can be further developed to suit such supportive interventions. Mirroring activities and group sessions may increase our insights into the variation in management practices. Also, professional supervision may be used to support individuals' insights and their control and handling of the complex and fragmented work situation as well of work-life balance.

CONCLUSIONS AND CONCLUDING REMARKS

How is it possible to make sense of this contradictory and complex world of health care management? Our research leads us to propose the usefulness of a theoretical perspective on managerial work that includes an understanding of different types of legitimacy and boundary-setting. Moral, pragmatic, and cognitive forms of legitimation coexist in such organizations when their managers (and others) negotiate the combination of health care work with administrative or managerial logics that also involve reputation and risks.

What are the implied consequences of the health care managerial work in this study? The coexistence of different structures is not without friction. Our analysis leads us to conclude that in such work there is a constant negotiation of boundaries: personal, relating to other employees; and professional, relating to goals from politicians and top management. It is difficult to offer normative interpretations of whether the patterns described are 'good' or 'need to be changed'. Management theorists sometimes have difficulty accepting the messy practice of managerial work. Most management is concerned with how to handle and relate to people – tasks that a model, checklist, or norm cannot teach. The manager criteria document is an example (see 'The setting of the study' section). Such models and discourse reduce the complexity experienced by the participants in a simplified attempt to make practice and theory 'manageable'. With the theoretical perspectives that we use in the study, complexity and constant negotiation are highlighted instead.

Our study thus adds to a conceptual understanding of the daily complexities of health care management and points to important consequences. In this respect, our study contributes new evidence for the conclusions in earlier interview-based studies that have described managers' understanding of their work as a compound of different identities, a choice of strategies for dealing with varying logics, or a communication between different perspectives using 'two-way windows'. This study shows that the consequence of handling different logics was often the prioritization of one logic over others, during different daily activities and in different situations. Our study builds on this tradition and shows how the managers relate to the possibilities and limitations offered by the legitimation, signification, and domination structures that they are part of.

Our study emphasizes that managerial work consists of, and is a consequence of, interactions in social systems. The managers participate in the many social relationships of their work using fluid, individual agency. This agency was part of a power-laden reproduction of structures such as financial and reputation management, hierarchy, professional groups, work-group interdependencies, and work/private life time allocation. We have described the negotiations as constant, on-going work, inherent and always present in the unavoidable structuration process that is never permanently resolved. This study also contributes to the literature on stress that regards boundary negotiations as an important means of ensuring time for recovery. These time and space negotiations are part of, and subject to, the social interactions of structuration in the daily life of the manager.

From a stress management and health maintenance perspective, it is important to acknowledge the fragmented working situation of managers instead of blaming them for it as simplified or idealistic models often do. It is likely that both contextual situations, individual perceptions of time, and approaches to changes affect how sustainable handling and coping styles form. By acknowledging and identifying central conflicts in managers' work, the challenges can be communicated and handled more constructively. Our study points to the need to argue *for* the legitimacy of time-use that is necessary for these complex tasks.

APPENDIX: METHODOLOGY

Collecting and analysing the data

We used non-participant, semi-structured observations (see Mintzberg, 1973) as the primary source of data for this study. Although we use quantified data to present some results, the study is qualitative in nature. In arguing for the validity of observational methods, Czarniawska (2007) refers to Niklas Luhmann's theory that the world seen as an actor is different from a world seen as an observer. Observers can see alternatives that actors can only see in the moment of reflection, that is, when they are *not* acting. Czarniawska (2007: 9) writes: 'It is in the field that the actual production of the accounts can be studied'. In addition, in support of the observation method, we note that accounts (produced and used) in the field are more plentiful than in interview situations. The argument in favour of the semi-structured observation is that it is sufficiently reliable for the empirical focus of this research (managerial work) and the qualitative nature of the research. Such observation avoids mainstream management literature conceptualizations, and inductively studies what managers do (Noordegraaf and Stewart, 2000: 432). According to Mintzberg (1973: 230): 'The focus [of such observations] is on the job rather than the man'.

We obtained permission to shadow the managers during their work and to make notes on what we saw and heard. We observed 2,473 activities during nearly 360 hours of observations. We used Mintzberg's work categories (1973) to divide the managers' work into discrete measures of time and then to describe how this time was used. The term 'activity' used here is consistent with his study. The categories used in the field were mostly self-explanatory and straightforward. These categories have been used in several earlier studies (e.g. Florén, 2005; Tengblad, 2006). We tested the categories in a pilot study in order to confirm their usefulness in the health care setting. After the testing, we made minor additions and adjustments to include time on breaks and time talking to the researchers. The data from the structured observations were analysed using descriptive statistics for the frequency (number of activities) and the duration (time-use). Following the observations, we qualitatively coded the data so that we could interpret a primary *purpose* of the managers' verbal communications. We acknowledge this qualitative coding of purpose is an estimate. Intentions are socially constructed and hence must be interpreted (Tengblad, 2006).

We also collected anecdotal, unstructured, and interpretative data. In addition, we briefly interviewed the participating managers at the end of their workday. We conducted two in-depth interviews – one at the end of the observation period and a follow-up approximately ten days later. The second in-depth interview was partially 'ethnographic' since we asked the managers to use their calendars to recount the week after our observations (Czarniawska, 2007). We analysed this data using qualitative content analysis focusing on communication practices (Arman et al., forthcoming).

We used a combination of observation and questionnaire techniques to measure stress. We measured observed stress by recording continuous heart rates for one or two days. We defined stress as a pulse rate exceeding 10–20 per cent of each manager's mean pulse rate measured over a period of three minutes. We assessed self-rated stress and energy four times/day for four days using the stress–energy scale (Wadman and Kjellberg, 2007). In the questionnaire, which listed seventeen adjectives descriptive of stress and energy, the managers selected the adjectives that described their stress/ energy level. We then analysed the 'stressful' time periods in terms of their activities, strategies, and contextual conditions.

We purposely selected the ten managers for the research. In order to obtain a broad range in our sample, in our selection process we aimed for a variety in positions, in professions, in health care manager experience, and in health care settings. We observed each manager during a four-day work period. Seven participants were first-line managers and three were second-line managers. The number of employees reporting directly to each manager varied from ten to forty-three persons. Eight managers were women and two were men. Their ages varied between 44 and 62 years, with an average age of 52. Six managers were nurses or nurse specialists, two were social workers, one was a MD specialist, and one was a psychologist. Four managers worked in outpatient settings, four managed hospital wards, and two managed both 24-hour wards and outpatient units. Most were experienced managers, with an average of nearly ten years in their position (Arman et al., 2009).

We received ethical approval for our research from the local ethics committee. We asked the managers to inform their co-workers, including people they manage, of the study and to obtain permission from them to take part. As researchers, we acknowledged that we could be asked to leave at any time. Therefore, there were some activities that we did not observe that represented a total of approximately eleven hours (approximately 3 per cent of observed hours). For ethical reasons, we usually did not observe the managers in direct patient contact. Moreover, this part of their job was outside the scope of our research.

PREVIOUSLY PUBLISHED RESEARCH

Arman, R., Dellve, L., Wikström, E., and Törnström, L. (2009). What health care managers do: Applying Mintzberg's structured observation method. *Journal of Nursing Management*, 17(6): 718–29.

Dellve, L. and Wikström, E. (2009). Managing complex workplace stress in health care organizations: Leaders' perceived legitimacy conflicts. *Journal of Nursing Management*, 17(8): 93–941.

Tengelin, E., Wikström, E., Arman, R., and Dellve, L. (2011). Regulating time commitments in healthcare organizations – Managers' boundary approaches at work and in life. *Journal of Health Organization and Management*, 25(5): 578–99.

Wikström, W. and Dellve, L. (2009). Contemporary leadership in health care organizations: Fragmented or concurrent leadership. *Journal of Health Organization & Management*, 23(4): 411–28.

NOTE

1. This variation was due, in part, to the fact that some HCMs worked longer hours in order to have a day off every other week.

REFERENCES

Allvin, M., Aronsson, G., Hagström, T., Johansson, G., and Lundberg, U. (2006). *Gränslöst arbete: Socialpsykologiska perspektiv på det nya arbetslivet* [Boundless work: social psychological perspectives on the new worklife]. Malmö: Liber.

Arman, R., Dellve, L., Wikström, E., and Törnström, L. (2009). What health care managers do: Applying Mintzberg's structured observation method. *Journal of Nursing Management*, 17(6): 718–29.

——Wikström, E., Liff, R., and Dellve, L. (forthcoming) Hierarchization of rivaling logics in the case of psychiatric care [submitted for publication].

Braithwaite, J. (2004). An empirically-based model for clinician-managers' behavioural routines. *Journal of Health Organization and Management*, 18(4): 240–61.

Bryson, L., Warner-Smith, P., Brown, P., and Fray, L (2007). Managing the work-life roller-coaster: Private stress or public health issue? *Social Science & Medicine*, 65: 1142–53.

Carlson, S. (1951/91). *Executive Behaviour*. Stockholm: Almqvist & Wiksell International.

Czarniawska, B. (2004). *Narratives in Social Science Research*. London: Sage.

——(2007). *Shadowing*. Copenhagen: Copenhagen Business School Press.

——(2008). *A Theory of Organizing*. Cheltenham: Edward Elgar Publishing Ltd.

Deetz, S. (1992). *Democracy in an Age of Corporate Colonization*. Albany: State University of New York Press.

——(1995). *Transforming Communication, Transforming Business: Building Responsive and Responsible Workplaces*. Cresskill, NJ: Hampton Press, Inc.

Degeling, P. and Carr, A. (2004). Leadership for the systematization of health care: The unaddressed issue in health care reform. *Journal of Health Organization and Management*, 18(6): 399–414.

Dellve, L. and Wikström, E. (2006). Hållbart ledarskap i sjukvården [Sustainable leadership in health care]. [Report] Göteborg: Västra Götalandsregionen, Sahlgrenska Akademin och Handelshögskolan vid Göteborgs Universitet.

—— ——(2009). Managing complex workplace stress in health care organisations: Leaders' perceived legitimacy conflicts. *Journal of Nursing Management*, 17(8): 931–41.

——Skagert, K., and Vilhelmsson, R. (2007). Leadership in workplace health promotion projects: 1- and 2-year effects on long-term work attendance. *European Journal of Public Health*, 17(5): 471–6.

Doolin, B. (2002). Enterprise discourse, professional identity and the organizational control of hospital clinicians. *Organization Studies*, 23(3): 369–90.

Edwards, J. R. and Rothbard, N. P. (1999). Work and family stress and well-being: An examination of person-environment fit in the work and family domains. *Organizational Behavior and Human Decision Processes*, 77(2): 85–129.

Eklöf, M., Pousette, A., Dellve, L., Skagert, K., and Ahlborg, Jr., G. (2010). Utveckling av ett variations- och förändringskänsligt frågeinstrument för mätning av stressorexponering, copingbeteende och copingresurser bland 1:a och 2:a linjens chefer inom offentlig vård och omsorg [Development of a questionnaire instrument, sensitive for variations and changes, to assess stressor exposures, coping strategies and coping resources among 1st and 2nd line managers in public health care organizations]. Gothenburg: Institute of Stress Medicine.

Evans, J. A., Kunda, G., and Barley, S. R. (2004). Beach time, bridge time, and billable hours: The temporal structure of technical contracting. *Administrative Science Quarterly*, 49: 1–38.

Ferlie, E., Ashburner, L., Fitzgerald, L., and Pettigrew, A. (1996). *The New Public Management in Action*. Oxford: Oxford University Press.

Florén, H. (2005). *Managerial Work and Learning in Small Firms*. Göteborg: Chalmers University of Technology.

Frankenhaeuser, M., Lundberg, U., Fredrickson, M., Melin, B., Tuomisto, T., Myrsten, A.-L., Hedman, M., Bergman-Losman, B., and Wallin, L. (1989). Stress on and off the job as related to sex and occupational status in white-collar workers. *Journal of Organizational Behaviour*, 10(4): 321–46.

Freidson, E. (1994). *Professionalism Reborn: Theory, Prophecy, and Policy*. Chicago: University of Chicago Press.

Giddens, A. (1984/6). *The Constitution of Society*. Berkeley, CA: University of California Press.

Hales, C. (1999). Why do managers do what they do? Reconciling evidence and theory in accounts of managerial work. *British Journal of Management*, 10(4): 335–50.

Hannaway, J. (1989). *Managers Managing. The Workings of an Administrative System*. New York: Oxford University Press.

Hernes, T. (2004). *The Spatial Construction of Organization*. Amsterdam: John Benjamins Publishing Company.

Hochschild, A. R. (1997). *The Time Bind: When Work Becomes Home and Home Becomes Work*. New York: Henry Holt & Company.

Holmblad Brunsson, K. (2007). *The Notion of General Management*. Portland, OR: International Specialized Book Services.

Hultberg, A., Hadžibajramovic, E., Pettersson, S., and Ahlborg, Jr., G. (2009). Stressrelaterad ohälsa bland anställda vid Västra Götalandsregionen och Försäkringskassan i Västra Götaland. Delrapport 3 [Stress-related ill-health among employees in Region Västra Götaland and Försäkringskassan in Västra Götaland Report 3: Four year follow-up May–June 2008]: Fyraårsuppföljning maj–juni 2008. *Institutet för Stressmedicin; ISM-rapport 5*.

Karasek, R. and Theorell, T. (1990). *Healthy Work: Stress, Productivity, and the Reconstruction of Working Life*. New York: Basic Books.

Kerosou, H. (2006). *Boundaries in Action. An Activity-Theoretical Study of Development, Learning and Change in Health Care for Patients with Multiple and Chronic Illnesses*. Helsinki: Department of Education, University of Helsinki.

Kitchener, M. (2002). Mobilizing the logic of managerialism in professional fields: The case of academic health centre mergers. *Organization Studies*, 23(3): 391–420.

Kotter, J. P. (1982). *The General Managers*. New York: The Free Press.

Kouzes, J. M. and Mico, P. R. (1979). Domain theory: An introduction to organizational behavior in human service organizations. *The Journal of Applied Behavioral Science*, 15(4): 449–69.

Kreiner, G. E. (2006). Consequences of work-home segmentation or integration: A person-environment fit perspective. *Journal of Organizational Behaviour*, 27: 485–507.

——Hollensbe, E., and Sheep, M. (2009). Balancing borders and bridges: Negotiating the work–home interface via boundary work tactics. *Academy of Management Journal*, 52(4): 704–30.

Kunda, G. (1992/2006). *Engineering Culture: Control and Commitment in a High-Tech Corporation*. Philadelphia, PA: Temple University Press.

Kurke, L. B. and Aldrich, H. E. (1983). Mintzberg was right! A replication and extension of the nature of managerial work. *Management Science*, 29(8): 975–83.

Larson, M. S. (1977). *The Rise of Professionalism - A Sociological Analysis*. Berkeley, CA: University of California Press.

Llewellyn, S. (2001). Two-way windows: Clinicians as medical managers. *Organization Studies*, 24: 593–623.

MacEachen, E., Polzer, J., and Clarke, J. (2008). 'You are free to set your own hours': Governing worker productivity and health through flexibility and resilience. *Social Science & Medicine*, 66(5): 1019–33.

Marquis, B. L. and Houston, C. J. (2006). *Leadership Roles and Management Functions in Mursing: Theory and Application*. Philadelphia: Wolters Kluwer Health/Lippincott Williams and Wilkins.

Maslach, C., Schaufeli, W., and Leiter, M. (2001). Job burnout. *Annual Review of Psychology*, 52: 397–422.

McEwen, B. (1998). Stress, adaptation, and disease. Allostatis and allostatic Load. *Annals of the New York Academy of Sciences*, 1: 33–44.

——(2005). Stressed or stressed out: What is the difference? *Journal of Psychiatry Neuroscience*, 30(5): 315–18.

Milliken, F., Morrison, E. W., and Hewlin, P. F. (2003). An exploratory study of employee silence: Issues that employees don't communicate upward and why. *Journal of Management Studies*, 40(6): 1453–76.

Mintzberg, H. (1973). *The Nature of Managerial Work*. New York: Harper & Row.

——(1991). Managerial work: Forty years later. In Sune Carlson (Ed.), *Executive Behavior*. Uppsala: Uppsala University.

——(2002). Managing care and cure - Up and down, in and out. *Health Services Management Research*, 15: 193–206.

Noordegraaf, M. and Stewart, R. (2000). Managerial behaviour research in private and public sectors: Distinctiveness, disputes and directions. *Journal of Management Studies*, 31(3): 427–43.

Nyberg, A., Alfredsson, L., Theorell, T., Westerlund, H., Vahtera, J., and Kivimäki, M. (2009). Managerial leadership and ischaemic heart disease among employees: The Swedish WOLF study. *Occup Environ Med*, 66: 51–5.

Öfverström, H. (2008). *Steget till chefskap. Om läkare som verksamhetschefer* [Path to leadership: Physicians as managers]. Gothenburg: BAS Publisher.

Östergren, K. and Sahlin-Andersson, K. (1998). *Att hantera skilda världar - Läkares chefskap i mötet mellan profession, politik och administration* [Dealing with different worlds: Professional, policy, and administrative leadership for physicians]. Stockholm: Landstingsförbundet.

Perlow, L. A. (1999). The time famine: Toward a sociology of work time. *Administrative Science Quarterly*, 44: 57–81.

Pina e Cunha, M. (2004). Organizational time: A dialectical view. *Organization*, 11(2): 271–96.

Pousette, A. (2001). *Feedback and Stress in Human Service Organizations*. Göteborg: University of Gothenburg, Department of Psychology.

Power, M. (2007). *Organized Uncertainty. Designing a World of Risk Management*. Oxford: Oxford University Press.

Reed, M. (1996). Expert power and control in the late modernity: An empirical review and theoretical synthesis. *Organization Studies*, 17(4): 573–97.

Siegrist, J. and Theorell, T. (2006). Socio-economic position and health. The role of work and employment. In J. Siegrist and M. Marmot (Eds.), *Social Inequalities in Health. New Evidence and Practical Implications* (pp. 73–100). New York: Oxford University Press.

Skagert, K., Dellve, L., Eklöf, M., Pousette, A., and Ahlborg, Jr., G. (2008). Leader's strategies for dealing with own and their subordinates stress in public human service organisations. *Applied Ergonomics*, 39(6): 803–11.

Stewart, R. (1967). *Managers and their Jobs*. Houndmills, UK: MacMillan.

——(1996). Managerial behaviour. In M. Warner (Ed.), *The International Encyclopedia of Business and Management* (pp. 3100–16). London: Routledge.

Suchman, M. C. (1995). Managing legitimacy: Strategic and institutional approaches. *Academy of Management Review*, 20(3): 571–610.

Tengblad, S. (2002). Time and space in managerial work. *Scandinavian Journal of Management*, 18: 543–65.

——(2003). Classic, but not seminal: Revisiting the pioneering study of managerial work. *Scandinavian Journal of Management*, 19: 85–101.

——(2006). Is there a 'New Managerial Work'? A comparison with Henry Mintzberg's classic study 30 years later. *Journal of Management Studies*, 13(7): 1437–61.

Tengelin, E., Kihlman, A., Eklöf, M., and Dellve, L. (2011). Chefskap sjukvårdsmiljö: Avgränsning och kommunikation av egen stress [Health care managerial work: Limiting and communicating one's own stress]. *Arbete och Hälsa*, 45(1).

——Wikström, E., Arman, R., and Dellve, L. (2011). Regulating time commitments in healthcare organizations – Managers' boundary approaches at work and in life. *Journal of Health Organization and Management*, 25(5): 578–99.

Theorell, T., Emdad, R., Arnetz, B., and Weingarten, A. M. (2001). Employee effects of an educational program for managers at an insurance company. *Psychosomatic Medicine*, 63: 724–33.

Tourish, D. and Robson, D. (2006). Sensemaking and the distortion of critical upward communication in organizations. *Journal of Management Studies*, 43(4): 711–30.

van Dierendonck, D., Haynes, C., Borrill, C., and Stride, C. (2004). Leadership behavior and subordinate well-being. *Journal of Occupational Health Psychology*, 9(2): 165–75.

VGREG (2009). *Leadership Criteria*. Webpage: http://epi.vgregion.se/upload/Handikappf%c3%b6rvaltningen/Habilitering/GoteborgOchsodraBohuslan/Dokumentbibliotek/Administrativ%20service/Personal/Personalf%c3%b6rs%c3%b6rjning/Ledarskap/050415%20VG%20reg%20grundl%20ledarskapskriterier%20.pdf?epslanguage=sv [Accessed 2009-06-16].

Wadman, C. and Kjellberg, A. (2007). The role of the affective stress response as a mediator of the effect of psychosocial risk factors on musculoskeletal complaints – Part 2: Hospital workers. *International Journal of Industrial Ergonomics*, 37(5): 395–403.

Wikström, E. (2008). Boundary work as inner and outer dialogue: Dieticians in Sweden. *Qualitative Research in Organizations and Management*, 3(1): 59–77.

——Dellve, L. (2009). Contemporary leadership in health care organizations: Fragmented or concurrent leadership. *Journal of Health Organization & Management*, 23(4): 411–28.

7

Leadership as muddling through: Site managers in the construction industry

Alexander Styhre

INTRODUCTION

This chapter reports on empirical data from studies of site managers – project leaders in construction projects – in order to show how the technical, economic, and administrative organization of the construction site has immediate implications for the organization and practice of leadership in the construction industry. Using the term 'muddling through', derived from policy research in political science, the evidence reveals that site managers engage in a particular form of leadership that requires detailed plans for scheduled activities as well as ad hoc solutions to unanticipated problems. It is suggested that in milieus characterized by tight couplings between processes and technologies, and loose couplings between organizational elements, leadership is best described in terms of 'muddling through'. A pattern similar to that of construction industry site management may also be observed in other industries that use complex project organization as the principal organization form.

The construction industry accounts for a substantial percentage of GDP in most OECD countries, about 10 per cent according to one estimate (Hillebrandt, 2000: 19). In the United Kingdom, the construction industry is the country's largest sector, measured both by its proportion of GDP and by the number of people it employs (Agapiou, 2002: 697). In Sweden, the industry is second in terms of turnover and number of employees, smaller only than the public health care sector. Because of its labour-intensiveness, politicians use the construction industry to manage the ebb and flow of the economy; as a result, the industry is often subject to political influence.

Despite its economic influence and central role in contemporary society, organization and leadership researchers have shown only marginal interest in studying the construction industry. The industry is often dismissed, as in Hawk's description (2006: 735), as 'dangerous, dirty and demeaning, and too low tech to be at the leading edge of anything'. Both insiders and outsiders often portray the construction industry as conservative, particularly in its reluctance to change. Fifty years ago Stinchcombe (1959) emphasized that construction work has retained a craft-like production form – a position thoroughly criticized by Eccles

(1981) – as opposed to the manufacturing industry that essentially restructured during the 'rationalization movement' orchestrated by an emerging group of professional engineers (Guillén, 1994; Shenhav, 1995). Eccles (1981: 451) points to four characteristics of the construction industry: (*a*) the 'small degree of diversification' (i.e. the delivery of approximately the same products and services); (*b*) the 'geographically limited markets', often present in just one country or region; (*c*) the relatively low entry barriers; and (*d*) the 'lack of concentration' in the industry (i.e. the many actors in the industry). Both internal and external industry critics emphasize that the construction industry is poorly equipped to produce innovations. When innovations are produced, there are setbacks and failed projects, both of which dampen the innovative spirit. In addition, in most countries, the industry is very fragmented. A few large companies, a number of medium-sized firms, and a rich variety of small companies (often single-employee companies) dominate the industry. This fragmentation further impedes innovation in the industry although it also produces a number of leadership practices interesting to researchers.

This chapter reports on the work of construction site managers who are the project leaders with full responsibility in construction projects. Their work requires that they have technical expertise, engineering know-how, knowledge of administrative routine, and leadership skills. They must also understand human resource management activities and juridical matters. In addition, site managers typically feel responsible for essentially all project events and activities. As a consequence, site manager work is sometimes considered one of the most demanding positions in the construction industry (Lingard and Francis, 2004, 2006; Styhre and Josephson, 2006). On the one hand, site managers have full economic and financial responsibility and, on the other hand, they are involved in all the everyday, nitty-gritty practices. Thus, the work exposes site managers to substantial amounts of stress, conflicts of interests, and the necessity of making trade-offs. According to Djerbarni (1996: 281):

> Site managers carry out one of the toughest and hardest jobs in the construction process. Site management is characterized by a high work overload, long working hours, and many conflicting parties to deal with including the management, the subcontractors, the subordinates, the client, etc. This trait of the job makes it very prone to stress.

Lingard and Francis (2004, 2006) show that individuals working on site in the construction industry are exposed to more stress, work longer hours, and are generally more cynical about pay and their work than other construction workers. They also '[s]uffer higher levels of work interference with family life' (Lingard and Francis, 2004: 998). For instance, one female engineer said: 'I find it hard to see myself staying in this field if I intend to start a family. Not only do I feel drained each day, it affects my relationship dramatically' (cited in Lingard and Francis, 2004: 998).

Site managers, like most members of other occupational and professional communities, work according to a set of individually entrenched beliefs and values that they have acquired during their years of work experience. There is a great diversity of leadership styles and work practices among them, but they share the common goal that the production phase will continue, no matter the circumstances. Their principal responsibilities are therefore handling the practical problems that threaten the pace and harmony of work and dealing with administrative and personnel problems as time permits. Often they deal with the latter problems in the early morning or in the late afternoon, before and after construction work (Styhre, 2006).

The purpose of this chapter is to show how historical conditions and the more recent lean production and 'decentralization' changes in the construction industry influence site manager work qua leadership work. I use Charles Lindblom's concept (1959) of 'muddling through', a term first used in policy research in the discipline of political science, to demonstrate that the site manager's work is largely 'skillful problem-solving' (i.e. 'muddling through') in the everyday work at construction sites.

This chapter is structured accordingly: First, a number of operational concepts are presented in some detail; thereafter, various methodological issues related to the study are addressed; third, the empirical data are reported; and lastly, there is a discussion of some implications of the study.

LOOSELY-COUPLED SYSTEMS, MUDDLING THROUGH, AND THE LEADERSHIP WORK OF SITE MANAGERS

Taking an organization theory perspective, the construction industry is composed of what Weick (1976) called *loosely-coupled systems* – organizational entities that are largely separate from one another but that still need to be aligned and coordinated. 'Loose coupling occurs', Weick (1979: 111) explains, 'when two separate systems have few variables in common or when the common variables are weak compared to the other variables that influence the system. Two systems that are joined by few common variables or weak common variables are said to be loosely coupled'. One domain where loosely-coupled systems are predominant is the school system:

> Loose coupling is evident in schools. Only a limited amount of inspection and evaluation occurs in schools. A principal who visits the classroom too frequently is accused of 'harassment'. Professionals are reluctant to give one another unsolicited feedback. As a result, poor performance persists in the name of professional autonomy. The goals of education are also indeterminate, which makes them difficult to use as hard standards to evaluate individual performance. Administrators and instructors work on variable raw materials with little control over supply; they have no firm standards by which to judge the impact of their work and no clear theory of causation that specifies the effects of the things they do. Schools have large spans of control. There are few employees and many students. Teachers find it hard to keep track of the students, let alone one another. Because the technology of education is not clear, educators make extensive use of specialists; every time a specialist is inserted between the teacher and a student, the control over the student is loosened. (Weick, 2001: 42)

Dubois and Gadde (2002) suggest that the construction industry is essentially such a loosely-coupled system. For instance, the construction process involves a variety of actors – architects, designers, construction workers, electricians, suppliers, and so forth – who enter and leave the site at different periods. In loosely-coupled systems, where problems may arise because of their lack of formal authority over these different actors, leaders with political skills and persuasive rhetorical powers are needed to coordinate the actors in their separate tasks. However, in the work procedures at the construction site, there is a *tight coupling* between the activities; in the close sequence of individual activities, following one after another, there is little room for deviation from plan.

Such tight couplings between activities are found in a number of settings: health care emergency wards (Timmermans and Berg, 1997), operating rooms (Edmonson, 2003), nuclear plants (Perrow, 1984), research laboratories (Rheinberger, 1997), manufacturing operations (Delbridge, 1998), and, of course, the construction industry. With its time constraints and lean production principles, the construction industry allows less and less time between activities in the production process. As a result of the combination of (*a*) the loose, informal couplings between actors and (*b*) the tight couplings between activities, the site manager works under considerable pressure.

To cope with this responsibility and this pressure, site managers appear to adopt Lindblom's work management practice (1959) of 'muddling through' by which, in addition to managing planned activities, they haphazardly cope with unpredictable events on an ad hoc basis. Lindblom (1959: 86) advocates what is called an *incrementalist* view of policymaking in which 'policy is not made once and for all; it is made and re-made endlessly'. Therefore, a policy should preferably evolve as '[a] process of successive approximation to some desired objective in which what is desired itself continues to change under reconsideration'. Lindblom continues:

> A wise policy-maker consequently expects that his policies will achieve only part of what he hopes and at the same time will produce unanticipated consequences he would have preferred to avoid. If he proceeds through a *succession* of incremental changes, he avoids serious lasting mistakes in several ways. (Lindblom, 1959: 86)

Policymaking requires striking a balance between various interests and planning horizons in ambiguous and uncertain conditions where policies evolve in successive steps that form a pattern over time. Policy decisions in the construction industry evolve under these ambiguities and uncertainties that Lindblom (1959) describes, with one major difference. Lindblom emphasizes negotiations and joint agreements in the policymaking processes so that the 'muddling through' is accomplished by mutual adjustments. In site managers' work, 'muddling through' describes work as a series of events, some of which are unforeseeable but nevertheless require immediate attention and quick decisions. Policymakers in Lindblom's account may discuss alternatives and choices, but site managers basically 'muddle through' by trusting to their intuitive knowledge acquired by experience.

Leadership as 'muddling through' is therefore a form of tinkering (Knorr Cetina, 1981; Clarke and Fujimura, 1992) in which a bricolage of available measures is used to solve practical problems. As Clark and Fujimura (1992: 11) write: 'Tinkering involves a kind of "indexical" (local or situational) logic and opportunism – using what is at hand, making-do, using things for new purposes, patching things together, and so on'. Technically speaking, site managers are middle managers, a management group positioned rather bleakly between top management's expectations and subordinates' need for daily supervision (Dopson and Stewart, 1990) and subject to the pressures of outsourcing, off-shoring, downsizing, and other cost-cutting programmes (Floyd and Woolridge, 1997). Floyd and Woolridge write of middle managers:

> Are middle managers becoming the dinosaurs of the business world? They once dominated the corporate landscape with salaries and perks that were the envy (and career goal) of every MBA. Now, like prehistoric reptiles, these behemoths of bureaucracy appear likely to succumb to a hostile environment. (Floyd and Woolridge, 1997: 47)

There are, however, a few studies that take a more positive view of middle managers and their long-term survival prospects (e.g. King et al., 2001; Huy, 2002; Delmestri and Walgenbach, 2005). In these studies, middle managers continue to play a central role as the bridge between the top management tiers and the operational levels of the organization. That appears to be the role of the site manager who, at the very centre of value-adding activities, is one of the most valuable resources in the construction industry. The site manager's daily fragmented work activity revolves around formal planning and skilful problem-solving en route (Fraser, 2000; Davidson and Sutherland, 2002). Theoretically, as well as practically, this is the general conception of site management in large construction projects. However, site managers themselves tend to be rather sceptical of an increased formalization of their role; they think of the construction industry as an idiosyncratic blend of formal planning and impromptu problem-solving. The value of experienced site managers is their ability to maintain a formal structure at the site and, at the same time, to handle emerging concerns.

In summary, site managers are in charge of all construction site operations. Constructions sites are a specific domain of an organization consisting of loosely-coupled management systems and tightly-coupled site activities. In order to balance this idiosyncratic tight/loose coupling structure, the site manager is responsible for both the process and the result. Taking an analogy from the shipping industry, the site manager is like a ship's captain who has responsibility for the whole command but not for the details of the crew's work. Unlike ship captains, however, who plan for exceptional events, site managers prefer to solve problems as they arise and take a somewhat sceptical attitude towards anticipating trouble. As a consequence, site manager work is characterized by a large degree of unpredictability and improvisation. Such an approach to site management work may serve its purpose in the industry on an aggregate level, but the human cost can be substantial. Excessive overtime, mental stress, physical health problems, and work–family imbalance are likely outcomes from this conventional view of site manager work.

The practice of muddling through: site managers at work

In most construction companies, the organization structure separates what Mintzberg (1983) calls the *strategic apex* – the top management and division management responsible for strategic decisions and client contacts – from the front-line work at the construction sites. The front-line work, as the site of the production work, is where the site manager commonly works with both the company's employees and with the sub-contractors, many of whom work on short-term contracts (contracts of a few hours, a few weeks, or the whole project). These people include carpenters, installation consultants, and sometimes designers and architects. One or more foremen supervise the construction workers and are their contacts to the site managers. However, in Sweden, where there is a rather small power distance between management and labour, construction workers may also speak directly to the site managers. The site managers also chair meetings with the foremen, with other construction site actors (where the discussion is about the progress of the work and upcoming events), and with external stakeholders such as clients and end-users. The site manager is thus the de facto project leader and the construction company's representative vis-à-vis the client.

The characteristics of site management work are (*a*) a high degree of unpredictability, (*b*) a strong focus on traditional project management dimensions such as time, quality, and cost, and (*c*) a complex process of integrating various kinds of activities. Site managers take pride in this work that is a creative process of turning formal documents (blueprints, contracts, etc.) into a structure that may be used for a hundred years, or even longer. Construction work is a creative collaboration of utility and aesthetics. One site manager said: 'What's most positive is that from this very blueprint and a time line, you see something grow out there, a physical effect. I consider that very rewarding'. Thus, in transforming materials and labour into structures, site managers think of themselves (and are so thought of by stakeholders and other occupational groups) as at the very centre of the activity – in short, they are in charge. One site manager expressed this idea: 'As site manager, I need to know what is going on at the site...I coordinate everything, and thus I need to know what everybody is doing'. Another site manager agreed: 'The site manager is the hub around which everything revolves'.

As the central figure at the construction site, the site managers have a great many activities and processes to manage. They work long hours and are reluctant to leave the site for any extended period of time, for example, to go to leadership training courses. As a result, the site manager is more or less tied to the construction site, certainly during the critical periods of the work. Although the site manager works closely with, and depends on, the foremen who are the 'middle managers' at the construction site, it is the site manager's responsibility to create a good work climate, as various site managers emphasized. In the following exchange, an interviewee described the leadership aspect of the site manager position:

Q: How do you create confidence in the workplace?
A: I think you need to demonstrate to the lads that they are needed.
Q: And how do you do that?
A: It depends how you talk to them. You speak in a certain manner. 'Now, you do like this', a bit like 'hierarchical ordering', if you like. When you do not get the response you asked for, you say, 'I need help to fix this and that, and I believe you can help me, right?' Then he thinks that he's really making a difference. In the same manner, if they are ill, they expect you to call them to ask how they are doing. That is very important. Especially regarding the lads who are ill quite often. You need to know whether there is somebody in the workplace responsible [for the illness].

One management technique that site managers use is spending time, everyday if possible, walking around and talking to the construction workers (those employed by the prime contractor and by the subcontractors) about the progress of the work. One site manager explained:

> I think you can go a long way if you are skilled in talking to people. You mustn't stay on you own and believe you know everything. There's always somebody who knows better than you. As a site manager you need, if not a safety net, then a number of people around you – people you know and you can call when things go wrong. That is very important.

Even though the foremen manage much of the everyday work, site managers still find being in charge of this broad range of activities and procedures stressful. One of the most troubling concerns for site managers is finding time to deal with the administrative work that has been decentralized to the site manager function. One site manager complained: 'You are always split between production and administration. I think, on the whole, that I enjoy a bit of both, but what's demeaning is that you are always split in halves. You often do not have the time to engage carefully with either of the two, so you do two things in equally mediocre fashion'. As a consequence, site managers must continually prioritize between production work and administrative work. An interviewee described this difficulty:

> What I prioritize most of all is the flow of production. If that works, we keep to a time schedule and everybody gets the chance to do their work. The administrative work is less prioritized. I'd rather take some complaints because of that than for delays in production. Administrative work can always be dealt with afterwards. You need to deal with what happens here and now. If that does not run as intended, you never catch up.

Like engineers who separate 'real engineering work' and 'everything else' (Perlow, 1999: 64; Faulkner, 2007), site managers often think of production work – the construction of the building or space – as the 'real site management work' and the rest as work that preferably belongs with the line organization. Therefore, some site managers deplore the loss of the old work regime where the site manger had a different role in the construction industry. According to one site manager:

> The old site manager role, back then, put more emphasis on the production management. I know that back then, you did not even see any invoices out there. Somebody else took care of them. What has happened over the years is that more and more administrative work has been decentralized and transferred to the projects while just as much production management work is still expected. This fragments your work.

However, the site managers do not think there will be a return to this former way of working.

Stress and workload

The site managers stated that 'no day is like another', with new things always going on at the work site. They also said that they have a difficulty isolating themselves from the turmoil of the work at the site, for instance, in order to deal with administrative work. One site manager emphasized this point:

> In a place like this, it is really hard to close the door and say, 'I need to be on my own for a while, because I have an agenda, or I have some things to take care of so I need a bit of calm'. Then the telephone rings or people come to see you all the time. But after four o'clock, things calm down and then you can gather all your thoughts.

Site managers generally come to work early in the morning (around 6 o'clock) so that they can get work done before their co-workers arrive; they also stay longer in the afternoon. This schedule makes for a long workday. In addition to the long work hours, the work is quite stressful at times. One foreman (a former site manager) emphasized the feeling of inadequacy, of never being able to finish anything: 'It is stressful. And you have this feeling that you never get a fair chance to finish anything. You may have ten different jobs going on at the same time, and you never complete them. In many cases, you have to use the night to shovel off things so you can start off fresh with the next thing [in the morning]'. Some site managers claimed the level of stress was cyclical, with calm periods in the construction processes followed by periods of more stability. However, they said the less stressful periods are fewer and fewer as a consequence of the compressed project times and the 'concurrent engineering' routines where work begins at a work site before the designers or even the client has made a decision on the structure to be built.

> The construction projects are shorter and shorter, and that's a negative thing . . . the real estate companies save some money that way . . . you don't let a project team of four persons run such a project a year in advance. Instead, you start the design work more or less at the same time as we start the production. It is a really slim organization these days, especially in this type of contracting [Total contracting, a specific contract form that gives more freedom to the contracting company].

Most site managers seem generally satisfied with their jobs. Many have substantial organizational tenure and some have even spent their entire lives in the industry, beginning with work in school vacations and then full time work after leaving school. However, they do have some criticism of the current work regime. Several of the relatively younger site managers (ages 30–45 years) pointed to the masculine culture that defines the site manager's role as a self-sufficient and largely autonomous figure. Such norms may be manifested in the rather autocratic leadership behaviour of older site managers. One interviewee said: 'The site managers need to play the role of the king of the construction site'. Others said the site manager is personally accountable for the entire construction project and should not ask for help from the head office when problems emerge. The consequence is typically burnout and costly overwork. However, the site managers expect that this masculine image of the self-sufficient, self-made man who requires no outside help will gradually disappear. For instance, some interviewees claimed that this amount of overwork among site managers would not be accepted by the new generation of site managers. Curiously, this masculine role goes very much against the grain of the actual work at the construction site where collaboration and close communication are imperative for long-term effectiveness. One site manager told a story about how his line manager introduced him to the work:

'Here, you have a bunch of blueprints, off you go! Do you know where the site is?' 'Not really'. 'Well, there's a map in there you can take so you can find your way. The client is at this address, and you can go see him' . . . And then you have manage it on your own, everything that you need to do. It is often taken for granted that the site manager is capable of operating on his own, right?

In this case, the assumption was that no proper introduction to the work was needed. Some site managers claimed that this kind of rather unsystematic use of site managers and their competencies has becoming increasingly problematic for the industry – not so much for the working conditions for current site managers, who are used to this tradition, but in the recruitment of newcomers. Another site manager made the following critical comments:

We [the construction industry] need to think in new terms. You can no longer devise your own solutions to everything. There is this problem in the construction industry: there is inadequate support of the managers. You become a site manager relatively soon if you are a bit ambitious and then—they give you a few courses, that is true— you're on your own. They give you the calculations and blueprints, and then say, 'Build this and make some money'. As long as that works satisfactorily, then no one really cares even though many things could be improved.

He continued:

It is of *critical importance* that construction companies take these things seriously. Younger people today question this way of working; nobody works as they used to. I don't think so. There is a need for a completely new organization. We need to think in new terms.

In summary, site managers supervise a world of continuous inflow and outflow of people and materials where dealing with expected and unexpected events is an everyday activity. Although the site managers delegate tasks to the foremen, they must manage a large number of people and activities, sandwiching that responsibility between frequent meetings arranged by, for instance, the client organization. In managing these different responsibilities, site managers work long hours and periodically experience substantial amounts of stress. Theirs is a work world where there is almost never any time where everything is in equilibrium; there are always activities requiring supervision or planning.

DISCUSSION

This study suggests that such settings, where there are tight couplings between technologies and practices and loose couplings between the horizontal and hierarchical organization elements, require a leadership practice described as 'muddling through'. Such 'muddling through' entails detailed planning of a sequence of interconnected and mutually dependent events while maintaining openness towards the future (i.e. the ability to handle unanticipated events as they occur). This leadership practice of 'muddling through' is highly practical because it calls upon the leader to deal with materials and polices and to execute direct authority, all of which are contingent on varying external conditions.

Site managers fit Frederick W. Taylor's definition of 'managers' – the officers who take full responsibility for the hands-on activities on the shop floor. Such leadership is observable in many industries characterized by many contingencies and unanticipated events. In the construction industry, site managers take pride in their ability to navigate in such environments where unpredictable events (e.g. sudden changes in weather or breakdowns in logistics) interrupt the work. While handling such events related to production demands the site manager's full concentration, site managers are increasingly responsible for handling administrative tasks and other 'office matters' as well. The situation blends what Orlikowski (2007) – referencing Suchman (2007) – calls *sociomaterial practice* and symbolic management that demand the presence of the manager. Therefore, site managers are generally critical about being in charge of desk assignments that they think would be better handled by administrative personnel.

Site managers are generally sceptical of the formalization of routines and knowledge because much of their expertise and experience is inherent in their decisions and choices. Like other construction industry representatives, they think that because the construction industry has relatively few repeated tasks, the value of standardizing work procedures and formalizing knowledge is lower than in large-scale, batch production (e.g. the automotive industry). Therefore, it is not expected that the skilled site manager will be able to anticipate and prevent problems (as in many other industries). Rather, the site manager should be able to deal with problems effectively as they occur.

At the same time, it is not suggested that site managers are unaware of possible future problems; on the contrary, the value of seasoned site managers lies precisely in their ability to act proactively, in accordance with institutionalized routines in the construction processes. However, the site manager learns such institutionalized routines by working at the site. Thus, day-to-day work largely consists of muddling through a series of events, one construction phase after another. The construction industry's loosely-coupled structure is not replicated at the construction site with its tightly-coupled sequence of activities. The diachronic and synchronic perspective of the site manager's role is a rather curious one. It is the craft production role of the *Meister* with a bird's-eye view of the workshop activities rather than the role of the hands-on manager who monitors and steers daily work using a variety of institutionalized managerial techniques and theories (e.g. Total Quality Management practices). Site managers must constantly shift their perspective between the nitty-gritty issues and more large-scale concerns; and, in all instances, they are responsible for the results. Many other leaders use symbolic interaction and communicative skills as the principal elements of their leadership role, but site managers have direct supervision over the transformation of raw materials into structures (houses, bridges, etc.). The site manager's work requires management of traditional work tasks as well as the more symbolic (e.g. motivation of co-workers) and administrative assignments (e.g. control of client/authority documents).

Previous studies of leadership activities by Carlsson (1951), Mintzberg (1973), Kotter (1982), and, more recently, Tengblad (2002) suggest that most leadership involves managing a series of disruptive events and brief meetings. The only major change in leadership activity since the early 1970s, Tengblad (2002) reports, is that leaders today spend more time travelling. The conclusion of these studies is that the work of most leaders is a form of muddling through, a 'sequential attention to goals' according to Cyert and March (1963). However, there is a significant difference in site managers' understanding of the leader's role. Site managers not only accept that such muddling is the most effective leadership, but they also think that this is the way leadership is *supposed to be*. Leadership, for the site manager, is not about trying to anticipate unforeseeable problems, an impossible task, but rather about handling a problem as quickly and as effectively as possible. As a consequence, the social capital in the community of site managers is critical in the efficient distribution of know-how. When site managers encounter problems they are unprepared to deal with, they call upon their contacts, or, as Granovetter (1973) labels them, the 'weak ties' – the network of former colleagues, friends, acquaintances, and other knowledgeable people in the construction industry. One site manager described this situation: 'At times, my mobile phone is red hot [from the extensive use]'.

This study contributes to the study of leadership by emphasizing the tactic of 'muddling through' in knowledge work, especially as used by construction site managers. In addition, the study focuses on the little-studied empirical domain of leadership practice in construction projects, in particular the idiosyncratic nature of the work (i.e. the unwillingness to standardize and formalize work procedures and know-how). In agreement with Stinchcombe's conclusion (1959) that construction work in part is based in a craft production regime that is now largely missing in many spheres of economic activity, this study suggests that site managers have an unusual position in business management. They are complete leaders in charge of nearly everything at the construction site.

CONCLUSION

Given the economic importance of the construction industry in the Western world, it is somewhat surprising that there has been so little systematic study of its leadership practices. This chapter suggests that construction site managers work in a setting where they muddle through activities and events that are mostly impossible to anticipate. Site management leadership work is a combination of ad hoc problem-solving, direct engagement with project co-workers, and dialogue with current and former colleagues (see e.g. Weick and Roberts, 1993; Thomas, 2006; Weick and Sutcliffe, 2006).

These dialogues with colleagues are essential when a problem that site managers have no experience with arises. Then, rather than jump to solutions – jeopardizing both materials and machinery – site managers contact other site managers or even other companies to request information and 'good advice'. For instance, in a major tunnel construction project in Western Sweden, the tunnel had to be connected to the rock foundation beneath the muddy terrain. In drilling into rock some 50 metres below ground level, an instrument called a 'hammer' stuck in the rock. It took the site manager and others in the contracting firm a week to collect information on how to solve the problem; once they had that information, the hammer was soon released and the work continued.

Such events are effectively dealt with in the construction industry through mindful as well as improvisational problem-solving. The distinguishing characteristic of 'muddling through' leadership is the ability of leaders to follow the project management model and timeline at the same time that they improvise as unanticipated situations arise. The project management model, that conventionally uses a Gantt chart to present time and activities sequentially, is the script for the work. While site managers tolerate brief deviations from the timeline, they take great pride in finishing projects on schedule. One the one hand, they look at improvisational problem-solving largely as a necessary evil for getting projects on track. On the other hand, improvisation is a much-praised feature of many construction war stories.

Consistent with many previous studies of managerial work (e.g. Mintzberg, 1973), this study describes the site manager's work as a sequence of short and overlapping assignments, some completed, others not. However, in comparison with other managerial work, site management work generally takes place in unfamiliar settings – new work sites, new materials, new social relationships, and new construction solutions. For construction site managers, a new setting is yet another 'prototype' where they have to learn new things. Therefore, site manager leadership requires always being ready for emerging problems and never assuming that things will go as planned. It is leadership practice in the form of thoughtful and innovative 'muddling through'.

APPENDIX: ON METHODOLOGY

The empirical material reported in this chapter comes from three construction industry research programmes, conducted in the years 2001–9. Using a collaborative research method (Adler et al., 2004; Shani et al., 2008), these research programmes were conceived of and articulated with representatives from the Swedish construction industry. For instance, the members of the research council of *Sveriges Byggindustrier* (the Swedish Construction Federation) commented a number of times on the research proposals and helped arrange the interviews and observations at the member companies. In addition, industry representatives offered insightful comments on the research proposals at the Center for Management in the Construction Industry (CMB) at Chalmers University of Technology, chaired by Professor Per-Erik Josephson. Moreover, executive committees of construction industry representatives formed the governing body for these research programmes and commented on the research results.

In general, this collaborative research setting encouraged open discussions between the academic researchers with their scholarly interests and the industry representatives with their expectations of 'actionable knowledge' (i.e. theoretical knowledge that can be used to inform day-to-day practices in construction firms). Collaborative research is a truly *relational* research method (see e.g. Dutton and Dukerich, 2006; Bartunek, 2007; Adler et al., 2008; Cunliffe, 2008). In conventional action research, the assumption is that academic researchers have 'something to teach' practitioners. Practical matters are not a major concern and the researcher takes a detached position vis-à-vis the object of study. However, in collaborative research, emphasis is placed on creating meaningful and enduring relationships between researchers and practitioners. The object of such research is to understand the complexities of a social practice.

The three research programmes used the case study methodology of interviews with site managers and internal documents examination. However, in one programme on the new role of the site manager in the construction industry, researchers studied a coaching method used to support site managers in their day-to-day work (see Styhre and Josephson, 2007). The coaching method was developed and used as a pilot study during a one-year period that included six site managers. During the coaching study, six site managers met individually on a regular basis with a professional coach who helped them developed their leadership skills and more generally their self-awareness. During this time, the research team interviewed the six managers three times each and the coach twice. The coaching programme was an explicit attempt to develop and use a practical, hands-on method for support of site managers in their day-to-day work. Taken together, the experiences from the coaching work were very positive and all the participating site managers endorsed the method as a tool for professional development of leaders in the construction industry.

In total, the three research programmes provide intriguing empirical data that show how site managers perceive, as well as criticize, their role and work in the industry. Most data were collected using semi-structured interviews although a significant amount of relevant experiences and observations came from the 'liminal events' of the research work – the informal discussions before and after the interviews, the guided walks around the work sites, the interviewees' body language, the jokes between site managers and other workers, and so forth. In short, the totality of such marginal or idiosyncratic experiences and observations is important in understanding the construction industry and the site manager's work. Typically, such data escape the formal documentation procedures of empirical research (see e.g. Law, 1994). Insight into the work of site managers derives less from direct observations of their work and more from their comments about their work.

REFERENCES

Adler, N. B., Shani, A. B., and Styhre, A. (Eds.) (2004). *Collaborative Research in Organizations: Foundations for Learning, Change, and Theoretical Development*. London, Thousand Oaks, and New Delhi: Sage.

Adler, P. S., Kwon, S-W., and Heckscher, C. (2008). Professional work: The emergence of collaborative community. *Organization Science*, 19(2): 359–76.

Agapiou, A. (2002). Perceptions of gender roles and attitudes toward work among male and female operatives in a Scottish construction industry. *Construction Economics and Management*, 20: 697–705.

Bartunek, J. M. (2007). Academic-practitioner collaboration need not require joint or relevant research: Toward a relational scholarship of integration. *Academy of Management*, 50(6): 1323–33.

Carlsson, S. (1951). *Executive Behaviour: A Study of the Work Load and the Working Methods of Managing Directors*. Stockholm: Strömbergs.

Clarke, A. E. and Fujimura, J. H. (1992). What tools? Which jobs? Why right? In A. E. Clarke and J. H. Fujimura (Eds.), *The Right Tools for the Job. At Work in Twentieth-Century Life Sciences* (pp. 3–45). Princeton, NJ: Princeton University Press.

Cunliffe, A. L. (2008). Orientation to social constructionism: Relationally responsive social constructionism and its implications for knowledge and learning. *Management Learning*, 39(2): 123–39.

Cyert, R. M. and March, J. G. (1963). *A Behavioral Theory of the Firm*. Englewood Cliffs, NJ: Prentice-Hall.

Davidson, M. J. and Sutherland, V. J. (2002). Stress and construction site managers: Issues for Europe 1992. *Employee Relations*, 14(2): 25–38.

Delbridge, R. (1998). *Life on the Line in Contemporary Manufacturing: The Workplace Experience of Lean Production and the 'Japanese Model'*. Oxford and New York: Oxford University Press.

Delmestri, G. and Walgenbach, P. (2005). Mastering techniques or brokering knowledge? Middle managers in Germany, Great Britain and Italy. *Organization Studies*, 26(2): 197–220.

Djerbarni, R. (1996). The impact of stress in site management effectiveness. *Construction Management and Economics*, 14: 281–93.

Dopson, S. and Stewart, R. (1990). What is happening to middle management? *British Journal of Management*, 1: 3–16.

Dubois, A. and Gadde, L-E. (2002). The construction industry as a loosely coupled system: Implications for productivity and innovation. *Construction Management and Economics*, 20: 621–31.

Dutton, J. E. and Dukerich, J. M. (2006). The relational foundation of research: An underappreciated dimension of interesting research. *Academy of Management Journal*, 49(1): 21–6.

Eccles, R. G. (1981). Bureaucratic versus craft administration: The relationship of market structure to the construction firm. *Administrative Science Quarterly*, 26(3): 449–69.

Edmonson, A. C. (2003). Speaking up in the operating room: How team leaders promote learning in interdisciplinary action teams. *Journal of Management Studies*, 40(6): 1419–52.

Faulkner, W. (2007). 'Nuts and bolts and people': Gender-troubled engineering identities. *Social Studies of Science*, 37(3): 331–56.

Floyd, S. W. and Woolridge, B. (1997). Dinosaurs or dynamos? Recognizing middle management's strategic role. *Academy of Management Executive*, 8(4): 47–57.

Fraser, C. (2000). The influence of personal characteristics on effectiveness of construction site managers. *Construction Management and Economics*, 18: 29–36.

Granovetter, M. S. (1973). The strength of weak ties. *American Journal of Sociology*, 78(6): 1360–80.

Guillén, M. F. (1994). *Models of Management: Work, Authority, and Organization in a Comparative Perspective*. Chicago and London: The University of Chicago Press.

Hawk, D. (2006). Conditions of success: A platform for international construction development. *Construction Management and Economics*, 24: 735–42.

Hillebrandt, P. M. (2000). *Economic Theory and the Construction Industry* (3rd ed.). Basingstoke: Macmillan.

Huy, Q. N. (2002). Emotional balancing of organizational continuity and radical change: The contribution of middle managers. *Administrative Science Quarterly*, 47: 31–69.

King, A. W., Fowler, S. W., and Zeithaml, C. P. (2001). Managing organizational competencies for competitive advantage: The middle-management edge. *Academy of Management Executive*, 15(2): 95–106.

Knorr Cetina, K. D. (1981). *The Manufacture of Knowledge: An Essay on the Constructivist and Contextual Nature of Science*. Oxford: Pergamon Press.

Kotter, J. P. (1982). What effective general managers really do? *Harvard Business Review*, Nov/Dec, 60(6): 156–68.

Law, J. (1994). *Organizing Modernity*. Oxford and Cambridge: Blackwell.

Lindblom, C. E. (1959). The science of muddling through. *Public Administration Review*, 19(2): 79–88.

Lingard, H. and Francis, V. (2004). The work-life experiences of office and site-based employees in the Australian construction industry. *Construction Management & Economics*, 22(9): 991–1002.

——(2006). Does a supportive work environment moderate the relationship between work–family conflict and burnout among construction professionals? *Construction Management & Economics*, 24(2): 185–96.

Mintzberg, H. (1973). *The Nature of Managerial Work*. New York: Harper & Row.

——(1983). *Structure in Fives: Designing Effective Organizations*. Englewood Cliffs, NJ: Prentice-Hall.

Orlikowski, W. J. (2007). Sociomaterial practices: Exploring technology at work. *Organization Studies*, 28(9): 1435–48.

Perlow, L. A. (1999). The time famine: Toward a sociology of work time. *Administrative Science Quarterly*, 44: 57–81.

Perrow, C. (1984). *Normal Accidents*. New York: Basic Books.

Rheinberger, H-J. (1997). *Toward a History of Epistemic Things: Synthesizing Proteins in the Test Tube*. Stanford: Stanford University Press.

Shani, A. B., Mohrman, S. A., Pasmore, W. A., Stymne, B., and Adler, N. (Eds.) (2008). *Handbook of Collaborative Management Research*. Thousand Oaks, London, and New Delhi: Sage.

Shenhav, Y. (1995). From chaos to systems: The engineering foundations of organization theory, 1879–1932. *Administrative Science Quarterly*, 40: 447–585.

Stinchcombe, A. (1959). Bureaucractic and craft administration of production: A comparative study. *Administrative Science Quarterly*, 4(2): 168–88.

Styhre, A. (2006). The bureaucratization of the project manager function: The case of construction industry. *International Journal Project Management*, 24: 271–6.

——Josephson, P-E. (2006). Revisiting site manager work: Stuck in the middle? *Construction Management and Economics*, 24: 521–8.

—— —— (2007). Coaching the site manager: Effects on learning and managerial practice. *Construction Management and Economics*, 25(10–12): 1295–304.

Suchman, L. A. (2007). *Human-Machine Reconfigurations: Plans and Situated Actions* (2nd ed.). Cambridge: Cambridge University Press.

Tengblad, S. (2002). Time and space in managerial work. *Scandinavian Journal of Management*, 18: 543–65.

Thomas, D. C. (2006). Domain and development of cultural intelligence: The importance of mindfullness. *Group & Organization Management*, 31(1): 78–99.

Timmermans, S. and Berg, M. (1997). Standardization in action: Achieving local universality through medical protocols. *Social Studies of Science*, 27(2): 273–305.

Weick, K. E. (1976). Educational organizations as loosely coupled systems. *Administrative Science Quarterly*, 21: 1–19.

——(1979). *The Social Psychology of Organizing*. New York: McGraw-Hill.

——(2001). *Making Sense of the Organization*. Oxford: Blackwell.

——Roberts, K. H. (1993). Collective mind in organizations: Heedful interrelating on flight decks. *Administrative Science Quarterly*, 38: 357–81.

——Sutcliffe, K. M. (2006). Mindfulness and the quality of organizational attention. *Organization Science*, 17(4): 514–24.

8

R&D managers leading knowledge workers with care

Ola Edvin Vie

INTRODUCTION

There are numerous studies in the Managerial and Work Behaviour (MWB) literature of executives and managers where the aim is to identify the characteristics of effective leaders. To that end, the research examines leaders in different work settings, different organizations, and different geographic locations in the search for similarities and differences in management actions and styles. The MWB research approach (Stewart, 2008) taken in such studies is a distinct approach that is both empirical and inductive (Noordegraaf and Stewart, 2000). Studies using this approach have focused on the form and content of managerial work by collecting behavioural data about individual managers with the intent of understanding managerial work as a whole. This approach, although sometimes criticized as too atheoretical and too concerned with variation in managerial work (Hales, 1986, 1999), takes a positional orientation to leadership through studying individuals formally appointed as managers (Noordegraaf and Stewart, 2000: 432).

In his well-known book, *The Nature of Managerial Work*, Henry Mintzberg (1973) described the tension between variation and commonalities in managerial work. Although Mintzberg made an empirical study of top executive behaviour, he also focused on the generalities of managerial work. Pointing to the similarities in the work of foremen, presidents, and other managers, Mintzberg wrote: 'In essence, managers work today as they always have' (1973: 161). Although strongly influenced by Mintzberg's classic study, many researchers now believe it is necessary to consider the potential differences in managerial work when the intention is to compare managers in different settings and at different levels.

In these leadership studies, one area where insufficient attention has been paid to such potential differences is management in knowledge-intensive firms. There are special conditions in such firms that require their managers to adopt special management styles. This chapter, which is based on my doctoral thesis (Vie, 2009), focuses on middle managers in the Research and Development (R&D) setting and examines both the distinctiveness and the commonality of R&D managerial work. First, I review MWB studies that describe managers at different levels and other studies that address the particularity of management in R&D organizations. Thereafter I detail the methodological approach, empirical setting, and empirical findings of this study. Using qualitative data, I show that 'care' is a natural part of the R&D manager's acceptance of personnel responsibility. The chapter concludes with a discussion of the theoretical implications of this study and makes suggestions for future research.

MANAGERIAL WORK AND BEHAVIOUR STUDIES

Mintzberg's 1973 book, which was followed by his award-winning article in the *Harvard Business Review* (1975), is still an important reference for management research. Underpinning his research is the argument that stable managerial characteristics are explained by the strength of the structural conditions surrounding all managers. His formulation of ten managerial roles is the book's most famous contribution, but his thirteen propositions about managerial work and his behavioural categories are also well known. Since Mintzberg described his method and categories in detail, later researchers have often been able to base their studies on his work. His general propositions have also enjoyed a rather universal and timeless appeal among researchers. A good example of his influence is the nearly identical replication of his work by Kurke and Aldrich (1983). The next section reviews some of these MWB studies, many of which were influenced in some way by Mintzberg's work. This review sets the background for my study of R&D managers that is reported on in this chapter.

Studies of top executives

In his study of top executives that depicts the considerable change in their work compared to the work Mintzberg described, Tengblad (2006) challenges the stability of managerial work concept that Mintzberg proposed. Tengblad supports his conclusions using empirical evidence grouped in two broad patterns: managers' decreased preoccupation with administrative work and their increased dialogue-oriented contact. Tengblad also argues that there has been a relative shift in behaviour from administrative management to the institutional leadership that Selznick (1957) had described. In this shift to institutional leadership, the relative importance of various managerial activities has changed as ceremonies and accounts of company history take priority over desk work. However, Tengblad argues that this change at the top executive level does not necessarily imply a similar change for other managerial groups.

Studies of middle managers

Researchers have also found a different pattern in the work of middle managers. In older MWB studies of middle managers (e.g. Burns, 1954, 1957; Guest, 1956; Horne and Lupton, 1965) and in more recent studies (e.g. Martinko and Gardner,

1990; Stewart et al., 1994; Hales and Mustapha, 2000), it is evident that middle managers spend much less time in scheduled meetings and much more time in unscheduled meetings than the top executives that Mintzberg (1973) and Tengblad (2006) described. Moreover, middle managers, like Mintzberg's executives although unlike Tengblad's executives, spend much of their time on desk work.

Leading in R&D settings

In addition to the influence of the management hierarchical level, noted above, there is another influence on R&D middle managers owing to the peculiarities of their work environment. In knowledge-intensive firms, managers are often in charge of large groups of expert employees who are not amenable to supervision (McAuley et al., 2000) or to managerial hierarchies (Oliver and Montgomery, 2000). Thus, R&D managers have to reduce their direct control over knowledge workers and allow them more freedom to organize themselves. The research in R&D and knowledge-intensive organizations therefore emphasizes the importance of indirect and facilitating leadership (Drucker, 1988; Alvesson, 1995; Mintzberg, 1998).

Beginning at least with Burns and Stalker's study (1961) of innovation management, researchers have recognized the need for 'softer' management practices in R&D and other creative settings (for a review of R&D leadership research, see Elkins and Keller, 2003). In leadership research, the study of leader support of employees begins even earlier. Studies at Ohio State University were the starting point with their focus on unravelling the behavioural indicators of effective leadership (see Stogdill, 1950). These studies also identified two leadership styles termed 'Consideration' and 'Initiating Structure' (Fleishman, 1953). The Initiating Structure management style focuses on production and work accomplishment. The Consideration management styles focuses on employees as human beings. Bass and Avolio (1990) included individualized consideration as one of the four dimensions of transformational leadership. However, taking the MWB approach, only Pavett and Lau (1985) have studied R&D managers. In their study, they found that R&D managers rated flexibility, good communication, and listening skills as the more important leadership characteristics.

The use of the term 'Consideration' in the leadership literature highlights the behavioural dimension of management and researchers' increasing recognition that 'emotions are an integral and inseparable part of everyday organizational life' (Ashforth and Humphrey, 1995: 98). However, the knowledge management literature has been more receptive to a discussion of the more emotional dimensions of leading than the leadership literature. In this context, Von Krogh (1998) has introduced the concept of 'care' that is discussed in the next section.

Leading with care

Since human beings make up the emotional core of organizations, understanding the emotional nature of work requires understanding the people who perform the work. Since human beings are the emotional creatures who constitute an

organization's emotions, understanding the emotional nature of work is a necessity in any organization (see Fineman, 2003). Assuming that human beings – and
the relationships between them – are fundamentally emotional, their personal
characteristics can never be totally separated from their professional characteristics. As noted by Solomon (1998), even though caring in corporations is
sometimes denied, people working in such corporations, including the leaders,
can, and do, care about one another.

The relational nature of care, with its focus on recognizing and understanding
other people's perspectives, explains why care has special relevance in sharing and
creating knowledge. Mayerhoff (1971: 1) says that to care for another person 'in
the most significant sense, is to help him grow and actualize himself'. Building on
this definition, von Krogh (1998) argues that care is essential for innovation in
companies because high-care relationships can overcome mistrust, fear, and
isolation as well as promote voluntary knowledge sharing. Care gives rise to
mutual trust, active empathy, access to help, lenience in judgement, and courage
(von Krogh, 1998; von Krogh et al., 2000). In a definition similar to Mayerhoff's,
Burns (1978: 20) says transformational leadership occurs when 'persons engage
with others in such a way that leaders and followers raise one another to higher
levels of motivation and morality'.

Although care usually is described positively, the responsibility for providing
care can be burdensome. According to Solomon (1998), at the same time that the
caregivers offer support and affection, they may become possessive, vengeful, and
hurtful. In addition, caregivers, in adopting another's interest as their own, may be
tempted to defend that interest despite the danger of personal reprisals.

According to Gabriel (2009), there is also a good deal of interest in the ethics of
care among scholars who study ethics from feminist and environmental perspectives (see also Gilligan, 1982; Tronto, 1993; Kittay and Feder, 2002; Held, 2006).
Gabriel (2009: 179) further explains: 'Care is attending to the needs of others to
whom we feel close and for whom we are prepared or expected to take responsibility. It is not a scripted emotional performance but involves a wide range of
actions, concerns, utterances and feelings that grow out of sensitivity and concern
for the needs of those close to us. Those close to us and in direct contact with us
are experienced as entitled to more care and attention than those distant and
unknown'.

In this chapter, where the focus is on R&D leaders who care about their
employees, care should not be viewed as a part of the 'highly romanticized, heroic
views of leadership' (Meindl et al., 1985: 79). Instead, care, as conceived of here, is
reflected in the more everyday leadership activities such as listening, chatting, and
being cheerful (Alvesson and Sveningsson, 2003). While the term 'Consideration'
in the leadership literature focuses on the behavioural dimension, the term 'care'
in the knowledge management literature highlights the emotional dimension.
Therefore, the central question of this research is: How does managerial care
work as an effective leadership technique in R&D settings?

To answer the question, I use parts of Cialdini's framework (2001) that
recognizes that the social influence process can be subtle, indirect, and outside
our awareness. This understanding supports the view that emotions can be spread
implicitly through emotional contagion (Hatfield et al., 1993). Such indirect
influence is also highlighted in more recent leadership research (e.g. George,

2000; Dasborough and Ashkanasy, 2002; Dasborough, 2006) that argues the social influence process of emotions is central in effective leadership.

According to Cialdini (2001), people tend to act according to fixed-action patterns, usually triggered by a single source of relevant information in a situation. In a world with more information than people can readily handle, the reliance on a single source of information helps the individual to decide on a course of action without having to analyse the situation carefully. The disadvantage of such automatic responses lies in the potential for making foolish and costly mistakes that compliance professionals, such as salespersons, may exploit.

In this chapter, I use the following assertions in my explanation of why R&D managers lead with care:

- Reciprocation is a powerful and influential process that makes people feel psychologically obligated to return favours (Cialdini, 2001: 19ff).
- Liking, which is influenced by physical attractiveness, similarities, and greater familiarity through repeated contact and association, works because people prefer to say 'yes' to individuals they know and like (Cialdini, 2001: 143ff).
- Authority is the process by which occupational titles increase compliance (Cialdini, 2001: 178ff).

I will return to an analysis of these assertions of influence in the 'Discussion' section following my presentation of the study's methodology, empirical setting, and some of its empirical findings.

METHODOLOGY

This study applies the structured observation method that Mintzberg described as 'a method that couples the flexibility of open-ended observation with the discipline of seeking certain types of structured data' (1973: 231). The method, which some managers in Mintzberg's book described as being 'shadowed' (Mintzberg, 1975: 50), can be considered a distinct research technique that combines quantitative and qualitative approaches (McDonald, 2005). It has been used as a research method in various social science fields (see Czarniawska, 2007, on shadowing). In using the flexibility that the method permits, I revise Mintzberg's original terminology as necessary. In following Martinko and Gardner's research recommendation (1985), my study includes recording data for more than one purpose and for more than one kind of participant in verbal contacts. In the study, I spent more time recording for different purposes than in verbal participant contact.

I shadowed four R&D managers for one week each, for a total of 191 hours. My direct observations were limited to managerial behaviour in the workplace or in transit to the workplace. Although work at home or on the weekends is excluded, eleven hours of work not directly observed (because of sensitivity or confidential issues) are included. This unobserved work is coded based on short interviews with the managers.

In addition to shadowing, I conducted thirty separate interviews. Eight interviews were with the four managers (for each manager, an interview before the shadowing and an interview after the shadowing), two were with superior managers, and twenty were with subordinates (five subordinates for each manager). Five subordinates were female and fifteen male; eleven subordinates had project management experience. I interviewed only two superior managers because one shadowed manager was a second-line manager above a shadowed manager and because two shadowed managers had the same superior manager. I collected data in the R&D departments of two companies at two time periods in 2006.

Research setting

The two R&D departments are in companies that produce advanced technical products for an international market. R&D activities are central to operations in both companies. The two companies are very similar in size. In 2006, each company had operating revenues of approximately 400 million Euros and around 2,000 employees. Their employees' ages and education levels are also similar. There is also similar gender distribution among the employees at the two companies. Most employees have a technical education. Nearly one-quarter of the employees have more than four years of higher education; about half the employees have up to three years of higher education. Both departments are part of other divisions. The larger department has about 150 employees working in seven sections, while the other department has about sixty employees working in four sections. Both companies are organized as matrix organizations.

The four shadowed managers are men between the ages of 36 and 51. Each has a Bachelor's, Master's, or PhD degree in engineering. Three managers are first-level managers and one is a second-level manager. The number of people they supervise varies between twelve and sixty persons. On average, the managers have been at their companies for fourteen years, have seven years' managerial experience, and have been in their current positions for three years.

Data analysis

In the data analysis, I took an unrestricted approach that allowed for a shift in focus when specific themes seemed interesting. My preliminary data analysis involved reading the interview transcripts and observational field notes several times. In the thematic analysis (see Bryman, 2008) and summarization of the interview data, I looked for illustrative examples. In the analysis of the interviews with the knowledge workers, I focused on their expectations of leadership in general and their relationship with their immediate manager in particular. I later compared these expectations to the perceptions of the four shadowed managers and their two superiors on the same issues. In addition, I analysed both the interview and observational data in order to reach a description of the managerial activities. Although I first categorized the observational data according to Mintzberg's taxonomy (1973), many activities did not fit into his categories. Therefore, I added a new category titled 'Care and consideration' for the activities of greeting people, using humour, talking informally, and exhibiting empathy.

Tables 8.1, 8.2, and 8.3 present the managers' time distribution according to the activities and verbal contacts.

EMPIRICAL FINDINGS

R&D managers' time distribution

Table 8.1 presents a comparison of time distribution for the R&D managers of my study with that of the top executives in Mintzberg's study (1973). The two sets of managers worked approximately the same number of hours, but the R&D managers were much more involved with administrative work, including desk work. While they spent less time in meetings in total, they spent more hours in unscheduled meetings and fewer hours in scheduled meetings. When managers have fewer scheduled meetings, they have more time for phone calls, tours, and unscheduled meetings.

As Table 8.2 shows, compared to Mintzberg's top executives, the R&D managers spent considerably more time talking with subordinates and superiors than with people outside their companies. Because more than one participant category could be involved in a single verbal contact, for both groups the total time spent with participants is higher than the total time spent in verbal contact (see the Appendix for individual results for the R&D managers). In general, the R&D managers attended either lengthy, scheduled meetings or short, unscheduled meetings. I argue that their personnel responsibilities partially explain this characteristic meeting pattern in which the R&D managers prioritize interactions with their subordinates.

Table 8.3 shows the various purposes of the verbal contacts. It is particularly noteworthy that the purpose of as much as 16 per cent of the R&D managers' verbal contacts is Care and consideration (such as social chit-chat, humorous exchanges, greetings, or expressions of concern for others). Since Mintzberg did not use the category of Care and consideration, there are no figures for his top executives. Care and consideration usually, although not always, appeared in private meetings between the R&D managers and other employees. Later in the chapter, I will return to this issue.

The three tables show that the managers in this study had activity patterns that, in many ways, are similar to those of the managers in earlier studies of executive work (e.g. Mintzberg, 1973) but different from the patterns of the executives in more recent studies and the middle managers in earlier and more recent studies. This conclusion is based on a comparison of the amount of time these managers and executives spent on desk work and in scheduled and unscheduled meetings. Like the executives in Tengblad's study (2006), the R&D managers in this study engaged in dialogue-oriented communication and exhibited a supportive leadership style. However, the R&D managers, like those in Mintzberg's study, were more involved with routine administration than the Tengblad executives. As Tengblad concludes, it is possible that the relative importance of supportive and dialogue-oriented leadership practice has increased, resulting in no radical changes in managerial behaviour. In a similar manner, the relative importance

Table 8.1 Total working hours average values per manager

	Vie (2010)			Mintzberg (1973)		
	Hours/week	Share* (%)	Range* (%)	Hours/week	Share (%)	Comparison (%)
1. Scheduled meetings	15.0	31	22–36	23.9	54	–37
2. Unscheduled meetings	8.2	17	13–23	4.0	9	106
1–2. *Total meetings*	23.2	49	45–48	27.9	64	–17
3. Tours	2.0	4	3–7	1.0	2	101
4. Telephone calls	3.8	8	7–9	2.6	6	48
5. Desk work	10.6	22	15–29	8.9	20	19
6. Transportation	7.9	17	5–20	3.5	8	125
7. Observer interaction and personal	3.2	7	6–8	–	–	–
Sum of activities	50.7	106	44–55	45.3	103	
Total working time per participant	47.7	100	44–54	43.9	100	9

* These shares are computed as a percentage of total sums of activities.

Table 8.2 Participants in verbal contact

	Vie (2010)				Mintzberg (1973)		
	Hours/week	Share* (%)	Share** (%)	Range** (%)	Hours/week	Share* (%)	Comparison (%)
1. Subordinates	18.5	44	64	33–90	15.2	48	22
2. Superiors	4.8	11	16	0–36	2.2	7	116
3. Peers	5.7	14	20	3–41	5.1	16	13
4. Others from others organizations	10.1	24	34	26–42	?	–	–
5. Client, supplier, associate	0.7	2	2	0–9	6.3	20	–89
6. Independent and others	1.8	4	6	0–12	2.5	8	–29
7. Unknown	0.5	1	2	0–5	–	–	–
Sum	42.1	100	145	138–167	31.3	99	35
Total time in verbal contact	29.0				31.6		–8

* Computed as a percentage of total time in verbal contact with participants.
** Computed as a percentage of total time in verbal contact.

Table 8.3 Purpose of verbal contact

	Vie (2010)				Mintzberg (1973)		
	Hours/week	Share* (%)	Share** (%)	Range (%)	Hours/week	Share (%)	Comparison (%)
1-4. Total secondary work	1.4	2	5	1-7	6.6	21	-80
5-8. Requests and solicitations	18.3	31	63	36-79	5.7	18	228
9-13. Total informational	29.1	49	100	84-119	12.6	40	134
14-15. Total decision-making	3.9	7	13	0.3-26	6.2	21	-37
16. Care and consideration	4.5	8	16	11-21	?	-	-
17. Resource allocation	1.4	2	5	1-9	?	-	-
18. Unknown	0.5	1	2	1-3	?	-	-
Sum	59.1	100	203	148-251	31.6	100	90
Total time in verbal contact	29				31.6		-8

* Computed as a percentage of total time in verbal contact with participants.
** Computed as a percentage of total time in verbal contact.

of administrative work may have declined without a radical change in preoccupation with administrative routines. Since it is highly improbable that routine, administrative work will disappear without some causal factor, someone should ensure that detailed tasks are completed. Such tasks may be as essential as ensuring that equipment functions properly or as minor as ordering the preferred tea for the lunchroom. For the R&D companies in this study, it appeared that, surprisingly, the subordinates left such administrative tasks to their managers. This reversal of roles may be interpreted as an illustration of managerial care that supports subordinates.

In the next section, I turn to the knowledge workers' expectations of their managers and the managers' explanations of their supportive and caring activities. In these descriptions, I quote several managers who talk about what it means to have responsibility for care of subordinates and how they demonstrate that care. For further discussion of the managers' comments quoted in this section, see Vie (2010).

Managing the personnel responsibility with care

> The personnel responsibility, which is perhaps the hardest part in this job, is solved mainly by being around to check on how people are doing and by listening to how they describe their project work.

This is one manager's view of himself and the care he shows to the subordinates he manages. The statement reveals not only his burden of personnel responsibility but also how he deals with this responsibility. In order to learn how the subordinate knowledge workers view their managers, I interviewed five knowledge workers for each of the four managers. When asked what characterizes a good leader, many subordinates responded that managers should have good personal skills. A good leader should be empathetic, understand human nature, be easy to talk to, have time to talk, and relate to employees as complete persons. The subordinates did not expect their managers to solve their personal problems. However, the subordinates felt they should be able to talk to their managers about private and sensitive issues so that the managers would try to shield them from excessive work demands during difficult periods. The subordinates also commented that it was only natural to involve a manager when their personal problems affected work. Several subordinates associated their expectation of managerial personal skills with the managerial competence to take actions and fix problems.

Another manager described the burden of being a manager as follows:

> When you are a line manager you have personnel responsibility, which means that you need to recognize that you are working with people. You have to take their personal needs, in their different phases of life, into consideration . . . You should also take care of all the formalities, all those little small matters that create bugs and annoyances for everyone doing the work.

The managers recognized the importance of solving employee problems. One solution mentioned was to organize the work conditions for the knowledge workers, for example, arranging for equipment, resolving administrative issues, and prioritizing their tasks. One manager explained the reason behind his caring behaviour:

> It is about greasing the engine, because if a subordinate is unable to do his work because of some obstacle, it is good business for the company to take care of the obstacle and get rid of it. If it takes me three minutes to fix it and get the person back to work, it is a good investment and preferable to my reviewing a document or working on some other task with a more long-term perspective.

Several managers said it is necessary to take individual considerations into account during the assignment process. They want to know about their subordinates' work and home lives so that they can strike a balance between the amount of work assigned and the subordinates' personal lives. Therefore, the managers take time to chat with and listen to their subordinates in informal meetings. Sometimes the subordinates initiate the conversations, but generally it was observed that the managers took the initiative. In addition, the managers usually eat lunch with their subordinates. During these lunch breaks, people usually talk about topics unrelated to work, such as their families and hobbies. Thus, through chatting and listening, the managers and subordinates get to know each other. Because the managers assign people to different projects and approve overtime, they can intervene on behalf of their subordinates. However, as the following statement by a manager shows, managerial care is not just about being nice. It may also mean being stern and authoritative.

> I see it as essential to have a fairly good sense of the social situation of people. When people have small kids at home and yet are too preoccupied with their work, I tell them to buzz off back home. I say: "You can't sit here and work overtime now. Now it's time for you to take care of your family."

As an example of managerial care, the following comments by a manager about one subordinate in particular and subordinates in general are representative. In his comments, the manager shows that care shown towards a subordinate can also have an effect on others.

> I am totally convinced that, so to speak, being engaged with and sustaining the well-being of the employees is the way this company can succeed...I have one employee, aged 63, who unfortunately was diagnosed with cancer. We sent flowers before we knew he had cancer. I visited him at home and we have talked over the phone several times. Our Unit bought him an iPod and volunteers downloaded music onto it. It is very important for me have a good relationship with him as I am very fond of him. I do not try to hide from others that I think it is important that we show that we really care about him. It is important for our employees to see that if they are in the same situation, the workplace will care about them. I genuinely care about him, but I know in the back of my head that it [my care] serves more than one purpose.

However, if managing is about influence, how do such everyday activities contribute to such influence? This is the subject of the following theoretical discussion.

THEORETICAL DISCUSSION

As the previous section argues, taking responsibility for the personnel in an organization and exhibiting care towards them seem to be central facets of managerial work. Thus, there is 'a significant emotional dimension to managerial work' (Watson, 1994/2001: 180). This issue is particularly important because many newly promoted managers are unprepared to handle subordinates' emotions. They are also generally surprised to learn how important this facet of their work is (Watson and Harris, 1999; Hill, 2003). The findings of this study show that while at least some managers are indeed concerned about the personal welfare of their subordinates, demonstrations of care to one subordinate may also have a significant complementary effect on other subordinates. In this respect, care can be an effective leadership technique.

The social influence of care

Based on Cialdini's description (2001) of influence tactics, the liking dimension seems to be very relevant and important in R&D organizations. Liking among people is influenced by physical attractiveness, similarities in interests, appearance, attitudes and values, and increased familiarity resulting from repeated contacts and associations. Tables 8.1, 8.2, and 8.3 show that the R&D managers spend considerable time with their subordinates when responding to requests and receiving short exchanges of information. In such exchanges, these managers demonstrate care that may cause their subordinates to increase their liking of the managers. When subordinates read a manager's distributed e-mails of support for another person, share in the common caring activities, and talk to their manager about the care of another person, their liking of, as well as trust in, the manager is strengthened. Heightened liking may lead to greater cooperation when the manager asks a favour or makes assignments.

Cialdini (2001) identified reciprocation as another powerful dimension that influences people since acting generously towards another person creates a psychological obligation to return the favour. For example, when a manager does a favour for a subordinate, the subordinate may feel obliged to respond in kind. This obligation may cause the subordinate to work harder in order to repay the favour. In such situations, it may also be argued that there is a complementary effect. Other employees, not under that specific obligation, may feel obliged to work more also. Having observed the manager's care in doing the favour, they may well assume they will receive equal treatment in the same or similar situation. This assumption may cause them to feel more committed to their manager.

The findings of this study support Alvesson and Sveningsson's conclusions (2003) on the importance of everyday work activities (e.g. listening and chatting). However, these researchers argue that because everyone influences others, the managerial influence of these activities is not extraordinary. This claim raises the question: Is the influence of managers actually the same as the influence of others? Admitting that the social influence dimensions of liking and reciprocation are indeed common to all people, I argue, however, that the processes of authority are more significant for managers than for others.

The manager's positional authority can have a more subtle form of influence. According to Cialdini (2001), the social influence process of authority can be subtle, indirect, and outside our awareness. When Fineman (2000) states that emotional processes may be subconscious, the implication is that managers can and do influence others by their daily activities, both intentionally and unintentionally. A further implication is that managers' care for others may have a positive and practical influence on subordinates. Kunda (1992) described this influence in his account of a manager who told his project managers to know and care for their employees in order to prevent burnout. According to Kunda, the manager stated: 'We need them [the employees] for a long, long time' (1992: 204). This account exemplifies normative control that Kunda (1992: 11) defines as an effort to direct organizational members by 'controlling the underlying experience, thoughts and feelings that guide their actions'.

The effectiveness of soft authority

Since a title by itself can increase subordinate compliance (Cialdini, 2001), the managerial title gave the R&D managers authority even though they worked to reduce power differences between themselves and their subordinates. However, they could not avoid their managerial roles. There is paradox when someone tries to decrease power differences. Such efforts actually confirm that such differences exist because if all employees were equal, there would be no need to engage in such work. In many ways, the R&D managers were like their subordinates as far as education and experience and tried to reinforce these similarities at lunch or other informal settings by talking about topics of general interest, unrelated to work. Nevertheless, the managers made the subordinates' project assignments and negotiated their salaries. Thus, the managers could not distance themselves from their formal positions or their managerial authority. There is an implication for knowledge workers. If they see their managers not just as individuals but also as organizational representatives, it is possible that the liking of managers and the reciprocal commitment to them may transfer to the organization as a whole.

Friendliness between managers and subordinates agrees with a basic view of authority. Authority, which is usually described as legitimate power (Clegg, 1989), can be traced to Weber's three forms of authority (1922/78): legal-rational, tradition, or charisma. Managers thus gain their authority, which involves rights, prerogatives, obligations, and duties (Yukl, 2002) from their position in a hierarchical organization rooted in laws. However, Weber's three forms of authority are ideal types that are separated in order to promote their understanding and discussion. This separation does not exclude the possibility that different forms of authority intervene. Barnard (1938), for instance, understands authority relations not as given, but as dependent on acceptance of all people involved. Thus, authority addresses the persons who define the acceptance or extent of authority, not the persons of authority.

The typical understanding of knowledge workers and creative people is that they value autonomy (Oldham and Cummings, 1996; Mumford et al., 2002). Knowledge workers do not dislike authority in itself, but dislike authority in the form of command-and-control management styles. The subordinates in this study said it was only natural to involve a manager in their personal lives when work is affected. They involve the managers who have the authority to control working hours and, if necessary, to provide special working arrangements. This means that when knowledge workers talk to a manager about both work and personal problems, the understanding is that they are not talking to just anyone. In this situation, the manager's authority is indeed very welcome.

In addition to taking responsibility for other organization personnel, managers have authority over them. Authority is not only about rights, but it is also about obligations and responsibilities. The implication of this understanding of authority is that the exercise of authority depends on its acceptance by employees who can influence managers' obligations and expectations. Such duality related to authority may explain why knowledge workers expect their managers to resolve their practical or administrative issues and why managers comply. As noted by Watson and Harris (1999: 172), the way in which managers 'manage is constrained by the expectations of their staff and the culture they are used to and are re-creating'. In other words, employees' expectations and construction of personnel responsibility influence managers' demands, constraints, and choices (Stewart, 1976, 1982). In short, managers show care towards employees because it is expected.

The manager's emotional burden

Drawing on series of manager interviews, Watson and Harris (1999) report on how recently promoted managers describe their experiences. Many of the interviewed managers talk about 'playing the part' of a manager, of controlling their feelings by 'biting their lips', and of finding ways to avoid confrontations and 'explosions'. Some managers talk about the importance of being seen as a supportive and compassionate person who has time to listen to others. They understand that showing care can have positive results. Nevertheless, according to one manager in the Watson and Harris study, although a good deed is an effective management action, 'that's not why you do it'. However, another manager questions whether supportive and caring acts are 'verging on the manipulative'.

It is of interest that standard definitions of care include both a burdened state of mind as well as assistance or treatment to someone in need. Thus, in caring for subordinates, a manager carries an emotional burden. In his study of care and compassion, Solomon (1998) writes that caring may bring out negative behaviours in managers as well as supporting and nurturing behaviours. In Hill's study (2003), managers said that taking disciplinary action is emotionally difficult because they realize the power they have over other lives. One manager in the Watson and Harris (1999: 174) study explained how she felt when she had to dismiss a person: 'I just felt like a bad person. But I wasn't. I was making a management decision for the best of the company. But as a person, I felt lousy for days'. Another manager in the same study talked about the difficulty of dealing with staff involved in personal crises and tragedies such as family illnesses and death. To this list, based on my findings, we may add relationship break-ups and child custody arrangements.

CONCLUSIONS

Tronto (1993: 157) writes:

> Care is a central but devalued aspect of human life. To care well involves engagement
> in an ethical practice of complex moral judgement. Because our society does not notice
> the importance of care and the moral quality of its practice, we devalue the work and
> contributions of women and disempowered groups who care in this society.

Although Tronto's statement refers to the particular framework of the ethics of
care, it is also appropriate to the findings of this research. Managers, like the R&D
managers of this study, who care about employees are also devalued. Although the
study's participants said managers were expected to show care, they expressed
doubt about the world's view of its importance. In general, researchers and the
media do not devote a great deal of attention to caring leaders.

Yet, as the findings of this study indicate, the exercise of care by managers in
R&D settings is a central element of their managerial behaviour. In addition to
being a genuine expression of concern for others, such care can be an effective
managerial tactic. Care, expressed by listening to and chatting with subordinates,
may influence others by the social processes of reciprocation, liking, and authority
(Cialdini, 2001). However, managers' authority implies the performance of certain
duties that are influenced by their subordinates' expectations. Because these duties
are not completely in the managers' control, their performance may become
burdensome. Care, for the manager, means accepting this emotional burden by
taking responsibility for subordinates.

In its close-up examination of R&D managers and their subordinates, this study
also highlights the emotional nature of managerial work that Fineman (2003) asks
managers to acknowledge and take into account. Like other managers, R&D
managers cannot leave their feelings at the gate when they enter the workplace.
Thus, R&D managers who lead knowledge workers have to cope with their own
and others' emotions in the workplace. By recognizing the need to exercise care
for subordinates, managers, and newly appointed managers in particular, may be
less surprised by the *burdens of managing and thus better prepared to bear them.*

SUGGESTIONS FOR FUTURE RESEARCH

This study suggests several future research areas. First, the study reaffirms the
usefulness of Mintzberg's original formulation (1973) of structured observation as
a flexible method where categories may be developed during and after observations. This research approach responds to Barley and Kunda's call (2001) for a
more solid empirical foundation, acquired through field studies, for organization
and management theories. Additional field studies may define yet more categories
of managerial activities.

Second, although the concept of care was developed in knowledge management
literature (see von Krogh, 1998; von Krogh et al., 2000), it is possible that
managers in R&D and other knowledge-intensive firms may offer more support
to personnel than managers in other types of organizations. For example, in

project organizations such as construction companies, the managers may focus more on fixing problems than supporting employees (see Styhre, this book, Chapter 7). In this regard, it seems that the R&D managers' attention towards their employees is more similar to that of the health care managers (see Arman et al., this book, Chapter 6). Thus, there is a need to examine whether managerial care is influenced or limited by industry sector.

Third, it is also possible that the burden of care is greater for managers who manage non-managerial employees instead of other managers. As both Watson and Harris (1999) and Hill (2003) noted, inexperienced and newly promoted managers, as first-line managers, are usually placed in charge of their former peers. Thus, there is a need for researchers to examine the extent of managerial care for non-managerial employees. Such research focus may link the MWB approach with more general organizational theory.

APPENDIX: INDIVIDUAL MANAGERS' VALUES

Table 8A.1 Total working hours

	Manager A1	Manager A2	Manager B1	Manager B2
1. Scheduled meetings (%)	32	29	22	36
2. Unscheduled meetings (%)	13	19	23	9
3. Tours (%)	7	3	3	3
4. Telephone calls (%)	7	9	9	6
5. Desk work (%)	29	15	20	21
6. Transportation (%)	5	19	16	20
7. Observer interaction and personal (%)	7	6	8	5
Sum of activities	*44.4*	*48.9*	*54.6*	*55.1*
Total working time per participant	*44.4*	*44.5*	*47.7*	*54.2*

Table 8A.2 Participants in verbal contact

	Manager A1	Manager A2	Manager B1	Manager B2
1. Subordinates (%)	33	78	51	90
2. Superiors (%)	21	8	36	0
3. Peers (%)	41	9	27	3
4. Others from other organizations (%)	27	40	42	26
5. Client, supplier, associate (%)	0	0	0	9
6. Independent and others (%)	12	2	10	0
7. Unknown (%)	5	0	1	1
Sum (%)	*139*	*138*	*167*	*130*

Table 8A.3 Purpose of verbal contact

	Manager A1	Manager A2	Manager B1	Manager B2
1–4. *Total secondary work* (%)	6	5	1	7
5–8. *Requests and solicitations* (%)	36	67	66	79
9–13. *Total informational* (%)	92	84	104	119
14–15. *Total decision-making* (%)	0	4	21	26
16. Care (%)	11	17	21	12
17. Resource allocation (%)	1	4	9	6
18. Unknown (%)	3	1	2	2
Sum (%)	148	181	224	251
Total time in verbal contact	26.0	29.2	30.9	30.1

REFERENCES

Alvesson, M. (1995). *Management of Knowledge-Intensive Companies*. Berlin: de Gruyter.
——Sveningsson, S. (2003). Managers doing leadership: The extra-ordinarization of the mundane. *Human Relations*, 56(12): 1435–59.

Ashforth, B. E. and Humphrey, R. H. (1995). Emotion in the workplace: A reappraisal. *Human Relations*, 48(2): 97–125.

Barley, S. R. and Kunda, G. (2001). Bringing work back in. *Organization Science*, 12(1): 76–95.

Barnard, C. I. (1938). *The Functions of the Executive*. Cambridge, MA: Harvard University Press.

Bass, B. M. and Avolio, B. J. (1990). Developing transformational leadership: 1992 and beyond. *Journal of European Industrial Training*, 14(5): 21–7.

Bryman, A. (2008). *Social Research Methods* (3rd ed.). Oxford: Oxford University Press.

Burns, J. M. (1978). *Leadership*. New York: Harper & Row Publishers.

Burns, T. (1954). The directions of activity and communication in a departmental executive group: A quantitative study in a British engineering factory with a self-recording technique. *Human Relations*, 7(1): 73–97.

——(1957). Management in action. *Operational Research Quarterly*, 8(2): 45–60.

——Stalker, G. M. (1961). *The Management of Innovation*. London: Tavistock Publications.

Cialdini, R. B. (2001). *Influence: Science and Practice* (4th ed.). Boston, MA: Allyn and Bacon.

Clegg, S. R. (1989). *Frameworks of Power*. London: Sage Publications.

Czarniawska, B. (2007). *Shadowing and Other Techniques for Doing Fieldwork in Modern Societies*. Malmö/Copenhagen/Oslo: Liber/CBS Press/Universitetsforlaget.

Dasborough, M. T. (2006). Cognitive asymmetry in employee emotional reactions to leadership behaviors. *The Leadership Quarterly*, 17(2): 163–78.

——Ashkanasy, N. M. (2002). Emotion and attribution of intentionality in leader-member relationships. *The Leadership Quarterly*, 13(5): 615–34.

Drucker, P. F. (1988). The coming of the new organization. *Harvard Business Review*, 66(1): 45–53.

Elkins, T. and Keller, R. T. (2003). Leadership in research and development organizations: A literature review and conceptual framework. *The Leadership Quarterly*, 14(4–5): 587–606.

Fineman, S. (2000). Emotional arenas revisited. In S. Fineman (Ed.), *Emotion in Organizations* (2nd ed., pp. 1–24). London: Sage Publications.

——(2003). *Understanding Emotion at Work*. London: Sage.

Fleishman, E. A. (1953). The description of supervisory behaviour. *Journal of Applied Psychology*, 37(1): 1–6.

Gabriel, Y. (2009). Latte capitalism and late capitalism: Reflection on fantasy and care as part of the service triangle. In C. MacDonald and M. Korczynski (Eds.), *Service Work: Critical Perspectives*. London: Routledge.

George, J. M. (2000). Emotions and leadership: The role of emotional intelligence. *Human Relations*, 53(8): 1027–55.

Gilligan, C. (1982). *In a Different Voice: Psychological Theory and Women's Development*. London: Harvard University Press.

Guest, R. H. (1956). Of time and the foreman. *Personnel*, 32(6): 478–86.

Hales, C. (1986). What do managers do? A critical review of the evidence. *Journal of Management Studies*, 23(1): 88–115.

——(1999). Why do managers do what they do? Reconciling evidence and theory in accounts of managerial work. *British Journal of Management*, 10(4): 335–50.

——Mustapha, N. (2000). Commonalities and variations in managerial work: A study of middle managers in Malaysia. *Asia Pacific Journal of Human Resources*, 38(1): 1–25.

Hatfield, E., Cacioppo, J. T., and Rapson, R. L. (1993). Emotional contagion. *Current Directions in Psychological Science*, 2(3): 96–9.

Held, V. (2006). *The Ethics of Care: Personal, Political, and Global*. Oxford: Oxford University Press.

Hill, L. A. (2003). *Becoming a Manager: How New Managers Master the Challenges of Leadership*. Boston, MA: Harvard Business School Press.

Horne, J. H. and Lupton, T. (1965). The work activities of 'middle' managers – An exploratory study. *Journal of Management Studies*, 2(1): 14–33.

Kittay, E. F. and Feder, E. K. (2002). *The Subject of Care: Feminist Perspectives on Dependency*. Lanham, MD: Rowman & Littlefield.

Kunda, G. (1992). *Engineering Culture. Control and Commitment in a High-Tech Corporation*. Philadelphia, PA: Temple University Press.

Kurke, L. B. and Aldrich, H. E. (1983). Mintzberg was right! A replication and extension of the nature of managerial work. *Management Science*, 29(8): 975–84.

Martinko, M. J. and Gardner, W. L. (1985). Beyond structured observation: Methodological issues and new directions. *The Academy of Management Review*, 10(4): 676–95.

——— (1990). Structured observation of managerial work: A replication and synthesis. *The Journal of Management Studies*, 27(3): 329–57.

Mayerhoff, M. (1971). *On Caring*. New York: Harper and Row.

McAuley, J. L., Duberley, J., and Cohen, L. (2000). The meaning professionals give to management . . . and strategy. *Human Relations*, 53(1): 87–116.

McDonald, S. (2005). Studying action in context: A qualitative shadowing method for organizational research. *Qualitative Research*, 5(4): 455–73.

Meindl, J. R., Ehrlich, S. B., and Dukerich, J. M. (1985). The romance of leadership. *Administrative Science Quarterly*, 30(1): 78–102.

Mintzberg, H. (1973). *The Nature of Managerial Work*. New York: Harper & Row Publishers.

——(1975). The manager's job: Folklore and fact. *Harvard Business Review*, 53(4): 49–61.

——(1998). Covert leadership: Notes on managing professionals. Knowledge workers respond to inspiration, not supervision. *Harvard Business Review*, 76(6): 140–7.

Mumford, M. D., Scott, G. M., Gaddis, B., and Strange, J. M. (2002). Leading creative people: Orchestrating expertise and relationships. *The Leadership Quarterly*, 13(6): 705–50.

Noordegraaf, M. and Stewart, R. (2000). Managerial behaviour research in private and public sectors: Distinctiveness, disputes and directions. *Journal of Management Studies*, 37(3): 427–43.

Oldham, G. R. and Cummings, A. (1996). Employee creativity: Personal and contextual factors at work. *Academy of Management Journal*, 39(3): 607–34.

Oliver, A. L. and Montgomery, K. (2000). Creating a hybrid organizational form from parental blueprints: The emergence and evolution of knowledge firms. *Human Relations*, 53(1): 33–56.

Pavett, C. M. and Lau, A. W. (1985). A comparative analysis of research and development managerial jobs across two sectors. *Journal of Management Studies*, 22(1): 69–82.

Selznick, P. (1957). *Leadership in Administration: A Sociological Interpretation*. New York: Harper & Row.

Solomon, R. C. (1998). The moral psychology of business: Care and compassion in the corporation. *Business Ethics Quarterly*, 8(3): 515–33.

Stewart, R. (1976). *Contrasts in Management*. Maidenhead: McGraw-Hill Book Company.

——(1982). *Choices for the Manager*. Englewood Cliffs, NJ: Prentice-Hall.

——(2008). A tougher world: Managerial work and behaviour. In S. Dopson, M. J. Earl, and P. Snow (Eds.), *Mapping the Management Journey: Practice, Theory, and Context* (pp. 49–62). New York: Oxford University Press.

——Barsoux, J.-L., Kieser, A., Ganter, H.-D., and Walgenbach, P. (1994). *Managing in Britain and Germany*. Basingstoke: Palgrave.

Stogdill, R. M. (1950). Leadership, membership and organization. *Psychological Bulletin*, 47(1): 1–14.

Tengblad, S. (2006). Is there a 'new managerial work'? A comparison with Henry Mintzberg's classic study 30 years later. *The Journal of Management Studies*, 43: 1437–61.

Tronto, J. C. (1993). *Moral Boundaries: A Political Argument for an Ethic of Care*. New York: Routledge.

Vie, O. E. (2009). *Shadowing Managers Engaged in Care: Discovering the Emotional Nature of Managerial Work*. Norwegian University of Science and Technology, Faculty of Social Science and Technology Management, Department of Industrial Economics and Technology Management, Trondheim.

——(2010). Have post-bureaucratic changes occurred in managerial work? *European Management Journal*, 28(3): 182–94.

von Krogh, G. (1998). Care in knowledge creation. *California Management Review*, 40(3): 133–53.

——Ichijo, K. and Nonaka, I. (2000). *Enabling Knowledge Creation. How to Unlock the Mystery of Tacit Knowledge and Release the Power of Innovation*. New York: Oxford University Press.

Watson, T. J. (1994/2001). *In Search of Management: Culture, Chaos and Control in Managerial Work* (Rev. ed.). London: Thomson Learning.

——Harris, P. (1999). *The Emergent Manager*. London, Thousand Oaks, CA: Sage Publications.

Weber, M. (1922/78). *Economy and Society: An Outline of Interpretive Sociology*. Berkeley, CA: University of California Press.

Yukl, G. (2002). *Leadership in Organizations* (5th ed.). Upper Saddle River, NJ: Prentice-Hall.

Part IV

Administrative managerial work

The four chapters of Part Four present managerial work at the senior and executive level. While the word administrative is used somewhat pejoratively these days, when managers are assumed to be leaders, it is still the best descriptor of this kind of managerial work. In everyday managerial work, there is almost a countless number of administrative tasks – scheduled meetings, routines, and, most important, information exchanges. However, owing to the sheer complexity of the work and the constant need for information exchange and adjustments, there is much less opportunity to act as transformative leaders or strategic decision-makers.

The first two chapters examine managerial work in the municipal sector, while the third and fourth chapters concern university managers and CEOs of large and medium-sized companies, respectively.

CHAPTER 9. MANAGERS AT THE MUNICIPAL TOP

Anna Cregård and Rolf Solli describe their research on the work of senior managers in Swedish municipalities (which usually have between 1,000 and 10,000 employees). They describe the special conditions that exist in this and other public sector areas, including the powerful influence of elected politicians on various municipal issues. Municipal managers/directors appear to yield power to the politicians who are the face of municipal government. Yet in such complex organizations, decision-making has a ritualistic character, and the leading managers have important ceremonial roles. As the head of administration, the municipality manager/director can be seen as the rubber band that holds the organization together.

CHAPTER 10. THE SWEDISH MUNICIPALITY DIRECTOR: A MANAGERIAL FUNCTION BETWEEN POLITICS AND ADMINISTRATION

Leif Jonsson reports on the work of the municipality director. In the main section of the chapter, he describes the work of nine directors, using their four-week diaries as his empirical data (much like Carlson's methodology in his CEO study of sixty years ago). The results of his study show that the directors work on average more than sixty hours a week at a large number of different activities. Decision-making is not one of the time-consuming activities. The chapter also discusses the importance of *anchoring* managerial work. This concept refers to the way managers gain acceptance for new ideas and thus overcome the *inertia* of the existing order.

CHAPTER 11. LEADERS OF MODERN UNIVERSITIES: *PRIMI INTER PARES* OR CHIEF EXECUTIVE OFFICERS?

Lars Engwall and Carin Eriksson Lindvall study the university managerial environment where new ideas about effective management challenge both leadership and collegial traditions. One focus of their research is the department level where management, which was once part-time work for scholars, has become increasingly professionalized. A second focus is the vice-chancellor level where the authors show that strategic planning is perceived by the vice-chancellors themselves as a more important task than the ceremonies and representation that occupy a huge proportion of their working time.

CHAPTER 12. MANAGERIAL WORK AT THE TOP: TRACING CHANGES IN WORK PRACTICES AND EFFORTS TOWARDS THEORY DEVELOPMENT

Stefan Tengblad presents his study of managerial work at the executive level that makes comparisons with the studies by Carlson (1951) and Mintzberg (1973). The chief executives in Tengblad's study experience less task fragmentation in their work, but as they travel more, their workspace has become more fragmented. These executives also work in a more decentralized way and typically are not much involved in functional issues like production, purchasing, and product development. As a response to the increasing focus on profitability and share prices, they are more involved in financial issues. Much time is spent on setting and meeting market expectations and maintaining good relationships with the actors related to the financial markets.

9

Managers at the municipal top

Anna Cregård and Rolf Solli

POINT OF DEPARTURE

How do senior managers in large organizations manage? This is a key question in management in both private and public organizations. Management strategies, management problems, and management actions are important factors in the consideration of management and leadership, for example, in a municipality. This chapter deals with management and leadership in local, public organizations.

High-ranking municipal employees are far too absent from the research despite their interesting proximity to political representatives and despite their key roles in the management of performance (Mouritzen and Svara, 2002). This chapter focuses on the employees who have the most contact with the political leadership, namely municipal directors, department managers, and finance managers. These are the top municipal employees who lead and manage the work in public administration. In the Nordic countries, they play a highly influential role in political decisions by preparing issues, giving advice, and implementing decisions. The municipal director's role is to manage the public employees in the central office – and sometimes the department managers as well. Municipal directors generally have the ears and trust of top politicians. This is also the case for the department managers as far as their 'own' politicians; therefore, they are also important actors in daily municipal operations. The finance managers, who play a key role in managing and interpreting financial information, have the ears of both politicians and department managers, although not to the same extent.

In this chapter, we ask the following question: What is typical of municipal top managers' management? To answer the question, we have conducted many studies on what managers do, how they do it, and why they do it. Our conclusions are particularly relevant since much of the management literature concerns private sector management and because the municipal sector still tends to implement management philosophies and reforms that are based on, and designed for, private sector corporations (Czarniawska and Solli, 2001).

Researchers have often tried to answer this simple question about management content and style (e.g. Stewart, 1967; Mintzberg, 1973; Kotter, 1982; Carlson et al., 1991). All have shown that it is difficult to describe such work. In a still relevant article reviewing the research on managers' actions, Hales (1986) asserts that very little research has actually investigated the effects and effectiveness of these actions from the point of view of the organizations.

Managerial work in the public sector is perhaps particularly complex. The demand for transparent communications and democratic decision-making clearly complicates the management context. Kellerman (2004) writes that the context has great significance since it determines the nature of the leadership that can be implemented. The context also influences the manager's position as well as the prospects of effecting organizational management. In municipal organizations, politics influence management in many ways. Managers who are not politically appointed have to adapt to their organization's democratic structure, which means, among other things, that high-ranking municipal employees are responsible for ensuring that the political will is implemented and that fundamental democratic principles – such as freedom of speech and the press, majority rule, and equality before the law – are respected. Consequently, the classic leadership literature may not always apply to managers in municipalities and county councils. Accordingly, in addition to this literature, in this chapter we also refer to the literature on managership in the public sector.

However, effective leadership requires more than a favourable context. Kellerman (2004) points out that, in addition to a leader in a particular context, leadership also requires followers. Without followers, there is no leader.

> The human animal resembles the baboon. We, too, have typically deferred to males whose strength and capacity to lead ostensibly have been proven. Still, there is no leadership without followership. Leaders *cannot* lead unless followers follow, passively or actively. (Kellerman, 2004: xiv)

This fundamental principle of leadership manifests itself in leaders' relationships with their followers. We translate and expand Kellerman's concept of followers by empirically viewing them as contacts. We make this translation and expansion for four reasons. First, the contact concept allows us to discuss other employees, who are not primary followers, as contacts. The employee concept is linked to the idea of formal managership in which employees are not required to be favourably disposed towards the manager. Second, the contact concept facilitates a discussion of other contacts (e.g. other managers) that are essential in the leadership of municipal and county council organizations. Third, the contact concept allows us to discuss the formal aspects of management since the follower concept generally places too much emphasis on the informal aspects of managership (important as they are in many organizations). Among these formal aspects, we include formal decision channels, the formal allocation of responsibility, and the formal division between politics and administration. Fourth, the contact concept accords well with an inspiration for this chapter – Kotter's concept (1982) of managerial work as four principal activities that link contacts and strategies in a relevant way. These four activities are: creating contacts, building an agenda, using the contacts, and implementing the agenda. Like the followers in Kotter's concept, the contacts are fundamental to managers' work and thereby to organizational management. In short, we examine how managers, using their contacts, implement the agendas that are broadly set by politicians.

It is not surprising that implementation of an agenda will differ among managers. Kotter believes that the more effective a leader, the greater the arsenal of strategies for managing the organization:

> 'Excellent' performers ask, encourage, cajole, praise, reward, demand, manipulate, and generally motivate others with great skill in face-to-face situations. They also rely more heavily on indirect influence than the 'good' managers, who tend to rely on a more narrow range of influence techniques and apply them with less finesse. (Kotter, 1982: 163)

In addition, since municipal managers have different expectations and different scopes for action, there are differences in how they manage. As a result, there is considerable variety in the descriptions of municipal directors, finance managers, and department managers.

In the following section, we briefly review the theories that inspire our work and also discuss the context that shapes management conditions. Following this section, we present our empirical research. We describe the municipal top managers' contacts and strategies in relation to three top management positions (municipal director, finance manager, and department manager). Our principal case is the municipal director; we describe the finance manager and department manager in terms of their similarities and differences. We follow these descriptions with an analysis of the typical characteristics of these top managers' management.

CLASSICAL THEORIES AND CONTEXT

In a famous article, Mintzberg (1975) suggests that much of the knowledge on management is unreflective and unsystematic and must be regarded as folklore. As examples, he gives four statements that contradict this management folklore. These contradictions focus on, among other things, the high pace of management, the lack of reflection, the preference for verbal communication, and the action orientation emphasis. He identifies ten management roles that can be classified into three categories: interpersonal roles (that are based on the formal authority of the manager), informational roles (that arise from the manager's many contacts), and decisional roles (that are interrelated with the information and formal authority in the other two categories). Of course, *how* these ten roles are performed depends on what is possible and relevant in the organization under consideration – that is, the management context. Here, we argue that four areas must be considered in the discussion of the typicality of management in the municipal sector: the domain structure, the objective-means dilemma, the political structure, and the professional features of many of the occupational groups. Next we discuss these four areas.

Handling several domains

A typical characteristic of the public sector is that several groups have a management function. At least three domains can be distinguished (Kouzes and Mico,

1979): the political, the administrative, and the professional domains. In the political domain, the fundamental principle is the consent of the citizens. Justice is the measure of success, which is achieved by arguing, voting, and negotiating (Wrenne, 1997). In the administrative domain, the fundamental principle is the hierarchy of management. Efficiency is the measure of success, which is achieved through a structure based on routines (i.e. the bureaucracy). The instruments for the work are large and complex systems (e.g. finance systems and quality management systems). In the professional domain, where services and sometimes goods are produced, the fundamental principle is autonomy, which is achieved by disengagement from other domains, both vertically and horizontally, and by a structure dependent on colleagues and client orientation. Quality, the measure of success, is measured by professional standards. However, quality is sometimes under challenge from the administrative (financial) domain, particularly by the reform ideas of New Public Management (Hood, 1991) and, in a Swedish framework, by the discussion of private alternatives (Almqvist, 2004).

One recent legislative trend is to require government cooperation with local, interested parties. An example is the European water framework directive that requires authorities in EU member countries to give citizens real influence in water management (Lundqvist et al., 2004). This trend of cooperation suggests the creation of a new citizen domain in public sector management that is in addition to the domain of elected officials. There is more evidence of this trend in political life where governance models with more direct democratic elements challenge or supplement the system of representative democracy. One such example is participatory budgets where citizens are invited to offer advice or to make decisions on such matters as planning issues (Allegretti and Herzberg, 2004). User councils in education, childcare, and health care are other examples.

Given the complexity of this context, management of communications is probably never easy. Many studies describe the difficulties managers encounter when they try to achieve communication coordination in organizations given this domain structure. Exerting influence may depend on the conflicting ways of looking at the organizational aims and goals. The difficulties in communication also mean that reaching a collective goal formulation is a challenging task, sometimes an impossible one. Managers' efforts to lead or manage often result in power struggles among the various domains.

Objective–means dilemma

Formulating an objective for an operation means identifying the achievement desired (Drucker, 1954). However, it can be difficult to formulate that objective. In addition, in practice, when conditions change, it may be unclear whether the original objectives are still valid (Rombach, 1991). The principle of enterprise is based on earning money (Taylor, 1911), generally through the conduct of some activity. The objective is financial gain, while the operations are the means used to achieve this objective. In principle, it does not matter what the activity is so long as it generates money. Since success is measured by profits, otherwise useful activities may be set aside in favour of more profitable ones. These indicators may be important sources of information for the manager, even if such information only confirms what the managers think they already know. Hard profits may also legitimize the operations, and, of course, the manager.

Financial budgets set limitations on public operations. In themselves, budgets can be extremely powerful. It is not advisable to continue operations for any prolonged period outside such financial limitations. Large and unexpected budgetary overruns can easily result in the replacement of managers (Wildavsky, 1975; Brunsson and Rombach, 1982; Cregård, 2004). However, other operational effects, not meeting financial budgets, are the objectives in the context of municipality management. While budgets are used to achieve certain results, management techniques that prioritize financial results are not necessarily always right for the public sector or for the manager. The logic of relevant indicators for the evaluation of leadership is naturally different if the nature of the objectives differs (Buck, 1983; Cohen, 1993). We suggest that success indicators in public operations should be the activity's usefulness, given its financial limitations. That is a big difference.

Is it important to managers if the accounting system cannot deliver information on the relevant goals of an organization? Such systems provide managers with hard figures on financial results, but not on goals. First, managers must distinguish between two kinds of information: the financial results and the operational goals. Then it is important to evaluate this information in combination. Second, management of subordinates requires non-financial control, perhaps informal control. This explains why we find many non-financial controls in the public sector (Czarniawska and Solli, 2001) even if such methods are not always successful (Solli et al., 2005).

Politics comes first

The most important feature of political organizations such as municipalities and county councils is that they are management bodies founded on the principle of representative democracy. There are many possible systems for political organizations. In their analysis of a political organization, Brunsson and Jönsson (1979) constructed a refined image of its characteristics. One type of political organization is a parliamentary or representative democracy where the ruling party or parties select the management. These managers sometimes have different opinions than the politicians, which may create difficulties for non-political managers.

As discussed above, political management is also complicated by the trend in which management forms, other than the traditional forms of representative democracy, influence public organizations. However, even in the traditional forms, the political influence on municipal organizations means there are clear implications for administrative management. In Mintzberg's terms (1975), one might say that politicians, in substance, take the decisional roles, especially in perhaps the most important of all governing decisions, the allocation of resources. This means that upper level managers in some respects have fewer decision-making opportunities. Furthermore, these decisions are made in a highly transparent environment since the entire process, before, during, and after, is open to public scrutiny. For managers, this transparent process is a consideration when they act in their informational roles.

Professional in most cases

Groups with strong professional traits populate the public sector. These groups are used to having extensive scope for action and a high degree of discretionary power (Cregård, 2000). These professional traits are particularly evident in education, health care, and some social services. It is difficult to evaluate the professional employees who work in these large-scale and resource-intensive activities. Their work cannot be simply routinized or measured; consequently, such professionals are generally given considerable work autonomy. There are also activities where the professional contributions are so essential that managers struggle to control the professionals (Cregård, 2007). In some cases, the professionals even control the managers. Thus, in most professional activities implemented by management, the interaction among the politicians, managers, and the professionals is characterized by the professionals' influence at both the general policy level and at the everyday, routine level. Of course, this situation may create difficulty in fulfilling Mintzberg's interpersonal roles, especially the leadership role.

Summary of the context: Always complex

An examination of the organizational context surrounding a high-ranking manager in municipal operations produces a picture of a managerial position that, by comparison with many other managerial positions, is very complex. A public sector manager has to handle paradoxical values and expectations (Czarniawska, 1992). Such management issues may be difficult or at least problematic. The size and variety of its activities make the municipal organization difficult to control and coordinate; the domains' different outlooks create communication issues; the objective-means dilemma and budgetary links make it difficult to measure and evaluate operations; among other things, politics gets in the way of consensus building; and substantial professionalization increases the autonomy of employees at the lowest level in the managerial hierarchy. Large, hard-to-measure operations involving players who are very different and who have difficulty understanding one another are not easy to manage. This is particularly true when many employees resist being managed, or, at least, resist being managed by their organization's managers. What, then, is typical for the high-ranking municipal managers? How do they handle their context as they try to fulfil their management roles?

In the next section, we present our empirical findings. We begin by introducing the municipal sector in Sweden and our research methodology. We then describe the managers' contacts that show the interrelationship between the three management categories of the research. We continue with a presentation of the municipal director's role, followed by comments on the roles of the finance manager and the department managers.

MANAGEMENT BY SWEDISH HIGH-RANKING MUNICIPAL MANAGERS

In Sweden, there are 290 well-established and independent municipalities called *kommuner*, a word that comes from the Latin *communis* and may be translated as *mutual*. The municipalities vary in size – the smallest has 2,516 inhabitants and the largest has 810,120 inhabitants. On average, a municipality has 32,000 inhabitants, about 2,500 employees, and a turnover of close to 2 billion SEK (around 280 million USD at average 2009 conversion rates). The municipal sector is characterized by strong self-government, which means the municipal council has autonomous decision-making authority in areas such as social services, roads and water, school and preschool, and eldercare. The Swedish Local Government Act regulates municipal activities, which are financed by local taxes, government grants, and fees. The Swedish Constitution mandates the municipalities' right of taxation. Since the municipalities are very important governance organizations with significant responsibilities, they require complex management systems with competent managers.

Methodology

Our empirical data are extensive. Within the framework of the entire project, we used several data collection techniques (see e.g. Hales, 1986). We studied municipal directors in three nationwide surveys (1995, 2000, and 2005) and in two interview series (1994 and 2003). We studied finance managers in similar nationwide surveys (1997, 2004, and 2009) and in two interviews series (1998 and 2006). We studied department managers (education directors) in a nationwide survey (2007), in an interview series with associated diary notes (1995), and in another interview series followed by shadowing (1999 and 2000). We interviewed the managers in one municipality twice, with a year between the interviews. In total, our data include approximately seventy 'in-depth' interviews and eight national surveys with close to 440,000 answers and observations. As these different research techniques naturally provided different types of data, we have different findings from them. Therefore, we present the managers' management styles and strategies from various perspectives.

The managers' contacts

As explained above, contacts are a requirement for the implementation of leadership. To introduce our empirical data, in Table 9.1 we tally the average frequency of contacts that managing directors, finance managers, and department managers have with other individuals and groups.

As the contact patterns reveal, leaders meet leaders, and they do so rather often. It may also be noteworthy that the municipal director meets the finance manager more often than the finance manager meets the municipal director. In the interview material, we see the opposite result: when the municipal directors

Table 9.1 High-ranking municipal managers and their contacts

	MDir	FinM	DeptM
Chairman of the municipal executive board	1.25	2.07	3.40
Opposition leader	2.48	3.36	3.82
Other politicians in the municipality	2.76	3.46	3.61
FinM	1.51		2.91
MDir		1.61	2.53
Other department managers	1.83	2.28	2.55
Other employees	1.87	1.81	1.98
Citizens	2.47	3.77	2.62
Journalists	3.34	3.94	3.45

Question: *How often do you communicate in normal circumstances (verbal communication, including meetings, phone calls, etc.) with the following persons/groups?*
1 = Daily, 2 = 2–4 times per week, 3 = once a week, 4 = 1–3 times per month, 5 = seldom/never.

name the attendees at a specific meeting, the finance manager is rarely mentioned, even if present. The municipal directors explain this omission by stating that the finance manager's presence is taken for granted. The fact that the municipal directors and finance managers meet department managers more often than the directors of education (department managers) meet the former is explained by the number of department managers – a typical municipality may have as many as ten department managers.

Excluding consideration of the politicians and the other employees, it is quite clear that the municipal director, the finance manager, and the department managers manage the municipalities. In the next section, we describe the management strategies used by each of the three groups. However, while we emphasize that the participation of both part-time and full-time politicians is a managerial requirement in municipal and county council operations, in this chapter our focus is on the high-ranking managers.

The municipal director

To outsiders, it appears that a municipal director has a complex work life of one meeting immediately after another. At each meeting, the director must be prepared to offer an opinion on issues discussed. This requires preparation outside office hours. For less experienced directors, this preparation takes place the evening before the next meeting(s).

In reality, the municipal director's work life may not be so complex. The same issues are discussed again and again in a repeated sequence of informal meetings and formal meetings. The municipal director is usually involved at all decision-making stages, and there is little that surprises him (or her, although in Sweden the municipal directors are usually male). This is how Tyrstrup (1993) describes the work of business executives and how Balle Hansen (1995) describes the work of Danish municipal directors. Tyrstrup compares this work to playing simultaneous games of chess: the municipal director plays multiple games at a time with a number of other players. One game may even influence another as decisions in meetings are combined.

It is typical that some meetings on any given day are quite routine. These may be meetings with employees, a department manager, several department managers, the working committee of the municipal executive board, the municipal council, a regional body, or some other individual or group. A schedule of two or three meetings per day or even twenty meetings per week is entirely normal. Such meetings, which are unavoidable and take up most of the director's daytime work hours, may range from less than an hour to the full day. Because of the number of meetings they attend, it is difficult to contact municipal directors. Most municipal directors are aware of this access problem but have no good solution for it.

In general terms, municipal directors say some meetings involve contacts external to the municipality. They describe these meetings as demanding because they are out of the ordinary and therefore require considerable planning and work. For example, a municipal visit by the Swedish King takes a lot of resources.

The aims of the meetings are naturally variable. It is the responsibility of the municipal director to chair the meetings so that the meetings are productive and focused on the agenda issues.

Others in the municipal organization are aware of the municipal director's close contacts and responsibility for tracking issues on numerous levels. The ability to anticipate the outcome of an issue increases with experience. One municipal director stated:

> The HR manager comes to me very often and asks what we can do. I know immediately, I think. It's very much about intuition, to be sure. You learn to say what is possible and what is not possible.

Anticipating the outcome of an issue means being able to sense the decision-makers' attitudes on other issues in order to adapt them to the current issue under discussion. This is an acquired and necessary skill; without it, a municipal director will not last in the position. Experience is an asset. One municipal director commented:

> If you have experience, you don't run into the wall or make a blunder. You sound things out tactically, inform, go back and get a feel for things. How are we doing? Can we proceed? What are the consequences? . . . And so you thrash things out.

If the community is dissatisfied in some way with services provided, or not provided, this dissatisfaction is frequently channelled to the municipal director who represents the municipality. If an angry citizen, for example, the chairman of the trade association, can not reach the chairman of the municipal executive board, the municipal director will do just as well. Sometimes action by the municipal director is required. In special cases, the required action means correcting the worst of the 'foolish ideas' coming from the municipal-governing structure. If it is possible to salvage an issue by taking rational rather than irrational action, it is the municipal director's job to take this step. However, such action must be performed in a 'nice way'.

The municipal director's main task therefore is dealing with issues in a steady stream of meetings. Since success in resolving issues amicably depends primarily on the directors' ability to mediate between differing views, they must be skilled in balancing the many viewpoints and the many personalities that make up munici-pal government.

One interpretation, which is hardly revolutionary, of the municipal director's work is that there is a pattern in the contact network. Some players appear more often in the municipal director's diary than others. For example, the municipal director meets prominent politicians, department managers, and various work colleagues frequently; they take the majority of the municipal director's time and energy.

The municipal director often meets with politicians. In particular, the munici-pal director meets with the municipal commissioners. These meetings, which may be formal or informal, frequently occur daily. The municipal director also travels with the commissioners to courses and conferences. Such close contact allows the director to have discussions with the 'heavyweight' politicians, one-on-one. Such contact gives the municipal director a position of power beyond the formal job description. In a private discussion, a municipal director can speak openly in order to convince politicians of what must be done or not done. Such influence, however, is exerted in private because a municipal director must appear loyal and impartial in public. It is not productive, or wise, to take a point of view that conflicts with views held by the local politicians; the municipal director can never emerge 'victorious' in such conflicts.

The municipal director understands that the politicians ultimately decide on the actions the municipality will take. The municipal director's responsibility is to ensure that matters are handled through an appropriate process and that the politicians are supplied with the right information at the right time. An additional task for the municipal director is to protect the organization from the unpredict-ability of politics. A municipal director stated:

> If we come into political conflict about a matter, it undoubtedly makes the work situation so much more difficult for the others. My task is to be able to send out clear signals for the operations on various matters. And if we then have an issue where the politicians are strongly divided, and where perhaps half of the politicians think this and the other half think that, then it makes it difficult to send out those clear signals.

Therefore, it is essential for the municipal director to achieve a balance between politics and management. In these meetings with politicians, which are numerous and frequent, experiences and ideas change 'owners' so quickly that it may be unclear who thought what and when. A municipal director is responsible for warning and guiding politicians in such instances.

It is also important to remember that the relationship between the municipal director and the politicians is not fixed. The blurred boundary between them is continually changing. A show of respect by the director to the politicians need not be troublesome (see Norell, 1989); this respect may simply be a matter of showing sensitivity to what politicians want, even if it is not always visible. There is no need for drama. Even a strong municipal director can work with strong politicians. According to one municipal director:

> You work together so much that you become real friends. You know that the other has a slight headache today, so I am the one to ask permission to speak and say this. You work well together.

Another municipal director expressed the strategy as follows:

> When it comes to major issues that you feel are beginning to go wrong, you need to seize them and try to put them right again. It may be time for reconsideration of something you feel has gone awry, when the politician is not assuming her or his role. You can, as it were, ask the commission chairman 'How do you want this? Do I need to worry about this?' You may speak psychologically by asking, 'You'll fix this, won't you? Have you been in contact at all?' That's getting hold of these things. Not everything is announced in a committee meeting. In this way you build up a confidence bank, and then politicians sometimes come and say 'What on earth are the others doing?' You are almost on your way to becoming a politician yourself. Sometimes you feel that, and then it is very difficult to maintain this neutral, civil servant role in this job. You have so much contact with politicians. You acquire so much information, some of which you can't pass on because it's so political.

The municipal directors say they should not push issues too hard. If they do, such issues may then 'come to a standstill' and nothing will happen. Over the years, municipal directors learn to take a more hardened view of the politicians. One municipal director observed:

> When I was new to the game, I tried to push my ideas more than I do now. I put forward proposals for reorganization. You may easily be rapped over the knuckles for such things.

In the following comments, a municipal director described the ideal process of the work:

> As the first stage of this matter we were able to explain the problem to the politicians and to get them to accept the solution. And then we had to get them to accept that the solution required a certain number of tasks, which we described to them. Our department managers have now outlined the tasks to a political management group. We are now doing an analysis of how the various tasks are being accomplished. That is what we will begin with, at this conference, by getting our politicians to agree to this analysis of these problems and how the operations will work in the future. In this way, we have come to accept certain things. We state that we don't accept this, that we want something else. And thus we approach a final picture of the organization in this way.

The ideal process is therefore based on rational decision-making – from problem identification to evaluation to decision. One important strategy is to narrow the number of alternatives. In this way, the outcome of the issue is more predictable.

The municipal director must be able to sense where the politics are heading. Consequently, the work is made more difficult when a problem is endlessly discussed and finally left unresolved when no political will is evident. In such cases, the director cannot possibly guess what course the matter will take.

The municipal commissioners' authority in relation to the municipal executive board and the municipal director is probably more complicated when a municipality is increasing in size. For example, one such municipality in our study had problems determining who was in charge and who made the decisions. Complications also arise when politicians make decisions informally without adopting them formally. Municipal commissioners may reach an agreement on 'applicable steps' at a coffee break or on a trip. When the municipal executive board then makes a decision with a different approach, people are surprised and disconcerted by the ambiguity in the decision-making process.

Relationships with leading politicians vary, depending on the prevailing culture. Most municipal directors think others do not have the same 'skeletons in the closet' they have. In one extreme situation, the municipal director worked in a municipality that does not really like managers. In this culture, the politicians make the decisions. As a result, the municipal director's relationship with the politicians was influenced by feelings of job insecurity.

The municipal director's formal relationships with department managers also vary, depending on the culture. In some communities, there is a clear link between the municipal director and the department managers. In the organization chart, this semi-formal, matrix relationship is in addition to the 'line' relationship. We found this informal connection consistently in all organizations in our study.

A municipal director has a responsibility to the department managers. They meet at formal meetings (e.g. the municipal executive board) and in other venues (e.g. internal conferences and temporary work groups). One municipal director described the relationship as follows:

> Well . . . I am *primus inter pares*. [first among equals]. You will no doubt hear that from other interviewees as well. That is how department managers see us. It is actually up to you individually to make sure that you have the respect and confidence of your department managers when you take on this role.

In a number of municipalities in our research, the municipal director was trying to remove an administration manager (Cregård and Solli, 1999). However, we also found municipal directors who were working to improve department managers' skills and to recruit others. One municipal director stated:

> One change, which is perhaps one of the issues I have pursued most, is boosting the department managers by trying quite simply to give them some muscle.

Municipal directors often 'use' the department managers to advance an agenda issue. Frequently, however, the opposite occurs. In individual meetings with the municipal director, department managers have the opportunity to influence the municipal director.

The internal conflict in the municipality between politics and action is reflected most clearly in the relationship between municipal management and administrative management. In this potential centre of conflict, taking a neutral position may sometimes be impossible. One prudent municipal director always takes the political side. 'It is better to be on bad terms with ten department managers than one municipal executive board', he stated. The implicit message is, unlike conflicts with an administrative manager, a municipal director can never win a dispute with the municipal executive board.

For most issues, the finance manager and the HR manager side with the municipal director. A problem arises when the employees do not act as expected, and then the municipal director has to get involved.

> By and large, I wrote the entire activity plan after listening to people on the staff who contributed some wording and so on. Then we went forward with the plan that the council, in the main, subsequently adopted. This year, as early as spring, I had an idea

that we should take further steps and work even more to improve the activity plan and try to make it a living target document.

With this strategy of seizing an issue, the municipal director is able to break new ground as well as show the employees the plans for the future. If employees are still puzzled, the municipal director can always raise the issue later.

Although it may sometimes be necessary to intervene in the employees' work, such action by municipal directors is not typical. For the most part, a municipal director trusts the employees and gives them freedom to work independently. The relationship between the municipal director and the employees is normally a trusting one.

The finance manager

Finance managers attend scheduled meetings – typically ten to twenty meetings per week of one to four hours each. The contacts in these meetings fall into the categories of politicians, the municipal director, administration managers, employees, colleagues, and others. We discuss these contacts next.

The finance managers meet with the following politicians: the municipal commissioners, the municipal executive board's working committees, and the municipal executive boards. Sometimes they also meet committee chairpersons. In general, they do not meet with part-time politicians. Although the finance managers have a relatively problem-free relationship with the politicians, they do have opinions on the politicians' activities. Their relationship is based on an unspoken but a clear allocation of responsibility. It is inconceivable that the finance managers would protest decisions made by the politicians. However, it is the task of the finance managers to make sure that financial issues are raised before decisions are taken. One finance manager commented:

> You don't protest against political decisions, but you have a responsibility to ensure that data is available before decisions are made. And that discussion then follows. That is what I am responsible for. At any rate, I think that municipal employees should not protest against political decisions after they are made. That is not their job, not at all.

One strategy a finance manager may use in dealing with politicians is to provide documentation, written and verbal, in any context where financial issues are applicable. Once finance managers have made the financial arguments, they have no responsibility to take further action.

A second strategy is to ask questions – the listener strategy (see Brunsson and Jönsson, 1979; Solli, 1988). This strategy allows the finance manager to test what is acceptable to the politicians and to see what they will take responsibility for.

A third strategy is the 'nagging strategy'. In this strategy, the finance manager repeats an idea or opinion that refers to a political decision. One common financial target is that the operation's costs must not exceed a certain proportion of the tax revenue. If such a financial target exists, the finance manager feels comfortable with mentioning it at every possible opportunity.

Finance managers may take certain liberties with politicians (e.g. by criticizing the political decision-making) so long as they do so privately. Offering public criticism in the media is a foolish action.

Finance managers need to achieve a balance in their work between establishing the financial facts and acquiring the politicians' trust (i.e. access to decision-makers' thinking). Such balance is acquired by experience. The price, if there is a price, for achieving this balance is keeping the conflict within the organization. Inward financial order is balanced against outward political neutrality.

There are primarily two occasions where the finance manager meets the department managers. They meet where general information passing to and from the municipal executive board is discussed. In these meetings, the finance manager is on an equal footing with the department managers. The second occasion is often linked to a project that the finance manager and a particular department manager are working on. The employees involved in these meetings are the person in charge of the budget, the person in charge of accounting issues, and sometimes an IT manager. In small communities, not all these positions exist; in that case, the finance manager assumes the missing role.

The finance managers frequently involve their closest colleagues. There is much exchange of information related to both past and future meetings. In principle, information meetings for either the finance office staff or its management team are held every week.

In our interviews, we noted the many telephone calls and e-mails the finance managers receive. Many of these communications are from journalists, consultants, local federations, and researchers. According to the finance managers, they are happy to meet with some of these people, others less so (e.g. journalists), and others not at all (e.g. consultants). The consultants want to sell their services to the communities, and the finance managers have no interest in dealing with such company representatives. Finally, it may be noted that finance managers rarely deal with citizens directly. Occasionally, they respond to a citizen telephone complaint about a municipal bill, but this is a rarity.

The department manager

The department managers say they have numerous contacts that provide resource assistance with their tasks. One department manager stated:

> There's a lot of discussion and an enormous amount of dialogue. Loads of contacts. From morning to evening.

In general, their contact patterns are similar to those of the municipal directors. One difference is that the employees may require even more of the department managers' time. In our interviews, some department managers said that, compared to the municipal director, they have relatively few external contacts. Most contacts are internal – contacts with people in the municipality as well as in administration offices. Much of their time is devoted to the work of their office that thus constitutes an important contact network. The other internal contacts – those in the municipality – are often spontaneously arranged. However, the department managers often schedule simultaneous meetings with numerous internal players since this promotes efficient dissemination of information.

All department managers emphasize that information management is an important task. One department manager stated:

> The most essential thing is to clarify the information system, for example, to the board of education. That is my most important duty – to provide the board of education with important decision-making data. I do that best, not by sitting here and brooding, but by being out in the organization and working and securing support as much as possible.

The department managers believe direct contact with employees is necessary for the management of employees' performance. They believe that good performance requires strong financial resources, good facilities, clear objectives, managerial support, and department unity. Thus, the department managers maintain close contact with their management teams and office staffs in order to provide this work environment. An education department manager believes it is a duty to ensure that everyone works towards the same objective of providing good education services, although achieving this unity of purpose is not always easy. This manager explains that the education sector has a long tradition of head teachers managing their areas independently, without any interference except that of the government. This situation makes it hard to lead and to establish the legitimacy of the management position.

The department managers use various strategies to manage their operations. Persuasion is one such strategy that one department manager described as follows:

> Nagging . . . I try to convince and persuade when I present data as I see it.

A second strategy is to delegate responsibility to employees for a project or issue while still overseeing its implementation or analysis. A third strategy is pre-announcement in which the department managers ask others to prepare for an upcoming project or issue. They use this strategy particularly in instances where, owing to the work required, it is essential to be prepared in advance or when they wish to secure support for future matters. Pre-announcement, which requires the department manager to have information that others do not, requires time and contacts. A fourth strategy, which is also very time-consuming, is 'proceduralization'. In this strategy, the department manager, with other employees, gradually works up an issue or a project over a prolonged period. Because of the time required and the many meetings involved, agreements are gradually reached. Therefore, proceduralization is most useful when a matter is controversial or complex. Like pre-announcement, proceduralization can be used outside the formal decision process so that no decisions are formally made until the matter reaches a formal arena. The department managers' position and extensive contact networks give them a fifth strategy known as dissemination. In this strategy, the department manager uses contacts to ensure that as many people as possible are informed about different projects, events, and issues in order to gain support for the decisions made by the politicians.

MANAGEMENT THROUGH ROLES

In this section, we examine the work of the high-ranking municipal managers of this study using Mintzberg's categories (1975) of interpersonal roles, informational roles, and decisional roles.

Interpersonal roles

This study of high-ranking municipal managers shows that they rely on extensive internal and external contact networks. In their external networks, for example, municipal directors meet other municipal directors, finance managers meet other finance managers, and department managers (especially education directors) meet other department managers through their professional associations. Of the three groups, the municipal directors have the most external contacts. In addition, contacts with politicians link the municipality with various parts of the political system. External contacts with citizens, users, and voters are also important (Bäck et al., 2006). The municipality is, of course, not a closed organization.

Mintzberg (1975) describes two interpersonal roles that he calls the figurehead role and the liaison role. The municipal managers, especially the municipal directors, take the figurehead role when they attend ceremonial activities where it is understood that the politicians will take the lead roles. In the liaison role, the municipal managers maintain more contacts with people outside the vertical chain of command than with their superiors. Nevertheless, since the vertical chain of command is crucial in municipal management, these liaison contacts are not the major work of the municipal managers. For the most part, the politicians take the liaison role. Thus, the municipal managers know to stay in the background in both their figurehead and liaison roles. Experienced managers know where the boundary between politics and administration lies; thus they are careful not to overstep that sensitive, and often blurred, boundary. Managers in this study who were too aggressive when they first assumed their jobs soon learned caution. Any manager who crosses the line between politics and administration will not last (Cregård, 2004).

Another interpersonal role that Mintzberg describes is the leader role. In this study, we found that the leader role is transformed, although differently, in all three managerial categories. The municipal directors describe themselves as *primus inter pares*, implying a somewhat vaguely defined relationship with the department managers and the finance managers. In formal, hierarchical terms, the municipal directors often act as equals, but in reality they hold a superior management position that is based more on trust than formal authority. The department managers, on the other hand, despite their formal authority over their subordinates, still find the leader role difficult. To achieve leadership legitimacy, they use various subtle strategies to influence their subordinates. The finance managers are more process leaders (e.g. in the allocation of resources and in accounting issues), and thus they establish their leader role through creating an environment of mutual respect with other employees and other managers.

Informational roles

Three informational roles are evident in municipality management: the monitor role, the disseminator role, and the spokesman role. Each role emphasizes the importance of promoting information flow through the use of contacts at different levels and in separate areas. Although the informational roles are important for the managers of this study, the organizational structure places specific demands on them with regard to their performance. Management in municipal administration involves networks of various contacts. Municipal directors, finance managers, and department managers are commonly in networks where administrative logic is the basis of the network patterns. In such networks, they are the principal players. The characteristics of these networks are efficiency, economy, and hierarchy. However, this administrative network is inextricable from the political network and from the professional network, each of which has its own logic. The top municipal managers, by providing information to these different networks, link the networks.

A common practice among the managers of this study is that they often work on issues or projects over a lengthy period of time. During this time frame, there are many meetings in and between the various networks, and matters are advanced by providing data, focusing on topics, nagging others, and using the strategy of proceduralization. The managers' tasks at these meetings are to present information to and between the networks, to determine possible development of issues, and to shift perceptions. It is delicate work since the managers cannot appear to promote an issue or project based on their own authority. The finance managers address this task by presenting a constant supply of financial numbers and considerations and by reminding others of financial limitations. The department managers involve their employees in the issues and projects. Both the municipal directors and the finance managers ask questions, listen to politicians (as well as others), and seek approval for their recommendations. In this way, the high-ranking municipal managers, who are at the centre of the interconnected networks, empower others – politicians and professionals – to perform their duties. As a result, the tasks of proposing initiatives and approving measures are widely spread among the networks.

Decisional roles

Municipal managers have fairly small interest in political theory. This lack of interest seems to be associated with the fact that municipal managers are not politicians but rather civil servants who must act apolitically in the performance of their activities (see Hagström, 1990). This means, for example, that municipal managers must perform their decisional roles in a special way. Mintzberg (1975) describes four decisional roles: the entrepreneur, the disturbance handler, the resource allocator, and the negotiator. In a municipality, the managers influence the decision-making process although they take no responsibility for decisions. Politicians are the primary decision-makers. (It may be noted that there are differences of opinion on what constitutes a decision; often the expected extent of a decision's impact is relevant.) Nevertheless, even though managers must refer decision issues to the politicians, they are still important in the decisional process. Their role is to facilitate the decision-making and to implement the decisions once made. Consequently, managers who do not make decisions in the way politicians do, still negotiate, handle unforeseen problems, and allocate resources, just as an entrepreneur would.

Our study shows that the municipal managers act respectfully towards the politicians in their communities and take care not to cross the line between political and administrative responsibilities. They are not politicians, but rather political players (see Högberg, 2002). Respect for the political system – towards democracy, as a whole – means that any top municipal manager has to act within limits that are different from those that top managers in other sectors face. Politics can be unpredictable, and the outcome of any issue or project is never certain. However, since the politicians take responsibility for decisions, top municipal managers have the opportunity to function out of the public eye. This position makes them clever tacticians who have enough flexibility to deal with municipal problems in knowledgeable and appropriate ways.

CONCLUDING DISCUSSION

Earlier in this chapter we referenced both Mintzberg (1975) and Kotter (1982) as possible sources of conceptual frameworks for this study of municipal management. However, we learned that the municipal manager holds a sensitive position, caught between politics and professionalism in the middle of an administrative logic that makes fulfilment of managerial roles in some ways different from Mintzberg's general description. In Kotter's analysis (1982), the typicality of management action means the development and implementation of an agenda are complex. However, Kotter offers no insight into the complex act required to balance politics with administration, to balance the logics of networks, or to balance the roles of entrepreneur and implementer. Therefore, we need additional concepts if we are to understand management in municipalities. Hales's criticism (1986) of the leadership research as too general seems to apply specifically to such organizations. Descriptions of top municipal managers' leadership must take into account the complex networks of contacts, the controlling position of politics, and the focus on dealing with municipal issues on a daily basis.

In this concluding section, we develop four partially overlapping themes that are applicable to the work of municipal managers: invisible and visible, multi-logic and contact-rich, ceremonial and informal, and ritually objective.

Invisible and visible

In Mintzberg's descriptions (1973) of the manager's role, the role of the figurehead is featured. In this role, managers act as representatives for their organizations, in particular at public events that have a considerable amount of symbolism. However, in this role, municipal managers appear rather anonymous and invisible

(Klausen and Magnier, 1998; Solli, 1999; Mouritzen and Svara, 2002). The implication is that such managers should be careful not to take too visible a role. Visibility should rest with the leading politicians (Brunsson and Jönsson, 1979). To some extent, we agree with this observation, but at the same time we take a more nuanced view of the municipal manager's role.

The assumption of responsibility by leading politicians gives them prominent visibility, but that does not preclude some attention falling on others. Since media representatives always want data and have short processing times (Solli, 1999), it is necessary that municipal managers always be prepared to answer questions on brief notice. They are the visible substitutes in the Swedish model of the division of labour between politicians and civil servants. Substitutes must also be prepared: changed, warmed-up, and ready to play.

Within the organization, the situation is different. When municipal directors describe themselves as first among equals, they are admitting to their visibility. All leading civil servants have this role in some sense, particularly when the politicians are absent. Municipal leadership, in such situations, is little different from leadership in the private sector.

Multi-logic and contact-rich

All leaders, including top municipal managers, attend meetings and act through networks. One interesting hypothesis is that the factor that most distinguishes municipal managers from other leaders is that they move both within and between domains (Kouzes and Mico, 1979) with different logics. Their job requires the ability to manage the transitions between these domains and to act appropriately in each domain. This means, for example, that top municipal managers have to speak the language of their own domain fluently, in both administrative and financial contexts (for development of this idea, see Rombach and Berglun, 2005). Yet they also need to understand and express themselves sufficiently well in the languages of the other domains (e.g. political language and professional language(s)). Otherwise, they risk not being taken seriously or risk being perceived as ill informed if they misuse words and terms in the different domains. However, facility in a language requires using the logic of its domain, not merely its words and terms. Capable managers learn the shades of meaning in the words they use. Such managers also understand why an issue that in financial or administrative terms seems neutral may appear positive in the political domain and negative in the professional domain. Thus, an important task for managers is to talk about issues using the language appropriate to the situation. Since municipal organizations have multi-logics that require managers to act multi-logically, accordingly this differentiated action contributes to increased cohesion and unity in the organizations. Metaphorically, the top municipal manager is the rubber band that holds the domains together.

Ceremonial and informal

Managers' meetings involve many and varied issues. Their work is both divided and full (see Mintzberg, 1973). Many issues are discussed over long periods of time, in different meetings, and at very different levels of clarity. As a result, such issues are also handled in informal arenas, before or in parallel with the formal arenas. Once an issue reaches the formal arena, the most important politicians are usually well informed about it since the managers have discussed it with them in numerous meetings. The politicians already know what the next step should be. Thus, many formal meetings take on the character of an arena for ceremonial decision-making.

Both the informal and the formal processes are essential. The informal process facilitates processing of the issue, where possibilities, problems, and potential solutions can be shaped by experts and the specially initiated (see Bartholdsson's description (2009) of the role of civil servants). This does not mean that the political element is missing, but rather that the 'heavyweight' politicians are consulted informally in private. This process allows the issue to be shaped and refined in a relaxed context. The manager's role in this informal process is thus to ensure that the issue moves forward, to involve individuals at the right time, and to maintain contact at the political level. The formal process, where the ceremonial decision-making takes place, constitutes an important reference point for an organization based on democratic values. In the context of formal meetings, the arguments are highly visible. This ceremonial decision-making has several implications: first, it shows that politicians take responsibility for the continuation and consequences of the issue; second, it signals to the managers (and others in the organization) that complaints of various kinds imply questioning of political decisions.

Ritually objective

The actions of high-ranking municipal managers reflect their objective attitude towards municipal issues (Lundquist, 1993; Blom, 1994). This objectivity contrasts with the subjectivity of politicians with their biased opinions. This idea of the objective civil servant is linked with the bureaucratic idea of the subjective public official (Bartholdsson, 2009). We do not know that much about the role of the elected public official since that role is a government device (Czarniawska-Joerges, 1986; Lundquist, 1998) and has a fairly different line of development from that of the municipal manager. The latter is more a clone of the early trustee role than a new entity derived from a legally based set of rules and regulations aimed at, among other things, separating politics and administration.

The municipal manager's role may be described as one coloured by *objective leadership*. It could be argued that such a conclusion is a paradox, and it is. It is impossible to lead and at the same time base your actions on objective facts. However, the myth of objectivity is essential in management. If municipal managers were perceived as subjective, they would be less effective. Others would study the political ideology the manager supported; if that ideology were found unsatisfactory, there would be indecision and even open conflict in the work. We are convinced that people know that the municipal managers are no less subjective than other people. However, in ritually based situations, people accept the myth of objectivity. Here, we are dealing with municipal managers whose management is based in ritually objective leadership.

The role of the municipal manager is, in other words, not completely straightforward. If these managers accomplish something, there is a risk they will be charged with being manipulative. If they accomplish nothing, there is a risk they will lose the confidence of those in the work environment. Typically, municipal managers must work within a framework of asymmetrical dialogue with ambiguous positions. In municipal top managers' management, asymmetry is widespread, making leadership complicated.

REFERENCES

Allegretti, G. and Herzberg, C. (2004). *Participatory Budgets in Europe: Between Efficiency and Growing Local Democracy*. TNI briefing series 2004/5.

Almqvist, R. M. (2004). *Icons of New Public Management: Four Studies on Competition, Contracts and Control*. Stockholm: School of Business Företagsekonomiska Institutionen.

Balle Hansen, M. (1995). Kommundirektørens roller i den kommunale organisation. *Kommunalpolitiske studier*, No. 7/1995, Odense Universitet.

Bartholdsson, K. (2009). *Hållbarhetens mänskliga byggstenar: Om betydelsen av engagerade tjänstemän i det lokala miljömålsarbetet*. Göteborg: Förvaltningshögskolan, Göteborgs Universitet.

Blom, A. P. (1994). *Kommunalt chefskap: En studie om ansvar, ledarskap och demokrati*. Lund: Dialogos.

Brunsson, N. and Jönsson, S. A. (1979). *Beslut och handling: Om politikers inflytande på politiken [Decisions and Action. About Politicians' Influence on Politics]*. Stockholm: LiberFörlag.

—— Rombach, B. (1982). *Går det att spara? Kommunal budgetering under stagnation*. Bodafors: Doxa.

Bäck, H., Heinelt, H. et al. (Eds.) (2006). *The European Mayor – Political Leaders in the Changing Context of Local Democracy*. Wiesbaden: VS Verlag für Sozialwissenschaften.

Buck, L. S. (1983). Executive evaluation – assessing the probability for success in the job. *Review of Public Personnel Administration*, 3(3): 63–72.

Carlson, S., Mintzberg, H. et al. (1991). *Executive Behaviour*. Uppsala, Stockholm University: Almqvist & Wiksell – International distributör.

Cohen, S. A. (1993). Defining and measuring effectiveness in public management. *Public Productivity & Management Review*, 17(1): 45–57.

Cregård, A. (2000). *Förvaltningschefers styrning: En studie av praktik och representation i skolans värld*. Göteborg: Centrum för forskning om offentlig sektor (CEFOS) Univ.

—— (2004). Abruption – Uppsägning som översättning och improvisation. KFi-rapport nr 71. Göteborg, Kommunforskning i Västsverige (KFi).

—— (2007). Att styra sin chef: disciplinering från centrum till periferi, *Demokratisk och effektiv styrning*. Siverbo, S., Lund: Studentlitteratur.

—— Solli, R. (1999). Framgångsrik och turbulent: En studie av en kommuns utmärkande egenskaper till vardags och under stress. *KFi-rapport, 51*. Göteborg: Kommunforskning i Västsverige (KFi): 74.

Czarniawska-Joerges, B. (1986). Förvaltningschefer – Politiker eller ledare? In N. Brunsson (Ed.), *Politik och ekonomi*. Lund: Doxa.

—— (1992). *Styrningens paradoxer: Scener ur den offentliga verksamheten*. Stockholm: Norstedts juridikförl.

—— Solli, R. (2001). Big city as a societal laboratory. In B. Czarniawska and R. Solli (Eds.), *Organizing Metropolitan Space and Discourse* (pp. 7–14). Malmö, Oslo: Liber.

Drucker, P. F. (1954). *The Practice of Management*. New York: Harper & Row.

Hagström, B. (1990). *Chef i offentlig verksamhet: forskning kring offentligt ledarskap*. Lund: Studentlitteratur.

Hales, C. P. (1986). What do managers do? A critical review of the evidence. *Journal of Management Studies*, 23(1): 88–115.

Hood, C. (1991). A public management for all seasons? *Public Administration*, 69(1): 3–19.

Högberg, Ö. (2002). *Kommunchefers tidsanvändning: en studie om kommunchefers funktioner och roller*. Linköping: Univ. Ekonomiska Institutionen.

Kellerman, B. (2004). *Bad Leadership: What it is, How it Happens, Why it Matters*. Boston: Harvard Business School Press.

Klausen, K. K. and Magnier, A. (1998). *The Anonymous Leader: Appointed CEOs in Western Local Government*. Odense: Odense University Press.

Kotter, J. P. (1982). What effective general managers really do. *Harvard Business Review*, 60: 156–67.

Kouzes, J. M. and Mico, P. R. (1979). Domain theory: An introduction to organizational behavior in human service organizations. *Journal of Applied Behavioral Science*, 15(4): 449–69.

Lundquist, L. (1993). *Ämbetsman eller direktör?: Förvaltningschefen i demokratin*. Stockholm, Norstedts juridik: Fritze distributör.

—— (1998). *Demokratins väktare: ämbetsmännen och vårt offentliga etos*. Lund: Studentlitteratur.

—— Jonsson, A., Galaz, V., Löwgren, M., and Olsson, J. A. (2004). Hållbar vattenförvaltning organisering, deltagande, inflytande, ekonomi. Rapport 5, VASTRA.

Mintzberg, H. (1973). *The Nature of Managerial Work*. New York: Harper & Row.

—— (1975). The manager's job: Folklore and fact. *Harvard Business Review* (July–August): 49–61.

Mouritzen, P. E. and Svara, J. H. (2002). *Leadership at the Apex: Politicians and Administrators in Western Local Governments*. Pittsburgh: University of Pittsburgh Press.

Norell, P.-O. (1989). *De kommunala administratörerna: en studie av politiska aktörer och byråkratiproblematik*. Lund: Studentlitteratur.

Rombach, B. (1991). *Det går inte att styra med mål!: En bok om varför den offentliga sektorns organisationer inte kan målstyras [Objective-based Management is not Possible! A Book about Why Objective-based Management cannot be Applied to Organisations in the Public Sector]*. Lund: Studentlitteratur.

—— Berglun, J. (2005). *Den framgångsrika ekonomiskan*. Stockholm: Santérus.

Solli, R. (1988). *Decentralisering i kommuner: Om politik och administration på lokal nivå*. Lund: Studentlitteratur.

—— (1999). *Lågmäld styrning: Perspektiv på kommunala ekonomers yrkesroll*. Stockholm, Studieförb. Näringsliv och samhälle.

—— Demediuk, P. et al. (2005). The namesake – On best value and other reform marks. In B. Czarniawska and G. Sevón (Eds.), *How Ideas, Objects and Practices Travel in the Global Economy*. Malmö, Köpenhamn: Liber.

Stewart, R. (1967). *Managers and Their Jobs: A Study of the Similarities and Differences in the Ways Managers Spend Their Time*. London: Macmillan.

Taylor, F. W. (1911). *The Principles of Scientific Management [Electronic resource]*. New York: Harper & Row.

Tyrstrup, M. (1993). *Företagsledares arbete: en longitudinell studie av arbetet i en företagsledning.* Stockholm: Ekonomiska forskningsinstitutet vid Handelshögsk (EFI).

Wildavsky, A. (1975). *Budgeting: A Comparative Theory of Budgetary Processes.* Boston: Little Brown and Co.

Wrenne, P. (1997). *Kontakter och förankring: en studie av kommunstyrelsens ordförande.* Göteborg: Centrum för forskning om offentlig sektor (CEFOS) Univ.

10

The Swedish Municipality Director: A managerial function between politics and administration

Leif Jonsson[1]

INTRODUCTION

The Swedish Municipality Director (sometimes also called the City Manager, and referred to in this chapter as the MD) is an appointed public official in charge of managing a municipality. The function, which exists in close relation to the elected politicians of the municipality, can be regarded as the highest civil servant function in the municipalities. The MD's function is to manage a public sector organization that may employ a few hundred people in small municipalities or more than 10,000 in large ones. The MD function requires its holder to be in contact with a broad area of the Swedish welfare system since the municipalities are responsible for several social service activities including eldercare, childcare, and much of the education system. The MD function[2] can be seen as a link between the political system and the administrative operations in Swedish municipalities (Källström and Solli, 1997). This chapter describes and analyses that function based on evidence from four studies that were conducted during a ten-year span (1999–2009). The discussion of this chapter focuses on this managerial function that is regarded as a link between politics and administration.

Researchers have sometimes argued that politically governed organizations differ from other types of organizations since in the former conflicts are a natural part of daily life (see e.g. Brunsson and Jönsson, 1979; Brunsson, 2002). Sometimes this difference is not given importance based on the argument that conflict-filled interests exist in politically governed organizations as well as in private ones (Christensen et al., 2005). In this chapter, the difference is highlighted since the focus is on a managerial function that is regarded as a linking function and since the chapter is built on four studies that had the same starting point – that municipalities are organizations that operate under different conditions than private companies. The main argument is that municipalities are governed by politics where there are two governing systems – one managed by politicians and one by public officials. These two types of governing actors are recruited through different proceedings and, as a consequence, have different conditions for their mandates. Politicians are elected based on the conditions of trust, and take their mandates from these prerequisites. Public officials, on the other hand, are employed by politicians, and receive their commissions based on the missions they are given.

The situation in which municipalities are controlled both politically and administratively can be understood by the fact that there are two kinds of institutions within municipality management. Brunsson (2002) calls these institutions 'The Political Organization' and 'The Firm'. The institutions differ from each other since they are based on different sets of rules, which in turn are founded in different ideas. The institutions can also be regarded as representing two types of logics: a political logic dealing with conflicts of interests and an administrative logic creating unity of action (Jonsson, 2008: 542).

Swedish municipalities are politically controlled by long tradition and are regulated by law. However, public officials who manage Swedish municipalities are not legally regulated. Regulation by law was discussed in the last revision of the municipality law (1992), but the legislators chose not to take action. The argument was that cooperation between political and administrative management should build on trust between the politicians and the public officials. Another way to express this statement is that the legislators left it to each local municipality to organize and regulate the cooperation between political and administrative control.

There are several reasons to study the MD function, beginning with the fact that the function is unregulated. A second reason is the fact that this management function, unlike management functions in the private sector, links the political realm with administrative operations. A third reason is the lack of articulated knowledge of the function as a link between political and administrative control.

There are two commonalities in the four studies that this chapter reports on. First, the studies share a common purpose of seeking to understand the MD function. Second, while the four studies use different methodologies, each study depends to a high degree on the same empirical foundation. Each study seeks to understand this managerial function in Sweden, especially as it links the political and administrative spheres. The studies can be regarded as a process of searching for understanding of this particular managerial function, especially its link between politics and administration in municipalities. The described process concerns what was found and how our understanding increased. The chapter concludes with a discussion on how this increased understanding was related to the methodologies and theoretical approaches used.

FINDINGS FROM THE FOUR MUNICIPALITY DIRECTOR STUDIES

Study 1: Understanding contents in the Municipality Director function

Since there is a lack of knowledge on the MD function, the purpose of Study 1, which began in 1999 and ended in 2002 (Jonsson et al., 2002), was to explore the contents of the MD function as it exists in municipalities of different sizes. All MDs in the study participated actively in generating concepts and descriptions of the function. We chose this methodological approach ('interactive knowledge building') in order to obtain the MDs' tacit knowledge of the function we believed they held (Jonsson, 2001). We also used empirically oriented management theories from the tradition of 'Managerial Work'.[3] The commonality among these theories is that each tries to describe the work of managers.

There are two principal findings from Study 1. The first result was a terminology for the MD function that may take place in four different contexts – a political context, an administrative context, an external context, and an individual context. The second result was a specific terminology used to describe the activities in each context.

This way of describing the MD function in terms of its location and the activities it performs was combined with ideas about the diverse missions of the municipalities in order to categorize local constructions of the MD function. This analysis showed the following so-called MD profiles:

- *The society builder* focuses primarily on long-term issues of societal development – often related to infrastructure issues. The work is performed primarily in external arenas.
- *The service manager/the professional administrator* focuses on education, health care, eldercare, and other municipal services. The work is typically performed in administrative arenas.
- *The local democrat* focuses on issues related to the workings of democratic government. The work is often performed in political arenas.
- *The official* focuses on the legality of political issues. The work is performed in both political and administrative arenas.
- *The strategic manager* works in a broad alignment to manage the municipality holistically. The work is performed in political and administrative arenas, as well as in external arenas.
- *The democratic society builder* focuses on the municipality mission of acting as a society builder in a democratic institution. The work is performed in the political arena, as well as in external arenas.

Although we found differences in the configurations related to the depictions of the MDs in their daily work lives, most MDs appeared to fit the profile of the 'service manager/professional administrator'. Using their statements as a starting point, we then searched the literature for studies related to the function of the MD. In summary, the literature commonly makes the following observations about this function:

- The MD function works in an overall position to manage all areas of activity in the municipality.
- The MD function has a political as well as an all-embracing administrative aspect that represents different kinds of rationality.
- The responsibility associated with the MD function, as specified by the appointing commission, is rarely clear.

- The municipal executive committee defines the MD function and specifies the extent of its power.
- The MD function is substantially communicative in nature.

These elements are common to the MD function at the end of the 1990s and the beginning of the 2000s. There are, of course, elements that differentiate how the function looks in one municipality from how it looks in another. This is expressed by the configurations presented above.

Study 2: Understanding the use of time in the Municipality Director function

In Study 2, which began in 1999 and ended in 2002, the terminology developed from Study 1 was used to explore how MDs allocate their time in their various work contexts and among their various activities (Högberg, 2002). This part of our research was inspired by Sune Carlson's classic study (1951) of how Chief Executive Officers spend their time. The study also focused on the various forms of communication that MDs use.

For the design, a combination of MDs' written diaries, direct observations of MDs' daily work, and interviews with the MDs were used. Nine MDs were asked to keep diaries for a four-week period in which they noted all activities that lasted more than five minutes. The diaries resulted in 1,835 diary sheets with notations of 3,532 activities, covering 1,935 hours (193 days, consisting of 170 work days and 23 weekend days, with no distinction between Saturdays and Sundays). During a four-month period, direct observations were made of the MDs for one to two days each, using shadowing. The purpose of the observations and shadowing (about 100 hours in total) was to see how the MDs used their time: what they did, whom they met, what they said, and where they were. The diaries and observations were compiled individually for each MD. In individual interviews, they were asked for their comments on this data in order to make additions if needed. This data was then compiled on an aggregate level for all nine MDs and presented to them with the results at a seminar.

The study reveals that MDs work a lot. See Table 10.1 for a breakdown of their working hours by weekday, weekend, and week. Since the diaries and observations show that most lunch hours are lunch meetings, the weekday hours and week hours in Table 10.1 include the lunch hours.

Why do the MDs work these long hours? Their response was that they have to use overtime hours if they want to work alone in the office; regular work hours are for meetings, networking, presentations, etc. One MD commented: 'You don't mind. It is expected that you will work these long hours'. Another MD said: 'If you are at the office, you are always hunted'. Most MDs said, however, that they control their working time and that they 'change hour for hour' as the opportunity occurs.

Where do the MDs work? For this study, a fifth context was added to the four contexts identified in Study 1. The new area is 'Other' – for travel time, work at home, or work at lunch. See Table 10.2 for the allocation of MDs' work time among these various work contexts.

Table 10.1 MDs' working hours

Work time	Mean (h)	Max (h)	Min (h)	Med (h)
Hours/weekday	10.8	11.8	9.2	10.8
Hours/weekend	4.7	11	0	1.9
Hours/week	63.1	81.2	46	60

Table 10.2 MD's time allocated by contexts

Context	Mean (%)	Max (%)	Min (%)	Med (%)
Political context	16	26	9	16
Administrative context	25	43	8	24
External context	14	36	5	8
Individual context	23	45	7	21
Other	20	43	8	14
Undefined	2	3	0	0
Total	*100*			

The MDs thought the *political context* (mean 16 per cent) figure was surprisingly low. They assumed they spent much more time on political matters. They explained the low political context percentage by the fact that political policy relates to nearly everything they do, and thus the 16 per cent figure was not really representative.

The MDs explained the *administrative context* (mean 25 per cent) figure as the time spent creating a homogeneous, administrative organization and in collecting information for political decisions. In addition, they said the administrative context figure included the time spent working through other persons.

The MDs explained the *external context* (mean 14 per cent) figure – which seems rather low – as the time spent working with politicians. For such work, specialists from the different departments are the main contacts with the politicians, not the MDs. Nevertheless, despite the MDs' wish to spend more time on external work, they said this is not always possible due to the necessity of creating a homogeneous, administrative organization.

The MDs thought the *individual context* (mean 23 per cent) figure was reasonable. However, they expressed a desire to spend even more time in this context. They said that they do not have enough time for their own work because the everyday work is so demanding with its many different activities. This observation is confirmed by the figures on the division of activities in the MDs' workday. It is rare that a MD can spend more than ten minutes on individual tasks without interruption.

What MDs do in these contexts? See Table 10.3 for the allocation of time among activities.

Table 10.3 lists a number of activities. The list is the result of the discussions with the MDs involved in both Studies 1 and 2. The activity list describes the work they preferred.

Table 10.3 MDs' time allocated by activities

Activity	Mean (%)	Max (%)	Min (%)	Med (%)
Disseminating information	12	29	4	9
Collecting information	16	36	5	15
Handling/working with information	5	10	1	4
Personal development	2	4	0	1
Distributing tasks	3	6	1	2
Making decisions	2	6	0	2
Carrying out decisions	1	2	0	0
Receiving others' decisions	1	4	0	1
Confirming others' decisions	1	2	0	0
Directing meetings	1	4	0	1
Acting as an representative for the employer	3	7	0	2
Private activity	2	3	0	2
Supervising matters	3	10	0	1
Presenting matters	2	7	0	2
Handling/managing matters	5	18	1	3
Representing the municipality	8	21	1	6
Controlling/supervising and following-up	2	6	0	1
Watching over municipal interests	2	9	0	1
Creating and maintaining relationships	8	17	3	6
Acting as a bridge between the political majority and the opposition	1	2	0	0
Acting as a bridge between municipal board and administration	1	5	0	0
Individual writing	4	16	0	1
Exchanging experiences	4	20	0	2
Negotiating	0	1	0	0
Undefined, other	11	27	2	11
Total	*100*			

As shown in Table 10.3, the MDs use the majority of their time handling information in different ways. Their major activities are *disseminating* and *collecting information*. The MDs also spend a good proportion of their time *representing the municipality* and in *creating and maintaining relationships*. Curiously, given their managerial role, it is also clear that the MDs generally do not think of themselves as managers who make or even execute decisions. An explanation may be that they think the politicians make the decisions and the lower-level managers and specialists carry out the decisions.

Lastly, how do MDs communicate? See Table 10.4 for a calculation of the different communication forms used.

Verbal communications (i.e. at meetings and in telephone calls) total 66 per cent. One MD explained: 'The principle of public access to official documents leads to increased verbal communication'. This MD meant it is better to communicate verbally since then there are fewer compulsory written records that the public has access to. Issues can be discussed verbally over a longer time period without involving external interests. Moreover, many smaller tasks can be dealt with informally without formal discussion. However, if a task is described in written form, it is available to the public as a government document. With such access, even simple tasks risk becoming complex and time-consuming.

Table 10.4 MDs' forms of communication

Communication forms	Mean (%)	Max (%)	Min (%)	Med (%)
Office visits	1	5	0	0
Letters/faxes	0	1	0	0
Various other communications	4	23	0	0
E-mails	3	6	0	3
Internet	0	3	0	0
Meetings	63	77	49	63
Reports/writings/papers/magazines/notes	8	22	2	6
Telephone calls	3	7	0	3

The direct observations in the study revealed that meetings initiated by people from the MDs' administrative departments are mainly unplanned and brief. In addition, the observations reveal a pattern in the kinds of people, mostly from the MDs' departments, who insist on the MDs' attention. This steady stream of people contributes to the fragmentation of the MDs' workday. It is a different situation with the planned meetings that the MDs initiate. Such meetings occur more rarely, take longer, and are more formal than unplanned meetings. It was observed that in meetings with the politicians, the MDs are rather passive; for the most part, they listen and speak only to deliver factual information. By contrast, in meetings with administrative personnel, the MDs seem to take control and participate actively. The MDs seem to 'take charge'.

Study 2 focused on how MDs spend their time in terms of location, actions, and communications. There are three main findings from the activities summarized above from Study 2 that increased our understanding of the MD function. First, the study confirmed Study 1's finding that the main MD profile is the 'service manager/professional administrator'. This is a time-bounded conclusion since the two studies were conducted in the same years between 1999 and 2002. Second, it was of interest that the MDs' main tasks are disseminating and collecting information, followed by representing municipalities and creating and maintaining relationships. These activities produced more understandings of the linking elements in the MD function. A third interesting result was the observation that the MD function involves making decisions only to a very small extent. This can be regarded as remarkable for a managerial function, but as a linking function it can be a confirmation that political assemblies make the decisions.

Study 3: Understanding management power in the Municipality Director function

The purpose of Study 3, which began in 2003 and ended in 2007, was to explore the MDs' power resources in order to call attention to the relationship between leading politicians and leading public officials and in particular to the assumption that politicians make decisions and that public officials carry them out. The study aimed to identify the power conditions linked to actions made by the MD.

The empirical material from Study 2 was used in this study, supplemented by data from a case study of how two municipalities organize their central management functions in the cooperation between leading politicians and leading public officials. The findings from Study 3 were originally published as a doctoral thesis (Högberg, 2007).

The purpose of Study 3 was to contribute to field of knowledge concerning the MDs' political actions and the power relations behind this behaviour. In focus were the questions of which power resources are identified as connected to the MD function, and of what and how these power resources allow the function to achieve certain effects.

For this study, the term 'power' was defined as the capacity to act that social agents have and which can be identified by virtue of MDs' lasting relationships to the underlying social structures between politics and administration and between politicians and public administrators (see Isaac, 1992). Power has thus been viewed as an explanatory element in understanding public managers' political behaviour.

The empirical material collected in Study 2 was used in Study 3, complemented with a case study of the leading politicians and the municipal managers (i.e. the leading public administrator in a municipality who moves in the immediate proximity of the overall political leadership and thereby acts in the interface between politics and administration). The case study was conducted using in-depth interviews of fifteen managers and twenty-one politicians. Furthermore, a study of documents was conducted. These documents describe an extensive change in the political organization in two municipalities.

The researcher developed an analytical model using the approach of critical realism to social structures and causality (e.g. Bhaskar, 1978; Sayer, 1992, 2000; Danermark et al., 2003). This model is founded on three analyses: structural analysis, causal analysis, and the analysis of understanding.

Using structural analysis, the researcher identified three structural power resources associated with the MD function – centrality, control over critical resources, and nearness to executive power. Centrality, as a power resource, stems from the central position of the function in municipalities that allows it to control the flow of work to leading political assemblies. The second power resource, control over critical resources, stems from the function's control over critical resources (i.e. resources the politicians depend on in the decision-making process). The main resources identified in Study 3 were the resources embedded in the administrative organization, such as administrative knowledge and expertise, which the function controls. The third power resource, nearness to executive power, is rooted in the function's close relationship to the executive political management function. The results of our structural analysis showed that the MDs, with their direct access, often act as a kind of right hand for the leading politicians (e.g. the chairman of the municipal board). In a broad sense, the MD function has direct access to the political management function.

Using causal analysis, the researcher explored how these power resources permitted the holder of the MD function to achieve certain desired effects. The analysis showed that the structural power resources allow the MDs to influence the political decision-making process in several ways. They control the delivery of official documents and decision-support data that describe problems; they present the different problem areas; and they describe the possible consequences of proposed solutions.

Using analysis of understanding, the political behaviour of MDs was studied. The critical realist approach revealed that the political behaviour of MDs is best understood in terms of a proactive, political role inherent in the managerial function. This role is strictly interconnected with the structural power resources because the role requires, for its existence, that those resources are associated with the municipal position.

Study 3 furthered the understanding of the MD function beyond what was learned in Studies 1 and 2 since it showed that the MD function has power resources and that such resources in practice are used to influence political decision-making.

Study 4: Understanding contextual impacts in the Municipality Director function

The purpose of Study 4, which was conducted during the years of 2006-9, was to gain an understanding of how the MD function develops (Jonsson, 2009). The study was based on the idea that the function is the interface between politics and administration.[4] This interface was assumed to have an impact on how the function is exercised. The question was how.

In the study, the MD function was regarded as constructed over time in social environments.[5] Two types of construction processes were observed in four municipalities of different sizes. The researcher followed the recruiting and hiring process for the function in three municipalities (2006-9) – from the discussion of the so-called specifications of demands to the point where the new proprietors of the MD function had been in the positions for about a year. In the fourth municipality (2006-8), the researcher studied an organizing process in municipality governance in which the MD function was one among several that were objects of the reorganizing discussions. In the process, the MD function was held by the same person. For all municipalities, the processes were empirically observed by conducting interviews and reading documents. Three rounds of interviews were made in three municipalities and four in the fourth municipality. Politicians, important civil servants, and union representatives were interviewed (in total, between ten and twenty-five persons) in each municipality.

In order to discuss the functions of the MD as contextually bound, certain concepts were developed concerning this type of management. The concepts were contextually influenced in two respects. First, the concepts were developed for use in discussions on the actual management. Second, the concepts were generated through discussions with municipal employees and politicians.

The concepts were related to three perspectives on the MD function: namely as conceptual construction, as shape of action, and as human shape. The first perspective – conceptual construction – focuses on the purpose of the MD function, expressed as three different links: the link between politics and administration, the link between municipal activities, and the link between the municipality and its environment. The second perspective – shape of action – focuses on the management function in action. There were two aspects to this perspective: (*a*) the issue function of actions (concerning the 'What' function) that is regarded as issue-oriented, distinguished from oriented-acting; and (*b*) the how function of actions (concerning the 'How' function) that differs between behaviour-oriented and oriented-acting. The third perspective – human shape – focuses on how the management function is expressed humanely in the management function and consists of competence and numbers of people.

The three perspectives represent three ways of focusing on the construction, and thereby the contextual impact, of the MD function. In this sense, the conclusions from Study 4 are the following:

- The conceptual construction of the MD function is contextually embedded in all Swedish municipalities generally, and in individual municipalities locally. The contextual effects differ from one municipality to another, depending on the political and administrative impacting forces bound to political and administrative circumstances. In general, there are established institutionalized ideas that state that the function of the MD today is more or less to fulfil all these above-mentioned links. The implication is that the proprietors of the function cannot influence the conceptual constructions of the function. This conclusion can be seen as a way to give the function legitimacy in the municipalities.
- The shape of actions of the MD function is mainly influenced by the proprietors of the function. This can be done by the use of experience, skills, and trust. However, frames for space of actions consisting of inertia in the shape of traditions and cultural circumstances exist.
- The human shape of the MD function is, of course, influenced by proprietors and their mandates. The possibilities for individual influence are naturally based on the competence connected to the individual in question.

Two concepts were used in Study 4 in order to increase the understanding of the influences on the MD function: (*a*) *inertia*, the institutionalized circumstances linked to the function; and (*b*) *instruments of anchoring*, which focuses on how new ideas are integrated into the construction. The concept of *inertia* focuses on historic institutionalization while the concept of *instruments of anchoring* focuses on institutionalization processes in a specific social content.

The study identified the following types of *inertia*:

- Common ideas on the MD function
- Established relationships (e.g. in terms of distribution of work and trust) between the leading politicians and the MD function
- Local political management culture
- Ideas about competence
- Local, administrative traditions
- Local, administrative management culture
- Physical work environment

These types of inertia can support or reject changes in the construction of the MD function, depending on the extent to which the constructions are challenged by instruments that try to anchor new ideas in the constructions. The study identified the following types of *instruments of anchoring*:

- Anchored specifications on demands related to recruitment
- Attendance to the recruited person
- Local politics
- Space for actions and mandate for proprietors of the MD function
- High degree of participation in the organizing processes of political and administrative municipal management
- Formal decisions on organizing the political and administrative municipal management
- Experience and skills of the proprietors of the MD function

The proprietors of the MD function have access to some of the identified *instruments of anchoring*. With the use of these, some space of action can be utilized.

Several *instruments of anchoring* relate to the recruitment and organizing processes. In day-to-day management, such work can be regarded as construction by small talks and actions (Ekman, 2003). In such situations, it appears most likely that the proprietors' skills in combination with space of actions should be the most relevant instruments of anchoring. Even change in local politics can have effect as an instrument for change in the constructions of the MD function.

Some *instruments of anchoring* can lead to inertia. It is in the nature of organizing regarded as institutionalizing (Czarniawska and Joerges, 1998). Instruments of anchoring will be established as new ingredients in institutions. Local politics and formal decisions on management organizations can appear as roots, and so can instruments of anchoring.

The study classified types of inertia and *instruments of anchoring* as conceptual structures, structures of actions, formal structures, and physical structures within constructions of the MD function.[6] Some types of *inertia* are mainly conceptual structures, namely common ideas concerning the function and ideas on competence. Other types of *inertia* can be understood as both conceptual structures and structures of actions. This is the case of the local relationships between the leading politicians and the MDs, local political management cultures, local administrative traditions, and local administrative management cultures.

The study characterized *instruments of anchoring* similarly. Anchored specifications on demands related to recruiting are a type of conceptual structure. Is this the case of attendance and choice of person in the case of recruiting? Even experiences and skills related to the proprietors of the MD function can be characterized as conceptual structures. The instrument of anchoring, which has been named as space for actions and mandates for proprietors of the function, can be regarded as a conceptual structure in close relation to action. A high degree of participation in organizing processes is a type of structure of action.

Study 4 increased our understanding of the MD function in several ways. First, new concepts were developed that provided opportunities to create contextual, conformed descriptions of the MD function in terms of its purpose, its shapes of actions, and its human shapes. These concepts increased the understanding of the function in its daily context. Second, the study reached an understanding of the function as a dynamic phenomenon that may change over time in its environment. Third, we learned how the MD function develops.

DISCUSSION

Understandings on the Municipality Director function

The four studies appear to complement the understandings of the MD function. The studies resulted in different understandings corresponding to their different focuses and purposes. These different results were also a consequence of the variations in theoretical approaches and methodologies of the four studies.

Study 1 and Study 2 created understandings on the content of the function. In these studies, our inspiration was the Managerial School (e.g. Mintzberg, 1973, 1994; Kotter, 1982; Hales, 1986). Using the conceptualizations from this School, Study 1 painted a picture of the specifics of the MD function mainly in terms of where the manager acts and what actions the manager performs. These pictures were presented in terms of contextual-related concepts. A methodology – interactive knowledge building – was used that consisted of a series of discussions and texts from interviews and discussions in groups with the proprietors of the MD function. This method proved to be successful in that it captured and registered the tacit knowledge that previously had not been articulated.

Study 2 provided more specific descriptions on the content of the MD function – how MDs allocate their time among different contexts, arenas, and activities. The study also showed which communications devices they use. By defining the MD function, according to time spent, in terms of what it entails and time involved, as well the context in which the work is performed, the understanding of the function was increased. This proved to be of importance not only for practitioners (e.g. proprietors of the function) but also for the researchers in the project. As an additional outcome, it was found that the results in this study proved to be important for the credibility and the sustainability that was developed in Study 1. The methodological approach in Study 2 was inspired by Sune Carlson's (1951) and Stefan Tengblad's (1999) studies.

Study 3 focused on another aspect of the MD function, namely the power resources related to the MD function. Data were used from case descriptions of the MD function obtained from traditional data collection methods as well as from analytical tools developed using concepts rooted in the perspective of critical realism (Bhaskar, 1978; Sayer, 1992, 2000; Danermark et al., 2003). This meant that the results of Study 3 (in terms of interpretation of the empirical material) would not have been detected by using more traditional forms of data collection.

Study 4 increased the understanding of how the MD function develops. This understanding was expressed using the terms *inertia* and *instruments of anchoring*. The study also resulted in an apparatus of concepts that was influenced by contextual circumstances that increased the understanding of the contents of the function. This study relied on a variant of Institutional Theory that focuses on institutional processes. It also was realized with a method using a series of interviews.

Figure 10.1 summarizes the understandings from the four studies as well as the theories and approaches used.

Understanding a managerial function

Figure 10.1 presents the understandings generated in the four studies on the three aspects of the managerial function: its content, its power resources, and its contextual impacts. These aspects provide a broad and rich understanding of the MD function, especially its position as a link between political and administrative control of municipalities. In addition, the aspects represent important ingredients in definitions of leadership that often say that leadership is a phenomenon that exists in certain contexts and consists of actions aimed at influencing others (see e.g. Yukl, 2006).

Figure 10.1 also shows that these understandings have been achieved by using different theoretical approaches and empirical methods. We note, however, despite these differences, the common denominator among the studies: the importance of the empirical material. However, the material was used differently in the four studies. Study 1 developed concepts on the MD function that were useful in capturing the content of the function, which, in turn, was of great importance for discussions in the municipalities and for further research. Thus, in Study 2, those concepts were used and were shown to be useful in the depiction of the MD function. Study 3 used the empirical material from Study 2 for the theoretical interpretations of the conceptualization of the power relations and actions between the MD function and the municipality politicians. In Study 4, empirical material – captured in real time during a three-year period – was significant for the development of the concepts necessary to understand the importance of the context and its effect on the MD function.

Thus, different scientific approaches and methods were used in the four studies. Studies 1 and 2 present a view of reality as something that requires the development of more knowledge. The approaches used in both studies were chosen because they aimed at gaining knowledge as empirically shaped depictions of reality. Studies 3 and 4 present a more critical view of reality as something that relates to the purposes of these studies. In Study 3, the concept of power approach was chosen since it relates to the strand of thought called critical realism. In Study 4, the idea was to explore how the MD function was constructed in social contexts. To do so, the approach used was Institutional Theory, in particular a Scandinavian type of this theory that emphasizes the importance of processes in understanding institutionalization in organizations (Czarniawska, 2008).

Despite the different specific purposes, approaches and theories of the four studies, they share the common purpose of increasing our knowledge about the MD function in municipalities. When our interest was first tickled regarding this phenomenon, knowledge about it was scarce. Because of the scarcity of knowledge, we were motivated to take a slightly less critical, social scientific approach. As our knowledge increased about the MD function, it was possible to be more

Understandings on:

	Contents	Power resources	Contextual impacts
Study 1 **Managerial School** **Interactive knowledge building**	Acting descriptions; acting where and what sort actions Acting profiles		Contextual-related concepts
Study 2 **Managerial School** **Written diaries, direct observations,** **interviews**	Detailed acting profiles Mainly an informing function Very little decision-making		
Study 3 **Critical realism**		Power through centrality, control over critical resources and proximity to executive power Influence on political decision-making by delivering support data in concise ways	
Study 4 **Institutional theory** **Interviewing over time**	Contextual descriptions in terms of purpose, shape of action, and human shape A dynamic phenomenon		Contextual-related concepts Contextual-related explanations on how the function takes shape and gives legitimacy

Figure 10.1 Understandings on the MD function

specific regarding our interests about this leadership function. This led to an increase in the use of the critical approach.

The four studies of this research focus on an important issue in the social scientific research agenda – the balance between, on the one hand, a critical, basic approach, filled with theoretical conceptualizations, and, on the other hand, an open and sensitive interest in finding social conditions through empirical material. In this balance it is important not to overemphasize the critical, basic approach because of the risk of elitism and insensitivity towards the rich amount of empirical material often offered. It is also important, on the other hand, not to exaggerate the empirical concentration by getting caught up in superficial phenomena and conventional performances, and thereby running the risk of losing the critical perspective (Alvesson and Deetz, 2000: 13–14).

In total, the four studies represent a balancing act where the critical foundation has gradually increased our knowledge about the MD function at the same time that the collection of empirical data has continually been important in the understanding of this function and in the generation of concepts.

NOTES

1. The author expresses his appreciation to Peter Gustavsson and Örjan Högberg for their contributions to the chapter.
2. In this chapter, the management function is regarded as just a function in order to open up the topic for broad discussion of its contents, aims, actions, and contextual influences. An alternative concept is position; however, as a concept, position raises associations with hierarchical circumstances and not the broad connotations intended.
3. Theorists and researchers describe managers' work differently, for example patterns of activities (Carlsson, 1951), roles (Mintzberg, 1973), networks (Kotter, 1982), and conceptualized models (Mintzberg, 1994).
4. The interface function, sometimes called the link, is discussed in the literature dealing with how municipal management differs from private company management. See e.g. Hood (2000) and Brunsson (2002).
5. The idea that a management function is socially constructed over time is inspired by institutional theory, especially the Scandinavian variant of Institutional Theory with its focus on institutional processes in which the main interests are on 'how institutions emerge, change, and vanish – not merely *that* they do' (Czarniawska, 2008: 773).
6. This classification is inspired by Löwstedt's discussion (1995) of organizations in structural ways.

REFERENCES

Alvesson, M. and Deetz, S. (2000). *Kritisk samhällsvetenskaplig metod.* Lund: Studentlitteratur.

Brunsson, N. (2002). Politisering och företagisering. In R. Lind (Ed.), *Ledning av företag och förvaltningar – Förutsättningar, former och förnyelse.* Stockholm: SNS förlag.

—— Jönsson, S. (1979). *Beslut och handling. Om politikers inflytande på politiken.* Stockholm: Liber förlag.

Bhaskar, R. (1978). *A Realist Theory of Science.* Hassocks, UK: Harvester Press.

Carlson, S. (1951). *Executive Behaviour.* Stockholm: Strömbergs.

Christensen, T., Laegreid, P., Roness, P. G., and Rövik, K. A. (2005). *Organisationsteori för Offentlig Sector.* Malmö: Liber.

Czarniawska, B. (2008). How to misuse institutions and get away with it: Some reflections on institutional theory (ies). In R. Greenwood, C. Oliver, K. Sahlin, and R. Suddaby (Eds.), *The SAGE Handbook Organizational Institutionalism.* London: Sage.

—— Joerges, B. (1998). Winds of organizational change: How ideas translate into objects and actions. In N. Brunsson and J. P. Olsen (Eds.), *Organizing Organizations*. Bergen-Sandviken: Fagboksforlaget.

Danermark, B., Ekström, M., Jacobsen, L., and Karlsson, J. (2003). *Att förklara samhället*. Lund: Studentlitteratur.

Ekman, G. (2003). *Från prat till resultat – Om vardagens ledarskap*. Malmö: Liber.

Hales, C. P. (1986). What do managers do: A critical review of the evidence. *Journal of Management Studies*, 23: 88–115.

Hood, C. (2000). *The Art of the State: Culture, Rhetoric, and Public Management*. New York: Oxford University Press.

Högberg, Ö. (2002). *Kommunchefers tidsanvändning. En studie om kommunchefers funktioner och roller*. Licentiatuppsats, FiF-a 56, Linköpings Universitet, Ekonomiska Institutionen.

—— (2007). *Maktlösa makthavare. En studie om kommunalt chefskap*. Doktorsavhandling, Linköping Studies in Arts and Science, No. 391, Linköpings Universitet, Institutionen för Ekonomisk och Industriell utveckling.

Isaac, J. (1992). Beyond the three faces of power: A realist critique. In T. E. Wartenburg (Ed.), *Rethinking Power*. New York: State University of New York Press.

Jonsson, L. (2001). *Kunskapsbildning i samverkan mellan forskning och praktik. En studie av interaktiv kunskaps bildning avseende kommunchefers chefskap*. Linköpings Universitet.

—— (2008). Ideas on organizing municipalities. *Public Management Review*, 10(4): 539–58.

—— (2009). *Kommunchefer blir till*. Nora, Sweden: Nya Doxa.

—— Gustavsson, P., Arnell, S-I., Högberg, Ö., and Jonsson, R. (2002). *Kommunchefers chefskap. Ett lokalt präglat chefskap i politisk miljö*. Nora, Sweden: Nya Doxa.

Källström, A. and Solli, R. (1997). *Med takt och taktik*. Göteborg: BAS.

Kotter, J. P. (1982). What effective managers really do. *Harvard Business Review*, 60(6): 156–67.

Löwstedt, J. (1995). Människan och strukturerna. Några utgångspunkter. In J. Löwstedt (Ed.), *Människan och strukturerna. Organisationsteori för förändring*. Stockholm: Narenius & Santerus förlag.

Mintzberg, H. (1973). *The Nature of Managerial Work*. New York: Harper & Row.

—— (1994). Rounding out the manager's job. *Sloan Management Review*, Fall: 11–26.

Sayer, A. (1992). *Method in Social Science. A Realist Approach* (2nd ed.). London: Routledge.

—— (2000). *Realism and Social Science*. London: SAGE Publications.

Tengblad, S. (1999). *Företagsledares Tidsanvändning – En uppföljning av Sune Carlssons klassika studie Executive Behaviour*. Paper presented at The Nordic Business Administration Conference in Helsingfors, Finland, 1999.

Yukl, G. (2006). *Leadership in Organizations*. Upper Saddle River, NJ: Pearson Prentice Hall.

11

Leaders of modern universities: *Primi inter pares* or chief executive officers?

Lars Engwall and Carin Eriksson Lindvall

INTRODUCTION

Universities are important organizations in modern society. Politicians and the business community have considerable expectations as far as universities' contributions to the public welfare and to economic growth. At the same time, there is great deal of scepticism on whether universities are managed in the right way. Different camps demand a greater say concerning university governance principles.

In relation to these circumstances, this chapter deals with the changing conditions of university leaders. For some time, there have been discussions on the demanding role of university leaders as stewards of complex and almost unmanageable organizations. As universities become increasingly complex, in an environment of greater dynamics and increased uncertainty, many observers argue there are even more demands on university leaders. In addition, with the increased demands for accountability, efficiency, and transparency in universities, the activities of reporting, analysing, measuring, monitoring, and evaluating have become central concerns at various university levels. Furthermore, the competition among universities, combined with technological, financial, social, and political changes, has placed new demands on university leaders. In response, university organizational structures have become more complex with greater specialization of functions, increased professionalization of roles, and the addition of more management layers.

All together, these changes create escalating demands on university leaders. At the same time, there are questions about their roles and the traditional ways in which they are appointed. The collegial form – when university leaders are appointed from among their peers and thus become *primi inter pares* – has been criticized for not providing the right type of leaders. Instead, it is often suggested, for example, that for state-funded universities, representatives from the general public (i.e. the state) should appoint the university leaders just as shareholders elect corporate boards to appoint executives.

This chapter begins with two sections that portray the general working conditions of university leaders. First, the chapter analyses the changing role of university leaders beginning with a discussion on the basic nature of universities, with reference to DiMaggio and Powell (1983). In this discussion, the chapter points to the complex position of universities that subjects them to the influence and control of states, professions, and markets. Based on this analysis, the chapter then elaborates on modern changes in the working conditions of universities as they move towards increasing environmental embeddedness. Empirical results from studies of university leaders at two levels – Vice-Chancellors (VCs) and Department Chairs (DCs) – are then presented in the third section. The final section presents our conclusions and discusses the implications of this research.

THE GOVERNANCE OF ACADEMIC INSTITUTIONS

By tradition, self-governance is a significant characteristic of academic institutions at the university level. Basically, such institutions are professional organizations, strongly influenced by insiders who make decisions on both the admission of outsiders and on the internal governance systems.[1] The admission mechanisms control the acceptance of new students and new faculty members and the approval of new disciplines. As a matter of fact, the reputation of academic institutions depends in part on the care they exercise in their selection/approval processes. It is expected that enrolling students have specific qualifications, that faculty members meet certain standards, and that new disciplines withstand any scepticism about their lack of scientific rigour. Similarly, internal norms govern academic institutions through the mechanism of internal quality control (i.e. student examinations, control of research, and faculty promotion).

This system of self-governance, of course, creates inevitable tensions in academic institutions. On one hand, since such institutions must stand behind the quality of their product (students and research), there is a strong incentive to comply with traditional academic rules. On the other hand, they are expected to be innovative, which may sometimes mean old rules have to be broken. As noted by Thomas Kuhn (1962), over time, scientists develop strong paradigms. Imre Lakatos (1970) refers to these paradigms as scientific research programmes. However, such paradigms, which provide norm systems for scientific work, may break down if the empirical evidence against them is too strong. Therefore, Kuhn argues scientific revolutions may challenge normal science with its puzzle-solving and mop-up work.

Although universities are not infrequently criticized as ivory towers, they are not disconnected from their environments. As Clark (1983) observed, universities have significant relationships with the state and the market. In other words, politicians make decisions that affect university policy and programmes, and people in the marketplace influence university priorities.[2]

Given this interplay between states, professions, and markets in the discussion of the university role, it is appropriate to recall DiMaggio and Powell's arguments (1983) concerning the governance of modern institutions. They argue that organizations are subject to three isomorphic forces (Table 11.1):

- Coercive
- Normative
- Mimetic

Table 11.1 States, professions, and markets

Variable	States	Professions	Markets
Force	Coercive	Normative	Mimetic
Signals	Rules	Norms	Models
Mechanism	Obedience	Socialization	Imitation

Source: Our summary and development of the reasoning in DiMaggio and Powell (1983).

The coercive force (Table 11.1, vertical column 2) – traditionally related to states – is associated with obligatory *rules* (laws or regulations). There are penalties if rules are violated. The basic enforcement mechanism is *obedience*.

Second, the normative force (Table 11.1, vertical column 3) – traditionally related to academic institutions – is associated with *norms* that are developed in certain cultures, such as professions. They are adopted through the mechanism of *socialization* (i.e. new entrants to the organization gradually adopt the dominant norms).

Third, the mimetic force (Table 11.1, vertical column 4) – in our view, a particularly strong force in markets – is associated with others' behavioural signals concerning pricing, product design, organization, etc.[3] In this way, *models* are diffused. Since most markets and organizational fields, as opposed to the models of free competition, are concentrated, governance by markets tends to lead to *imitation*. Thus, homogeneity is reinforced.

Needless to say, these three governance systems interact and influence each other. Figure 11.1 is a schema of this influence and interaction. In terms of the signals presented in Table 11.1, the following conclusions may be stated:

- States influence professions and markets through rules.
- Markets influence states and professions institutions through models.
- Professions influence states and markets through norms.

The basic issues in the governance of academic institutions, then, are the significance of the three governance signals (rules, norms, and models) and the change in their importance over time. In Europe, the governance in academic institutions has traditionally been a mix of rules and norms with few market models. While the states defined the role of academic institutions with rules, insiders governed them with norms. In short, the politicians enforced the entry controls for academic institutions while the academic hierarchy managed the performance controls. With the passage of time, however, we see the growing effect of market models as states increasingly use market solutions rather than rules to allocate resources. The result is that academic institutions are also adopting such market models.

This development appears to reflect a movement towards an academic governance system similar to that in the United States. Figure 11.2 is based on Clark's representation (1983) of the state governance of many European higher education systems in the early 1980s – with the notable exceptions of Italy and the United Kingdom where the professions governed – and of the market governance in the US higher education system. However, in the nearly three decades since Clark's

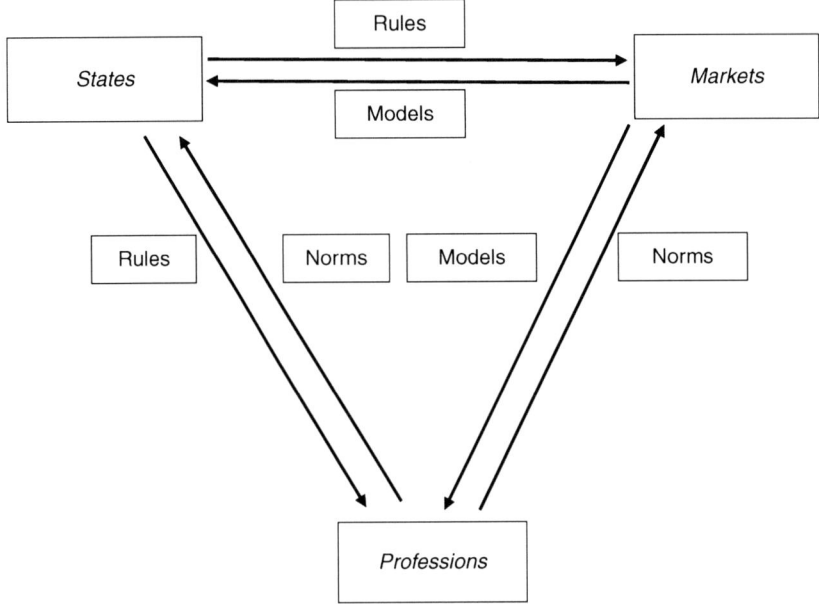

Figure 11.1 States, professions, and markets

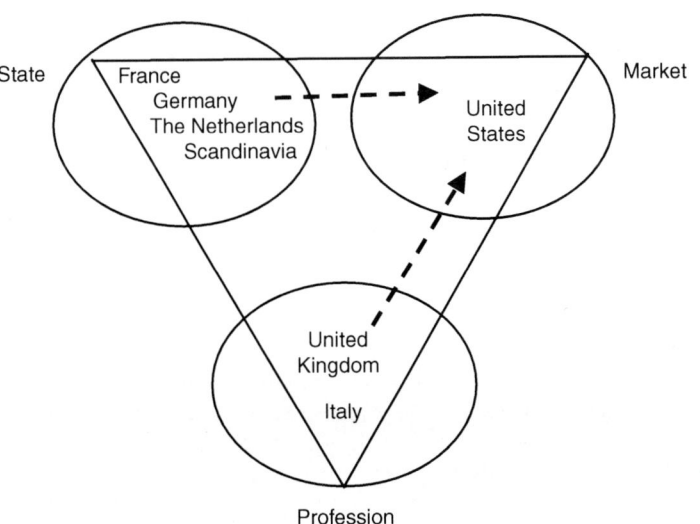

Figure 11.2 Variations in university systems (based on Clark, 1983: 143)

book on cross-national higher education, Europe has moved towards a more market-oriented system. The dashed lines in Figure 11.2 depict this movement.

The literature in the sociology of science, which argues that the production of knowledge has changed radically in recent years, examines such changes. Gibbons et al. (1994) argue there has been a shift from an exclusive focus on scientific relevance (Mode 1) to an increase in the consideration of external factors (Mode 2). In addition to the need to recognize scientifically reliable knowledge, Nowotny et al. (2001) argue that we should develop 'socially robust knowledge'.[4] Etzkowitz and Leydesdorff (1997) develop the argument by claiming that a triple helix of close relationships among governments, universities, and industry has emerged in the production of knowledge. In the same vein, Rooney (2005) provides a perspective on the knowledge economy, and Drori et al. (2003) discuss the scientification of society. It is clear that that knowledge production and its diffusion have become increasingly embedded in society.

This increased societal embeddedness of universities means there are now more performance controls in what Power (1999) describes as 'the audit society'. As concepts like transparency, accountability, and efficiency are used more in the public discourse, actors in the political and economic spheres have increasingly scrutinized universities. Evaluations of university scholars and rankings and accreditations of universities are increasingly common in most European countries. As a corollary, competitive funding is replacing lump sum grants.

In summary, it appears today that a mix of state rules, professional norms, and market models govern universities. The mix varies, and has varied, by country and by time period. In general, however, we have observed in recent decades both an increase in market models in Europe as well as more interest by the states in university governance. These changes, and the permanent interaction between states, professions, and markets in the governance of universities, are important to keep in mind as we examine the working conditions of university leaders.

THE EMPIRICAL EVIDENCE

There have been a number of studies on academic leadership, including research by Middlehurst (1993) and Bargh et al. (2000). More recently, the journal *Leadership* devoted a special issue to 'Leadership in Higher Education' (Bolden et al., 2009).

Middlehurst (1993) used questionnaires and interviews in the 'old' university sector. She assembled responses from questionnaires she sent to 175 academics (all of whom had participated in leadership courses) and conducted interviews with academics at ten universities in the United Kingdom. Her purpose was to analyse the relevance of contemporary ideas of leadership in academic institutions. As a result of her research, she called for a better balance between leadership and management in Academia.

Bargh et al. (2000) used (*a*) biographical information about 341 Vice-Chancellors, (*b*) questionnaire responses from university presidents in California and Georgia and from rectors in Sweden and the Netherlands, and (*c*) case studies. Their results suggest that although university leaders face new economic and financial pressures, the CEO (Chief Executive Officer) model is not widespread in Academia.

The special issue of *Leadership* (Bolden et al., 2009) is a collection of articles on different aspects of leadership in higher education. Gosling et al. (2009) discuss the effects of increasing managerialism in Academia; Middlehurst et al. (2009) deal with the practical implications of research in higher education leadership; Gronn (2009) points to the varying characteristics of such leadership; Bryman and Lilley (2009) report on a study of department heads; de Boer and Goedegebuure (2009) focus on deans; and Collinson and Collinson (2009) study leadership in the further education sector. Taken as a whole, these articles describe the specific characteristics of academic leadership and call for additional research in the area.

We supplement these studies with our evidence on academic leadership. As examples of academic leaders, we look at university VCs as well as DCs who, using a military metaphor, are the captains in the field. Leadership research typically focuses on top managers, but we also direct our research to university managers below presidents and rectors.

The context of the empirical studies

Since the studies of this research take place in the Swedish context, it is appropriate to explain the system of higher education in Sweden. At the outset, we note that in Sweden, as in most countries, the system has experienced considerable expansion during the past century. One hundred years ago in Sweden there were two state universities (one in Uppsala and one in Lund), two local university colleges (one in Gothenburg and one in Stockholm), and a few institutions for professional studies. Today, Sweden has sixteen universities and twenty-three university colleges (in general, university colleges do not confer doctoral degrees). In addition, there are a number of institutions that provide training in the performing arts, health care, etc. In total, sixty-one Swedish academic institutions are now authorized to award higher education degrees. Most such institutions are state-funded and are under the jurisdiction of the Higher Education Act and the Higher Education Ordinance. Section 2 of the Ordinance gives the state a strong voice in the programmes and policies of these institutions. However, as Section 2 states, since the early 1990s, with some exceptions, there has been a trend towards decentralization in higher education with less direct state control and more market-influenced solutions. A manifestation of this trend is the increasing emphasis on seeking managerial talent in the recruitment of university leaders.[5]

Three empirical studies

Of the three studies reported on in this chapter, two focus on VCs and one on DCs. These studies were reported separately in Eriksson (1997, 1999), Engwall et al. (1999), and Engwall (2008*b*).

The first study (Engwall et al., 1999) was the Swedish part of a larger study by Bargh et al. (2000). For the Swedish part, a standard questionnaire was used to interview the VCs of the thirty Swedish universities and university colleges.[6] All VCs agreed to participate. Most interviews were personal interviews and lasted between sixty and ninety minutes.

The second study (Engwall, 2008*b*), which focused on the development of university media relations, was based on archival material and interviews with various university leaders. In order to analyse differences as a result of institutional age, fourteen VCs and registrars were interviewed: four interviewees employed by old institutions, four by semi-old institutions, and six by young institutions. Seven information officers distributed over the three categories of institutions as well as two information professionals outside the universities and university colleges were interviewed.

The third study (Eriksson, 1997, 1999) focused on the working conditions of DCs in the 1990s at Uppsala University. This study concerned four departments: one small liberal arts department, one small bio-technical department, one medium-sized social science department, and one large science and technology department. All four departments were involved extensively with teaching (at the bachelor's, master's, and doctoral levels) and research. The study used three interview categories. Four deans and fourteen administrators from central administration were in the first category. Forty-nine employees from the four departments were in the second category. For these two categories, interviewers took detailed notes that were transcribed immediately after the interviews. The four DCs were in the third category. They were interviewed on four occasions during a period of eighteen months. Each of these four DCs kept a time allocation diary for a two-week period.

VICE-CHANCELLORS IN ACTION

The mandate

In an examination of the working conditions of university leaders, it is appropriate first to consider how they are selected. The process of leader selection is clear in corporations. In the corporate governance model, the shareholders select board members to represent their interests and boards in turn select executives for the same purpose. For universities the process is less clear since it varies over space and time, depending on the balance between state, professional, and market forces. However, it seems fair to say that historically the selection of VCs involves significant participation and commitment by the professions. Although the state often makes the formal appointments, the professors through a collegial process select the appointees from amongst themselves. However, in recent decades, university trustees have tended to select leaders from outside the universities.

Notable examples of such outside appointments have occurred in the last decade at both Oxford University and Cambridge University. In 2003, Cambridge University appointed the former Yale University provost and anthropology professor, Alison Richard, as VC. In 2004, Oxford University appointed New Zealander, John Hood, as the VC, the first external VC in Oxford's long history. However, Hood's efforts to change the governance structure of the university were unsuccessful, and he left his position in 2009. Andrew D. Hamilton, a Yale

University chemistry professor and provost, succeeded Hood as VC at Oxford University.[7] Thus, at present, former professors from the United States lead both old UK universities. These appointments support the theory that there is a movement in Europe towards the US university governance system.

Outsiders were selected at both these UK universities even though there were many qualified candidates for the VC positions among their professors. Some academic institutions, however, which lack qualified internal candidates, are forced to look for candidates outside their own ranks. This has been the case, for example, in Sweden where university colleges have mainly recruited for VC positions externally. In several cases, chairpersons at Swedish universities – externally appointed since 1998 – have followed suit by employing search consultants to find VC candidates on the open market. In this way, with their recruitment model for top academic jobs, university colleges have become a role model for VC hiring practices.[8] This development is particularly interesting since, using DiMaggio and Powell (1983) reasoning, the prediction is instead that universities would become the role models for university colleges.

The implication of this discussion is that university leaders are in a rather different position than their corporate counterparts. Owing to the special character of universities, with their need for academic prestige, university leaders require the support of the academic professions. Corporate boards demand market share and profits from their executives while university trustees demand an academic reputation for excellence from their leaders. Since the measure of such excellence is largely dependent on the research of individual scholars, university leaders can only manage this reputation to a limited extent. They can neither order nor control the research. Primarily, and increasingly, the research is funded by external grants that researchers have been awarded.[9]

It is of interest to examine how VCs, as chief academic and executive officers, think about the universities that they manage. In the study of thirty Swedish VCs, the respondents were asked to choose the one definition among four that they thought best fit their institution (Engwall et al., 1999: 83–4):

- *A complex organization*: Institutions of higher education are complex organizations: the rector's leadership role is to manage this complexity to ensure that the institution survives and flourishes.
- *A company*: Institutions of higher education are managerial organizations: the rector's leadership role is to create a clear sense of corporate purpose and direction.
- *A creative organization*: Institutions of higher education are creative organizations: the rector's role is to create an ethos and environment that stimulate innovation.
- *A collegial organization*: Institutions of higher education are collegial organizations: the rector's leadership role is to protect the procedural integrity of the institution and to build consensus.

Seventeen of the thirty respondents said their institutions were creative organizations, eight said complex organizations, four said company organizations, and one said a collegial organization.

The work of university leaders

In the study of the thirty Swedish VCs, the respondents were asked to rank the university leaders' tasks by order of importance and by the amount of time spent on each. The thirty VCs were also invited to indicate their views about the future importance of these tasks (see Table 11.2 for mean rankings of the six tasks). The questionnaire described the following six tasks for their consideration (Engwall et al., 1999: 82):

- *Human resource management*: Appointing senior individuals and developing commitment to institutional goals and values.
- *Representation, lobbying, and ceremonial activities*: Ensuring the institution reflects the respect of its regional/national/international communities; lobbying on behalf of the university interest.
- *Control systems*: Designing and implementing procedures to control and direct institutional activities and monitoring academic/financial performance.
- *Entrepreneurship and competitive advantage*: Positioning the institution within the higher education sector and engaging in successful competition with other institutions.
- *Strategic planning*: Creating a clear institutional vision/mission in relation to present and future developments in its external environment.
- *Cultural change*: Encouraging staff to embrace change and innovation throughout the university.

The VCs identify strategic planning as their most important task (mean rank = 1.6) followed by entrepreneurship and competitive advantage (mean rank = 2.8). Least important tasks are representation, lobbying, ceremonial activities (mean rank = 4.1), and control systems (mean rank = 5.6). Tasks that rank in the middle as far as importance are human resource management (mean rank = 3.0) and cultural change (mean rank = 3.9).

There are clear differences in the ranking of tasks by importance and their ranking by time spent on them. Strategic planning takes the most time (mean value = 2.7 vs. 1.6), in the importance ranking. The task of representation, lobbying, and ceremonial activities takes the second-most time, although it is one of the tasks ranked least important (mean value = 2.9 vs. 4.1). Human resource management (mean value = 3.3 vs. 3.0), entrepreneurship and competitive advantage (mean value = 3.3 vs. 2.8), and cultural change (mean value = 4.3 vs. 3.9) rank in the middle range for both time spent and importance. Control systems are least important in both categories although time spent ranks higher than importance (mean value = 4.5 vs. 5.6). As far as the importance of future development of the six tasks is concerned, entrepreneurship and competitive advantage rank first (mean value = 0.57), control systems rank last (mean value = 0.13), and the other four tasks rank in the middle with mean values between 0.37 and 0.47.

Two conclusions may be drawn from this analysis. First, it is evident that VCs have to spend more time on tasks they rank as less important than others. For example, strategic planning may suffer because of the attention given to the more

Table 11.2 The mean rankings of VCs based on the importance and time spent on six tasks and their views on future development

Task	Importance	Time Spent	Difference	Future
Human resource management	3.0	3.3	−0.3	0.37
Representation, lobbying, and ceremonial activities	4.1	2.9	1.2	0.43
Control systems	5.6	4.5	1.1	0.13
Entrepreneurship and competitive advantage	2.8	3.3	−0.5	0.57
Strategic planning	1.6	2.7	−1.1	0.47
Cultural change	3.9	4.3	−0.4	0.47

Note: Scale of importance and time spent: 1 = most important/most time and 6 = least important/least time. For future development, respondents were asked whether the importance of the task would increase (+1), be stable (0), or decrease (−1). Table 11.2 is based on tables 3, 4, and 7 in Engwall et al. (1999).

short-term tasks of control systems and of representation, lobbying, and ceremonial activities. This conclusion is consistent with earlier findings on executive behaviour by Carlson (1951) and later researchers. Second, it is clear that VCs foresee that their jobs will be even more demanding in the future. There are no negative mean values for future development of the six tasks.

Of the six tasks, all of which are assumed to increase in importance in the future, the task of representation, lobbying, and ceremonial activities shows the highest disparity between present importance and time spent. This may indicate that the VCs are aware of the increasing importance of their public roles in the promotion of their institutions. This conclusion is consistent with Stefan Tengblad's study where he found that CEOs 'participated more frequently in ceremonies (business dinners, inaugurations, and other social gatherings)' (2006: 1448).

It is also notable that the VCs exhibit a rather negative attitude towards control systems. They do not consider them important, they do not devote much time to them, and they do not consider their importance will increase much in the future. This is a remarkable finding since modern society, as Power (1999) observes, is an audit society with powerful demands for transparency and accountability. Such demands are acute in Academia with public control exerted through evaluations, accreditations, rankings, etc. (see e.g. Wedlin et al., 2009).

The protection of university leaders

In his study of CEOs, Tengblad (2002) reports findings that conflict with findings in studies by Carlson (1951), Stewart (1967), Mintzberg (1973), and Kotter (1982). Tengblad shows that the executives of his study have fewer work disturbances than the executives in the earlier research. Studies of modern corporations provide a likely explanation for this change in executive working conditions. Such studies suggest that various administrative units responsible for external relations buffer the executives (see Engwall, 2006). Pallas (2007) reports this is the case in particular with media relations.

Engwall's study (2008*b*) of media strategies in universities reveals a similar development. For example, in the 1960s, the old Swedish institution studied hired its first information officer. By 2006, the information department of the same university employed more than a dozen people. Moreover, the additional employees had more professional training, such as in journalism or communications. At the same time as university information activities expanded, titles were upgraded. For example, when the Head of Information at one of the old Swedish universities retired in early 2009, a Director of Communications succeeded her.

It is evident from Engwall's study (2008*b*) that the expansion in university media relations is a result of the increasing public interest in universities as societal actors. Universities today are more and more in the media, especially compared to former times when the media did not cover universities to any significant extent. This is particularly true in the media's reporting on academic research results and on academic organizational problems. Although some university leaders in this study complain of the media coverage, on the whole they feel well treated by the media. This attitude may reflect the successful protective work by their media relations units. First, such units have developed rules for handling upcoming media issues. Second, media training is now a standard procedure for university leaders, from deans upwards. Third, the units act as buffers to protect VCs and to direct questions to other university personnel. As one registrar commented: 'We want to save the VC for the positive things; I take care of those things that are not so positive'.

It was also evident that another task of the media relations units is to promote the universities. We observed two promotional strategies – *branding* and *boosting*. The first of these strategies, *branding*, means being proactive in creating a favourable picture of the university. To that end, the media relations units establish permanent relationships with journalists, issue press releases, and hold press conferences. In recent years, the web has also become an important means of communication. One VC in the study even writes a blog that attracts considerable public attention. The second strategy, *boosting*, means creating a sense of pride inside the organization. For example, one VC stresses the importance of developing internal communications that advance the organizational culture and the strategic thinking processes.

The three forces (coercive, normative, and mimetic) of the governance framework presented above are instrumental in the development of the universities' information activities. The increase in competition for students and for research resources has stimulated protective and promotional efforts with the state. In addition, academic norms are now more positive about media coverage, not least because of student requests. Finally, there are considerable mimetic elements in the comparisons with other universities and in the exchange of experiences by information officers from various institutions.

Conclusions on university leaders

Our analysis of the roles of the thirty VCs points to significant differences in their mandates in comparison with corporate executives. These differences derive principally from their different missions: market share and profit versus a reputation for academic and research excellence. Furthermore, unlike the appointments of corporate executives that reflect market demands, the appointment of university VCs reflects the influence of the state, the professions, and the market, all of which have a voice even as their individual influence varies in space and over time. Despite these differences, however, it appears that university leaders experience the same hectic work life that corporate executives do. For example, university leaders would like to take a more long-term perspective even as they are required to take short-term actions. Yet, like corporate executives, university leaders are able to shield themselves somewhat from external disturbances by the creation of special buffering organizational units.

DEPARTMENT CHAIRS IN ACTION

Introduction

In the previous section, we noted that universities have created media relations units to protect VCs from external disturbances. However, there is also another administrative layer that protects the VC. Middlehurst (1993: 189) comments:

> [Universities have] tightened their coordination and control systems; streamlined their decision-making processes; integrated their academic, financial and physical planning; improved their cost-control procedures; devolved many managerial functions from institutional to the basic unit and individual level; restructured operational units; created new functions and posts (public relations, marketing, a development office); developed new policies; and shifted from collective to individual managerial responsibility and accountability.

Reporting, analysing, measuring, monitoring, and evaluating have thus become central concerns at all levels in all areas of the university. Managing such challenging activities requires skilled leadership. One administration leader charged with these tasks is the DC who copes daily with demands from both above and below in the organizational hierarchy.[10] These demands arise from various expectations in different arenas – education, research, and administration. The explanation for the importance of the DC's leadership role is that because of changes in university administration, the university departments have often acquired greater authority, and the DCs, as department managers, have had to assume larger responsibilities.

In an academic department, while there may be a department tradition surrounding the DC position, it is also likely that its members have different expectations and experiences of leadership. The special nature of the DC position, owing to the characteristics of the university, may also create problems. DCs are appointed to a term of office during which time they lead their peers. At the completion of this term, the DCs resume their former positions as colleagues. The DC position is rarely for the long-term. Moreover, since most DCs are faculty members, they have little or no administrative experience. Their expertise is in an academic discipline, such as English literature, mathematics, or chemistry; management is a new responsibility for them.

The Work of Managers

Expectations of DCs

The interviews in the four departments at Uppsala University (Eriksson, 1997, 1999) revealed that the department members had many expectations of their department leaders. Table 11.3 lists these various expectations in two columns. The left column lists the administrative roles DCs are expected to assume: able administrator, skilled economist, and strategist. Their tasks require them to be coordinators, problem-solvers, and conflict-solvers. As diplomats, communicators, and decision-makers, they must lead. The right column lists a different set of DC roles that are more related to the profession. The DC is expected to be a colleague who mentors, advises, and inspires. The DC should also act as a mediator, servant, and facilitator for the department. In addition, the DC should be an experienced teacher, established researcher, and well-considered professional. High performance ratings on the professional roles may partially explain high performance ratings on the administrative roles, but the opposite relationship is less likely.

The analysis of the study's interviews reveals that the department members take three perspectives about the DC role:

- the professional perspective
- the collegial perspective
- the conflictual perspective

The *professional perspective* primarily relates to the *legitimization* process for leaders. Many interviewees described the specific skills and expertise they (and others) need to exert influence and authority. DCs should be able to inspire and lead their colleagues. As a representative for the professionals in the department who require research funding, DCs should be able to attract resources. DCs should be well regarded for their scholarship in the department's field. In order to lead the department, DCs should also understand the profession and its professionals – that is, DCs should know the department from the inside.

The *collegial perspective* relates to the process of creating a collegial environment in which DCs support the work of individuals and of the group. Such leadership is based on facilitation and consultation, with the leaders viewed as servants – and never as masters. DCs are involved in consensus decision-making as they represent the department members' interests and opinions; such a process

Table 11.3 Expected DC roles

Able administrator	Colleague
Skilled economist	Mentor
Strategist	Advisor
Coordinator	Provider of inspiration
Problem-solver	Mediator
Conflict-solver	Servant
Diplomat	Facilitator
Communicator	Experienced teacher
Decision-maker	Established researcher
Leader	Well-considered professional

Source: Eriksson (1997: 42–3).

reflects the idea that 'we need to make all the important decision together'. In this perspective, the best DCs embrace the group's commonly shared values and goals fully even as they recognize there will always be people in the group who reject those values and goals. In describing the presidency of the American college, Cohen and March (1974: 3) explain the natural discord in the academic institution:

> The organization appears to operate on a variety of inconsistent and ill-defined preferences. It can be described better as a loose collection of changing ideas than a coherent structure. It discovers preferences through action more than it acts on the basis of preferences.

However, it is no simple matter to identify the values and goals related to the dual mission of teaching and conducting research. Various interpretations of values are possible; achievements of goals are difficult to measure. At times, when the DC can distinguish no common values and goals, the fragmentation in the department poses a severe challenge to the collegial perspective.

The *conflictual perspective* relates to the circumstances where opposing goals, values, and expectations among department members sometimes create departmental tension. Just as in other organizations, conflicts may occur for many reasons in an academic department.[11] Three types of conflict emerged in this study. The first conflict is caused by the diversity and allocation of work tasks. For example, a director of studies may ask a colleague to teach in a term that the colleague planned to use for research, or an administrator may ask others to do work they think unnecessary or boring, or a teacher may adopt teaching methods not used by others in the same field. A second conflict arises out of career-oriented concerns. Examples are disagreements about the distribution of career-enhancing tasks and of resources (new computers, rooms, equipment, funding, etc.). The third conflict may result when people simply 'can't get along'.

The majority of the interviewees emphasize that DCs must be able to manage these complex situations and difficult conflicts. A good DC, they say, listens to others and respects the diversity of their opinions, but is unafraid to make a decision when the situation warrants it.

The work of the DC

The four DCs in the study confirm the other interviewees' opinion that they are expected to play many roles. However, they also agree they cannot meet all expectations, some of which seem either impractical or incompatible with others. One DC said:

> I believe I handle this job rather well – I am tough enough for it. It is a matter of recognizing that one cannot satisfy all demands. It is also necessary to be able to choose what one wants to prioritize and sometimes dare to make unpopular decisions.

Another DC said:

> I am not the manager type. I do not want to make decisions and control others in the department. I know that I am expected to take a stand and get involved with university issues, but I am not that type of person. I serve as a department chair only

Table 11.4 Working conditions of the DCs

Activity	DC1	DC2	DC3	DC4	Average
Total work hours per week	54	50	53	43	50
Activity ≤15 minutes (%)	61	59	58	81	65
Paper work (%)	15	29	21	34	24
Meetings (%)	4	18	17	16	14
Discussions and social interaction (%)	30	17	27	49	28
Research (%)	1	24	31	1	16
Teaching (%)	50	12	4	0	18
Own office (%)	50	48	27	46	43
Elsewhere in the department (%)	24	10	10	41	20
Home (%)	21	11	10	2	12
Other (%)	5	31	53	11	25

because I feel it is my turn to bear the responsibility, but it is oppressive knowing that I cannot live up to the demands.

The four DCs, with their different personalities, confront their conflicting role expectations in different ways. Their management styles are reflected in how they use their time, where they work, and with whom they work. Table 11.4 presents their time allocation on management activities based on their two weeks of diary entries.

The DCs work an average of fifty hours per week. These hours include teaching and research as well as departmental administration. While they think that they have enough time to complete all their work as DC, the time officially designated for DC-related work is insufficient. Thus, certain important tasks have to be set aside in order to attend to those with a higher priority. Their diaries also show that a large portion of the DCs' activities take fifteen minutes or less. DC4, in the largest of the four departments, has the most fragmented workday with 81 per cent of his activities taking fifteen minutes or less. On average, he was interrupted every eleven minutes by a knock at the door or a telephone call. The three other DCs were not interrupted as often. About 40 per cent of their time could be spent on activities taking longer than fifteen minutes.

On average, the DCs spend the highest proportion of their time (28 per cent) in discussions and social interaction. Paper work, which includes reading, answering mail, and other administrative activities, is second (24 per cent). Formal meetings take 14 per cent of their time.

Two DCs have very little time for research (1 per cent each) compared to the other DCs: one at 31 per cent and the other at 24 per cent. One DC spends a significant part of his time in teaching (50 per cent) while others spend far less. One DC does no teaching. The DC who teaches the most emphasizes the importance of student contact. Conversely, another DC stresses the greater importance of his external contacts. In their complaints that they lack time for long-term planning, the four DCs confirm the classic findings by studies on executive work behaviour.

On average, the DCs spend about two-thirds of their time in their departments, either in their own offices (43 per cent) or elsewhere in the department (20 per cent). At the extreme, DC4 spends 87 per cent of his time in the department while DC3 spends only 37 per cent in the department.

Conclusions on the work of DCs

The motivation for this research was the examination of university leadership at an administrative layer below that of university VCs. The leader role selected was the DC who administers and leads an academic department. The DC, who is the administrator closest to the teaching and research activities of the university, is a key figure in the university hierarchy.

We conclude that DCs, in their managerial and professional roles, are the focal points for diverse expectations. They are expected to be administrators who understand economic issues, who can devise and implement strategy, and who can communicate effectively both within and without their departments. In addition, they are expected to have achieved excellence in scholarship and teaching. Yet they should also be colleagues who can manage departmental personalities and conflicts. Their work environment in the midst of these multiple expectations is often one of constant interruptions with many and varied demands. In brief, DCs have to act according to both corporate (i.e. market) and collegial (i.e. professional) norm systems as described above.

CONCLUSIONS

Universities of today are not ivory towers, and perhaps never were. They have always depended on the community for funding – from the Sovereign, wealthy benefactors, or the State. Thus, university leaders have always been subject to the conflict between their professional values and the interests of their financiers. However, the twentieth and the twenty-first centuries have created new scenarios for university leaders that pose new leadership problems.

First, owing to state initiatives in many countries, national university systems have expanded significantly. The last 100 years have witnessed the founding of new universities and the growth of established universities with many more students and faculty members. Second, the development of large corporations and the rapid diffusion of management concepts worldwide have made corporate leaders role models whose behaviour other leaders are expected to emulate. Third, as scientific fields have developed, the academic disciplines have become professionalized with professional associations, journals, annual meetings, etc.

As posited by the framework of this chapter, today state, professional, and market forces strongly influence the programmes and policies of universities. The effect on university leaders, obviously, is significant. It has long been established in leadership studies that the work of leaders is demanding in many respects. One particular problem is the difficulty in making long-term plans when work is constantly interrupted by short-term disturbances. More recent studies indicate that corporate leaders as well as academic leaders are increasingly protected from such disturbances by various buffering arrangements. However, such arrangements may be less effective for academic leaders than for corporate leaders since the former are required to manage professional issues as well as state and market concerns. While this problem exists at the VC level, it is more pronounced at the DC level since DCs have less administrative support.

An interesting feature in university hiring is that markets for university leaders, including VCs, are developing. This development is part of the professionalization of university leadership that is related to the three changes discussed above. Formerly, the position of the VC circulated among faculty members, often with an annual term of office. With the passage of time, as the position became more demanding, faculty members were elected and re-elected as VCs for longer terms. Today it is common to recruit VCs externally. As noted above, even the two tradition-steeped UK universities of Cambridge and Oxford recruited externally for top administrative positions! While we expect to see more such hiring activity in the future, academic reputation is likely to remain a required qualification of university top leaders who seek administrative posts.

By contrast, DCs today are rarely recruited externally although this situation may change in the future as department mergers increase, and ranking surveys and accreditation results are more publicized. These trends may require DCs to make more external contacts and to expand the marketing of their departments. The DC of the future will remain an important university leader, but one with perhaps a broader range of skills and expertise than the traditional professor with little or no administrative experience.

Taking the findings of this and other chapters in this book into consideration, it is natural to ask if universities are moving towards a mainstream corporate model of organization and leadership. To a certain extent, this appears to be the case. The corporate model is penetrating universities as a result of a movement towards market models and the introduction of different kinds of management control systems. However, at the same time, universities, like other professional organizations dealt with in this book, will continue to have a strong professional component. This conclusion means that university leaders will face problems and standards different from those of their corporate counterparts.

Finally, we call for further research into the leadership of academic institutions, particularly because such institutions in recent years have been exposed to the management philosophy of New Public Management (NPM). This philosophy, with its methods and ideas that typically are applied to the public sector, is not necessarily applicable to academic governance. The adaptation of NPM to academic institutions requires more intensive studies of academic leaders at all levels. As such research is undertaken, it is appropriate to place the recent developments in an historical perspective in order to demonstrate the changes in the working conditions of university leaders. In addition, such studies should take an international perspective in order to demonstrate the effects of regulation on university leadership. Two strategic aspects in that context are the development of recruiting principles and the growth of administrative support functions in academic institutions.

NOTES

1. On professions, see e.g. Larson (1977), Abbott (1988), Burrage and Torstendahl (1990), and Torstendahl and Burrage (1990).
2. Economists point to a similar dichotomy for business entities – that is, whether the organizational hierarchy or the market is the more efficient way to make certain transactions (Williamson, 1985). In this tradition, Ouchi (1980) introduced the concept of 'clan' for the intermediate form between the market and the organizational hierarchy.
3. The argument that markets are linked to mimetic forces may appear to depart from DiMaggio and Powell's distinction between competitive and institutional isomorphism. However, in the former case, these authors refer to a 'free and open competition' (1983: 150) that seldom exists. Instead, most markets have a limited number of actors who can observe and copy their competitors.
4. For a critical view of the argument of a radical change in science production, see e.g. Whitley (2000: xiii–xxii).
5. For a fuller account of the Swedish system for higher education and research, see Engwall and Nybom (2007).
6. The questionnaire was in five parts. Part one asked basic questions about the interviewees and their institutions. Part two asked about the interviewees' professional qualifications. Part three focused on interviewees' previous professional experience. Part four dealt with the interviewees' external commitments. Part five asked ten questions on interviewees' attitudes.
7. http://www.admin.ox.ac.uk/po/vc/biog.shtml, http://www.ox.ac.uk/media/news_stories/2008/080616a.html, and http://www.admin.cam.ac.uk/offices/v-c/richard.html. As the first web link reveals, Hood had previous experience as a VC in New Zealand but had a limited scientific record other than his doctoral research. In contrast, both Hamilton at Oxford University and Alison at Cambridge University have considerable research records.
8. See further Engwall (2007).
9. See further Engwall (2008a).
10. Instead of the term, Department Chair (DC), some universities use the term Department Head. While it is possible to distinguish between the terms in order to reflect the selection patterns or organizational images in different university systems, that distinction is unnecessary for this analysis.
11. Organizational theory more often uses the metaphor of the 'political system' to refer to this situation. The metaphor implies that individuals and groups of individuals compete and have different wills, values, interests, and norms (e.g. Cyert and March, 1963; Pfeffer, 1981).

REFERENCES

Abbott, A. D. (1988). *The System of Professions: An Essay on the Division of Expert Labor.* Chicago, IL: Chicago University Press.

Bargh, C., Bocock, J., Scott, P., and Smith, D. (2000). *University Leadership: The Role of the Chief Executive.* Buckingham: Open University Press.

Bolden, R., Petrov, G., Gosling, J., and Bryman, A. (Eds.) (2009). Special Issue of *Leadership*, 5(3): 291–394.

Bryman, A. and Lilley, S. (2009). Leadership researchers on leadership in higher education. *Leadership*, 5(3): 331–46.

Burrage, M. and Torstendahl, R. (Eds.) (1990). *Professions in Theory and History: Rethinking the Study of the Professions*. London: Sage.

Carlson, S. (1991/51). *Executive Behaviour: Reprinted with Contributions by Henry Mintzberg and Rosemary Stewart*. Acta Universitatis Upsaliensis, Studia Oeconomiae Negotiorum 32. Stockholm: Almqvist & Wiksell International.

Clark, B. R. (1983). *The Higher Education System: Academic Organization in Cross-national Perspective*. Berkeley, CA: University of California Press.

Cohen, M. D. and March, J. G. (1974). *Leadership and Ambiguity, The American College President*. New York: McGraw-Hill.

Collinson, D. and Collinson, M. (2009). 'Blended leadership': Employee perspectives on effective leadership in the UK further education sector. *Leadership*, 5(3): 365–80.

Cyert, R. M. and March, J. G. (1963). *A Behavioral Theory of the Firm*. Englewood Cliffs, NJ: Prentice-Hall.

de Boer, H. and Goedegebuure, L. (2009). The changing nature of the academic deanship. *Leadership*, 5(3): 347–64.

DiMaggio, P. J. and Powell, W. W. (1983). The iron cage revisited: Institutional isomorphism and collective rationality in organizational fields. *American Sociology Review*, 48(2): 147–60.

Drori, G. S., Meyer, J. W. Ramirez, F. O., and Schofer, E. (2003). *Science in the Modern World Polity: Institutionalization and Globalization*. Stanford, CA: Stanford University Press.

Engwall, L. (2006). Global enterprises in fields of governance. In M-L. Djelic and K. Sahlin-Andersson (Eds.), *Transnational Governance: Institutional Dynamics of Regulation* (pp. 161–79). Cambridge: Cambridge University Press.

—— (2007). The universities, the state and the market. Changing patterns of university governance. *Higher Education and Policy*, 19(3): 87–104.

—— (2008a). The university: A multinational corporation? In L. Engwall and D. Weaire (Eds.), *The University in the Market* (pp. 9–21). London: Portland Press.

—— (2008b). Minerva and the media: Universities protecting and promoting themselves. In C. Mazza, P. Quattrone, and A. Riccaboni (Eds.), *European Universities in Transition: Issues, Models, and Cases* (pp. 31–48). Cheltenham: Edward Elgar.

—— Nybom, T. (2007). The visible hand versus the invisible hand: The allocation of research resources in Swedish universities. In R. Whitley and J. Gläser (Eds.), *The Changing Governance of the Sciences. The Advent of Research Evaluation Systems* (pp. 31–49). Berlin: Springer.

—— Levay, C., and Lidman, R. (1999). The roles of university and college rectors. *Higher Education Management*, 11(2): 75–93.

Eriksson, C. B. (1997). *Akademiskt ledarskap* (Academic Leadership), Acta Universitatis Upsaliensis. Studia Oeconomiae Negotiorum 43. Uppsala: Almqvist & Wiksell.

—— (1999). Role conflict and ambiguity at the department level. *Higher Education Management*, 11(1): 81–96.

Etzkowitz, H. and Leydesdorff, L. (Eds.) (1997). *Universities and the Global Knowledge Economy: A Triple Helix of University–Industry–Government Relations*. London: Pinter.

Gibbons, M., Limoges, C., Nowotny, H., Schwartzman, S., Scott, P., and Trow, M. (1994). *The New Production of Knowledge: The Dynamics of Science and Research in Contemporary Societies*. London: Sage.

Gosling, J., Bolden, R., and Petrov, G. (2009). Distributed leadership in higher education: What does it accomplish? *Leadership*, 5(3): 299–310.

Gronn, P. (2009). Leadership configurations. *Leadership*, 5(3): 381–94.

Kotter, J. P. (1982). *The General Managers*. New York: Free Press.

Kuhn, T. S. (1962). *The Structure of Scientific Revolutions*. Chicago, IL: The University of Chicago Press.

Lakatos, I. (1970). Falsification and the methodology of scientific research programmes. In I. Lakatos and A. Musgrave (Eds.), *Criticism and the Growth of Knowledge* (pp. 91–195). Cambridge: Cambridge University Press.

Larson, M. S. (1977). *The Rise of Professionalism*. Berkeley, CA: University of California Press.

Middlehurst, R. (1993). *Leading Academics*. London: Open University Press.

—— Goreham, H., and Woodfield, S. (2009). Why research leadership in higher education? Exploring contributions from the UK's leadership foundation for higher education. *Leadership*, 5(3): 311–29.

Mintzberg, H. (1973). *The Nature of Managerial Work*. New York: Harper & Row.

Nowotny, H., Scott, P., and Gibbons, M. (2001). *Re-Thinking Science: Knowledge and the Public in an Age of Uncertainty*. Cambridge, UK: Polity Press.

Ouchi, W. G. (1980). Markets, bureaucracies and clans. *Administrative Science Quarterly*, 25 (March): 129–41.

Pallas, J. (2007). *Talking Organizations: Corporate Media Work and Negotiation of Local Practice*. Uppsala: Department of Business Studies, Uppsala University (Doctoral thesis No. 133).

Pfeffer, J. (1981). Management as symbolic action: The creation and maintenance of organizational paradigms. In L. L. Cummings and B. M. Staw (Eds.), *Research in Organizational Behavior* (Vol. 3, pp. 1–52). New York: JAI Press.

Power, M. (1999). *The Audit Society*. Oxford: Oxford University Press.

Rooney, D. (Ed.) (2005). *Handbook on the Knowledge Economy*. Cheltenham, UK and Northampton, MA: Edward Elgar.

Stewart, R. (1967). *Managers and Their Jobs*. London: MacMillan.

Tengblad, S. (2002). Time and space in managerial work. *Scandinavian Journal of Management*, 18(4): 543–65.

—— (2006). Is there a 'New Managerial Work'? A comparison with Henry Mintzberg's classic study 30 years later. *Journal of Management Studies*, 43(7): 1437–61.

Torstendahl, R. and Burrage, M. (Eds.) (1990). *The Formation of Professions: Knowledge, State and Strategy*. London: Sage.

Wedlin, L., Sahlin, K., and Hedmo, T. (2009). The ranking explosion and the formation of a global governance field of universities. In L. Wedlin, K. Sahlin, and T. Hedmo (Eds.), *Exploring the Worlds of Mercury and Minerva. Essays for Lars Engwall* (pp. 317–33). Acta Universitatis Upsaliensis. Studia OeconomiaeNegotiorum 51. Uppsala: Uppsala University.

Whitley, R. (2000). *The Intellectual and Social Organization of the Sciences* (2nd ed.). Oxford: Oxford University Press.

Williamson, O. E. (1985). *The Economic Institutions of Capitalism*. New York: Free Press.

12

Managerial work at the top: Tracing changes in work practices and efforts towards theory development[1]

Stefan Tengblad

BACKGROUND TO THE STUDY

At the end of the last century, I had the opportunity to replicate Sune Carlson's study that he had published in *Executive Behaviour* in 1951. As a preparation for my replication study, I had the privilege of interviewing Carlson in December 1998, a year before he passed away. Although he had made his study many years before, in the interview Carlson remembered and shared important information about the study with me (not least, the names of the participating Chief Executive Officers (CEOs) and other behind-the-scenes data). This interview allowed me to gather more information about the challenges the CEOs of his study faced, given the context of their times. In this chapter, I summarize the results of my study and the articles that resulted from it. I also comment on the study's findings in relation to a recent study of top executives at large German companies (Matthaei, 2010).

Sune Carlson, who was born in 1909, was a true pioneer in Swedish business administration research. He began his academic career in 1932 at the Stockholm School of Economics as an assistant teacher in economics to Bertil Ohlin (later a Nobel Prize Laureate for his work in the field of international trade). Carlson earned his PhD at the University of Chicago in 1936 where he became friends with many prominent intellectuals, including Milton Friedman (Carlson, 1983). With his appointment as Professor at the Stockholm School of Economics in 1947, he became the first professor in Sweden in the field of administrative science.

In 1998, Sune Carlson was living as a retiree with his wife in a large, book-filled apartment with a spectacular view of central Uppsala. His physical health had deteriorated at the time of my interview, but he was still very acute mentally. He shared his current reading with me – a long biography of Czar Peter the Great, written in French. His lifelong curiosity about geography, history, economic affairs, and culture is probably what made him such an innovative scholar.

During World War II, Carlson was the secretary of the Swedish National Price Control Board where he made contacts with a group of prominent Swedish business leaders. He used these contacts when he formed The Administrative

Problem Study Group (the A-group) in 1944 that consisted of about a dozen senior business executives. The members of the A-Group were from the Swedish business elite, including CEOs for the largest banks, insurance companies, and metal producers in the country. Moreover, the chairmen of the Swedish Employers' Association and the Federation of Swedish Industry were members (Tengblad, 2003).

In 1946, Carlson made a study trip to the United States on behalf of the A-Group. This trip gave him the idea of studying CEOs' hourly activities at work, their meetings, their reading, and their leadership styles. Carlson presented this idea to the head of the American Management Association, Alvin Johnson, and to his research director. They thought the idea was fascinating but doubted whether any CEOs would participate (Tengblad, 2003: 89). On his return to Sweden, in a meeting with the A-Group, Carlson described the Americans' reaction to his idea and then challenged the Swedish CEOs to take part in such a study: 'The Americans don't think you'll dare to do it!' (ibid.). No one in the A-Group wanted to appear cowardly, especially to foreigners, and thus almost all members agreed to the study. Thanks to Carlson's brilliant initiative, a new research field was established.

The purpose of this chapter is to summarize the research into executive work with a particular focus on the changes in managerial work. The chapter reviews the progress and future of this work – the various developments to date and the areas yet to be investigated.

THEORETICAL FRAMEWORK: THE CEO AS EXPECTATIONS HANDLER

One problem in the design of my study that replicated Carlson's study was the choice of a theoretical perspective. Carlson used Henri Fayol's theories and the scientific management movement in his design; the normative purpose of his study was to suggest improvements in planning processes, flow of communications, and decision-making. In interpreting his results, which were very different than he had expected, Carlson took a rudimentary, cultural, and external control perspective that presented the CEOs mainly as victims of inhumane work pressures and excessive task fragmentation. Such work conditions prevented them from working in a reflective and deliberate way. Carlson (1951: 73–4) wrote that CEOs scarcely had time 'to sit down and light a cigarette before they were interrupted by a visitor or a telephone call'. In another classic bit of imagery, Carlson wrote that before the study he imagined the business leaders as orchestra conductors or ship captains, but after the study he saw them more as puppets in a marionette theatre.

Henry Mintzberg, who faced a different situation more than twenty years after Carlson's research, had the benefit of many later studies and much more development in the field of administrative science. Mintzberg's theoretical framework (1973) consisted mainly of management science theory that he used to support his goal of standardizing managerial work practices to make them more effective using rational decision-making models and programming of comparable work tasks. Like Carlson, Mintzberg concluded that executives work reactively and informally instead of reflectively and formally. The executives in his study worked superficially because of the relentless work tempo, their attraction to verbal media, and their orientation towards current events; as a result, they had neither the interest nor time to think about the past or to plan for the future.

My solution to the problem of choosing a theoretical perspective for my research was to avoid taking an explicit perspective in the beginning, especially on how effective management should be performed. I also wished to be sensitive to the meaning of the concepts used to measure executive work and the theoretical underpinnings of the Carlson and Mintzberg studies. The concepts in themselves really suggest that management should be a structured and deliberate process.

In Herbert Simons' book, *Administrative Behavior* (1947), probably the most influential theoretical perspective in management research, the manager is a decision-maker. The manager's chief responsibility is to process information in order to make, confirm, or correct decisions in a goal-oriented way. Thus, the manager is a rather autonomous and powerful administrator who should be able to handle a huge amount of information in a thoughtful and organized manner.

However, in the Carlson and Mintzberg studies, field notes and diary/observational data revealed that decision-making took only about a tenth (9–10 per cent) of the CEOs' work time, and therefore was not a very time-consuming activity for them.[2] With one exception, the CEOs in my research did not see themselves primarily as decision-makers either. Rather they thought they were leaders or in-charge managers with much broader responsibilities than just decision-making. Being in charge meant taking an overview of the organization, communicating with others, and motivating (as well as following-up) the management group and the workforce. The CEO role also meant working to institutionalize the organization's values by instilling the spirit of achievement, cooperation, responsibility, and innovation in employees (Tengblad, 2004). The role had two other dimensions as well that are not normally included in the concept of leadership: maintaining good relations with shareholders, creditors, unions, and other important stakeholders, and interpreting financial reports from various units in the company. To conclude, decision-making, according to my research, was only one of the CEO's many responsibilities.

The theoretical concept that best described the CEO role in my study was *expectations handler*. The role of CEO meant taking responsibility for multidimensional expectations about the organization's financial returns, its environmental and social performance, and its leadership. This view of the CEOs' responsibilities might be seen as adhering to a general stakeholder perspective, but, interestingly enough, the CEOs were most concerned with the expectations from one particular group – the stakeholders with a stock market connection. Thus, the CEOs tried to develop a business agenda that was both appreciated externally (possibly a rather short-term outlook) and yet was good for the company in the long-term. The CEOs addressed this dual task by making sense of these expectations in collaboration with the Board of Directors and the executive group, and then communicating the business agenda strategically. In this communication, realistic promises and achievable forecasts for financial performance were considered essential since failure to meet expectations could easily lead to a crisis of confidence, plummeting stock prices, and negative business press (Tengblad, 2004).

The challenge for the CEOs was to communicate a sound strategy to actors in the financial community and then to meet forecasts. It was considered wiser to present a conservative projection that could be met – or even better, surpassed – than to promote an overly optimistic vision of the future that would disappoint observers if not achieved.

Dealing with expectations required working with two parallel processes. First, the CEOs performed *identity work* in communication with important stake-holders, which involved defining their roles and the organization mission. Second, the CEOs dealt with *alignment processes*, which involved aligning their organization with this mission.[3] In taking responsibility for these tasks, the CEOs devoted the main part of their time to communicating these expectations, to monitoring how well the expectations were being met, and to rewarding and punishing managers accordingly. At time of this study, financial market actors were placing intense pressure on most of the companies to reach quarterly forecasts; this pressure contributed to a conformist climate that left little room for open and creative discussion (ibid.: 598).

METHODOLOGY

At first, I chose a basic research design for this study that would permit comparisons, as much as possible, with Carlson's study, in which the design was to study ten CEOs for four weeks each, using the diary method. Then I decided to add direct observations in order to make comparisons with Mintzberg's study in which he observed five executives for a week each. At this point, there was a possibility that my study would to be too large and too time-consuming. The solution was to study eight CEOs: direct observations of four CEOs for a week each, and 1–2-day observations of the other four CEOs. This fieldwork was conducted between April 1998 and May 1999. I recorded almost 2000 hours of executive work, of which more than 300 hours were based on direct observation. See Table 12.1 for comparisons of the three studies' participant numbers and other fieldwork data.

The eight CEOs in my study worked in various sectors: *media, banking,* insurance, *retailing,* energy, the paper industry, medical equipment, and *manufacturing.* (Industries in italicized print are industries in which CEOs observed for a full week.) Six of the eight companies were listed on the Stockholm Stock Exchange, one was state-owned, and one was family-controlled. Four companies were Swedish-oriented, three employed more than 90 per cent of their employees outside Sweden, and one company had the bulk of its operations in a single urban region. In 1999, the eight companies in total employed more than 40,000 people and had a total market value of close to 25 billion US dollars. See Tengblad (2002, 2006) for additional details on the methodology of this study.

Table 12.1 Comparative figures for the three studies of executive behaviour

Number of	Carlson	Mintzberg	Tengblad
participants	9	5	8
weeks of work studied	45	5	40
days of work studied	About 200	25	159
hours of work studied	About 2000	202	1965
hours observed	–	202	332
hours self-recorded	About 2000	–	1633
activities registered in total	1500–2500	547	1748
activities self-recorded	1500–2500	–	1040
activities observed	–	547	708

MAIN RESULTS

The study generated several findings. While there may be disagreement on which are the most important findings, I believe three findings are most significant:

- A different kind of fragmentation: from time to space
- Stakeholder relations change over time
- Managerial work as a rather stable craft

Next I describe these findings and discuss their implications.

A different kind of fragmentation: from time to space

Fragmentation is definitely one of the most reported results in studies of managerial work. Therefore, it was a great surprise to learn that the CEOs of this study experienced less fragmentation (e.g. interruptions of work, changes in work tasks, initiation of new activities) than many managers in other studies. As other chapters in this book clearly illustrate, managers in the middle and front tiers, as well as owners of small companies, work in a rather fragmented way. As other chapters in this book also indicate, it seems unlikely that managerial work in general has changed in this regard; rather it seems that the work of top managers has become less fragmented in nature.

Figure 12.1 compares the times CEOs work alone (without interruption) in this study to the times in Carlson's study (Tengblad, 2002: 558). In the Carlson study, the most common working alone time is one to six minutes while in my study it is twenty-eight minutes or more. Carlson complained that this excessive fragmentation left little room for reflection and planning. In the longer working alone time that the new study reveals, the CEOs could use that time for preparing speeches, planning for board meetings, and/or writing monthly letters to their employees. Their time alone work was as intense and as varied as other kinds of CEO work, but it was no longer as fragmented as that of lower level managers. They avoided daily disturbances with the assistance of secretaries and other close co-workers.

However, in another important aspect, the CEOs in the new study had more fragmented work, namely the aspect of space. The CEOs in Carlson's study were based either in central Stockholm or in smaller, regional towns where their

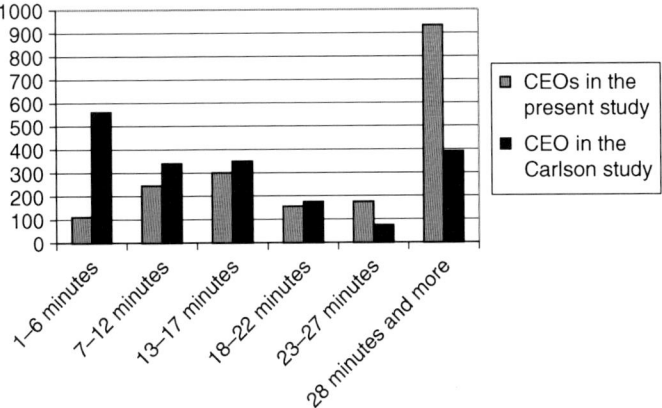

Figure 12.1 Length of periods before interruptions occur when working alone (Tengblad, 2002: 558)

companies' main operations were located. The CEOs in Stockholm were within short walking distances to most meetings while the CEOs outside Stockholm made regular train trips to Stockholm for meetings. The CEOs in Carlson's study only travelled outside Sweden on extraordinary occasions. However, in the new study, three of the eight companies had more than 90 per cent of their operations outside Sweden. Thus, Stockholm was still an important meeting venue for the CEOs in the new study, but it was not as important as in Carlson's study.

One consequence of the increased geographical dispersion of company operations and of stakeholder locations was the increased time CEOs spent travelling (see Table 12.2). Compared to the Mintzberg study, the new study shows that the CEOs spent three times as much time travelling. The CEOs in the new study travelled more than seven times as much as the CEOs in Carlson's study. One reasonable conclusion is that the increase in efficient means of transportation has made global business operations much easier to conduct. Emilio Matthaei (2010) examined the work behaviour of twelve German top executives for large firms (four weeks per executive) and found a pattern of executive work that is similar to the pattern I found in my study; the executives' average workweek was 65.5 hours; their time distribution was 64 per cent meetings, 17 per cent transportation/tours, 9 per cent telephone calls, and 10 per cent other.

An important aspect of the new travelling pattern that the new study revealed was that the CEOs often worked at places besides their offices – for example, hotel rooms, airport lounges, conference rooms, and guest offices. On average, they spent three-fourths of their working time away from their offices. The CEOs at the four international companies of the new study spent about 40 per cent of their working time outside Sweden. The picture of busy executives in their offices, issuing orders like generals in staff rooms, was no longer valid. Instead, the emerging picture was the busy executive travelling the globe in order to manage and control the company.

Table 12.2 Total working time: Average values per participant (Tengblad, 2006: 1446)

		Tengblad			Mintzberg		Comparison
		Hour/ week	Share (%)	Range (%)	Hour/ week	Share (%)	Hour/week (%)
1.	Meetings	45.7	63	59–71	28	64	63
2.	Tours	0.9	1	0–4	1	2	–10
3.	Telephone calls	5.4	7	2–16	2.6	6	108
1–3.	*Total verbal*	52	72	62–80	31.6	72	65
4.	Desk work	9	12	4–23	8.8	20	2
5.	Transportation	11.2	16	7–21	3.6	8	211
	Total working time per participant	*72.2*	*100*		*44*	*100*	*64*

Matthaei (2010) reaches similar conclusions. However, the work of the executives in his study was even less fragmented as far as time, and even more fragmented as far as space is concerned. Indeed, they worked in almost any physical location.

Carlson noted that the CEOs' out-of-the-office travel, especially absences of several days, created disturbances in administrative routines since the approval of many activities required their presence. One might assume that this problem would have intensified since the new study showed the CEOs' travel time had increased substantially, but this was not the case. On the contrary, the problems associated with CEO absenteeism seemed greater in companies where the CEOs spent more time in their offices! It is possible to use the time CEOs spend in their offices as a proxy for how centralized/decentralized their leadership styles are. The leadership style of the CEOs who spent 39–52 per cent of their time in their offices was based on centralized authority, while the CEOs who spent 18–23 per cent of their time in their offices had adopted a leadership style based on decentralized authority.

As a company grows in size, the need for decentralization increases. In a company with 1,000 employees, a top manager can exert much more hands-on control than in a company with 100,000 employees. Since Carlson made his study, new management techniques have been developed for facilitating more decentralized control based on monitoring economic activity rather than on monitoring physical/functional activity. One important finding in my comparison with the Carlson study was that the CEOs in the new study were much less occupied with the more hands-on functional activities such as purchasing, production, product development, marketing and sales, and personnel (see Table 12.3). Instead, they dealt more with financial activities and issues. Typically, this meant that instead of discussing how a production or purchasing problem should be handled, the CEOs in the new study spent time reviewing financial reports and discussing financial matters, for instance, what could be done in order to increase a certain key ratio. When the need for finding solutions for unsatisfactory production numbers or for purchasing problems became apparent, subordinate managers were assigned to deal with these tasks rather independently. The CEOs were not closely involved in finding, approving, or rejecting such solutions. In many cases, the accounting systems and the financial targets were designed to hold subordinate managers

Table 12.3 The functional area of activities (Tengblad, 2002: 555)

	Tengblad			Carlson
	Time spent per day	% of total	Range (%)	Share
1. Finance, legal	3.05	25	13–45	10
2. Accounting	0.14	2	1–5	*
3. Purchasing	0.19	2	0–7	8
4. Production	0.58	8	3–13	21
5. Product development	0.31	4	1–7	11
6. Marketing, sales	1.16	10	5–15	16
7. Personnel	1.19	11	4–21	15
8. Public/investor relations	1.35	13	3–23	13
9. Organizing, planning	1.05	9	4–14	7
10. Others, not defined	1.59	16	11–21	0
Total (hours and minutes per day)	*12.22*	*100*		*100*

*Included in 'Finance, legal'.

accountable for their actions, absent instructions from the CEO. One CEO commented:

> We have a very fast accounting. In eight days we have a monthly performance report. It's very good because is there a problem one month which also appears the following month, then they know I will be calling them. So actually, you don't have to interfere much, it regulates itself. (Tengblad, 2004: 594)

As Table 12.3 shows, the decreased emphasis on most functional activities (Tengblad study vs. Carlson study) was not true of the category of 'Public/investor relations'. The explanation seems to be the expectation that today's CEOs should be heavily involved in this area; they cannot delegate such responsibilities to lower level managers as easily as they delegate other functional tasks.

In the comparison of the two studies, there is also a clear difference in time usage by CEOs at companies organized mainly as business areas or as parent-subsidiary structures and by CEOs at companies organized mainly along function lines. The second CEO group was more involved in areas related to production, purchasing, product development, marketing and sales, and personnel (see Table 12.4).

Another way to describe this difference is that the work of a CEO has become more generic and less dependent on the particular contexts of production, technology, and customer and industrial relations. When Carlson made his study, the notion of general management – the idea that a skilled manager can manage in many different settings – did not exist. This notion did not become popular in Swedish business life until the 1970s. The present focus on financial control and the decentralization of business problems to managers with special expertise has surely made it easier for CEOs to move between industries. However, it is an open question – indeed, a controversial one – whether it is necessary for top managers to have expert knowledge of their industry and its technology in order to do a good job. Whatever the answer to this question, effective cooperation and good

communications between the management generalists and the various management specialists are still needed. The generalists understand the more universal
ingredients of company success, and the specialists have the expertise in important subareas related to the specific company in question.

A comparison of my study with Mintzberg's study suggests that a more
decentralized leadership style develops over time. As Table 12.5 shows, the
CEOs in the new study devoted less time to decision-making, requests, and
solicitations, and more time to ceremonies and information exchange. These
CEOs think supporting a motivated and well-informed management group and
acquiring knowledge about general company operations were more important

Table 12.4 Financial and functional work tasks in functional and multidivisional
organizations (Tengblad, 2002: 564)

	Carlson: functional organizations (%)	Tengblad: functional organizations (CEOs 1–4) (%)	Tengblad: business area organizations (CEOs 5–8) (%)
Finance activities (items 1–2 in Table 12.3)	10	20	35
Functional activities (items 3–7, except public relations)	70	39	30
Other activities (items 8–10)	20	40	35
Total	*100*	*100*	*100*

Table 12.5 Purpose of contacts (Tengblad, 2006: 1449)

		Tengblad			Mintzberg		Comparison
		Hour/ week	Share (%)	Range (%)	Hour/ week	Share (%)	Per cent
1.	Organizational work	0	0	–	0.6	2	–
2.	Scheduling	0.7	1	1–2	0.9	3	–22
3.	Ceremony	8.2	16	8–23	3.8	12	116
4.	External board work	1.9	4	0–8	1.6	5	19
1–4.	*Total secondary*	*10.8*	*21*	*18–25*	*6.6*	*21*	*64*
5–7.	*Requests and solicitations**	*4.3*	*8*	*5–10*	*5.7*	*18*	*–25*
8.	Observational tours	0.9	2	0–5	0.3	1	200
9.	Receiving information	11.4	22	17–30	5.1	16	124
10.	Giving information	10.1	19	16–23	2.5	8	304
11.	Review	9.1	18	15–25	5.1	16	78
8–11.	*Total informational*	*31.5*	*61*	*59–62*	*12.6*		*150*
12.	Strategy (important decision-making)	3.6	7	3–10	4.1	13	–12
13.	Negotiation	1.8	3	0–7	2.5	8	–28
12–13.	*Total decision-making*	*5.4*	*10*	*5–14*	*6.6*	*21*	*–18*
	Total	*52*	*100*		*31.6*	*100*	*65*

than being involved in approving/rejecting micro-suggestions. In many respects, this change reflects a relative shift from a focus on *administrative management* towards *institutional leadership* (Tengblad, 2006).

The German executives in Matthaei's study (2010) also spent around 60 per cent of their contact time on information tasks. But they also spent more time on decision-making than on ceremonies, which may reflect a difference in management traditions. It may also mean that the shift away from administrative management is less profound in some countries than Tengblad (2006) suggests.

Stakeholder relations change over time

The business environment in Sweden in the late 1940s and early 1950s was very different from that of the late 1990s. When Carlson made his study, only a few years after the most devastating war in human history, there was an enormous demand in Europe for raw materials, investment products, and consumables. However, there was a severe shortage of foreign currency across the continent that made overseas trade a challenging prospect. The Marshall Plan was only in its earliest phase, and Sweden's rapid growth of the 1950s was still a few years ahead. Since there were no properly functioning markets, especially across borders, political intervention was necessary. Such intervention, already institutionalized in Sweden after the outbreak of the war, continued for years. A significant context of Carlson's study was the fierce, political struggle in Sweden between those who wanted to permantize and even increase political control over industry and finance and those who wanted to return to the pre-war institutional arrangements. Several participants in the Carlson study were actively engaged in this political struggle (Tengblad, 2003).

Neither government nor military officials acted as the primary coordinators in the Swedish economy during World War II. Rather, prominent business executives and established industrial leaders coordinated the economy through trade associations and various committees (e.g. the National Price Control Board where Carlson was secretary). The need to coordinate the distribution of raw materials among firms, or to ensure the availability of capital and other resources needed for investments, or to allocate foreign sales among companies meant that the CEOs spent a lot of time at trade association meetings and on committees under governmental influence (see Table 12.6). In these years, it is understandable that trade associations and contacts with the governmental agencies and committees took more of the CEOs' time than meetings with other stakeholders.

The CEOs in the new study rarely met politicians, governmental officials, suppliers, or customers, and seldom took part in trade association activities. Instead, they met regularly with managers who reported to them directly, and frequently attended various internal meetings and external board meetings. The new study revealed two new categories of important contacts for the CEOs – the press and the financial analysts/institutional investors. Three CEOs in the new study met these actors more frequently than they met any other external parties. Satisfying the financial markets was an integral part of the work

Table 12.6 Four-week distribution of meetings (Tengblad, 2002: 553)

	Tengblad			Carlson	
	No. of meetings	% of total meeting time	Range (%)	No. of meetings	% of total meeting time
Own secretary	9	2	0.4–4	30	3
CEO assistant	–	–	–	22	7
Directly reporting managers	42	30	9–64	42	30
The owners, the board	3	4	0–10	4	3
Personnel/union meetings	3	5	0–11	1	2
Other internal meetings	19	18	4–32	28	8
Internal meetings, total	*78*	*59*	*23–79*	*127*	*52*
Customers and suppliers	5	6	0–10	9	9
Competitors/colleagues	3	5	0.4–15	5	2
Governmental agencies/ committees	3	3	0–24	9	8
Trade associations	1	1	0–4	14	19
Press contacts	2	2	0–8	0	0
Investors, analysts	3	4	0–12	0	0
Other public relations	3	3	0–5	0	0
External board meetings	2	8	0–19	1	2
Other external meetings	6	10	1–27	11	8
External meetings, total	*27*	*41*	*21–77*	*49*	*48*
Total	105	100		176	100

of the CEOs at listed companies. Demanding organizational climates resulted (Tengblad, 2004).

The new study noted the powerful influence of the stock market on CEOs' work. In the Mintzberg study, shareholders are referred to as a group of little strategic importance. On the whole, the new study confirmed that 'the shareholder value movement' (Davis and Thompson, 1994) has had an influence on managerial work practices in Sweden. Before 1993, traditional institutional investors (e.g. fund managers) had very little influence on corporate governance issues that were controlled by a network of industrialists linked to a few influential owner-groups and to a few commercial banks (Tengblad and Ohlsson, 2010).

Managerial work as a rather stable craft

To this point in the chapter, the discussion concerns the major differences among the three studies as far the work of CEOs. These differences are evidence of the very large changes in the business environment and in technologies for communication and transportation in recent decades. In addition, the differences strongly suggest that more decentralized and less fragmented management practices have occurred in these years. Do these changes imply the arrival of a radically different kind of managerial work? My response is, despite the above-mentioned differences, 'no'. In particular, I disagree with those who claim that managerial work based on flexible, non-hierarchical network organizations has emerged (Drucker, 1988; Handy, 1989; Kanter, 1989; Peters, 1989). In my opinion the CEO is as powerful a figure today as in decades past. Today the CEO's work, with its control responsibilities – informing, delegating, and attending ceremonies – does not mean that CEO control has diminished, only that it has changed in character. Moreover, both bureaucratic and managerial work practices – built on tradition (taken-for-grantedness) and selection (elimination of inadequate practices such as loose network organizations) – have remained relatively stable. Neither the hierarchy nor the bureaucracy of the CEO role has been challenged to any substantial degree.

To test the stability of managerial work practices, I compared the results of the new study with Mintzberg's thirteen propositions or, more accurately, his twelve testable propositions (see Tengblad, 2006). My test supports eight of Mintzberg's propositions and partially supports two of his propositions. The two propositions my test does not support are: (*a*) interruptions are commonplace and (*b*) managers appear to prefer brevity and interruptions. This test clearly underscores the fact that there are many aspects of managerial work that are rather independent of particular contexts and technologies. Executives' increased air travel and their use of mobile phones and electronic communications have made their work more hectic, geographically dispersed, and communicatively intense.

CONCLUDING DISCUSSION

Expectations handler: Developing a realistic view of managerial work

The authors in this book argue against the view of managerial work as a rather structured, pre-planned, and ordered activity. They support this argument by highlighting the prevalence of emotions, political processes, symbolic actions, ambiguity, and uncertainty in the everyday work of managers. However, this argument should not be interpreted to mean that management is the opposite of 'rational order' – unstructured chaos where actors only pursue selfish interests in order to satisfy emotional needs. Management can be seen as the effort to create order out of chaos, even if such order is likely far from fully achievable. When order is really achieved, the outcome will probably be stiff and inert management practices, performed by grey and faceless bureaucrats, best suited for tightly regulated markets.

Expectations handler, as a concept, suggests the limitations of looking at the CEO role from an either/or perspective – the rational decision-maker or the powerless figurehead. The concept of expectations handler reflects more recent research about leadership and organizational culture. This research has shown the importance of human interaction and the symbolic/emotional aspects of managerial work while still retaining the view of the CEO as a purposeful actor accountable to outside parties for actions and results. Expectations handling implies a leadership style that avoids rigid planning and decision-making processes; instead, expectations handling can be performed in a much more adaptive and instructive way through experimentation, dialogue, negotiations, and a willingness to make changes. Some CEOs in the new study had developed such a view of their work through reflection. Top managers can be reflective practitioners, as one CEO made clear:

> One thing I learned at Handels (i.e., the Stockholm School of Economics) concerns an idea that is totally wrong – that a manager can lead any kind of organization. I have really come to this conclusion through my own experience, and I wonder why highly gifted persons thought so wrongly in the first place. I think the main reason was that they saw top management as something very structured and planned. The problem with this model is that managerial work is much more chaotic. You simply cannot plan all your time and your actions in advance. Unexpected events always occur. People come to me regularly and ask: 'How the hell should we deal with this [situation]?' When I look back on the important decisions I have made over the years, a great many were made on the following basis: 'Let's do it like this!' All such decisions have unknown side effects and consequences [...] Since there is much chaos in managerial work, it is very important to be knowledgeable about operations in order to take part in the dialogue on how the company should proceed. (CEO of a finance company in a feedback session on the 8th of October 2000.)

To conclude, it is my conviction that it is time to establish an alternative in management science better suited to the true nature of managerial work that is characterized by the ubiquity of complex and ambiguous work tasks and uncertain outcomes. This is also a matter of highest relevance for educators. Why should we teach students textbook management techniques that are of little or no use outside the classroom, and which they often are required to unlearn after graduation? Instead, we should teach students how successful managers of today work and how modern organizations function. Put simply, our teaching and our writing should be based on studies of how successful managers work – adaptively/ inductively, interactively, and creatively. Our primary teaching goal should not be to pass on the scientific community's traditional and enduring view of how managers work – rationally/deductively, sequentially/systematically, and objectively. While the rational/deductive, sequential/systematic, and objective ideals are central to the craft of the researcher/academic, instilling them in managers will only make them more science-like and not more scientific. If the study of management is to be a respected subject in business science, we need to break with the view of the manager as an untrained scientist and instead embrace the chaotic view of the role. Formal rationality falls short in a world that is complex and ambiguous and where results are uncertain. There are practitioners, ignorant of management theory, who are enormously successful. Let us allow their experiences to influence our discipline in a profound way.

Dissemination of results

To date, this study has been reported in two articles in the *Scandinavian Journal of Management* (*SJM*), one in *Organization Studies* (*OS*), and one in the *Journal of Management Studies* (*JMS*). The *SJM* articles (*a*) replicate the Carlson study (Tengblad, 2002) and (*b*) revisit the Carlson study (Tengblad, 2003). The *OS* article develops the theoretical perspective of the study and presents the most interesting findings from the field notes data (Tengblad, 2004). The *JMS* article makes a systematic comparison with Mintzberg's study on the question of whether a more post-bureaucratic managerial work has been institutionalized among top managers (Tengblad, 2006).

DELETED SCENES

As a postscript to this chapter, I present some research observations that were not included in the published articles because of space limitations. These observed episodes provide some additional information about managerial work, apart from normative management models and in particular apart from the participative and equality-oriented management style often referred to as Scandinavian Management. The episodes should not be taken as evidence that Scandinavian Management does not exist. Instead, the episodes reveal that management indeed is a very broad and open-ended set of activities and that the repertoire of the CEOs includes practices related to Scandinavian values as well as something very different.

Unexpected events at a management training session: A female manager embarrassed by her manager and a rowdy Viking Party

During a two-day management training session at a company's Swedish main manufacturing unit, two unexpected events occurred. The first event was at the beginning of the session when a young and beautiful management assistant introduced herself to the participants. The following exchange took place:

> 'You are very welcome to our next training session in Sweden. My name is Johanna Borg, and I am 28 years. If you have any questions about the session, please contact me.'
> The manager responsible for the training program [and Johanna Holm's boss]:
> 'Are you married?'
> [General laughter]
> Someone: 'Unfortunately, yes.'
> [More laughter]
> Johanna: [Blushes]

The second event occurred at a Viking Party at a downtown restaurant cellar that was arranged by the Swedish host. I very much regret I was unable to take a picture (or even better, a video clip) of the Group CEO (who has since become one of Sweden's most successful industrial leaders in recent decades) dressed as a Viking, in helmet and brown kilt, swigging from an enormous beer keg while singing a rowdy song. I wondered what image the foreign participants had of Swedish culture in general and of Swedish management culture in particular.

Executive rage

The following episode illustrates how a CEO expresses angry dissatisfaction with a subordinate manager's work performance. This episode concerned an acquisition of company in a regional town distant from Stockholm where the national manager lived. In the following telephone conversation, only the CEO's comments are presented. After receiving several unsatisfactory answers, the CEO raised his voice. Leadership is not always considerate.

> CEO: 'How big are the savings you are counting on in the next three years?'
>
> CEO: [Raising his voice] 'You haven't made any calculations? This is unacceptable! You have to be engaged in this deal. I have felt before that you are so tired and uncommitted. If I were in a deal like this, I would have worked day and night. Haven't I the right to demand that you work your guts out? [...]'
>
> CEO: [Shouting]: 'I will not accept that you are reluctant to take charge of the cost structure and to move to City X. You should be prepared to move to Africa if I ask you! I will call you back at four o'clock and then you damned well better be informed about the deal. Put everything else aside.'

The CEO then slammed the receiver down, shouting at me about his manager: 'Lazybones!'

Pushing down budgetary responsibility with laughter

The following episode is from a meeting about the status of an Internet venture with an open and easy-going partner. The CEO wanted, quite unexpectedly, the project group to adopt an ambitious economic goal for the venture:

> The CEO rises and begins to sum up the meeting: 'OK. Time is running out ... [summarizing a few points and continuing]. There is a demand from the Board that the local channels should breakeven within 18 months. That should apply to our Internet venture as well. Can we all agree on that?'
>
> Manager in charge of the venture [MCV]: [Surprised] 'But ... have we decided that?'
>
> CEO: 'Is it possible to reach breakeven in 99?'
>
> MCV: 'I don't think so, seen as an independent product. But together with cost reduction in our core business, it can be possible.'
>
> [Silence]
>
> CEO: 'Because nobody else says so, I say breakeven in 1999!'
>
> Administrative manager: 'Is it realistic to reach 12 million in revenue in 1999?'
>
> MCV: 'If we can make the savings, then it can work. But we have to see this as a long-term investment.'
>
> CEO: 'Our Chairman used to say: "If you don't take care of your short-term profit, you won't survive in the long-term."'

The CEO then ended the meeting with a witty remark that supported the decision. Earlier in the meeting the administrative manager had pointed out that all operational initiatives had to be contained within the existing budget framework. The CEO said that this restriction should be 'written on the forehead' of every manager in the company. Thus, his final words at this meeting were:

CEO: 'Remember this: Breakeven in 99!' [Drawing a finger across his forehead].
[Laughter].

NOTES

1. This study of managerial work was made possible by Professor Sten Jönsson who prepared the funding application and by the Swedish Council for Research in the Humanities and Social Sciences (HFSR) who funded the research. I also express my appreciation to the eight CEOs (and their secretaries) who generously took time to keep the diaries. Finally, I thank my wife, Malin, who looked after Erik when I was away studying the CEOs.
2. Carlson's figure for decision-making is 9 per cent in total – 7 per cent for decision-making and 2 per cent for confirming or correcting the decisions of others. Mintzberg's figure for decision-making is 10 per cent (Tengblad, 2002: 557; 2006: 1449).
3. The concepts of alignment and identity work are from Munro (1996).

REFERENCES

Carlson, S. (1951). *Executive Behaviour*. Stockholm: Strömbergs.
—— (1983). *Studier utan slut*. [Studies without end]. Stockholm: Studieförbundet Näringsliv och Samhälle.
Davis, G F. and Thompson, T.A. (1994). A social movement perspective on corporate control. *Administrative Science Quarterly*, 39: 141–73.
Drucker, P. (1998). The coming of the new organization. *Harvard Business Review*, 66 (January/February): 45–53.
Handy, C. (1989). *The Age of Unreason*. London: Business Books.
Kanter, R. M. (1989). The new managerial work. *Harvard Business Review*, 67 (November/December): 85–92.
Matthaei, E. (2010). *The Nature of Executive Work*. Wiesbaden, Germany: Gabler.
Mintzberg, H. (1973). *The Nature of Managerial Work*. New York: Harper & Row.
Munro, R. (1996). Alignment and identity work. In R. Munro and J. Mouritsen (Eds.), *Accountability: Power, Ethos and the Technologies of Management* (pp. 1–19). London: International Thomson.
Peters, T. (1989). *Thriving on Chaos*. London: Pan.
Simon, H. (1947). *Administrative Behavior*. New York: The Free Press.
Tengblad, S. (2002). Time and space in managerial work. *Scandinavian Journal of Management*, 18(4): 543–65.
—— (2003). Classic, but not seminal: Revisiting the pioneering study of managerial work. *Scandinavian Journal of Management*, 19(1): 85–101.
Tengblad, S. (2004). Expectations of alignment: Examining the link between financial markets and managerial work. *Organization Studies*, 25(4): 583–606.
—— (2006). Is there a 'New Managerial Work? A comparison with Henry Mintzberg's classic study 30 years later. *Journal of Management Studies*, 43(7): 1437–61.
Ohlsson, C. (2010). The framing of CSR and the globalization of business system. *Journal of Business Ethics*, 93: 643–69.

Part V

Managerial work in small businesses

The three chapters of Part Five present studies on managerial work in small businesses. In many ways, such managerial work resembles the work of operational managers. However, compared to operational managers, they are more informal, work more closely with operations (e.g. as substitute operators), have much more deskwork, and are far more powerful.

CHAPTER 13. MANAGERIAL BEHAVIOUR IN SMALL FIRMS: DOES IT MATTER WHAT MANAGERS DO?

Henrik Florén and Joakim Tell report on their research that compares entrepreneurial work behaviour in fast- and slow-growing firms using Mintzberg's structured observation method (1973) to study twelve entrepreneurs. In general, they found more similarities than differences in the work behaviour of the leaders in these groups. However, the study concludes that entrepreneurs in fast-growing firms spend less time on decision-making and control; they also trust their employees more. The implications of the study are that the way in which managers perform work is more important than the work itself, and that good leadership provides employees with opportunities for initiative-taking and personal growth, which in turn may lead to company growth.

CHAPTER 14. THE DUALITY OF STRATEGIC MANAGERIAL WORK IN SMEs: A STRUCTURATION PERSPECTIVE

Anders Nilsson, Mats Westerberg, and Einar Häckner's study of strategic management in small businesses relates to one of the book's theme – managerial work as a social practice. They describe and analyse three episodes of strategic management in companies in different contexts using Giddens' structuration theory (1984). The authors conclude that strategic management in small businesses should be understood as 'a social practice that is ingrained with symbolism, emotions and power, and is thus multifaceted and complex'. One important contextual factor described is strategic intensity, which moderates the interplay between structures and managerial action.

CHAPTER 15. MANAGERIAL PRACTICES IN FAMILY-OWNED FIRMS: STRATEGIZING ACTORS, THEIR ARENAS, AND THEIR EMOTIONS

Ethel Brundin and Leif Melin describe managers who work in small, family-owned companies. The chapter integrates strategy as practice perspective with insight into the importance of emotions in managerial work and strategy development. The authors demonstrate that the entrepreneurs' relationships with shareholder family members, with their employees, and with their business partners are all of crucial importance to understanding the strategic development of family businesses. Their research reveals that an entrepreneur's behaviour in displaying or hiding emotions has important consequences for the strategic development of the company. The chapter concludes that there are potential benefits to recognizing the importance of emotional aspects in strategy research that typically focuses only on the so-called cognitive aspects.

13

Managerial behaviour in small firms: Does it matter what managers do?[1]

Henrik Florén and Joakim Tell

INTRODUCTION

The question of why some small firms outperform others is central in small firm research. The question is generally answered in one of two ways. One explanation, which relates to a main issue in organization theory, maintains that organizational performance is largely dependent on environmental forces; the other explanation argues that managers' strategic actions have the greater influence. This debate has resulted in various management theories, for example, natural selection theories (Hannan and Freeman, 1977), resource dependence theory (Pfeffer and Salancik, 1978), and strategic management theory (Child, 1972).

It is possible to place these theories on a spectrum with the natural selection theories at one end, strategic management theory at the other, and resource dependency theory somewhere in the middle (Romanelli and Tushman, 1986: 608). The natural selection theories propose that early in their lives, firms become tangled in complex webs of commitment and interdependencies that inhibit their capacity to make changes. Strategic management theory emphasizes that managerial choice is instrumental in shaping firms' domains and their competitive characteristics. Resource dependency theory takes an intermediary position between these two views in explaining organizational performance.

The principal aim of this chapter is to increase our knowledge of the reasons behind the growth of small firms. Our research design (direct observation of managers) is a behavioural comparison of top managers in fast- and slow-growing small firms, in particular in relationship to the more general question of the importance of managerial agency. This approach allows us to investigate the extent to which managerial behaviour influences firm performance (in terms of small firm growth).

BACKGROUND

Numerous researchers have tried to explain why some small firms outperform others. The explanations include the following: the entrepreneur's personality (Miller and Toulouse, 1986; Delmar, 1996), the firm's organization and strategy (Covin and Slevin, 1989; Wiklund, 1998), the firm's resources (Zander and Zander, 2005), and the entrepreneur's experience (Dyke et al., 1992). Some researchers have focused more specifically on the behaviour of the entrepreneur (Gartner, 1988; Gartner et al., 1992; Sarasvathy, 2001). The implicit assumption of this behavioural focus is that the *actions* of the manager-entreprenuer are critical to firm performance (Delmar, 1996; Sadler-Smith et al., 2003). Since the research on small firm growth has been reviewed elsewhere (see Davidsson et al., 2006; Dobbs and Hamilton, 2007), we will not discuss it further here. We note instead, despite this large body of research, some researchers maintain that the evidence on small firm growth is both insufficient and contradictory. Research on the relationship between managerial behaviour and small firm performance is suggested as a way to gain a better understanding of why some small firms outperform others (Gartner et al., 1992; Sarasvathy, 2001).

In an attempt to bring some clarity to this issue, we look at managerial behaviour in fast- and slow-growing firms. Our ambition is not to relate managerial behaviour to firm growth in a comprehensive manner. Rather, our goal is to identify differences in the behaviour of the managers in these two groups of firms. The main contribution of this research is its comparison of managerial behaviour in fast- and slow-growing small firms using two homogenous samples of six firms each. We chose these twelve firms so as to avoid the difficulty of trying to make generalizations about the very heterogeneous population of small firms. The twelve firms in this research are of similar size and operate in similar industries. On a group basis, the managers in the two groups are of similar age and have similar management experience.

THEORETICAL FRAMEWORK

Since we required a research design that would allow us to understand what managers 'do', we took theoretical inspiration from the research stream on managerial work that began with Sune Carlson's study (1951) of executive behaviour in large companies.[2] The principal characteristics of such research, which have rarely been used in the study of managerial behaviour in small firms, are, first, the interest in the fundamental, everyday work of managers and, second, the conclusion that managerial work is quite different than expected (Hales, 1986).

Researchers have used various terminologies in the study of what managers 'do' (for a discussion of this conceptual turmoil, see Stewart, 1989). For example, some researchers study the manager's 'work' while others study 'managerial activities' or 'managerial behaviour'. For our research, we use the general term 'managerial activities' that was introduced by Carlson (1951) and developed by Mintzberg (1973). Therefore, we compare what managers in fast- and slow-growing firms do

Table 13.1 Managerial work as roles (Choran, 1969; Mintzberg, 1973)

Managerial roles	Interpersonal roles	Figurehead
		Leader
		Liaison
	Informational roles	Monitor
		Disseminator
		Spokesman
	Decisional roles	Entrepreneur
		Disturbance handler
		Resource allocator
		Negotiator
Operational roles		Specialist
		Substitute operator

on a daily basis. In our search for the similarities/differences in the managerial activities of these two groups, we ask the following questions about managers in such firms: What are their work activities? How do they allocate their time amongst deskwork, telephone calls, scheduled/unscheduled meetings, and factory visits? Whom do they work with? Where do they work? As we are also interested in the 'how' as well as the 'what' of managerial behaviour, we take the approach often used in the managerial work research that investigates the brevity, variety, and discontinuity of managerial work (Mintzberg, 1973; Hales, 1986).

In addition to investigating the similarities/differences in managerial activities, we also compare managers' roles in the two groups. In this investigation, we adopt the conceptualization of the managerial role developed by Mintzberg (1973). According to Mintzberg, there are three elements fundamental to this role – interacting with other people, processing information, and making decisions. Prior to Mintzberg's analysis of the managerial role, Choran (1969) had identified another element: managers' engagement in operations. See Table 13.1 for Mintzberg's ten managerial roles and Choran's two operational roles that are associated with managerial work.

DEVELOPING CONJECTURES

In the following section, we explore the postulated relationships between managerial behaviour and small firm growth. These relationships, which originate in various arguments and findings in the literature dealing with small firm growth, are the starting points for our investigation. As we are not developing and testing a sophisticated model, we use the term 'conjectures' to describe our assumptions instead of 'hypotheses' (see Miller and Toulouse, 1986). Before stating our four conjectures, we reference the literature that led to each conjecture's development.

BEHAVIOURAL ORIENTATION AND SMALL FIRM GROWTH

Managerial vs. operational roles

Previous research has identified the transition from the small 'one-man-show' firm to a larger, functional organization as a major hurdle in growing the firm (Greiner, 1972; Mintzberg, 1983). Successful transition depends on the top manager's ability to delegate authority and to develop coordinating mechanisms that allow the firm to operate without direct managerial supervision (Mintzberg, 1983). In short, firm growth requires increased decentralization of managerial responsibilities and tasks. It may be conjectured that such significant changes in organizational structure will be reflected in the behaviour of the top manager. We expect to be able to test this conjecture by observing the behaviour of such managers in business settings.

The literature on managerial behaviour shows that managers in small firms, in addition to their managerial roles, often assume an operational role (Mintzberg, 1973). Choran (1969) describes two operational activities associated with managers' work in small firms. First, because of firm size, small firm managers have to perform specialist tasks (e.g. marketing, purchasing, and product development). In larger firms, there are trained people responsible for these areas. Second, small firm managers are sometimes required to work as 'substitute operators' (Choran, 1969) when additional operational resources are needed to meet the demands of the market. These managers must be available to 'fill-in-the-gaps' when there are resource constraints. In fast-growing firms, with a self-sufficient organizational structure in place, we conjecture this phenomenon may be less evident. In the fast-growing firm, the structure provides, at minimum, basic support. We therefore conjecture that managers in fast-growing firms spend less time in operational roles since they have delegated such activities to subordinates.

C1: Managers in fast-growing firms spend less time in operational roles and more time in managerial roles than managers in slow-growing firms.

Specifically, we expect to find that managers in fast-growing firms spend less time acting as specialists or as substitute operators.

Degree of formalization

There is a debate in the literature on the importance of planning in small firms. One side argues that strategic planning generally has a positive effect on firm performance (Orpen, 1985; Miller and Cardinal, 1994). For example, Duchesneau and Gartner (1990) find a correlation between firm success and the time devoted to planning. On the other side, the argument is that small firms without formal planning processes perform as well as their counterparts with such processes. For example, Robinson and Pearce (1983) reach this conclusion in their study of small banks.

However, despite the debate, most research supports the assertion that planning helps a firm organize for growth (Hart, 1992). Early research on small firm growth clearly indicates that firm growth presupposes that the degree of formalization will increase (Greiner, 1972; Mintzberg, 1983). Since informality in planning does not fit the model of firm growth, we therefore conjecture that managers in fast-growing firms will act more formally than managers in slow-growing firms.

C2: Managers in fast-growing firms exhibit more formal behaviour than managers in slow-growing firms.

Specifically, managers in fast-growing firms are expected to spend more time in scheduled meetings, where planning occurs, and less time in unscheduled, impromptu meetings. As a result, managers in fast-growing firms experience fewer work interruptions.

External vs. internal networking

Successful small firm managers manage their firms in relation to the environment as well as the internal operations. Both tasks require the manager to be a successful networker – internally with employees and externally with customers, suppliers, and business partners. The evidence from the literature indicates there is a positive relationship between networking and small firm growth (Hansen, 1995; Lee and Tsang, 2001). In their study of food manufacturers, Dyke et al. (1992) find a positive correlation between a firm's growth and the number of its external partners. Muse et al. (2005) argue that commitment to employees is a crucial element in growing, small firms. Duchesneau and Gartner (1990) show that managers in successful firms are likely to spend more time communicating with their business partners, customers, suppliers, *and* employees than managers in less successful firms.

We therefore conjecture that managers in fast-growing firms devote more time to interaction with both their employees and outsiders. Our expectation is that managers in fast-growing firms have a larger external network and more intense interaction in their firms than managers in slow-growing firms.

C3: Managers in fast-growing firms spend more time communicating with partners, customers, suppliers, and employees than managers in slow-growing firms.

Proactiveness and reactiveness

One of the most common explanations of small firms' growth is their proactiveness – managers anticipate rather than react to events. Numerous studies support the conclusion that small firm growth is positively related to such proactiveness (e.g. Miller, 1983; Covin and Slevin, 1989; Lumpkin and Dess, 1996; Becherer and Maurer, 1999). We therefore conjecture that managers in fast-growing firms are more likely to take a proactive management role than managers in slow-growing firms.

C4: Managers in fast-growing firms initiate more activities than managers in slow-growing firms.

METHODOLOGY COMMENTS

For this research, we observed twelve top managers at small, manufacturing firms (between 10 and 43 employees each): six managers at fast-growing firms and six managers at slow-growing firms. All the managers are men between 35 and 65 years of age. Their years of experience as managers vary from 1 year to 28 years. Following Henry Mintzberg's design (1973),[3] we used structured observations to collect our data – in the Winter of 2002/3 for the six slow-growing firms and in the Winter of 2006/7 for the six fast-growing firms. We observed each group during two six-week periods: one week per manager for the slow-growing firms and three days per manager for the slow-growing firms. Using Mintzberg's design for chronology, contacts, and mail records, we observed approximately 330 hours of work and 2,500 managerial activities. We observed and categorized these activities according to the managers' activity patterns and their roles. We also took extensive field notes during our observations as support for our recounting of the managers' 'stories' and 'events' (see Appendix 2 for a more detailed description of our methodology).

MAIN RESULTS

As we note at the beginning of this chapter, the principal aim of our research was to increase our knowledge of the possible importance of managerial behaviour for the growth of small firms. We undertook this research by investigating the similarities and differences in work activities of top managers in fast- and slow-growing small firms.

Similarities and differences in work activities

On an aggregated level, there is little difference in the number of hours managers at fast- and slow-growing firms work. Excluding lunch and work breaks, the average time at work for both groups is eight hours (nine hours if lunch and work breaks are included). They also spend an average of one hour in the evenings at home reading work material, for example, in preparation for meetings (see Table 13.2).

As far as work location, managers in the slow-growing firms spend 62 per cent of the workday in their offices, 14 per cent in the outer office, 8 per cent in the factory, and 16 per cent outside the firm. Managers in the fast-growing firms spend about 72 per cent of the workday in their offices, 20 per cent in the outer office, 6 per cent in the factory, and 2 per cent outside the firm. The main differences between the two groups are that the managers in fast-growing firms

Table 13.2 A comparison of managerial activities of small firm managers

	Slow-growing firms (range)	Fast-growing firms (range)
Working hours/day (including lunch and breaks)	9.1 (8–10)	8.9 (7–12)
Hours during evenings/day	1 (0–1)	1 (0–2)
Place (% of activities) – office/outer office/production/ outside company	62/14/8/16	72/20/6/2
Initiative (% of activities) – others/own/scheduled (planned meetings)	53/45/2	53/44/3

spend more time in their own offices and spend less time outside the firm. However, these differences are minor.

As far as the initiation of activities, to our surprise we observed no differences between the two groups. The results of our observations show that managers in slow-growing firms initiate the same proportion of activities that managers in fast-growing firms do.

The results for the activities lasting fewer than nine minutes are as follows: 80 per cent for the managers at slow-growing firms and 75 per cent for the managers at fast-growing firms. For managers in slow-growing firms, 51 per cent of their time is spent interacting with subordinates; for managers of fast-growing firms, the figure is 52 per cent (see Table 13.3).

The two groups also spend approximately the same amount of time with clients (10 and 11 per cent) and with suppliers, associates, and others (39 and 37 per cent).

Table 13.4 accounts for how the managers allocate their time to (*a*) deskwork sessions, (*b*) telephone calls, (*c*) scheduled meetings, (*d*) unscheduled meetings, and (*e*) factory visits. A comparison of the activities between the two groups reveals only minor differences.

Using quantitative data to illustrate managerial work in a small firm context, however, does not by itself produce a complete understanding of the 'everyday' work life of top managers in small firms. As a qualitative illustration of the

Table 13.3 A comparison of managerial activities of fewer than nine minutes, of more than sixty minutes, and of verbal contacts by small firm managers

	Slow-growing (range)	Fast-growing (range)
Proportion of activities lasting:		
Less than 9 minutes	80% (76–81%)	75% (70–84%)
More than 60 minutes	1% (0–3%)	2% (0–6%)
Proportion of time in verbal contact with:		
Subordinates	51% (32–72%)	52% (32–78%)
Clients	10% (3–19%)	11% (2–22%)
Suppliers and associates	28% (15–33%)	17% (6–51%)
Other (lawyers, financial support, governmental inspectors (e.g. work health inspectors) and job interviews)	11% (7–24%)	20% (3–37%)

Table 13.4 A comparison of managerial activities, including range of data for small firm managers, excluding lunches and breaks

	Average slow-growing firms	Range slow-growing firms	Average fast-growing firms	Range fast-growing firms
No. of activities per day	57	48–66	51	41–69
Deskwork sessions				
Number per day	13	8–20	14	7–21
Proportion of time	46%	34–50%	50%	36–63%
Average duration (min)	16	11–21	18	10–32
Telephone calls				
Number per day	17	11–21	15	8–19
Proportion of time	13%	10–16%	13%	9–16%
Average duration (minutes)	3	2–4	4	3–5
Scheduled meetings				
Number per day	1	0–2	1	0–3
Proportion of time	15%	7–19%	17%	1–22%
Average duration (minutes)	88	27–165	75	20–210
Unscheduled meetings				
Number per day	22	12–26	16	4–33
Proportion of time	19%	7–22%	16%	5–36%
Average duration (minutes)	4	3–5	4	2–7
Factory visits				
Number per day	4	2–8	2	1–5
Proportion of time	7%	2–10%	6%	1–9%
Average duration (minutes)	7	5–9	13	5–20

numbers presented in the chapter's tables, we therefore include an episode from the study (see Appendix 3) that complements the quantitative data in its description of the fragmented features of managerial work.

This episode depicts the constant change of activities in the small firm manager's workflow; we found this depiction representative of the workflow in both groups. In the space of about two hours, the manager in the episode had (as usual) several unscheduled meetings, worked at his desk, took telephone calls, and visited the factory floor. During this time he engaged in several functional areas – marketing, quality control, production, maintenance, human relations, leadership issues, customer contacts, and safety and health questions. He interacted with more than ten persons with almost no time to himself.

This episode, together with the quantitative data from the observations, provides a good summary of our observations of the managers. To a large extent, managerial work in small firms is generic, consisting of many different tasks.

Table 13.5 A comparison of small firm managers' work roles

		Slow-growing (%)		Fast-growing (%)	
		Average	range	Average	range
Interpersonal roles	Figurehead	0	0–2	2	0–9
	Leader	6	2–10	16	1–50
	Liaison	7	0–16	1	0–5
		14		19	
Informational roles	Monitor	10	6–19	14	9–28
	Disseminator	3	1–4	2	0–4
	Spokesman	2	0–4	4	1–10
		15		20	
Decisional roles	Entrepreneur	10	1–28	5	0–20
	Disturbance handler	4	1–7	2	0–5
	Resource allocator	12	3–27	9	0–14
	Negotiator	1	0–4	6	0–29
		28		21	
Operational roles	Specialist	38	12–63	29	6–53
	Substitute operator	1	0–4	7	0–45
		40		36	
	Other	3	1–6	4	1–8
		3		4	

Similarities and differences in work roles

After identifying the activities of the twelve managers, we classified them according to Mintzberg's role categories. As Table 13.5 reveals, while there are significant commonalities between the two groups, there are some differences. One difference is that managers in slow-growing firms work more hours in the specialist role. Another difference is that managers in fast-growing firms assume the leadership role to a greater extent than managers in slow-growing firms.

On a general level, however, the similarities outweigh the differences. In terms of how the managers in the two groups allocate their time in the interpersonal, informational, decisional, and operational roles, the differences are small.

THEORETICAL DISCUSSION

We began the research with four theoretical conjectures. Next, we examine these conjectures based on the analysis of our data.

> C1: Managers in fast-growing firms spend less time in operational roles and more time in managerial roles than managers in slow-growing firms.

Our observations reveal no difference between the two groups in the time managers spend on operational vs. managerial roles. Hence, our first conjecture is not supported. One interpretation of this finding is that managerial work in small firms includes a generic element of operational work that requires managers to shoulder operational roles. In order to compensate for scarce resources in small firms, managers also need to assume the roles of the specialist and the substitute operator. It seems that the simple, organizational structure of the small firm requires that all small firm managers be deeply involved in firm management, on both the strategic and operational levels.

C2: Managers in fast-growing firms exhibit more formal behaviour than managers in slow-growing firms.

Our observations reveal no difference between the two groups in the formality of managerial behaviour. Hence, our second conjecture is not supported. One possible explanation for this finding is that organizational size and industry type are more important predictors of formalization than firm performance. This explanation suggests that formal behaviour is a result of, rather than a require-ment for, firm growth.

C3: Managers in fast-growing firms spend more time communicating with partners, customers, suppliers, and employees than managers in slow-growing firms.

Our observations reveal no difference between the two groups in managerial networking behaviour. Hence, our third conjecture is not supported. According to the results of our study, interaction patterns do not explain small firm growth. On a general level, the interaction with employees and external actors is the same, independent of firm growth. One explanation for this finding is that it is the content of the interaction and not its frequency that matters.

C4: Managers in fast-growing firms initiate more activities than managers in slow-growing firms.

Our observations reveal no difference between the two groups in managerial proactiveness. Hence, our fourth conjecture is not supported. This result chal-lenges the traditional view of the high-performing, small firm top manager as a proactive individual. One interpretation of this finding is that managers in fast-growing firms do not need to take all the proactive steps themselves; what is important is that they create a culture and an organization that encourage proactive employees to anticipate rather than to react to events.

In summary, none of our conjectures is supported by our observations of managers in fast- and slow-growing firms. The managers are more similar than not. One possible explanation for this similarity is that there are methodological and conceptual errors in the study. Our study may fail to identify behavioural differences because relevant data was not obtained during the periods observed or because certain behaviours mask others.

In addition, the similarity may reflect the assumptions of the natural selection theories. Small firms may grow, not as a consequence of strategies practiced by their agents, but rather because of exogenous factors that 'create' a fit between what the firms do and the market demands. This explanation is consistent with Carlsson's observation (1951) that managers are more like marionettes than orchestra conductors – an observation that indicates firm success, to a large extent, is dependent on the environmental context. This is not to say that managerial behaviour/agency is irrelevant; we only suggest that managers' influ-ence is limited by their operating environments and the history of their firms.

From the perspective of natural selection, the results of this study suggest that fortuitous circumstances play a role in firm growth.

However, taking a strategic management theory perspective, which argues that managerial agency is influential, two alternative explanations of our results are then possible. These explanations differ from those reflecting the natural selection theories. First, it is possible that there really is no difference in the managerial behaviour of managers in fast- and slow-growing firms. Second, and more theoretically plausible, it is possible that managerial behaviour matters, but that a large part of the manager's job in small firms is generic. This explanation agrees with Sadler-Smith et al.'s research (2003) that divides managerial behaviour in small firms into three types: (*a*) generic managerial behaviour, (*b*) non-entrepreneurial managerial behaviour, and (*c*) entrepreneurial managerial behaviour.

From this theoretical perspective, one interpretation of the results of this study is that the generic and non-entrepreneurial aspects of managerial behaviours, which represent the greater part of managerial work in small firms, do not differentiate fast-growing from slow-growing firms. Instead, these behaviours are generic to many small firms, independent of their growth performance. If this conclusion is true, it may be that our observations fail to capture the entrepreneurial behaviours that Sadler-Smith et al. (2003) argue is a performance predictor. This seems a plausible explanation since these entrepreneurial behaviours may be more irregular and infrequent than the generic and non-entrepreneurial behaviours. Hence, such behaviours are more difficult to observe in observational studies.

CONCLUSION

Contrary to our expectations, our results show that there are more similarities than differences in the behaviour of managers in fast- and slow-growing firms. In the previous section, we proposed several explanations for the rejection of our conjectures that we would find differences. In this section, we develop our conclusions and discuss the implications for future research as well as the managerial implications.

One important result from this research is that it seems generic to small firms that their top managers, to a large extent, assume non-managerial roles – for example, the role of a specialist or the role of the substitute operator. Given the hectic, relentless pace of work and the need to focus on immediate problems, managing in small firms often requires managers to behave 'non-managerially' (adopting generic managerial behaviour and non-entrepreneurial behaviour using Sadler-Smith et al.'s vocabulary (2003)). Thus, our first conclusion is that a large portion of the manager's work is generic, regardless of the growth performance of the small firm. Although earlier research (e.g. Choran, 1969) reached this conclusion, we re-emphasize the importance of this characteristic of small firm management.

Drawing on previous research that argues in favour of taking an upper echelon perspective on organizations (e.g. Hambrick and Mason, 1984), we suggest that a reasonable and relevant avenue for future research is to investigate whether top managers influence the growth of the firm in particular circumstances. As dis-cussed above, while this study may give details about the generic aspects of small firm management, it may not consider the non-generic behavioural aspects that may explain why some firms outperform others. Hence, future research may examine specific behaviours that may explain the growth of fast-growing firms.[4] To capture these 'critical incidents', longitudinal research designs and close-up studies aimed at observing these small differences in behaviour over time are necessary. One specific suggestion is to use methods such as the critical incident technique (Butterfield et al., 2005; see also Chell et al., 1991) to identify behaviours that are important to firm growth and can be explored in observational studies.

Our second conclusion is that small firm growth depends on other factors than the behaviour of the top manager. Management in small firms seems to be a more complex, collective achievement than expected, involving many people working with the top manager. Hence, firm growth also depends on the actions of others, not just those of the top manager. In this study, we observed that the top managers at each of the twelve firms interacted frequently with a small group of individuals working closely with them in the decision-making. Hence, future research may take a more comprehensive approach that defines managerial behaviour more broadly. Such research should also examine the behaviour of the key individuals who support the top managers.

Given the results of this study, we offer the following managerial implications. Operational work seems to be generic to managerial work in small firms. From this conclusion, it follows that small firm managers should not overstate the importance of acting only 'managerially'. In small firms, managers need to demonstrate operational as well as managerial behaviour. Additionally, in our observations we did not identify any differences in the level of formalization in the managerial behaviours between fast- and slow-growing firms. We therefore con-clude that the level of formalization is not a factor correlated with growth. Even if this result is inconclusive, it seems advisable that managers see formalization as a consequence of firm growth rather than as a key ingredient in the achievement of firm growth.

The need for research in the field of managerial behaviour in small and growing firms is considerable, given all the internal and external challenges that their managers face. Much work remains to be done in order to better understand these challenges in managing a growing firm and developing the tools necessary to facilitate firm growth. Our hope is that the study reported on in this chapter will contribute to such future research.

APPENDIX 1: DISSEMINATION OF RESULTS

Previous presentations of this (and related) research (in reverse order of publication):

- Andersson, S. and J. Tell (2009). The relationship between the manager and growth in small firms. *Journal of Small Business and Enterprise Development*, 16 (4): 586–98.

- Florén, H. and J. Tell (2009). Managerial behavior in slow and fast growing small firms. In S. Å. Hörte (Ed.), *Research on Technology, Innovation and Marketing Management 2007–2008* (pp. 109–23). Stockholm, Sweden: Halmstad University.
- Andersson, S. and H. Florén (2008). Exploring managerial behavior in small international firms. *Journal of Small Business and Enterprise Development*, 15(1): 31–50.
- Florén, H. and J. Tell (2007). Managerial behavior and small firm performance, Presented at the 20th SEAANZ Conference, Auckland, New Zealand.
- Florén, H. (2006). Managerial work in small firms – Summarizing what we know and sketching a research agenda. *International Journal of Entrepreneurial Behaviour & Research*, 12(5): 272–88.
- Florén, H. (2005). *Managerial Work and Learning in Small Firms.* Thesis for the Degree of Doctor of Philosophy, Chalmers University of Technology, Department of Project Management, Gothenburg, Sweden.
- Florén, H. and J. Tell (2004). What do owner-managers in small firms really do? Differences in managerial behavior in small and large organizations. *Small Enterprise Research*, 12(1): 57–70.

APPENDIX 2: METHODOLOGY

There is a danger in this study's approach to exploring the relationship between managerial behaviour and small firm growth. The danger is that the conclusions from a sample population are not generalizable to a larger population owing to the number of variables influencing the results. We have therefore invested time and effort in identifying small firms that have similar characteristics in order to keep as many variables as possible constant.

SAMPLE DESCRIPTION

We first selected six slow-growing manufacturing firms from a list of firms that had participated in a previous research project. We then selected six fast-growing, small manufacturing firms for this research from a list of 'Gazelle firms' created by the Swedish financial newspaper *Dagens Industri*. Table 13.6 summarizes the key characteristics of the twelve managers and their firms.

In our observations, we noted all the managers' activities contemporaneously, minute by minute in chronological order. We then summarized and presented this data to the managers in focus groups for our joint analysis. We used these focus groups to verify the 'normality' of the data and of the sense-making related to the data. In short, these sessions helped us understand the data at a higher level than that of mere activity patterns.

An advantage of direct observation compared to interviews is that observational data are less subject to participant constraint and interpretation (McDonald, 2005). It is, however, necessary to consider the 'researcher effect' (or the 'Hawthorne effect' as it is often labelled). Although this effect is neither avoidable nor measureable (Snow and Thomas, 1994), it is important to recognize that the presence of the researcher in

Table 13A.1 A comparison of the no/slow growth firms and the fast growth firms

Study	Focus of study/ number of employees	Sex/age	Time as manager	Empirical data
No/slow growth	6 top managers	Male/ between 43 and 58 years	Between 1 and 28 years	1 week of observation
−3% average decrease in turnover during the six-year period prior to observations	(17–43 employees) Manufacturing industry			A total of approx. 204 hours of observation. A total of 1,634 activities documented.
Range: −61% to + 28%	*Average 26 employees*	*Average 49.3 years*	*Average 14 years*	Data collected in 2002/3
Fast growth +241% average increase in turnover during the six-year period prior to observations	6 top managers (10–38 employees). Manufacturing industry	Male/ between 35 and 65 years	Between 3 and 20 years	3 days' observation. A total of approx. 125 hours of observation (+2 days of observation of four of the managers (approx. 67 hours) by Master's students). A total of 855 activities (+418 activities by students) documented.
Range: +93% to +406%	*Average 24 employees*	*Average 49.3 years*	*Average 12 years*	Data collected in 2006/7

observations may affect the data and the research results. Burgoyne and Hodgson (1984) state it is necessary to discuss how observer effects have influenced the data and those who are observed. In this research, we dealt with possible distortions from the researcher effect by frank discussions with the managers, both individually and in groups.

We conclude that our presence had only a limited effect on the data and results. We explain this conclusion by the fact that in many cases someone who was unaware of our presence initiated the managers' activities (e.g. incoming telephone calls, incoming e-mails, or scheduled meetings). Some managers, however, indicated our presence meant there were fewer unplanned meetings or the scope of planned meetings was reduced. Our presence may also have had a structuring effect on the managers' workdays since they would not wish to appear ineffectual or uninvolved.

During the observations, we took turns observing the managers and we shared the task of typing each day's data into Excel spread sheets the day after each observation. In this way, we recapped more fully each day's observations.

APPENDIX 3: A TYPICAL MORNING: THURSDAY, THE 17TH OF OCTOBER

8.29 The owner-manager (OM) arrives at his office.

8.30 The factory manager comes into the OM's office. He needs the drawings for one of the company's products. The OM gives him the drawings and exchanges a few friendly words.

8.31 The OM checks his e-mail. He notes that one e-mail says an employee will soon become a father. The other e-mails are SPAM.

8.32 An employee enters the OM's offices to ask whether the meeting with the health care representatives will take place. This employee had not read the OM's e-mail stating that the meeting had been delayed a week.

8.33 The manager of the company's largest customer telephones. This manager and the OM discuss business and informal topics and also arrange a meeting date for the following week.

8.44 The factory manager enters the OM's office to tell him that his mother, who works in a hospital near Stockholm, has heard that the hospital does not want to buy products from the company's largest customer because of a bad experience with that company's salesman. The factory manager asks the OM if he thinks they should do something about this situation. Nothing is decided on this issue. Instead, the OM tells the factory manager about his telephone call with the manager at their largest customer in which he learned about the product development in other markets (Norway and Holland).

8.50 The quality manager enters the OM's office to ask about the management group meeting (with the OM, the factory manager, and himself) that was supposed to take place at 8.45. The meeting is delayed until 10 o'clock.

8.51 Since the company has received an important order, the OM goes to the factory floor to see if they have all necessary items for that particular product.

8.52 At the factory, the OM talks to an employee about materials for the order. It is a rush order, and the OM suspects that they do not have everything in inventory.

8.55 Since some items are not in inventory, the OM asks another factory employee if he has the necessary items at his workstation. This employee replies he has some, but he does not have enough.

Then the OM asks him to manufacture the additional items needed. The OM tells this employee he did not find the right size brush that the employee has asked him to buy on his way home the day before. The employee then tells the OM that the chemical paint does not work properly because iron phosphate was mixed with the clean water owing to a malfunctioning valve. When another employee joins the discussion, the OM tells him that the items he has asked for will be manufactured that day. The OM then approaches a third employee to discuss the possibility of manufacturing an item that the company usually buys but is too expensive to manufacture internally. Following their discussion, they decide to produce the item in-house. Before returning to his office, the OM asks how the work on the new lathe looks for the rest of the month.

9.09 On the way to his office, the OM talks to an employee about the internal failure in production that resulted in a missing item for a larger project.

9.15 Returning to the factory, the OM meets with an employee about the lack of some items. This leads to an internal report (that the OM sends by e-mail to the quality manager).

9.20 The OM sends an e-mail postponing the management meeting to Friday. The quality manager comes into the OM's office to ask about a project; the factory manager enters at the same time to ask about another project. The OM then asks about an item that the company has subcontracted and that was supposed to be completed the previous week. The OM also talks about the chemical paint problem. The factory manager, who was present when the machine was cleaned in the summer, wonders if the area has forgotten to clean the filters. The OM tells the factory manager to fix the problem at once.

9.35 The OM talks with the quality manager about the chemical paint problem. He asks if there is a risk of a problem in the production phase if the colour does not adhere properly to the manufactured items.

9.50 There is a discussion about the phosphate problem. The quality manager had checked into the source of the problem. While the filter is supposed to be cleaned daily, it has only been cleaned when the water is changed; that is not often enough. The quality manager agrees that the clean water is contaminated, which could mean that the colour will not stick to the products. There is a discussion about what must be done. The decision in the problem is so serious that this particular machine must be shut down and cleaned.

10.00 The factory manager enters the OM's office. The OM asks why the chemical painting has not been cleaned properly. Where is the problem? This is a serious obstacle. The OM wants to make an example of the situation to show the employees that the machinery must have proper maintenance. The factory manager leaves in order to arrange for shutting down the machine and cleaning it properly.

10.07 The OM informs a group leader that there will be delays in assembly due to the shutdown of the chemical paint machine. The OM wants the group leader to stay alert and not let the tempo slacken in the assembly group. If the tempo does slacken, the OM wants the factory manager to move some employees to other work stations.

10.15 The factory manager enters the OM's office and says that after lunch they will begin cleaning the chemical paint machine.

NOTES

1. The authors gratefully acknowledge the financial support of KK-Stiftelsen (the Knowledge Foundation).
2. For reviews, meta-studies, and conceptual studies, see Martinko and Gardner (1985), Hales (1986, 1999), Willmott (1987), Stewart (1989), Whitley (1989), Fondas and Stewart (1994), Mintzberg (1994), and O'Gorman et al. (2005).
3. See Appendix C of Mintzberg (1973) for a full description of this methodology.
4. In Chapter 3 of this book ('Managerial leadership as event-driven improvisation'), Holmberg and Tyrstrup hypothesize that specific behaviours involve the balance between a focus on opportunities and a focus on problems. This hypothesis suggests that the manager's ability to respond both reactively and proactively to critical incidents, such as opportunities and disturbances inside and outside the firm, is critical to firm success.

REFERENCES

Becherer, R. C. and Maurer, J. G. (1999). The proactive personality disposition and entrepreneurial behaviour among small company presidents. *Journal of Small Business Management*, 38(1): 28–36.

Burgoyne, J. G. and Hodgson, V. E. (1984). An experiential approach to understanding managerial action. In J. G. Hunt, D-M. Hunt, D-M. Hoskings, C. A. Schriesheim, and R. Stewart (Eds.), *Leaders and Managers: International Perspectives on Managerial Behaviour and Leadership*. New York: Pergamon.

Butterfield, L. D., Borgen, W. A., Amundson, N. E., and Magilio, A-S. (2005). Fifty years of the critical incident technique: 1954–2004 and beyond. *Qualitative Research*, 5(4): 475–97.

Carlson, S. (1951). *Executive Behaviour: A Study of the Work Load and the Working Methods of Managing Directors*. Stockholm: Strombergs.

Chell, E., Haworth, J. M., and Brearley, S. (1991). *The Entrepreneurial Personality: Concepts, Cases and Categories*. London: Routledge.

Child, J. (1972). Organization structure, environment and performance: The role of strategic choice. *Sociology*, 6: 2–22.

Choran, I. (1969). The manager of a small company. Unpublished MBA thesis, McGill University, Montreal.

Covin, J. and Slevin, D. (1989). Strategic management of small firms in hostile and benign environments. *Strategic Management Journal*, 10(1): 75–87.

Davidsson, P., Achtenhagen, L., and Naldi, L. (2006). What do we know about small firm growth? In S. Parker (Ed.), *Handbook of Entrepreneurship Research* (Vol. 3). New York: Springer.

Delmar, F. (1996). *Entrepreneurial Behavior and Business Performance*. Stockholm: Stockholm School of Economics.

Dobbs, M. and Hamilton, R. T. (2007). Small business growth: Recent evidence and new directions. *International Journal of Entrepreneurial Behaviour & Research*, 13(5): 296–322.

Duchesneau, D. and Gartner, W. (1990). A profile of new venture success and failure in an emerging industry. *Journal of Business Venturing*, 5(5): 297–313.

Dyke, L. S., Fischer, E. M., and Reuber, A. R. (1992). An inter-industry examination of the impact of owner experience on firm performance. *Journal of Small Business Management*, 30(4): 72–87.

Flanagan, J. C. (1954). The critical incident technique. *Psychological Bulletin*, 51(4): 327–58.

Fondas, N. and Stewart, R. (1994). Enactment in managerial jobs: A role analysis. *Journal of Management Studies*, 31(1): 83–103.

Gartner, W. B. (1988). 'Who is an entrepreneur?' is the wrong question. *American Journal of Small Business*, 12: 11–32.

—— Bird, B. J., and Starr, J. A. (1992). Acting as if: Differentiating entrepreneurial from organizational behaviour. *Entrepreneurship Theory and Practice*, 16(3): 13–31.

Greiner, L. E. (1972). Evolution and revolution as organizations grow. *Harvard Business Review*, 50(4): 37–46.

Hales, C. P. (1986). What do managers do? A critical examination of the evidence. *Journal of Management Studies*, 23(1): 88–115.

—— (1999). Why do managers do what they do? Reconciling evidence and theory in accounts of managerial work. *British Journal of Management*, 10(4): 335–50.

Hambrick, D. C. and Mason, P. A. (1984). Upper echelons: The organization as a reflection of its top managers. *The Academy of Management Review*, 9(3): 193–206.

Hannan, M. and Freeman, J. (1977). The population ecology of organizations. *American Journal of Sociology*, 82: 929–64.

Hansen, E. L. (1995). Entrepreneurial networks and new organization growth. *Entrepreneurship: Theory and Practice*, 19(4): 7–19.

Hart, S. L. (1992). An integrative framework for strategy-making processes. *The Academy of Management Review*, 17(2): 327–51.

Lee, D. and Tsang, E. (2001). The effects of entrepreneurial personality, background and network activities on venture growth. *The Journal of Management Studies*, 38(4): 583–602.

Lumpkin, G. and Dess, G. (1996). Clarifying the entrepreneurial orientation construct and linking it to performance. *The Academy of Management Review*, 21(1): 135–73.

Martinko, M. J. and Gardner, W. L. (1985). Beyond structured observation: Methodological issues and new directions. *The Academy of Management Review*, 10(4): 676–95.

McDonald, S. (2005). Studying actions in context: A qualitative shadowing method for organizational research. *Qualitative Research*, 5(4): 455–73.

Miller, C. C. and Cardinal, L. B. (1994). Strategic planning and firm performance: A synthesis of more than two decades of research. *Academy of Management Journal*, 37(6): 1649–65.

Miller, D. (1983). The correlates of entrepreneurship in three types of firms. *Management Science*, 29(7): 770–92.

—— Toulouse, J. (1986). Strategy, structure, CEO personality, and performance in small firms. *American Journal of Small Business*, 10(3): 47–62.

Mintzberg, H. (1973). *The Nature of Managerial Work*. New York: Harper & Row.

—— (1983). *Structure in Fives: Designing Effective Organizations*. Englewood Cliffs, NJ: Prentice-Hall.

—— (1994). Rounding out the manager's job. *Sloan Management Review*, 36(1): 11–26.

Muse, L., Rutherford, S., Oswald, J., and Raymond, J. (2005). Commitment to employees: Does it help or hinder small business performance? *Small Business Economics*, 24(2): 97–111.

Orpen, C. (1985). The effects of long-range planning on small business performance: A further explanation. *Journal of Small Business Management*, 23(1): 16–23.

O'Gorman, C., Bourke, S., and Murray, J. A. (2005). The nature of managerial work in small growth-orientated businesses. *Small Business Economics*, 25(1): 1–16.

Pfeffer, J. and Salancik, G. (1978). *The External Control of Organizations: A Resource Dependence Perspective*. New York: Harper & Row.

Robinson, R. B. and Pearce, J. A. (1983). The impact of formalized strategic planning on financial performance in small organizations. *Strategic Management Journal*, 4: 197–207.

Romanelli, E. and Tushman, M. (1986). Inertia, environments, and strategic choice: A quasi-experimental design for comparative-longitudinal research. *Management Science*, 32(5): 608–21.

Sadler-Smith, E., Hampson, Y., Chaston, I., and Badger, B. (2003). Managerial behavior, entrepreneurial style, and small firm performance. *Journal of Small Business Management*, 41(1): 47–64.

Sarasvathy, S. D. (2001). Causation and effectuation: Toward a theoretical shift from economic inevitability to entrepreneurial contingency. *Academy of Management Review*, 26(2): 243–63.

Snow, C. C. and Thomas, J. B. (1994). Field research methods in strategic management: Contributions to theory building and testing. *Journal of Management Studies*, 31(4): 457–80.

Stewart, R. (1989). Studies of managerial jobs and behaviour: The ways forward. *Journal of Management Studies*, 26(1): 1–10.

Whitely, R. (1989). On the nature of managerial tasks and skills: Their distinguishing characteristics and organization. *Journal of Management Studies*, 26(3): 210–44.

Wiklund, J. (1998). Small firm growth and performance. Doctoral thesis, Jönköping International Business Schooyl, Jönköping University.

Willmott, H. (1987). Studying managerial work: A critique and a proposal. *Journal of Management Studies*, 24(3): 249–70.

Zander, I. and Zander, U. (2005). The inside track: On the important (but neglected) role of customers in the resource-based view of strategy and firm growth. *Journal of Management Studies*, 42(8): 1519–48.

14

The duality of strategic managerial work in SMEs: A structuration perspective

Anders Nilsson, Mats Westerberg, and Einar Häckner

INTRODUCTION

The intellectual foundations of research in the managerial work tradition date from the heyday of scientific management and administrative rationalization in the early twentieth century (e.g. Taylor, 1911). A distinguishing characteristic of several later pioneering studies is their instrumental perspective on managerial work. One such study is Carlson's classic study (1951) of executive behaviour. When Carlson conducted his empirical study, the role of the scientist was 'to study work behaviour and to determine whether that was effective or not' (Tengblad, 2003: 99). Such an instrumental perspective tends to be associated with the practical question: *Does it serve?* (Law, 1996: 286).

Later studies, including the highly influential work of Henry Mintzberg (1973), have a strong empirical orientation with more interest in answering the question: *Is it true?* The title of Mintzberg's famous book on executive behaviour, *The Nature of Managerial Work* (emphasis added), illustrates his ambition to report adequately on what is out there from an empiricist perspective (Law, 1996: 286f.).

Regardless of which of the two perspectives taken, one common trait of most research on managerial work is its orientation towards the large firm (e.g. Carlson, 1951; Mintzberg, 1973; Tengblad, 2002) and its orientation towards detailed descriptions of managerial work life (Barley and Kunda, 2001: 84). Often inspired by the Carlson (1951) study, research in this tradition tends to concern the important question of which activities are most conspicuous on the executive agenda, the stimuli that cause managers to respond to their environment through their activities, and the extent to which these activities change over time (e.g. Tengblad, 2006).

This chapter differs in two important respects from the managerial work tradition referred to above. First, we adopt a structuration perspective (Giddens, 1976, 1979, 1984) rather than an instrumental or empiricist one. From this point of view, our interest is in contributing to the knowledge about the dualistic features of managerial work where managers act on the basis of cognitive frames of reference, existing control mechanisms, and moral considerations, and where their actions and such structural circumstances co-evolve over time, in a dynamic interplay (e.g. Law, 1996: 286f.). Our intent is mainly to supplement and enrich the traditional literature on managerial work rather than to criticize it. Like the strategy-as-practice perspective that Brundin and Melin (this book, Chapter 15) apply, our orientation allows us to focus more on the subtleties of the processes in which strategizing actors are involved than on the visible and countable aspects of managerial work. Second, like Brundin and Melin and Florén and Tell (this book, Chapter 13), we aspire to extend the research on managerial work to the domain of small and medium-sized enterprises ('SMEs'). SMEs are an important part of our economy and deserve greater recognition in the research on managerial work.

Conceptually, we draw on the rich tradition of approaching strategy from a behavioural point of view (e.g. Pettigrew, 1977; Quinn, 1980; Mintzberg, 1987). A main point of departure in this chapter is that we regard strategic managerial work in SMEs as a social practice with symbolic, power-related, and emotional dimensions. The visualization of this multifaceted practice requires the adoption of an alternative theoretical framework, which to our knowledge has not been employed previously in the managerial work literature. In applying Giddens' structuration theory (1976, 1979, 1984), we empirically highlight the multifaceted nature of work among SME managers when they strategize in social situations. In doing so, we aspire to contribute to a broader understanding of the emotional, symbolic, and political aspects of strategic managerial work than provided by conventional approaches, while illustrating how managerial work in SMEs is dualistic in the sense that it consists of an interplay between reactions to environmental stimuli and proactive design (Boland and Collopy, 2004).

Compared to large firms, SMEs as a group are more cautious in certain respects, for example, in the matter of ownership. To preserve the organization, SMEs – family-owned SMEs especially – typically take fewer risks than large firms (Gómez-Mejía et al., 2007). On the other hand, SMEs are characterized by a stronger entrepreneurial influence that involves discovering, evaluating, and exploiting opportunities through proactiveness, risk taking, and innovation (Covin and Slevin, 1991). Thus, the notion of duality in the structuration framework in which actors can both draw upon established structures (i.e. be conservative) and produce new structures (i.e. be entrepreneurial) is central (Giddens, 1976). Furthermore, social interaction is an important means for maintaining as well as changing structures in SMEs (see Ekanem and Smallbone, 2007). As structuration theory is largely a social process theory, it should fit well with strategic managerial work in SMEs.

Even if structuration theory seems unconventional when compared with previous studies in research on managerial work, it is receiving increasing attention in the SME and entrepreneurship literature. Responding to Gorton's call (2000) for overcoming the agency–structure divide, researchers are using structuration theory to examine such issues as owner-manager learning (Down, 1999), entrepreneurial learning more broadly (Taylor and Thorpe, 2004), the embeddedness of the entrepreneurial process (Jack and Anderson, 2002), and autocratic management in small firms (Jones, 2003). More recently, Sarason et al. (2006) offer three reasons, beyond those offered in the traditional entrepreneurship literature, that explain why structuration theory may offer new insights on entrepreneurial processes. First, while the traditional view is that the entrepreneur fills market gaps, structuration theory suggests that the entrepreneur and the social system co-evolve. Second, the traditional view is that the entrepreneur creates ventures *ex ante*, whereas the structuration view is that ventures evolve through processes where the entrepreneur engages with sources of opportunity. Third, the traditional view distinguishes between the entrepreneur and opportunity, whereas structuration theory considers these as interdependent. Accordingly, while agreeing with Sarason et al. (2006) that structuration theory offers a largely untested opportunity to take processual dynamics into consideration, we extend their argument into the domain of strategic managerial work in SMEs.

This chapter synthesizes key findings from our empirical studies of strategic managerial work in SMEs. We draw mainly upon our empirical evidence (see Häckner, 1985, 1988; Nilsson, 1998, 2008; Westerberg, 1998, 2001) where we studied strategy development, managerial information use, and management behaviour in turbulent SME situations.

THEORETICAL FRAME OF REFERENCE

The concept of the institution, with its origins in sociological theory (Parsons, 1951; Selznick, 1957), has proven useful for organization research (Meyer and Rowan, 1977; Zucker, 1977, 1983; DiMaggio and Powell, 1983; Powell and DiMaggio, 1991; Scott, 1995). Institutional theory, in its relevance to cultural influences on actions and formal structures, emphasizes values, norms, beliefs, assumptions, habits, and scripts that are taken-for-granted by the individuals who construct and enact them (Barley and Tolbert, 1997). In this chapter, we understand institutions as the shared normative and taken-for-granted assumptions that identify categories of human actors and their relevant activities and relationships (Burns and Scapens, 2000: 8). Thus, we accept Hamilton's definition (1932: 84) of the institution:

> A way of thought or action of some prevalence and permanence which is embedded in the habits of a group or the custom of a people.

Institutional studies have so far provided rather little evidence in the analysis of how institutions are created, altered, and reproduced. However, Giddens's notion (1984) of 'structure' resembles the concept 'institution' as defined above, and Barley and Tolbert (1997) conclude that institutionalization can be considered a structuration process. Giddens discusses three key characteristics for institutional orders, namely (A): systems for (*a*) signification, (*b*) domination, and (*c*) legitimation. These institutional characteristics correspond to 'the realm of action' in the real world of practice with its day-to-day interactions, namely (B): (*a*) communication, (*b*) power, and (*c*) sanctions. Furthermore, Giddens specifies three 'modalities' – that is, the dimensions of the rules and resources individual actors draw upon in linking A to B through 'interpretive acts' (Boland, 1993). First, signification in institutions (i.e. signs, signals, and symbols) is mediated by cognitive, 'interpretive schemes' as bases for communication and sensemaking (Weick, 1995). Second, systems for domination in institutions translate to power in social relations by control of 'facilities' (i.e. resources). Third, norms are the modalities that link legitimation in the institutional realm to sanctions in the realm of action. Norms that articulate how tasks should be addressed and performed define the legitimate means to reach goals.

Based on the above, it is possible to discern three ways in which the use of structuration theory (Giddens, 1976, 1979, 1984) contributes to a more complete understanding of the multifaceted social practice of strategic managerial work. First, the semantic dimension provides insights into the symbolic aspects of managerial work. Second, the power dimension assists in capturing its political aspects. Third, the moral dimension concerning 'what is right and what is wrong' is useful for understanding deeply held values, which are indicative of the emotional characteristics of managerial work (see Table 14.1).

Our conception of strategic managerial work, therefore, emphasizes strategy as patterns of thought and action, where power matters and sensemaking are facilitated by stories and legends that signal what is important (Pettigrew, 1977). Strategizing may be more or less deliberate and emergent (Mintzberg, 1987). The processes involved are often continuous and incremental (Quinn, 1980), although radical paradigm shifts will occur from time to time (Hedberg and Jönsson, 1977).

From a structuration and entrepreneurship perspective, we draw on Sarason et al. (2006) when we relate strategic managerial work, in SMEs in particular, strongly to the discovery, evaluation, and exploitation of opportunities. Individuals can use domination and legitimation to exercise social control when they rely on the social mechanisms that regulate individual and group behaviour. From a business point of view, the strategic goal is to create vision, motivation, trust, a

Table 14.1 Structure and agency in the strategic managerial work of SMEs (Macintosh and Scapens, 1990, elaborated)

Dimensions of structuration	Structural properties	Modes of mediation	Agency	Outcomes
Semantic	*Signification*	*Interpretive schemes*	*Communication and discourse*	*Meaning*
	Abstract cognitive dimension of social life whereby agents communicate	Cognitive means by which each actor makes sense of what others say and do	Speech acts	Sensemaking
Moral	*Legitimation* The moral constitution of social action	*Norms* How to operationalize the values of what is a virtue, what is important, what ought (not) to happen	*Sanctions* Rewards and punishments	*Morality* Morally meaningful action
Power	*Domination* A social system's capacity to achieve outcomes, produce power	*Resources* Allocative: The rights to hold command over material objects and knowledge about thoseAuthoritative: The rights of some agents to command others	*Power* Facilities brought to and mobilized in interaction for purposes of influence	*Influence* Coordination and control

business culture and business policies, as well as maintain *conformity* and compliance with the rules, norms, and scripts of the organization (e.g. Simons, 1995). *Norms* and *values* are internalized by positive and negative reinforcements (i.e. sanctions) that can be either positive (*rewards*) or negative (*punishments*).

THREE EPISODES

This section presents three strategic managerial cases featuring episodes derived from our empirical findings (see also Häckner, 1985, 1988; Nilsson, 1998, 2008; Westerberg, 1998, 2001). We selected the episodes from these three cases to illustrate supplementary aspects of the complex social practice of strategic managerial work by presenting very different situations under which such work is conducted (Lukka, 2005). The episode in our first case, GRAFAB, illustrates a financial crisis situation where new survival measures are critical. The episode in the second case, Smalltown House, illustrates a situation where the company is under no immediate financial threat. The focus in this episode is on the exploitation of the current business idea, despite a challenging market situation. The episode in the third case, CRAFT, involves a company neither under direct threat nor in a steady exploitative mode. This episode illustrates the management team's evaluation of a potential business opportunity. In each episode, we use the following coding scheme: Aspects that relate to structural properties are coded in **bold**, aspects that concern modes of mediation are coded in ***bold italics***, and features linked to agency are coded in underlined. For each episode, we present relevant case background material to set the scene.

Episode 1. GRAFAB: Negotiations with union representatives in a financial crisis

GRAFAB is a Swedish, medium-sized printing company. The company had been very successful for many years due to a clear niche strategy that was based on very close specialization (i.e. differentiation). Another important reason for the company's success was its charismatic CEO – Adam, a true entrepreneur. Adam started the company, but after some years sold it to a silent partner, Bertil. Later, Bertil decided to take a leadership position in the company. By then the company had become a group with several operating entities, including the main unit on the Swedish West Coast and a branch in Stockholm. Bertil made changes in organizational and authority structures as well as changes in strategy. The ramifications of these measures were unfortunate. Key actors, including Adam, left the company and profitability declined severely. After a couple of years, the company was in severe financial distress. Faced with the threat of bankruptcy, Bertil agreed to sell the company to Cesar, a key actor who had left the company. A radical turnaround process was needed, but at the time of this episode, it was still very uncertain if the new management could save the company. The episode concerns the negotiations with the local unions for the main unit and for the branch unit. Management wants the unions to accept a drastic turnaround programme, including considerable cuts in salaries and wages. Cesar represents the company management during the two separate negotiations with the union teams.

Cesar opens both negotiations with a description of the company's distressed financial situation by referring to financial accounting figures as well as the next year's budget. His intention is clearly to activate *interpretive schemes* by the union teams through **signifying** the severe extent of the crisis situation and the necessity to reduce the labour force as well as cut wages and salaries in order to survive. At the same time, an objective of this discourse is to **legitimate** the suggested turnaround programme with implicit references to morality and *norms*, such as loyalty to the company. The threat of job losses can be interpreted as sanctions if the suggested measures are turned down. It is clear that Cesar is trying to de-emphasize aspects of power and authority. Nevertheless, management's capacity for **domination** through control of *resources* is implicit in the negotiations and undoubtedly influences their outcome. Both union teams try to exercise **domination** by drawing on power since they can force management into a situation where bankruptcy and loss of *resources* are inevitable. Both union teams **legitimate** their positions by reference to union *norms*, traditions, and loyalties. They claim that many union employees will be unable to pay their bills if wages are cut, some key employees may leave, and still others may lose the motivation to do good work (sanctions). Consequently, the union teams argue, on moral grounds, it is unacceptable to cut wages and salaries. The intentions of the union teams' discourses are clearly to activate Cesar's *interpretive schemes* through **signifying** the meaning of social responsibility. Both sides in the negotiations hold to the discursive level of consciousness. However, the two union teams act a bit differently in the two negations. The union team for the branch unit is tougher in the negotiations than the union team for the main unit. At first, the branch unit team rejects the general cuts in salaries and wages while the main unit team accepts them. Yet the branch unit union team eventually accepts some salary/wage cuts as well as other measures (e.g. reduced working hours with reduced overtime compensation) under the condition that lay-offs should be fewer than recommended by the management plan.

The outcome of the negotiations saves the company and allows Cesar to change strategies. Parts of the differentiation strategy (specialization) from the start-up phase of the company are reintroduced. In addition, the company takes a step forward technologically by implementing advanced production computer hardware and software. As a result, delivery to customers is now faster and more reliable. With the success of these strategic actions, the company's financial position is secured.

The episode illustrates a situation characterized by a very severe crisis that jeopardizes the company's survival and requires drastic changes in institutions and structures. In this situation, the CEO has a rather weak power base. Furthermore, as structures must be drastically changed, it is difficult for the CEO to rely on the existing structures. Since management and the unions have different and, initially, opposing expectations of the negotiations, each side is very sensitive to the other's intentions and partially hidden agenda. Thus, the negotiations are very emotional. The episode illustrates how strategic managerial work in such situations involves skilful persuasion in discourse if the preferred action is to be approved. Management's arguments are not only practical and calculative (financial and accounting figures) but also moral and normative.

Management strategies changed profoundly at GRAFAB in two instances. The first instance was when Bertil abandoned the original specialization strategy. The second was when Cesar reintroduced specialization and implemented advanced computer-aided production equipment. The first change occurred gradually as an emergent strategy. The second, and more dramatic, change occurred under the time pressure of the severe financial crisis. The GRAFAB case illustrates how strategic managerial work depends on an acquired repertoire of recipes that may result in the (partial) reactivation of structures created in the past.

Episode 2. CRAFT: Deliberations concerning the introduction of a new product and a strategic investment

CRAFT is a small Swedish manufacturing company in the eyewear industry. The CEO founded the company in 1979 as an entity in a family-controlled company group with foreign subsidiaries and international joint ventures. The CEO has a creative background as a designer and is known for his innovative and unconventional ideas for growing the company. After the company's considerable expansion in the 1980s, competition had intensified considerably. The episode concerns a management team meeting in the early phase of planning for the introduction of a new, patented product that the CEO had designed.

After discussions about the composition of the project group, the discussion turns to capital investment financing and human resources related to the adoption of new CAD/CAM production technology. The highly influential CEO emphasizes – in strongly emotional tones – that 'this mustn't be like Northtown' (**signification**, communication, intentionality, *norm*). The management team members nod in agreement and seem to understand this statement (meaning, reflexivity). Subsequent interviews reveal that the interpretations of 'Northtown' by the management team are rather uniform, have a sequential character, and concern events that the actors relate to the case of 'Northtown' (*interpretive schemes*). Although there are small differences in the actors' interpretations of Northtown concerning the level of detail in those interpretations, the Northtown reference cues cognitive scripts among them. The team members reach a general understanding of what is important and what must not be allowed to occur (**legitimation**, *norm*) given the experience referred to in the script. A long and common history of events and occurrences produces numerous shared experiences on which to base analogies (*interpretive schemes*). The team's response to the Northtown reference is also positive because of the CEO's influential position in the company (***authoritative resources***, power). The actors suggest that the advantages of making analogies (**discursive practice**) include smoothness in work and a reduced distance between thinking and acting (rationalization). However, because of a taken-for-granted attitude, the possibility of seeing issues from new and different perspectives may be limited.

This episode concerns a situation in which the degree of change in institutions and structures is moderate. While a change in production technology is underway, the company's fundamental values are stable with no change in the CEO leadership. The episode reveals that in a small firm setting, where management team members have an extensive stock of implicit knowledge to draw upon for sensemaking purposes and where the CEO is charismatic and powerful, strategic managerial work may consist of activating the 'right' interpretive schemes in the team. Because of these schemes, it is unnecessary for the CEO to explicitly communicate the norms he considers desirable in the situation under discussion. Rather, those norms are part of the interpretive schemes activated. In turn, the activation of interpretive schemes contributes to their reproduction. Hence, the episode illustrates how a powerful CEO can control sensemaking processes through argumentation (speech acts) rather than by rational calculation. Another interesting feature of this episode is that the strategic managerial work focuses more on the intentional reproduction of existing structures than on the creation of new ones.

Episode 3. Smalltown House: Handling a market downturn and changing industry regulations

Smalltown House originated as a joinery factory in Sweden, founded by the present CEO's father and a friend some sixty years ago. In the early 1960s, the joinery factory became a manufacturer of prefabricated wooden houses. Through cooperation with other companies, Smalltown House could sell to customers using a turnkey concept with its houses in ready-to-use condition. From the beginning, the company's vision was clear – to maintain low manufacturing costs in which the company would control every step from 'log to cabin' and as much work as possible would be finished indoors. The present CEO and chief owner succeeded his father in 1979 and continued with the same basic vision. Today, Smalltown House designs, produces, and markets one-family, prefabricated wooden houses that are sold directly to the individual homebuyer. The production is based on an assembly line. The episode begins with a description of the present CEO and then deals with how he acted when the company was faced with a drastic downturn in sales following new regulations in the industry.

When Stan, the present CEO, began in the company, under his father's supervision, he wanted to master every task better than anyone else (**legitimation**). Over the years, as he worked at every station in production and at every position in management, he became a master of just about everything at the company. He acquired a comprehensive knowledge of the business that no one else at the company could match. Based on this knowledge, he installed systems to ensure that employees would perform their tasks efficiently (**domination**). For instance, most production tasks were on piece rate contracts (*resources*), the sales people were mostly independent (yet closely controlled) entrepreneurs, and all managers had stringent targets. Stan's management style was 'management by exception', and if targets were not met, sometimes he would be very critical (**sanctions**). His philosophy was that the employees should always prioritize the company's best interests (**legitimation**, *norm*). Since the company was prosperous, he was confident in his role as CEO, and others perceived him to be effective. Then a crisis occurred in the housing industry although it did not come out of the blue. There were many warning signs of a collapse in the industry that Stan had noted. For instance, he communicated frequently with a government minister who alerted him to the impending crisis (**signification**). To control the crisis, Stan decided to lower production and work with longer delivery times. However, houses that had once 'sold themselves', without any real marketing, no longer did. Reluctantly, he saw the need for change and so brought in a professional marketing manager. Since marketing was an area that Stan never had focused on, the marketing manager was the first manager who had a competence that Stan did not (**resources**). To handle the situation, Stan directed the marketing manager to devise a plan for marketing and sales. The plan was later discussed, but mainly in terms of desired outcomes (**signification**), and then the plan was formalized as a 'contract' (**domination**) between the marketing manager and Stan – if the manager delivered according to plan, he would be rewarded; if not, he would be dismissed (**domination, legitimation**, sanctions). The result was that the marketing manager made significant changes in the way Smalltown House worked with customers and made the company a market leader.

In the Smalltown House case, the change in structures and institutions is modest. We can see, in its general terms, that Stan has an impressive system for controlling the work force. The company has strong domination structures in which resources are distributed such that Stan has full control over events (even when he does not understand the means). These domination structures are supported by legitimation structures indicating what is right at Smalltown House (i.e. a strong work ethic and a norm that prioritizes work). Communication is downplayed since systems of legitimation and domination set the rules of the game. The needed change in the marketing function is accomplished with little alteration to these systems. Even in a rapidly changing market, the marketing manager has to conform to the overall system. This case exemplifies strategic managerial work where the manager (mainly acting as he has in the past) restricts actions of others substantially while still producing desired and needed change. Strategic managerial work is shown to be effective when based on power, fundamental managerial values, and efficient control mechanisms.

INTERPRETATIONS OF THE THREE EPISODES

In this section, we present the patterns of strategic managerial work derived from the three episodes. Specifically, the patterns concern (*a*) structural properties of strategic managerial work, (*b*) strategic intensity as a contingency factor for strategic managerial work, and (*c*) strategic managerial work as a multifaceted social practice.

Structural properties of strategic managerial work

Despite the different conditions for the SME managers in our three episodes (discovery in GRAFAB, evaluation in CRAFT, and exploitation in Smalltown House), as a whole the episodes show that managerial work is characterized by significant elements of power and influence, symbolic and occasionally political features, and emotional aspects that are important for persuasion and commitment. Although the importance of the semantic, power, and moral dimensions varies in the episodes, to some extent all dimensions are at play in each episode. Thus, these dimensions seem to work in a figure/ground relationship (Boland and

Table 14.2 Structural properties of strategic managerial work in SMEs

	Discovery (GRAFAB)	Evaluation (CRAFT)	Exploitation (Smalltown House)
Signification	Discourse (often symbolic) aimed at the break up of existing structures and the discovery of new ones	Speech acts convey norms and values, thus reflexively activating interpretive schemes	Means for formulating and monitoring authoritative contract with subordinate(s)
Legitimation	Normative beliefs concerning why it is justified to break up existing structures and replace them with new ones	Norms and values (often emotionally charged) used to influence interpretations of what is (un)desirable	Norms and values as basis for rewards and punishments with respect to contract fulfillment
Domination	Power dimension downplayed although implicitly present in communication	Control of sensemaking processes	Allocative and authoritative resources used to control the process of value capture (absence of politics)

Pondy, 1983) where one dimension dominates in one situation but is background in another. When oriented towards discovery, strategic managerial work appears to be highly discursive and symbolic, with power and emotion as background parameters. When concerned with evaluation, strategic managerial work draws heavily on emotionally charged norms and values. As far as exploitation is concerned, strategic managerial work appears dominated by the power dimension that directs resources in the appropriate direction (see Table 14.2).

Strategic intensity as a contingency factor for strategic managerial work

The environments in the three episodes differ significantly. GRAFAB is in a financial crisis with the possibility of bankruptcy. The problem must be dealt with immediately. CRAFT and Smalltown House are not faced with such severe crises. However, Smalltown House has to deal with environmental hostility due to changes in industry regulations. The situation at CRAFT is more stable.

There are also differences with respect to the viability of the business idea in the three episodes. At GRAFAB, the company must consider new opportunities; not even basic beliefs can be taken-for-granted (Hedberg and Jönsson, 1977). At Smalltown House, the company is considering the exploitation of the pre-existing business concept. At CRAFT, the company is considering the evaluation of a capital investment opportunity.

Based on this discussion, the three episodes can be mapped in two dimensions that (*a*) denote the perceived viability of the business idea among the companies' actors and (*b*) denote the threat level from their environments. Although the environment at Smalltown House is quite hostile, the company still operates in a

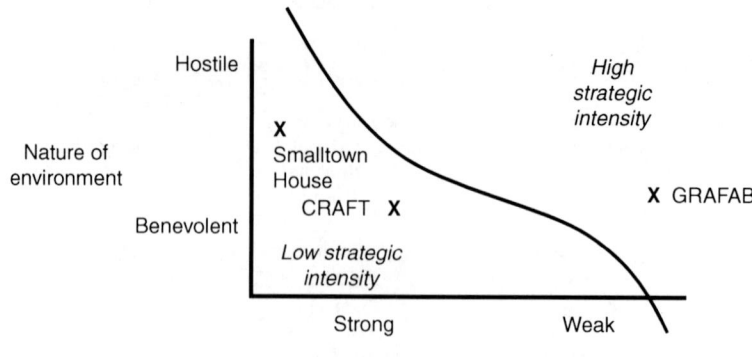

Figure 14.1 Strategic intensity as a result of environmental conditions and belief in the business idea

strongly exploitative mode. There is little overall debate on strategic issues because of the strong belief in the company's business idea. At GRAFAB, while the environment is less hostile, nevertheless the company's actors have little faith in their current business idea. Therefore, there is an intense strategic discourse about the future. At CRAFT, where the belief in the business idea and the threat from the environment are both moderate, a situation results where strategic issues are discussed but not debated.

Figure 14.1 displays the three cases. We suggest that the strategic intensity is relatively low in the area below the curved line. In this area, a company will make no attempt to radically change its business idea. In the area above the curved line a company will test, and probably change, its business idea. We suggest that the perceived viability of the business idea is the dominant dimension. If there is a strong belief in the business idea, the nature of the environment may be quite hostile without causing high strategic intensity (as evidenced at Smalltown House). If, however, the belief in the business idea is weak, high strategic intensity may result even if the environment is far from hostile (as evidenced at GRAFAB).

Strategic managerial work as a multifaceted social practice

Although our results show how power, influence, symbolism, and emotion are present in strategic managerial work, the varying dimensions of structuration in the episodes illustrate how multifaceted and complex the social practice is. One such dimension that has a varied effect is power. At GRAFAB, since the CEO is new and does not have a strong power base, instead of using power as a main management tool, he tries to persuade his opponents through discourse. At CRAFT, and even more so at Smalltown House, the CEOs have strong power bases. They manage the action (or non-action) without using persuasion – the actors understand and follow the CEOs' directions even in the absence of explicit orders. The CEOs have set domination and legitimation structures (Giddens, 1979) firmly in place in earlier time periods. Signification, then, becomes an especially important managerial tool for building legitimation and domination for the future when the power base may weaken. When the power base is strong, signification can assist in directing action (or non-action); however, in such situations, the predominant features of strategic managerial work in SMEs appear to be legitimation and domination.

A second factor characterizing strategic managerial work is the duality between structure and action. Existing structures are of less value at GRAFAB than they are at CRAFT and Smalltown House. Since larger changes are necessary at GRAFAB, the actors question the reliance on existing structures. At CRAFT and Smalltown House, the CEOs use existing structures, the actors accept the strong institutions, and the processes operate without any strong agency component. The actors monitor their own and others' social behaviour by implicitly following their knowledge of how to act and how to interpret events and the actions of others (Macintosh, 1994: 171). In contrast, at GRAFAB, where the processes rely heavily on agency, the actors can rationalize their actions and explain how situations should be interpreted (ibid.).

A third factor characterizing managerial work is the element of politics. At CRAFT and Smalltown House, managerial agendas are transparent. At GRAFAB, such agendas are implicit and/or partially hidden. A game-like situation results. For example, the unions see the negotiations as a zero-sum game, while the management, using discourse, tries to create a common understanding of the situation as a potential win-win opportunity. Thus, there is a stronger political dimension to managerial work at GRAFAB than at CRAFT and Smalltown House. Such a political emphasis calls for discourse.

A fourth factor characterizing managerial work is that the processes that rely less on agency tend to exhibit traits of strategic managerial work as a craft (Mintzberg, 1987). At Smalltown House, mastery of detail and quality of performance resulting from intimate familiarity with every aspect of the company are highly valued. At CRAFT, it is evident that the CEO, acting as a 'pattern recognizer', is attuned to stories from the past and their relationship to the company's current situation. When strategic managerial work in SMEs relies heavily on structure, it appears that it is the owner/manager's experientially acquired frames of reference that most strongly influence action.

PROPOSITIONS ABOUT STRATEGIC MANAGERIAL WORK IN SMES

In this section, taking a structuration viewpoint based on the interpretations of our findings, we offer eleven propositions on strategic managerial work in SMEs. These propositions concern the structural properties of strategic managerial work, strategic intensity as a contingency factor for strategic managerial work, and strategic managerial work as a multifaceted social practice.

As illustrated in our episodes, strategic managerial work has symbolic, emotional, and power-related characteristics. Yet the relative importance of these characteristics may differ from one managerial work situation to another. In particular, the extent to which managerial work is oriented towards discovery, evaluation, or exploitation is likely to be an influential component in the composition of such a 'mix'. Thus, we propose:

P1: When discovery-oriented, strategic managerial work in SMEs is predominantly discursive and symbolic, while power and emotion have less influence.

P2: When evaluation-oriented, strategic managerial work is predominantly based on norms and values with an emotional content, while symbolism and power have less influence.

P3: When exploitation-oriented, strategic managerial work is predominantly power based, while symbolism and emotion have less influence.

As the episodes in our three cases suggest, the level of strategic intensity may relate to the use of different structural properties. In situations of high strategic intensity, the reliance on signification is greater since it is a tool for making sense of an ambiguous situation. When strategic intensity is lower, sensemaking is not the main issue. Instead, domination and legitimation are used to coordinate, control, and create meaningful action. Thus, we propose:

P4: The higher the strategic intensity, the greater the extent to which strategic managerial work in SMEs relies on signification.

P5: The lower the strategic intensity, the greater the extent to which strategic managerial work in SMEs relies on domination and legitimation.

Regarding the link between strategic intensity and managerial work with opportunities, it seems clear that the more intense situations require discovery, while less intense situations relate more to evaluation and exploitation of opportunities. Thus, we propose:

P6: The higher the strategic intensity, the greater the extent to which strategic managerial work in SMEs is oriented towards discovery of opportunities.

P7: The lower the strategic intensity, the greater the extent to which strategic managerial work in SMEs is oriented towards exploitation and evaluation of opportunities.

While previous research offers important contributions to knowledge about managerial work (e.g. Carlson, 1951; Mintzberg, 1973), such research offers little guidance on its structural and agency properties. Our use of structuration theory sheds some light on the dualistic nature of managerial work. The agency properties are especially apparent at GRAFAB (i.e. when the strategic intensity is high). Our findings suggest that processes to a large extent are agency based when the current situation is not deemed viable and changes of structures and institutions are necessary. In contrast, at Smalltown House, where the strategic intensity is low, we see that the structural properties dominate. Thus, we propose:

P8: The higher the strategic intensity, the greater the extent to which strategic managerial work in SMEs relies on agency.

P9: The lower the strategic intensity, the greater the extent to which strategic managerial work in SMEs relies on structure.

Finally, we suggest that the extent to which a CEO is firmly established as a company leader is likely to affect the extent to which managerial work draws on the structural properties of signification, legitimation, and domination. We also posit that there are fewer demands for political and democratic processes in SMEs since their CEOs generally have ownership positions. Therefore, the latter two structural properties (i.e. legitimation and domination) are especially pronounced in the strategic work of SMEs. Thus, we propose:

> P10: The more firmly established that the CEO is in the company, the greater the extent to which strategic managerial work is based on domination and legitimation.

> P11: Domination and legitimation are more influential components of strategic managerial work in SMEs than in large corporations.

CONCLUDING REMARKS

We conclude this chapter with some comments on our theoretical contributions to a richer understanding of strategic managerial work in SMEs. Our contributions concern the following themes: (*a*) the understanding of strategic managerial work in SMEs as a social practice that is ingrained with symbolism, emotions, and power, and is thus multifaceted and complex; (*b*) strategic intensity as a contingency factor for strategic managerial work; and (*c*) the non-sequential nature of strategic managerial work in SMEs as evidenced by the duality of structure and action.

Related to our first theme, our findings suggest that strategic managerial work in SMEs contains symbolic, emotional, and power-related aspects that tend to overlap. Although our propositions suggest that one or two of these aspects dominate in certain situations, all are present to some extent. The impact of symbolism, emotion, and power, which may be subtle and difficult for outside observers to discern, makes strategic managerial work in SMEs both multifaceted and complex. As a result, a successful manager may require a broad action repertoire. In addition, management education may need to take this requirement into consideration.

Related to our second theme, our findings suggest that strategic intensity may be crucial to an understanding of important aspects of strategic managerial work in SMEs. The intensity level seems to act as a contingency factor since the content of work varies sharply depending on the level of intensity. Thus, an accurate perception of the firm's internal and external environments may be important for managers so that they can fit their actions to the situations. Also, it is important for researchers to acknowledge this contingency factor if they are to understand strategic managerial work.

Related to our third theme, our findings suggest that strategic managerial work in SMEs can be understood as a duality involving structure and action. Structure sometimes drives the way forward while action takes a back seat. This pattern clearly contradicts the traditional sequential management models (plan, implement, and follow-up) since structural elements constrain what is possible. This path dependency constrains current actions based on the organization's history while the current situation constrains future actions (Kimberly and Bouchikhi, 1995).

In sum, we conclude that structuration theory, as a frame of reference for understanding strategic managerial work in SMEs, is a promising research avenue. We claim that structuration theory has the requisite variety (Ashby, 1958) needed to understand the subtle complexities of strategic managerial work. Therefore, studies of managerial work from a structuration perspective can supplement and enrich more instrumental or empirical approaches. Our hope is that this study will provide a starting point for such work.

REFERENCES

Ashby, W. R. (1958). Requisite variety and its implications for the control of complex systems. *Cybernetica*, 1(2): 83–99.

Barley, S. R. and Kunda, G. (2001). Bringing work back in. *Organization Science*, 12(1): 76–95.

—— Tolbert, P. (1997). Institutionalization and structuration: Studying the links between action and institution. *Organization Studies*, 18(1): 93–117.

Boland, R. (1993). Accounting and the interpretive act. *Accounting, Organizations and Society*, February/April: 1–24.

—— Collopy, F. (Eds.) (2004). *Managing as Designing*. Stanford, CA: Stanford Business Books.

—— Pondy, L. R. (1983). Accounting in organizations: A union of natural and rational perspectives. *Accounting, Organizations and Society*, 8(2–3): 223–34.

Burns, J. and Scapens, R. (2000). Conceptualising management accounting change: An institutional framework. *Management Accounting Research*, 11(1): 3–25.

Carlson, S. (1951). *Executive Behavior: A Study of the Work Load and the Working Methods of Managing Directors*. Stockholm: Strömbergs.

Covin, J. G. and Slevin, D. P. (1991). A conceptual model of entrepreneurship as firm behavior. *Entrepreneurship: Theory & Practice*, 16(1): 7–25.

DiMaggio, P. J. and Powell, W. (1983). (Eds.) *The New Institutionalism in Organizational Analysis*. Chicago: University of Chicago Press.

Down, S. (1999). Owner-manager learning in small firms. *Journal of Small Business and Enterprise Development*, 6(3): 267–80.

Ekanem, I. and Smallbone, D. (2007). Learning in small manufacturing firms: The case of investment decision-making behavior. *International Small Business Journal*, 25: 107–28.

Giddens, A. (1976). *New Rules of Sociological Method*. London: Hutchinson.

—— (1979). *Central Problems in Social Theory*. Berkeley, CA: University of California Press.

—— (1984). *The Constitution of Society*. Berkeley, CA: University of California Press.

Gómez-Mejía, L., Haynes, K., Núñez-Nickel, M., Jacobson, K., and Moyano-Fuentes, J. (2007). Socioemotional wealth and business risks in family-controlled firms: Evidence from Spanish olive oil mills. *Administrative Science Quarterly*, 52(1): 106–37.

Gorton, M. (2000). Overcoming the structure-agency divide in small business research. *International Journal of Entrepreneurial Behavior & Research*, 6(5): 276–92.

Hamilton, W. (1932). 'Institution'. In E. Seligman and A. Johnson, A. (Eds.), *Encyclopaedia of the Social Sciences* (Vol. 8, pp. 84–9). New York: Macmillan.

Hedberg, B. and Jönsson, S. (1977). Strategy formulation as a discontinuous process. *International Studies of Management and Organizations*, 7: 89–109.

Häckner, E. (1985). *Strategiutveckling i medelstora företag*. Göteborg: BAS förlag.

—— (1988). Strategic development and information use. *Scandinavian Journal of Management*, 4(1–2): 45–61.

Jack, S. L. and Anderson, L. R. (2002). The effects of embeddedness on the entrepreneurial process. *Journal of Business Venturing*, 17: 467–87.

Jones, O. (2003). The persistence of autocratic management in small firms: TCS and organisational change. *International Journal of Entrepreneurial Behavior & Research*, 9(6): 245–67.

Kimberly, J. R. and Bouchikhi, H. (1995). The dynamics of organizational development and change: How the past shapes the present and constrains the future. *Organization Science*, 6(1): 9–18.

Law, J. (1996). Organizing accountabilities: Ontology and the mode of accounting. In R. Munro and J. Mouritsen (Eds.), *Accountability: Power, Ethos and the Technologies of Managing*. Copenhagen: Copenhagen Business School Press.

Lukka, K. (2005). Approaches to case research in management accounting: The nature of empirical intervention and theory linkage. In S. Jönsson and J. Mouritsen (Eds.), *Accounting in Scandinavia – The Northern Lights* (pp. 375–99). Copenhagen: Liber and Copenhagen Business School Press.

Macintosh, N. B. (1994). *Management Accounting and Control Systems: An Organizational and Behavioral Approach*. Chichester: John Wiley & Sons.

—— Scapens, R. W. (1990). Structuration theory in management and accounting. *Accounting, Organizations and Society*, 15(5): 455–77.

Meyer, J. and Rowan, B. (1977). Institutional organizations: Formal structures as myth and ceremony. *American Journal of Sociology*, 83(2): 340–63.

Mintzberg, H. (1973). *The Nature of Managerial Work*. New York: Harper & Row.

—— (1987). Crafting strategy. *Harvard Business Review*, July–August: 66–75.

Nilsson, A. (1998). The analogy as a management tool (p. 13). PhD thesis, Luleå University of Technology.

—— (2008). Walking between decision models: Analogising in strategic decision-making. *Qualitative Research in Organizations and Management: An International Journal*, 3(2): 104–26.

Parsons, T. (1951). *The Social System*. New York: Free Press.

Pettigrew, A. M. (1977). Strategy formulation as a political process. *International Studies of Management & Organization*, New York, Summer: 77–87.

Powell, W. and DiMaggio, P. (Eds.) (1991). *The New Institutionalism in Organizational Analysis*. Chicago, IL: University of Chicago Press.

Quinn, J. B. (1980). *Strategies for Change: Logical Incrementalism*. Homewood, IL: Richard D. Irwin.

Sarason, Y., Dean, T., and Dillard, J. F. (2006). Entrepreneurship as the nexus of individual and opportunity: A structuration view. *Journal of Business Venturing*, 21: 286–305.

Scott, W. (1995). *Institutions and Organizations*. Thousand Oaks, CA: Sage Publications.

Selznick, P. (1957). *Leadership in Administration. A Sociological Interpretation*. Evanston, IL: Row, Peterson and Company.

Simons, R. (1995). *Levers of Control: How Managers Use Innovative Control Systems to Drive Strategic Renewal*. Cambridge, MA: Harvard Business Press.

Taylor, F. W. (1911). *The Principles of Scientific Management*. New York: Harper & Brothers.

Taylor, D. W. and Thorpe, R. (2004). Entrepreneurial learning: A process of co-participation. *Journal of Small Business and Enterprise Development*, 11(2): 203–11.

Tengblad, S. (2002). Time and space in managerial work. *Scandinavian Journal of Management*, 18: 543–65.

—— (2003). Classic, but not seminal: Revisiting the pioneering study of managerial work. *Scandinavian Journal of Management*, 19: 85–101.

—— (2006). Is there a 'New Managerial Work'? A comparison with Henry Mintzberg's classic study 30 years later. *Journal of Management Studies*, 43(7): 1437–61.

Weick, K. (1995). *Sensemaking in Organizations.* Thousand Oaks, CA: Sage Publications.
Westerberg, M. (1998). *Managing in Turbulence: An Empirical Study of Small Firms Operating in a Turbulent Environment* (p. 43). Luleå University of Technology, PhD thesis.
—— (2001). Tillväxt i turbulens: Vad krävs av småföretagaren i tider av omvälvning? Exempel från svenska trähus- och snickerifabriker. In P. Davidsson, F. Delmar and J. Wiklund (Eds.). *Tillväxt: Svensk forskning om företags expansion.* Stockholm: SNS Förlag.
Zucker, L. (1977). The role of institutionalization in cultural persistence. *American Sociological Review,* 42: 726–43.
—— (1983). Organizations as institutions. In S. Bacharach (Ed.), *Research in the Sociology of Organizations* (pp. 1–47). Greenwich, CT: JAI Press.

15

Managerial practices in family-owned firms: Strategizing actors, their arenas, and their emotions

Ethel Brundin and Leif Melin

INTRODUCTION

This chapter focuses on managerial work in the upper echelon of business organizations where one or several members of the management team are also owners. Often such firms are family owned, and, in some cases, one family member is the sole owner. Where ownership and management are interlaced in such family-owned firms, the owners are usually both visible and active. These and other characteristics legitimize family-owned firms as a specific population of business firms.

In this chapter, we look exclusively at managerial practices in the family-owned firm, with the owner-managed firm (with one or several owners) as a special case of the population in focus. We define the family-owned firm as a firm where family members control the company through ownership of more than 50 per cent of the voting shares, where at least one family member holds a top management position, and where the leading representative(s) of the family perceive the business to be a family firm (cf. Westhead and Cowling, 1999). We argue that this combination of active ownership and active management participation shapes the firm's managerial practices in different and unique ways.

A number of researchers have reported on the wide distribution (as well as successful performance) of family-owned firms (e.g. La Porta et al., 1999; Anderson and Reeb, 2003; Miller and Miller, 2005). Family-owned firms, the most common form of business organization worldwide, account for 50–90 per cent of the GDP in free market economies. Within the small- and medium-size enterprise (SME) population, 70–80 per cent of the firms in many countries are family businesses (e.g. 75 per cent in Holland). Family firms create a large portion of private sector jobs (e.g. 60 per cent in the United States). On many stock markets, the market value of family-controlled firms is quite high. For instance, in Chile, fifteen family groups account for over 50 per cent of the market value of the Santiago stock exchange. In Austria, Germany, and Belgium, families control around 60–65 per cent of all listed companies. In Finland, over 30 per cent of the largest 500 corporations are family firms. In India, sixteen family groups control 65 per cent of the total assets in the private sector. While there are many family-owned firms that are SMEs, there are also many large family-owned firms, many of which are listed on stock markets. In Sweden, approximately 90 per cent of all private and closely held firms are owner-managed; 70 per cent of them are family owned (NUTEK, 2004). The purpose of this chapter is to discuss and illustrate managerial practices and their implications in family-owned firms.

In the next section, we describe the main characteristics of the family-owned firm resulting from the family ownership logic and its influence on managerial practices. In the following section, we take a strategic view of managerial practices in family-owned firms. In taking this view, we introduce a strategy as practice perspective on managerial work and argue that family owners act in several arenas, both inside and outside the firm. We argue that the emotional aspect of management practices should be integrated with the strategy as practice perspective. Then we illustrate two integrated themes that develop these two arguments on managerial practices in the context of family-owned firms. We examine family owners as strategizing actors, their specific arenas, and their emotions as crucial elements of strategizing practices. In the concluding section, we discuss the theoretical and practical implications of our research.

FAMILY OWNERSHIP SHAPES MANAGERIAL PRACTICES

Family-owned and owner-managed firms are not a homogeneous population. There are many varieties of such firms – not only because of differences in firm age, size, and industry but also because of differences in their ownership and governance structures. Despite these differences, there are nevertheless a number of characteristics that most family-owned firms share. Thus, it is reasonable to study them as a specific business firm category. We label these common characteristics *the family ownership logic* that leads to the overarching, emotional bonding by family owners with the family firm (Brundin et al., 2008*a*). Next, we identify and describe seven main characteristics of the family ownership logic. The meaning of some of these characteristics may be quite obvious. However, the full meaning of the family ownership logic is both the combination of the seven characteristics and the strong manifestation of each.

- *Active and visible ownership.* Family business owners are visible and are actively committed to and involved with the firm.
- *Stability in ownership and power.* There is a high degree of continuity in family ownership and top management where it is evident that the ultimate control is concentrated among a few, closely related owners.
- *An industrial and long-term focus.* Family business owners have in-depth knowledge of their firm's industry and often have hands-on industry experience. They are inclined to take a long-term business perspective owing to the trans-generational character of their firms. Therefore, such owners typically

identify themselves with long-term strategic development in order to pass on their firms to future generations.

- *Multiple ownership goals.* Family business owners also have goals other than purely financial ones as evidenced by their heightened sense of responsibility to their employees, to their communities, and to past and future family generations.
- *Autonomy towards capital markets.* To fund their firms, family business owners prefer to use their own resources rather than to rely on resources from outsiders. This attitude reflects the importance of independence and freedom to family business owners.
- *Flexibility in governance structures.* Family business owners value rapid decision-making, which is less possible in large and listed firms with their often more hierarchical and unwieldy governance structures. The role of the board differs, but few family-owned firms follow the strictly hierarchical governance structure with an independent board that controls top management as advocated in codes of conduct that regulate the governance of listed companies. This view does not fit very well with the situation where majority owners act as top managers.
- *Identification.* Family owners have a strong, emotional commitment to their firms. They are therefore willing to put a great deal of effort into the firm. Since they identify closely with their firms, generally they cannot imagine selling their firms. Since the family ownership logic reflects this strong emotional bonding with the firm (Brundin et al., 2008a), a sale of the firm to outsiders would mean the loss of identity.

The long-term orientation of the family ownership logic especially influences the strategy process and related managerial practices and activities in family-owned firms (Miller and Le-Breton-Miller, 2005, 2006; Lumpkin et al., 2010). This orientation differs from the more short-term, shareholder value logic – with its emphasis on quarterly results – that is found in many listed firms. These two logics lead to quite different managerial practices and ways of working. The family ownership logic is reflected in many ways – for example, in the owners' deeply rooted involvement in the firm; in the close interest they take in its development; in the variety of roles open to them (owner, manager, and family member) that may even lead to role conflict (Ashforth, 2001); in their many rights, obligations, and responsibilities (to past/future family members as well as to any external stakeholders); and in the emotional investment of self in the firm (cf. Pierce et al., 2001).

A STRATEGY AS PRACTICE PERSPECTIVE

Because of their special characteristics, family-owned and owner-managed firms may be studied as a special case of strategic management. The ownership dimension influences the practices and processes of the managerial work in these firms in particular ways (Sharma et al., 1997; Nordqvist and Melin, 2010). In this chapter, we look at such managerial work strategically by applying the emerging strategy as practice perspective. This perspective directs researchers into the daily activities of actors when they strategize – that is, when they are 'doing strategy'. Johnson et al. (2003: 3) define strategizing as 'the detailed processes and practices which constitute the day-to-day activities of organizational life *and* which relate to strategic outcomes' (emphasis in original).

The strategy as practice perspective focuses on what managers do as they interact with various actors in specific arenas that are critical to strategic development (Johnson et al., 2003; Johnson et al., 2007). The strategic arena is defined 'through the dialogues around issues that are strategic to the individual organization' (Ericson et al., 2001: 68). This means there are 'multiple appearances' of the strategic arena – that is, there are 'several and simultaneous meeting places for strategic dialogues at and across different layers' (Achtenhagen et al., 2003: 70). All actors who play a crucial role in some part of the strategy process are strategic actors (Ericson et al., 2001). To summarize, the strategy as practice perspective directs our attention to the actors involved in the strategic activities – not only who they are but also when, where, and how they engage in this work. The focus is on their interaction with others and their relationships to the specific practices they use (Jarzabkowski, 2003; Whittington, 2003, 2006; Nordqvist, 2005).

The application of the strategy as practice perspective to family-owned firms is useful as a way to identify and examine the specific managerial activities and practices typical of such firms. Furthermore, this perspective incorporates the emotions involved in strategizing (i.e. those emotions connected to the strategists and their actions where these emotions become practices with implications for the strategic outcomes). Since the emotional states of strategists engaged in managerial work are important aspects of their strategic practices (Jarzabkowski et al., 2007), we integrate our discussion on actors and arenas in family-owned businesses with their work emotions.

The study of managerial work from the strategy as practice perspective implies that the researcher takes a micro approach in field studies. Only by coming close to actual activities and emotions, is it possible to explore the connection between managerial activities and strategic outcomes. For data collection in such field studies, qualitative methods that allow for close scrutiny are required. For our research, these methods include participant and non-participant observations, interviews as conversations, self-reports, and joint interpretations. Our empirical data are longitudinal in character and are based on numerous interviews and conversations, many days of observations, and a substantial number of self-reports (Brundin, 2002; Hall, 2003; Nordqvist, 2005). Our choice of approach also responds to recent calls in family business research for the use of in-depth, qualitative research methods that provide a sound base for theory generation and refinement (Goffee, 1996; Sharma et al., 1997; Chrisman et al., 2005).

Next, we present examples of important (and typical) managerial practices that illustrate two related themes: (*a*) *family firm owners as strategizing actors in their arenas* and (*b*) *emotions in managerial practices with a strategy as practice perspective*. These related themes are closely connected to the family ownership logic. The first theme concerns family owners and family owner-managers who are active and visible in formal and informal arenas where they strategize. Thus, external (i.e. non-family) managers in family-owned firms, who are usually excluded from some of these arenas, do not participate in strategic activities in the fullest sense. The second theme concerns the strategic display of emotions by managers in family-owned firms. In the illustrations of this theme, we argue that the display of emotions may have different implications in family firms when used by a family owner-manager than when used by non-family member manager.

TWO RELATED THEMES ON MANAGERIAL PRACTICES IN FAMILY-OWNED FIRMS

To develop the themes on managerial practices in family-owned firms, we show how various family members as owners, and sometimes as owner-managers, are actively involved in the on-going strategizing. This involvement occurs both in formal arenas, such as the management team and the board of directors, and in more informal arenas where the involvement is often invisible to other, non-family firm actors. This focus on actors 'doing strategy' results from the need to humanize strategy research and to bring the individual back in. Research that applies the strategy as practice perspective is concerned with placing human actors, their actions, interactions, and emotions at centre stage (Jarzabkowski and Spee, 2009). This perspective is critical of mainstream strategy research as well as most family business research that marginalizes human actors and neglects their emotions that shape strategy (Jarzabkowski and Spee, 2009).

We next illustrate these two related themes. We begin with the family owners and their interactions in different arenas as examples of managerial practices in the family-owned firm. Thereafter, we focus on the emotions displayed in these interactions. In the discussion that follows, we integrate the two themes.

Family owners as strategizing actors in their arenas

The family ownership logic means that one or several family members are influential strategists in the on-going strategic development of the family-owned firm. In their strategizing, the family member(s) may likely prioritize family interests over personal interests. The sense of belonging to the family group often causes family members to be actively involved in dialogues on strategic issues even if they are not active in the daily management of the firm (Nordqvist, 2005). In Hall's study (2003) of the impact of family relationships on the on-going strategizing in family firms, the findings show that the genuine (i.e. close, life-time) relationships between family members influence the outcome of specific strategic issues. Thus, intergenerational family members often take an active role in strategizing activities, for example, when a new generation tries to strategically renew the family firm while still preserving the core business values adopted by the earlier generation(s). Both Nordqvist and Hall base their conclusions on their longitudinal, qualitative studies. Nordqvist builds on empirical data acquired in fieldwork of three in-depth case studies, each followed over a period of two to three years, in which the data were collected in ninety-eight semi-structured interviews, unstructured conversations, and observations of different meetings.

Hall builds on empirical data acquired in fieldwork of three in-depth case studies, each followed over several years, in which the data were collected from more than fifty interviews as well as unstructured conversations.

The family ownership logic reflects the values and interests of the family owners as well as their emotional bonding with the firm. One powerful interest is the desire to exert strategic autonomy by preserving the independence of the family-owned firm. As a result, the family ownership logic translates into the family members' active efforts to influence the strategic future of the firm (Brundin et al., 2008a). This logic, however, may result in negative practices, such as nepotistic recruitment, an unwillingness to delegate power to non-family managers, and a strategically introverted orientation that eventually leads to inertia when necessary strategic adaptation is called for (Nordqvist, 2005).

Influential actors and arenas in family-owned firms

In studying the managerial practices in family-owned firms, we need to look not only at the influential actors (both family and non-family actors) but also at the strategic arenas where they act (Ericson et al., 2000; Melander et al., 2010). Mainstream strategy research typically focuses on certain formal arenas where the top management team and the board of directors conduct the strategic conversations and make the strategic decisions. In family-owned firms, however, there are other influential strategizing arenas – formal arenas such as family meetings (the family assembly) and family councils (Melin and Nordqvist, 2007) as well as more informal arenas such as family weekends, family holidays, the Sunday family dinner, family parties, etc.). As these informal arenas usually are located outside the firm, non-family members are usually excluded from them. In particular, the family council is a governance structure absent in non-family-owned firms. '[T]he fundamental purpose of a family council is to provide a forum in which family members can articulate their values, needs, and expectations vis-à-vis the company and develop policies that safeguard the long-term interest of the family' (Gersick et al., 1997: 237).

In family-owned firms, family members who hold top management positions exert their very visible influence on the firm through their direct participation in the daily operational and strategic activities. The additional influence of non-manager family owners with family relationships to these top managers is often invisible to other managerial actors such as the non-family members who hold top management and/or board positions. Such influence takes place in family-specific arenas. In his in-depth study of the role of family ownership in strategizing, Nordqvist (2005) concludes that the family ownership is 'channelled' to different formal and informal arenas that are populated by either a mix of family and non-family members, or exclusively by family members. The influence of this 'channelling' of ownership on the actual strategizing in different arenas takes place through the social interactions among the various actors.

In addition to the increased formalization of the ownership governance structure in family-owned firms (e.g. new formal arenas such as the family council), the continuous interaction among family members provides an important arena for influential strategizing. Thus, ownership influence is affected by 'this every day, informal interaction and conversation between actors involved in strategic issues' (Nordqvist, 2005: 286). Nordqvist's study argues convincingly that family members participate actively in strategizing based on their ownership positions in order to promote certain values and interests. We have also found evidence of the same practice in our studies (which are also longitudinal, in-depth case studies). A telling example is the following story. A father and his two sons from a Swedish, family-owned firm made a business trip to China. It was the first such trip by the younger son. The elder brother commented to us about the younger brother: 'We will show him how it works in China, and we will also go to Hong Kong for three days. And during lunches and dinners, when we will eat in good restaurants and discuss business and the company's future, that will end up in an on-going discussion for the rest of the trip' (Brundin et al., 2008b).

In general, all business firms have a mix of formal and informal arenas where strategic conversations take place (Sjöstrand et al., 2000). The interplay between different arenas, where strategizing occurs, is crucial for effective strategy work. In family-owned firms, however, the risk of 'arena confusion' is much higher than in non-family-owned firms since some arenas in family-owned firms are closed to non-family members (see also Melander et al., 2010). Family members may 'act in different arenas at different points in time, without making clear their respective roles...this can play a considerable role for how the strategic work unfolds' (Nordqvist, 2005: 259).

Figure 15.1 (from Nordqvist, 2005) summarizes the managerial practices related to the strategizing by different actors in different arenas. Figure 15.1 shows how ownership shapes and influences strategy work in family-owned firms. The combination of 'familiarizing' with both 'informalizing' and

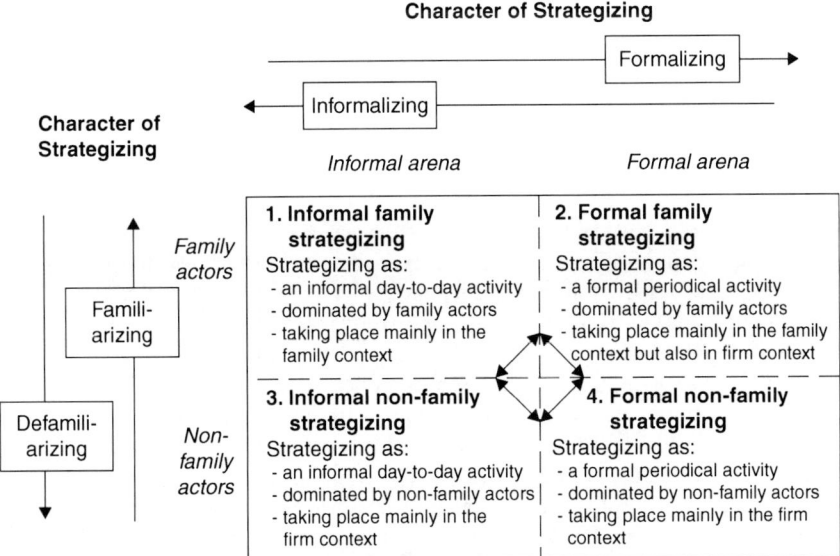

Figure 15.1 A model of actors and arenas showing the character of strategizing in family firms (figure 5 in Nordqvist, 2005: 263)

'formalizing' is a characteristic of family-owned firms where important strategic activities take place in family arenas and where non-family managers and board members are excluded. The strategizing by family owners shapes specific rules and managerial practices in family-owned firms.

Emotions are an important aspect of both formal and informal strategizing. The family ownership logic includes emotional bonding with the firm, beyond facts and figures, where emotions are an integral part of all managerial interaction. Next, we focus on emotions as a significant and integral dimension of managerial practices in the context of family-owned firms.

Emotions as part of strategizing in managerial practices

Although researchers have studied emotions in various disciplines and have recognized that organizations are emotional arenas (Fineman, 1993), surprisingly little research has addressed emotions as they relate to managerial practices. There is little discussion of emotions in the management literature. Yet it is well established that emotions are strong driving forces that influence managerial processes (Brundin, 2002).

In general, emotions are described as short-term in character with intentional affects of, for example, fear, joy, and anger (Parkinson, 1995). However, emotions may also be long-term in character. Viewed in a long-term context, they constitute the glue in human interactions. Thus, they are of special interest in family-owned and owner-managed firms. Over time, emotions experienced over long periods of time lead to high or low emotional energy levels where there is a shared focus, for example, among family owners. High emotional energy typically leads to relationships characterized by solidarity, commitment, trust, and confidence. Low emotional energy, on the other hand, leads to relationships characterized by alienation, stress, and depression (Collins, 1990, 2004).

Emotional energy is reflected in facial displays, verbal expression, mimicry, and body language. Individuals' high emotional energy is evidenced by their commitment, attentiveness, good eye contact, strong voice, and a focus on the issue at hand. Individuals' low emotional energy is evidenced by their resignation, avoidance, poor eye contact, subdued voice, and a lack of focus. This analysis of emotional energy has implications for the managerial practices in family-owned firms since managers who are also active owners often have high emotional energy. Others regard the owner-manager, who is usually very resourceful, as the evident leader. Furthermore, such an owner-manager is typically involved in many events and in much of the social interaction related to the firm. For these reasons, the owner-manager is rendered both power and status (cf. Collins, 1990, 2004). By contrast, it is difficult for managers with low emotional energy to make their voices heard and to exercise dominance. As a result, such managers, who lack power and status, are rarely regarded as leaders.

Depending on the situation, the same owner-manager may exhibit high or low emotional energy – or forms in between. In general, however, managerial practices that reflect a manager's high emotional energy are more likely to lead to positive outcomes (Collins, 2004). Different arenas therefore may influence a manager's level of emotional energy. For these reasons, we argue that there is a special need to study the role of emotions vis-à-vis managerial practices in family-owned firms managed by family members.

Emotional displays as managerial practices

In the micro-processual approach that focuses on individuals as key actors in strategy as practice, emotions are considered natural, integral, and important elements in most day-to-day managerial activities. Since they influence managerial practices, emotions have strategic implications. In this section, we examine the role of emotions in family-owned firms by drawing on two in-depth field studies of the display of emotions by two managers (both are chief executives: one a family member and one a non-family member). We argue that the way in which these two managers display their emotions and the interpretation of those emotions by those in their immediate surroundings determine the role the emotions play. Emotions are thus viewed as socially constructed and situational (Averill, 1980; Denzin, 1984, 1990; Cornelius, 1996), depending on the relationships and social interactions at the micro level where the arenas also play a role. In addition, emotions are performative (see the discussion of reasoning about power by Latour, 1998). Thus, people do not have emotions; rather, emotions stem from others' interpretations. Emotions are an effect, rather than a means. Accordingly, people who cry are assumed to be sad since others in their environment interpret the act of crying as an expression of sadness. This understanding of emotions is of special relevance since the interpretation of managers' display of emotions may lead to actions that promote or jeopardize their strategic intent.

The display of emotions refers to observable changes in face, voice, body, and activity level that are accompanied by emotional states (Lewis, 1998). An authentic display of emotion means the inner, subjective experience of the emotion is consistent with the displayed or expressed emotion (Waddington, 2005). An inauthentic display of emotion means the displayed emotion may mask, hide, or control the experienced emotion. In this case, the emotional display, which is then inconsistent with the experienced emotion, in the long run may lead to emotional dissonance, with stress or burnout as a likely consequence (Hochschild, 1983; Middleton, 1989; Grandey, 2003; Grandey et al., 2005).

The display of authentic emotions is also called deep acting; its opposite is called surface acting. Both are part of the emotional labour (Hochschild, 1983) for managers, that is, the adaptation and management of emotional displays that comply with professional rules. This compliance has been especially observed in the service sector (Hochschild, 1983; Rafaeli and Sutton, 1987, 1989). Humphrey (2002) and Ekman (2003) argue that the display of emotions by managers is more effective in influencing employees' performance than verbal communications. Viewed this way, emotional displays become part of managerial practices where the interpretation of these displays has a decisive influence on results.

THE EMPIRICAL SCENE AND METHOD

We followed two top managers at different companies for eighteen months. One researcher collected data as the two managers reported on events in real time as they occurred (Brundin, 2007). Two managers were identified, William, the non-family, chief executive officer at Company A, and Ted, the owner-manager at Company B. Company A, a member of a family-owned group of companies, is a manufacturer that operates in a mature market. The company, which had introduced a new product in a segmented niche, employed forty-five people at the beginning of the study and thirty-five people at the end of the study. During our study, Company A reported a declining trend in sales and profits. Company B is a high-tech, owner-managed firm that develops advanced quality assurance equipment. During our study, Company B reported an upward trend in sales and profits, and increased its number of employees from forty-five to one hundred.

Our research methodology for the two studies consisted of interviews with the two managers and their management teams, document examination, observations, informal conversations, and self-reports by the managers. In total, seventy conversations were held and interviews were conducted during thirty-six full days of fieldwork. We made more than ninety hours of audio tape recordings, which were transcribed as more than a thousand pages of text. In addition to their statements, these recordings revealed interviewees' laughter and hesitations and suggested their smiles and frowns. In addition to the firms' printed material, we also compiled several files of the managers' notes, e-mail correspondence, and self-reports. The self-reports gave us thirty pages of field accounts that we interpreted, looking for patterns and consequences of emotional displays and experiences.

Displays of emotions and strategizing

Below we present two illustrations of emotional display: one from Company A (the manufacturer) and one from Company B (the equipment developer).

Company A: Display of emotions that counteracts strategizing

At an information meeting for production personnel, William presents the figures (sales, production, and profit and loss) for the third quarter of the year. Before the meeting, William conveys to the researcher his irritation, frustration, and worry regarding the result. However, at the meeting, he displays confidence as he reassures the employees that the company's liquidity is acceptable, that the parent company supports them financially, and that the Board firmly believes in the new strategy. In subsequent interviews, people who were at the meeting interpret William's remarks as a display of confidence.

At a later stage, a few months later, William expresses his worry and frustration concerning the attitude of the employees. Many of them have been at Company A all their working lives and are used to the company's ways of working. William feels this cultural embeddedness of the employees puts a damper on the strategy process since they are inclined to resist change.

In his self-report, William writes: 'Then there is another thing that is important that I am looking into right now. I have a feeling that there is something wrong in the organization, either that something is missing or there is discontent in the organization – I have a feeling that people in the organization do not work well together, I cannot give you an explanation of what is wrong. But I have that feeling . . . the organization does not work smoothly, people watch each other . . . Sometimes it is all so frustrating . . . Probably there are some people who do not fit in. This way we do not get the creative and dynamic organization we so badly need'.

These are thoughts that are not communicated to the employees. At the staff meeting, William's employees instead hear the following: 'We have good workers. When it comes to production, you work fine and we have good products and so on. There are many positive things, and the owner believes in us'.

This is interpreted by the employees as confidence. (Adapted from Brundin and Melin, 2006)

In this illustration, William does not display his honest emotions. What he says privately to the researcher or writes in his self-reports differs from his public statements. Rather than display his frustration and worry, he instead reassures the employees that he has confidence in the company's future. He makes a conscious effort to express his confidence to his personnel despite his concerns.

Ultimately, the dissonance between William's displayed and felt emotions dissipates his emotional energy and creates confusion among the employees. They perceive the incongruence between his displayed emotion and expressed emotion since they sense his lack of confidence as revealed in his facial expressions and body gestures. They are bewildered by his verbal communications. They are uncertain about the company's future and wonder what actions they should take. Eventually, their confusion leads to inertia in the company that counteracts William's strategizing efforts.

William's frustration and worry may be the result of performance pressure from the company owners. This pressure is evident in certain informal arenas such as in the phone calls between William and the Chairman of the Board (a family business owner) and in formal arenas such as in the Board meetings. Initially, William, however, assumes a cheerful front and does not display his authentic emotions. Gradually, as his emotional energy decreases, he openly displays frustration and even despair to the family management, resulting in a breakdown in trust between him and the family members. In the formal arena with his employees, William has been strategizing by displaying dishonest emotions, whereas in the informal arena in the contacts with the researcher, he dares to express his honest emotions.

Company B: Display of emotions that drive strategizing

Immediately before a meeting of the management team, where the forecasts of sales and production for the coming year are to be discussed, Ted remarks to the researcher:

'[My role today is] to get things moving. Development is too slow. The actual forecasting process is of minor importance. The important thing is to get the right products out at the right time. Costs are not that important'.

During the meeting Ted says:

'I mean, if we are to be dynamic about this, we need not have bothered about asking the agents, and just made everything up ourselves . . . I can't believe this. No, I don't think this is good. It's far from good. It's just a summary of what a bunch of agents have told you without your own viewpoint coming into it'.

Directly after the meeting Ted confirms his frustration to the researcher:

'It was a waste of time because none of the dynamics were there that should have been. It has not given us any direction for the future. The discussion put no emphasis on the products we should develop and prioritize . . . . They are all technocrats. They make and summarize their calculations without giving any real thought to them. So it was an utter fiasco. As I see it, anyone can make a forecast like this. The risk is that there is little dynamic behind it'.

A Logistics and Marketing director confirmed to the researcher that people had interpreted Ted's displayed emotions of frustration:

'I can understand Ted's frustration, because he had expected a particularly good result, and now he thinks that this forecast should be spectacularly dynamic. This places pressure on the R&D department. That's what was on his mind, and what was most important to him. So, of course, he was irritated. What he had decided in his own mind did not happen'.

(Adapted from Brundin and Melin, 2006)

In the second illustration, Ted displays his honestly felt emotions, not only in words but also by his facial expressions and by his body language. His public comments are confirmed in his private conversations with the researcher and in his self-reports. His employees accurately perceive his frustration and impatience. There is no difference between his public display of emotion in the formal arena in the budget meeting and his private display of emotion in the informal arena. He communicates his emotions clearly and authentically; as a result, his emotional energy increases. In the long run, this consistency allows the employees to 'read' their manager and to understand what actions they should take. Eventually, this leads to a dynamic atmosphere in the organization since Ted's emotional displays drive the strategic intent (strategizing).

The two managers in the studies work at very different companies, each with its specific cultures and conditions. Even so, we are able to discern two different patterns of managerial behaviour that are relevant to a description of the role of emotions in managerial practices (Brundin and Melin, 2006).

1. A persistent discrepancy between a manager's displayed and experienced emotions creates a low level of emotional energy in the manager and in the other employees. The effect is to thwart the manager's strategic intent. As the Company A illustration shows, emotional dissonance thus counteracts strategizing.
2. A persistent conformity between a manager's displayed and experienced emotions creates a high level of emotional energy in the manager and in the other employees. The effect is to support the successful realization of the strategic intent. As the Company B illustration shows, authenticity of emotion drives strategizing.

It is possible that the difference in personalities of the two managers is a contributing factor that leads to their authentic and inauthentic emotional displays. However, we argue that the company ownership difference is also an influential factor. As an owner-manager, Ted at Company B is motivated to push the budget process, to place new products in the market, and to earn a profit. When these efforts are jeopardized, he displays his frustration. He owns the company and acts in its direct interest without even giving a thought to managing or disguising his emotions. As an owner-manager, Ted can act directly since there is no higher-level pressure on him. Therefore, he forcefully exerts his right to motivate his employees using overt emotional displays. For this CEO, felt emotions are thus mirrored directly in the displayed emotions. His display of authentic emotions can be linked to the family ownership logic and can be seen as a result of his active and visible ownership, his strong industrial focus, and his identification with the firm.

The role of ownership comes through also in the illustration of the external CEO, William, in the second firm. In illustration A, the CEO is dependent on the ownership power of the group. He needs to produce the expected results that require the motivation and commitment of his employees since he cannot show results without them. He is limited by his decision to display authentic emotions that he believes would probably make the employees less motivated. If he were only accountable to himself and not to the owners of the company, he would probably have shown his worry and frustration before the employees.

Looking at the findings in these two studies, it might be easy to conclude that emotional authenticity is a positive managerial practice and emotional inauthenticity is a negative managerial practice. However, organizations are not rational and neither are managers. Brunsson (2002) writes that talk, decisions, and actions are not always consistent; we can say the same applies to experienced and displayed emotions. According to Brunsson, decisions may be taken to avoid action. In this way, employees are relieved of the burden of their actions. Similarly, the display of inauthentic emotions may allow a manager to avoid responsibility by allowing the employees to interpret these displayed emotions and then to act accordingly.

This chapter shows that the display of emotions is important for managers when they strategize. They need to recognize that emotional displays influence their managerial practices. Inauthentic displayed emotions may jeopardize organizational goals since employees interpret and act on these emotions. In this perspective, managerial practices are group efforts rather than individual efforts. For the manager, a mismatch between role expectations and experienced emotions places high demands on managerial practices; inauthentic, surface actions may lead to low emotional energy levels that create the risk of dysfunctional behaviour, such as apathy and burnout. For managerial practices in family-owned firms, emotional displays are of particular interest when the managers are also owners and act according to the family ownership logic (Brundin et al., 2008a) in a variety of formal and informal arenas.

294   *The Work of Managers*

CONCLUSIONS

In this chapter, we show how managerial practices are important characteristics of family-owned firms where actors, arenas, and emotions exert a high degree of influence on such practices. Managerial practices, as performed by family managers, non-family managers, or by both family and non-family managers, appear in very different arenas. These arenas have both formal and informal settings. We have shown that managers' emotions are influential in day-to-day activities where they inform strategic outcomes. In our discussion of managerial practices in family-owned firms, we draw the following conclusions.

First, we extend Carlson's more straightforward (1951), albeit complex, view of managerial practices. Carlson's research, which undoubtedly prepared the groundwork for much of the later investigation of managerial practices, is enjoying a renewed interest. Researchers now recognize that in order to understand managerial practices we also need to study organizations' human actors and their interactions. While we still need to examine the visible and countable managerial practices, we also need to examine the underpinnings of subtler social and psychological processes that, although often neglected, are strong influences on managerial practices. In this chapter, applying a strategy as practice perspective, we acknowledge the human actors by 'placing' them in arenas that are not commonly used, and we include the dimension of emotional strategic practices. A combination of emotional displays in a variety of arenas in the family-owned firm might cause non-family firm managers (perhaps without their being aware of it) to change their emotional displays, depending on the arena. The family firm owner-manager may not be under the same pressure. The family ownership logic explains this difference in how emotions are displayed.

Second, ownership of the firm plays a key role in the adoption of managerial strategic practices. Since family-owned firms have a visible and active ownership and are frequently owner-managed, this ownership structure has implications for how, where, and why certain managerial practices are exercised. Family ownership makes a difference since family owners are deeply and emotionally involved in their firms because of their close identification with their firms. They live and act the culture of the firm, rather than merely influence it. The conclusion is that managerial strategic practices are context-bound – their special characteristics distinguish them from more general management practices. In general, the literature on leadership and managerial work has not emphasized this aspect of managerial practices in family-owned firms. In seeking to fill this gap, this chapter examines the strong influence of emotions in family owner-managers' strategic practices.

Third, managerial practices in family-owned firms might not always have a positive effect on the firm. As this chapter illustrates, at times, managers may exercise complex managerial practices subconsciously. Such practices may lead to unintended consequences when family members in family-owned firms exclude non-family managers from arenas where important strategizing takes place. Furthermore, non-family managers can be manoeuvered away from positions of authority when managerial roles are transferred to family members (who perhaps do not even want these roles). Non-family managers may also lose emotional energy when they feel obligated to hide their authentic emotional displays in critical strategy situations. Therefore, it is not always easy for the parties involved to understand managerial practices in family-owned firms, and perhaps even less so for the observing researcher.

Fourth, by pointing to the subtle familial influences in the family-owned firm and the kinds of strategic management practices exercised in this context, and by including 'new' arenas, we highlight the importance of taking care in drawing conclusions on managerial practices in general and on strategic leadership in particular. For instance, currently leadership is subject to considerable (and deserved) criticism. Yet we temper that criticism with the observation that managerial practices, especially those involving strategizing, at times may be just messy. Furthermore, strategic actors who work in different arenas may be recognized as more competent if we acknowledge the importance of displays of emotions in the management practices.

In summary, we argue for an alternative and complementary view of managerial practices by focusing on the family-owned firm. Our interest is the effect of family ownership as it shapes managerial practices. By applying a strategy as practice perspective to our empirical data, we argue that strategizing takes place in what may sometimes seem insignificant events in the daily interaction between owners and managers. We also argue that strategizing is not reserved for specific arenas. Moreover, our two studies of managers in family-owned firms respond to the call that the human element should be considered in the study of strategizing. This is especially necessary when studying strategic practices in family-owned firms that are strongly interlaced with emotions. Our findings support the call by Jarzabkowski et al. (2007) and Jarzabkowski and Spee (2009) that the emotional dimension of strategic management practices should be studied further.

We also call for more studies of managerial practices in family-owned firms. Such firms provide a major part of many countries' wealth and thus deserve closer examination. In particular, we need to know more about the managerial practices in these firms where the special family ownership logic puts special management practices into play. To better understand these practices, we need more detailed observations from close interaction with the strategists in different arenas.

Practitioners who analyse our findings may gain a better understanding of the diverse set of actors and arenas that appear in strategizing processes. They may also realize the crucial role displays of emotions play when actors act strategically. By increasing their awareness of these actors, arenas, and processes, practitioners may increase their strategizing competence.

REFERENCES

Achtenhagen, L., Melin, L., Müllern, T., and Ericson, T. (2003). Leadership: The role of interactive strategizing. In A. Pettigrew, R. Whittington, L. Melin and Associates (Eds.), *Innovative Forms of Organizing: An International Perspective*. London: Sage.

Anderson, R. and Reeb, D. (2003). Founding family ownership and firm performance: Evidence from the S&P 500. *Journal of Finance*, 58: 1301–29.

Ashforth, B. E. (2001). *Role Transitions in Organisational Life: An Identity Based Perspective*. Mhawah, NJ: Lawrence Erlbaum.

Averill, J. R. (1980). A constructivist view of emotion. In R. Plutchik and H. Kellerman (Eds.), *Emotion*. New York: Academic Press.

Brundin, E. (2002). Emotions in motion. The strategic leader in a radical change process. JIBS Dissertation Series No. 12. Jönköping: Jönköping International Business School.

—— (2007). Catching it as it happens. In H. Nergaard and J. P. Ulhoj (Eds.), *Handbook for Qualitative Methods in Entrepreneurship Research*. Camberley: Edward Elgar.

—— Melin, L. (2006). Unfolding the dynamics of emotions: How emotion drives or counteracts strategizing. *International Journal of Work Organisation and Emotion*, 1 (3): 277–302.

—— Florin-Samuelsson, E., and Melin, L. (2008a). The family ownership logic: Chore characteristics of family controlled businesses. Jönköping: Jönköping International Business School, Center for Family Enterprise and Ownership, CeFEO Working Paper, ISSN 1654-8612; 2008:1.

—— Melin, L., and Nordqvist, M. (2008b). *Strategic Dialogue as an Important Practice of Strategizing*. Paper for 24th EGOS Colloquium in Amsterdam, 10–12 July 2008.

Brunsson, N. (2002). *The Organization of Hypocrisy: Talk, Decisions and Actions in Organizations*. Malmö: Liber ekonomi; Copenhagen: Copenhagen Business School (translated by Nancy Adler).

Carlson, S. (1951). *Executive Behaviour*. Stockholm: Strömbergs.

Chrisman, J. J., Chua, J. H., and Sharma, P. (2005). Trends and directions in the development of a strategic management theory of the family firm. *Entrepreneurship, Theory and Practice*, 29(5): 555–75.

Collins, R. (1990). Stratification, emotional energy, and the transient emotions. In T. Kemper (Ed.), *Research Agendas in the Sociology of Emotions*. Albany, NY: State University of New York Press.

—— (2004). *Interaction Ritual Chains*. Princeton, NJ: Princeton University Press.

Cornelius, R. R. (1996). *The Science of Emotion. Research and Tradition in the Psychology of Emotion*. Upper Saddle River, NJ: Prentice-Hall, Inc.

Denzin, N. K. (1984). *On Understanding Emotion*. San Francisco, CA: Joey-Bass Inc.

—— (1990). On understanding emotion: The interpretive-cultural agenda. In T. Kemper (Ed.), *Research Agendas in the Sociology of Emotions*. Albany, NY: State University of New York Press.

Ekman, P. (2003). *Emotions Revealed: Recognizing Faces and Feelings to Improve Communication and Emotional Life*. London: Weidenfeld & Nicolson.

Ericson, T., Hellqvist, A., Melander, A., and Melin, L. (2000). *Shaping New Strategies in Professional Organizations: The Strategic Arena Approach*. Presented at EGOS, Helsinki, July 2000.

—— Melander, A., and Melin, L. (2001). The role of the strategist. In H. W. Volberda and T. Elfring (Eds.), *Rethinking Strategy*. London: Sage.

Fineman, S. (1993). *Emotion in Organizations*. London: Sage Publications.

Gersick, K. E., Davis, J. A., Hampton, M. M., and Lansberg, I. (1997). *Generation to Generation: Life Cycles of the Family Business*. Cambridge, MA: Harvard Business School Press.

Goffee, R. (1996). Understanding family businesses: Issues for further research. *International Journal of Entrepreneurial Behaviour & Research*, 2(1): 36–48.

Grandey, A. (2003). When 'the show must go on': Surface acting and deep acting as determinants of emotional exhaustion and peer-rated service delivery. *Academy of Management Journal*, 46(1): 86–96.

—— Fisk, G. M., and Steiner, D. D. (2005). Must 'service with a smile' be stressful? The moderating role of personal control for American and French employees. *Journal of Applied Psychology*, 90(5): 893–904.

Hall, A. (2003). Strategizing in the context of genuine relations: An interpretative study of strategy formation in the family business. Dissertation, Jönköping International Business School, Jönköping.

Hochschild, A. R. (1983). *The Managed Heart. Commercialization of Human Feeling.* Berkeley and Los Angeles, CA: University of California Press.

Humphrey, R. H. (2002). The many faces of emotional leadership. *Leadership Quarterly,* 13(5): 493–504.

Jarzabkowski, P. (2003). Strategic practices: An activity theory perspective on continuity and change. *Journal of Management Studies,* 40(1): 23–55.

—— Spee, A. P. (2009). Strategy-as-Practice: A review and future directions for the field. *International Journal of Management Reviews,* 11(1): 69–95.

—— Balogun, J., and Seidl, D. (2007). Strategizing: The challenges of a practice perspective. *Human Relations,* 60(5): 5–27.

Johnson, G., Melin, L., and Whittington, R. (2003). Micro strategy and strategizing: Towards an activity-based view. *Journal of Management Studies,* 40(1): 3–22.

—— Langley, A., Melin, L., and Whittington, R. (2007). *Strategy as Practice. Research Directions and Resources.* Cambridge: Cambridge University Press.

La Porta, R., Lopez de Silanes, F., and Shleifer, A. (1999). Corporate ownership around the world. *Journal of Finance,* 54: 471–517.

Latour, B. (1998). *Artefaktens återkomst. Ett möte mellan organisationsteori och tingens sociologi.* Stockholm: Nerenius och Santérus Förlag.

Lewis, M. (1998). The development and structure of emotions. In M. F. Mascolo and S. Griffin (Eds.), *What Develops in Emotional Development?* London: Plenum Press.

Lumpkin, G. T., Brigham, K., and Moss, T. W. (2010). Long-term orientation: Implications for the entrepreneurial orientation and performance of family businesses. *Entrepreneurship & Regional Development,* 22(3/4): 241–64.

Middleton, D. R. (1989). Emotional style: The cultural ordering of emotions. *Ethos,* 17(2): 187–201.

Melander, A., Melin, L., and Nordqvist, M. (2010). The strategic arena approach to strategy process research. In F. Kellermanns and P. Mazzola (Eds.), *Handbook on Research on Strategy Process.* Cheltenham: Edward Elgar.

Melin, L. and Nordqvist, M., (2007). The reflexive dynamics of institutionalization: The case of the family business. *Strategic Organization,* 5(3): 321–33.

Miller, D. and Le Breton-Miller, I. (2005). *Managing for the Long Run: Lessons in Competitive Advantage from Great Family Businesses.* Boston, MA: Harvard Business School Press.

—— —— (2006). Family governance and firm performance: Agency, stewardship, and capabilities. *Family Business Review,* 19(1): 73–87.

Nordqvist, M. (2005). Understanding the role of ownership in strategizing. A study of family firms. JIBS Dissertation Series No. 29. Jönköping: Jönköping International Business School.

—— Melin, L. (2010). The promise of the strategy as practice perspective for family business strategy research. *Journal of Family Business Strategy,* 1(1): 15–25.

NUTEK (2004). *Ägarskiften och ledarskiften i företag. En fördjupad analys.* (Ownership and leadership succession in businesses. A deepened analysis). Stockholm: Verket för näringslivsutveckling.

Parkinson, B. (1995). *Ideas and Realities of Emotion.* London: Routledge.

Pierce, J. L., Kostova, T., and Dirks, K. T. (2001). Toward a theory of psychological ownership in organizations. *Academy of Management Review,* 26(2): 298–310.

Rafaeli, A. and Sutton, R. I. (1987). Expression of emotion as part of the work role. *Academy of Management Review*, 12(1): 23–37.

—— —— (1989). The expression of emotion in organisational life. In L. L. Cummings and B. M. Staw (Eds.), *Research in Organisational Behaviour* (Vol. 11). Greenwich, CT: JIA Press Inc.

Sharma, P., Chrisman, J. J., and Chua, J. H. (1997). Strategic management of the family business: Past research and future challenges. *Family Business Review*, 10(1): 1–35.

Sjöstrand, S-E, Sandberg, J., and Tyrstrup, M. (Eds.) (2000). *Invisible Management*. London: Thomson Business Press.

Waddington, K. (2005). Behind closed doors – The role of gossip in the emotional labour of nursing work. *International Journal of Work Organisation and Emotion*, 1(1): 35–46.

Westhead, P. and Cowling, M. (1999). Family firm research: The need for a methodological rethink. *Entrepreneurship: Theory and Practice*, 23(1): 31–56.

Whittington, R. (2003). The work of strategizing and organizing: For a practice perspective. *Strategic Organization*, 1(1): 117–25.

—— (2006). Completing the practice turn in strategy research. *Organization Studies*, 27(5): 613–34.

Part VI

The way forward

Two of the three chapters of Part Six deal with methodological and theoretical issues and are directed towards future research. The first chapter offers guidance about the use of the shadowing method; the second chapter offers advice on how to narrow the gap between the theory and practice of management; and the third chapter synthesizes the book's ideas and findings.

CHAPTER 16. REFINING SHADOWING METHODS FOR STUDYING MANAGERIAL WORK

Rebecka Arman, Ola Edvin Vie, and Håvard Åsvoll present a discussion on the use of shadowing in managerial studies in which they focus on abduction and theoretical development and offer practical advice to the future 'shadower'. They combine their theoretical discussions with 'tales from the field' and their valuable experiential knowledge gained from their fieldwork. The richness of data and the complexity of managerial work processes challenge the researcher since it is not possible to explain theoretical results in simple formulas or in 'boxes and arrows models'. One way of dealing with such complexity, these authors claim, is to be open to complementary interpretations.

CHAPTER 17. BRIDGING THE MANAGEMENT THEORY AND PRACTICE GAP

Seven authors and researchers who participated in an Academy of Management plenary session – Rob B. Briner, Lars Engwall, Tina L. Juillerat, Henry Mintzberg, Frederick P. Morgeson, Michael G. Pratt, and Stefan Tengblad – write about the problematic divide between theoretical management research and management in practice. Their propositions for closing this gap concern:

- The importance of observing actual management practices
- The importance of studying the impact of external relations
- The interaction between work context and work content

- The development of evidence-based management that promotes good management practices
- The redefinition of the meaning of rigorous research with careful attention to real management practices
- The need to strengthen interactive aspects of management research

CHAPTER 18. CONCLUSIONS AND THE WAY FORWARD: TOWARDS A PRACTICE THEORY OF MANAGEMENT

Stefan Tengblad develops the book's main contributions into a broad theoretical framework for an empirically solid, practice-based theory of managerial work/behaviour. The conclusion is that the often-neglected aspects of managerial work and behaviour – emotional work, symbolic behaviour, and political behaviour – are topics as relevant for management research as the contextual factors (e.g. intense work pressure, complex work tasks, and uncertain outcomes). Mainstream management theories cannot be empirically validated by real management practices because such theories are grounded in an out-of-date ideal based on the philosophical and scientific reasoning of formal logic. While the processes of formal rationality may prevent chaos, they cannot create managerial excellence. Researchers need to view exemplar management as a reflective practice based on experiential learning, contextual awareness, and artistry.

16

Refining shadowing methods for studying managerial work

Rebecka Arman, Ola Edvin Vie, and Håvard Åsvoll

A BASIC YET COMPLEX AND PROMISING METHOD

Historically, methodological debates have figured prominently in the research on managerial work and behaviour (MWB) (Stewart, 2008). It is quite possible to view Carlson's pioneering work (1951/91) on executive behaviour as methodologically motivated owing to the lack of earlier descriptions of executive work. However, this research focus could have unintended consequences. According to Hales (1986, 1999), studies taking this approach are rather atheoretical and rarely move beyond the purely descriptive. In a quite daring statement, Hales (1999: 336ff.) claims that MWB studies are evidence in search of an explanation, while management theories are in search of evidence. Barley and Kunda (2001) also note a general discrepancy between theories and empirical evidence. In their plea to bring work back into organizational studies, they call for more empirical data on what people actually do in organizations.

Despite calling for greater use of field techniques to gather detailed data and arguing for the value of grounded quantitative data to supplement qualitative field studies, Barley and Kunda (2001) do not mention Mintzberg's methodological (1973) contribution. Similarly, in her article on shadowing methods, McDonald (2005) omits a fuller treatment of the Mintzberg tradition. This is understandable when we note that Mintzberg labelled his method 'structured observation', a somewhat unfortunate label since it de-emphasises the openness and flexibility of a method that he described as coupling 'the flexibility of open-ended observation with the discipline of seeking certain types of structured data' (1973: 231). Alternatively, the method may be called semi-structured observation (Noordegraaf, 2000), which is a type of shadowing (Mintzberg, 1975). Semi-structured observation and shadowing are the terms used in this chapter.

Shadowing is a technique used for learning, especially in apprentice training programmes, and for collecting material for research purposes. In a straightforward definition, shadowing means following people, wherever they are, whatever they are doing. The research activity of shadowing may seem reasonably uncomplicated, but in actuality there are considerable demands on the researcher's stamina and concentration when recording constantly for eight hours or more, several days in a row. In her book on shadowing, Czarniawska (2007) describes this field technique as a valuable method for obtaining a personal account of various experiences encountered in fieldwork. In her review of shadowing studies, she found that in the beginning there were researchers who did not seem to know about each other's work and who used the method in several different fields.

Shadowing is both a distinct methodological research approach and a possible aspect of other research designs and strategies such as case study design or grounded method studies. As noted by Czarniawska (2007), Mintzberg's codifying procedure may illustrate grounded theory. Mintzberg observed: '*The categories are developed as the observation take place and after it takes place*' (1973: 231) (italics in the original). Also, Mintzberg's illustration (1973) of an iterative process of recording, tabulating, coding, recoding, and analysing on a daily basis may describe the abductive process. Czarniawska exemplifies abduction by describing Sherlock Holmes' investigative process. She writes that Holmes is an abductive investigator 'who collects observations with which he produces a conjecture, a hypothesis, and then experiments, which sometimes leads to refutation of certain elements or the whole hypothesis. Finally, he presents the solutions' (1999: 81–2). Alvesson and Kärreman (2007) also argue for the use of abductive research approaches that explore new terrain by developing novel ideas that surprise both the researcher and other interested audiences. They claim the approach involves 'the imaginative articulation of a new interpretive rule (theory) that resolves the surprise' (ibid.: 1269).

In summary, these debates in the literature underscore the need for a discussion of the shadowing methodology as applied in MWB research. In this chapter, we discuss how researchers can analyse and make sense of data produced from shadowing, in particular, by using the abductive research approach. The methodology of abductive research allows us to focus on the preparatory, tentative, and surprising aspects of shadowing that are often less discussed and understood. This analysis supports the development of theory through a reflective dialogue with empirical materials (Alvesson and Kärreman, 2007). Our main purpose in this chapter is to suggest ways to refine and expand the shadowing methods that have developed in MWB studies.

We next present the background to abductive research together with a literature review of the discussions on shadowing as well as reflections from our own experiences. The following section contains suggestions for possible refinements of a methodological nature that relate to the discussion on the methods we review in the literature. These suggestions for refinements are also based on our own experiences.

SHADOWING AND ABDUCTION

Concerns and concepts

Before Mintzberg's research into managerial work (1973), researchers used either the *diary method* (Carlson, 1951/91; Stewart, 1967/88) or *structured observation* (e.g. Guest, 1956; Jasinski, 1956) in their MWB studies. Mintzberg

(1973) was critical of diary studies because they require managers to record their activities on timesheets according to the researcher's predefined categories. This naturally means that managers match their activities to those job categories. In addition, there is the risk of unreliable data when managers self-report their activities. Mintzberg also criticized shadowing studies that only used predefined categories because the research method 'offers, at a higher cost, little more than the diary method' (ibid. 1973: 227). However, Mintzberg did not favour an ethnographical method because he felt the method was unstructured and non-systematic and because researchers cannot replicate or validate their findings. Martinko and Gardner (1985) and Hales (1986) agreed with this criticism and called for consistency in the categories used in MWB studies.

By structuring observations, observers direct and delimit their 'gaze' when watching managers since it is not possible to observe 'everything'. This structure, as a way to focus on a preconceived understanding of managerial behaviour, also permits the observer to analyse what managers do *not* do (leading to refutations of theories). However, the categories used in structured observations involve an operationalization of predetermined ideas of what managers do. As a result, such studies may not capture important contextual and new knowledge – they risk adding incrementally to old 'normal' knowledge without questioning or even refuting the conjectures they are based on. This is the concern of Mintzberg (1973) and others (e.g. Hales, 1999; Noordegraaf and Stewart, 2000). For example, nearly twenty years after his 1973 study, Mintzberg (1990, 1991) expressed disappointment that later researchers had mainly replicated his work. When researchers follow a replication strategy too closely they may miss the opportunity to generate rich, contextually sensitive data through direct observation of informants in their natural work setting.

Despite Mintzberg's use of structured observations, Martinko and Gardner (1985) criticized his 1973 study from a positivistic and quantitative perspective based on the small sample size and the lack of reliability checks. Noordegraaf and Stewart (2000: 432) responded to this criticism by pointing out that 'qualitative, inductive, observational and thus less reliable research is not an inferior kind of research, it is a different kind'. Kotter (1982: 152), relying heavily on Whyte (1943/ 93), explained that field research in general cannot be done in a 'clean way that fits traditional notions of "science"'. Several studies have followed Mintzberg in striking a fine balance between *both* structure and open-ended coding (Stewart, 1982; Noël, 1989; Tengblad, 2006).

These studies in the MWB tradition also differ somewhat, depending on how the researchers have collected and analysed their data and presented their findings. For instance, Mintzberg (1973) described roles and functions, illustrated by anecdotal examples, supported by small samples of raw data. Certain data – table summaries of structured observations according to time use – appear in an Appendix in his book. Some studies replicating Mintzberg's work have used quantitative descriptive analysis with a focus on the presentation of the structured data (e.g. Kurke and Aldrich, 1983; Florén, 2005; Tengblad, 2006). Other scholars have used more typical qualitative styles of analysis and presentation of findings. Stewart (1982) described a theoretical model of constraints, demands, and choices to summarize her analysis. Kotter (1982) described managerial life in a narrative style including career histories. Noël (1989) portrayed managers using psychological analysis of their subconscious obsessions.

Thus, many studies reveal a struggle in the MWB research that is similar to that in other qualitative research – that is, the difficulty of finding ways to analyse and present findings that are grounded, illustrative, and theoretically informed. There is a particular challenge in trying to balance an a priori imposed structure with openness to new and interesting data. Openness and structure are two strategies that should be mediated more as ideal types[1] than as reflections of concrete methodologies in managerial research.

According to McDonald (2005), researchers have used shadowing to gather quantitative or qualitative data (or both) by taking a positivistic or interpretive research approach. The 'deductive' model is mostly found in various 'quantitative' approaches (i.e. time frequency studies with statistical analysis methods), whereas the 'inductive' model is predominantly found in qualitative analysis (in the search for descriptive and explorative patterns). This is the traditional, although not necessarily valid, distinction because the emphasis on deductive or inductive approaches also varies considerably within the domain of qualitative research (i.e. structured and semi- or unstructured designs). Hence, we claim that practical managerial work research cannot be based on either pure deduction or pure induction. We propose using the concept of abduction because it provides a good description of the qualitative research processes of shadowing.

The concept of abduction, originally introduced by Aristotle, was developed into a theory of inference by the American pragmatist, Charles Sanders Peirce. Peirce (1934/60) explained that the traditional modes – induction and deduction – should be complemented by a third mode – abduction, which he conceived of as a process of gaining new knowledge in a pragmatic way. As Czarniawska's (1999) Sherlock Holmes' example shows, abductive logic results in an explanation based on some general rule deemed worthy of testing. It is crucial that abduction appeal to aspects of context (making abduction the polar opposite of deduction). Some areas of a phenomenon may be relatively easy to understand and interpret such that the additional time required for formulating abductive hypotheses is unwarranted. However, other inaccessible and incomprehensible areas may emerge that therefore require time-consuming abductive interpretations. Prior to the collection of empirical material, there is usually no indication of which mode should be applied. Alvesson and Kärreman (2007) suggest using theory not only as a tool for direction or control but also as a way of opening up sensitive constructions and interpretations. Research approaches that are actively sensitive and open to mysteries (incoherencies, surprises, breakdowns) are stronger than open approaches used passively only when extraordinary possibilities or unavoidable situations arise. We suggest that MWB research should move towards the sensitive and open-to-mystery approaches.

The inferential step that is central to any scientific process, including shadowing in MWB, is the step from some initially puzzling data to a theoretical and explanatory hypothesis. Such inferential processes are typical of abduction. Thus, the use of this concept may raise an awareness of how deductive categories and interpretations can be used in shadowing in order to strike a balance between structure and openness in the research process. The concept of abduction may show how a researcher on a daily basis proposes a trial hypothesis prior to deduction (which spells out the theoretical consequences) and induction (which tests the hypothesis based on observations). Thus, it is possible to understand shadowing as based on everyday sense-making in terms of abduction since unexplained or surprising/anomalian phenomena are included. The process involves actively working with alternative constructions (Alvesson and Kärreman, 2007). Later in the chapter, we distinguish between abductions that are followed up and abductions that are not supported by theory, showing the inherent value of both. In the following section, we deal with the issue of structure-openness based on our experiences in two doctoral projects that used the shadowing method.

Experiences of shadowing

We used shadowing methods in two doctoral projects aimed at the study of managerial work. One study was conducted in the Swedish public health care sector (see Chapter 6, this book) and the other in a Norwegian corporate research and development setting (see Chapter 8, this book). As we experienced the managers' workdays, alongside them, we were both exhausted and amazed by the number of tasks and problems the managers dealt with daily. It was only in the calm, almost boring, workdays that sometimes occurred that the managers had time to reflect and catch up.

In the chapter, we enclose descriptions of our personal experiences in boxed frames to distinguish this data from other text in the chapter.

Abductive ideas in the field

We found it most difficult to shadow managers when they had many brief, closely spaced activities. We could write freely about what was being said and how it was being said only after we had completed certain basic coding for each activity. Even when there was enough time to record nearly all that was being said, it was hard to distinguish subtleties in the interactions (e.g. when managers spoke ironically). We often thought about the managerial work we observed – when there was idle time during observations, when recording interpretive and extra anecdotal material after observations, or when trying to fall asleep after a day 'in the field'. In general, we reflected on abductive ideas about managerial work and the learning that could be gained from the shadowing. However, most of our reflection and categorization occurred after we were in the field. In the health care study, we did not categorize the main purpose of each activity as Mintzberg had. Even in short conversations, multiple activities (e.g. negotiations, requests, socializing, and discussing 'information') were observable. The difficult process of categorizing such activities was only possible once we left the field and were back at our desks.

The abductive reasoning we used in the final analysis, where we searched for connections to theory, occurred after the longer processes of discussing, reading, and thinking. Our reflections in the field were often about *what* to pay attention to. We wondered why we found some things interesting and others not. In this respect, we questioned our own 'gaze', or early abductions, by trying to remain open to, or aware of, our preconceptions. Some of our many abductions became working hypotheses while others were never followed up.

In two difficult shadowing situations, the observed managers experienced some quite serious work problems. One manager left her position only a few months after our observation because of the physical and mental stress she experienced in her job. A second manager took long-term sick leave, in part because of a conflict with a key employee. In our subsequent analysis, we found that managerial communication contradictions, conflicts, and negotiations were important parts of these managers' work.

Our strangest shadowing experiences occurred in our observations of the subordinate role in authority relationships. In observing such relationships, one may see how others react to authority. We observed both respect and resistance towards managerial authority in the subordinates' oral communications and body language. In the corporate setting, such observations were most evident when the managers met their superiors; in the health care sector, these observations were most evident when the managers met with employees. Possibly this behaviour could be an indication of 'distorted critical upward communication' caused by fear and strategic reasoning, which was one abduction that resulted from watching these interactions (e.g. Tourish and Robson, 2006).

The research experience of shadowing gave us embodied knowledge that may be difficult to articulate and to share with others, a phenomenon that Blackler (1995) has commented on. While we may not always be able to communicate such knowledge precisely, it will always be a part of how we understand the work of managers. Thus, this knowledge is a form of embodied tacit knowing to be used as a base for developing abductions. In agreement with Polanyi's statement (1967: 4) – 'We can know more than we can tell' – we recognize the embodied and non-specifiable element in the process of knowing and in the (abductive) formation of hypotheses. Embodied knowledge or abductive knowing is therefore always more than that which appears in the mind's eye (see Mullins (2002) for further discussion on the connection between abduction and embodied knowledge).

Polanyi (2002) also introduces the term 'commitment' (referring to intellectual passions) to explain the unspecified aspect of scientific (personal) knowledge. Commitment can be regarded as the indispensable foundation of the movement *from* the proximal body *to* the distal awareness and (empirical) observation. Polanyi (1967) envisages the researcher as one who, in wrestling with a problem/anomaly, is sensitive to clues in experience. A personal commitment sustains the brain-racking effort required for solving a problem. Hence it is interesting to examine why shadowing researchers are passionate about and committed to observations of surprising facts and how they pursue these embodied abductions in order to explain these surprising facts that they discover.

REFINING THE METHODS

The researcher faces several challenges in using the investigative processes of shadowing and semi-structured observations. Our focus here is on the combination of structure with unstructured field notes, followed by a description of the challenges involved in recording empirical materials, using multiple perspectives, and developing theory based on this data. We intersperse examples from our experiences in the discussion with our recommendations.

Combining structure with simultaneous unstructured field notes

Unlike McDonald (2005), we think that quantitatively recording work activities certainly has value as a research method. Comparisons across national cultures, sectors, hierarchical levels, functional specialties, and time can increase our knowledge of managerial work. We also believe it is feasible to take field notes on how managers use their time and to make richer, more detailed descriptions of their work in accordance with Mintzberg's semi-structure (1973). On this basis, researchers can defend their choice of a mixed data collection, including time distribution, combined with an interpretive research approach primarily directed at understanding different perspectives on MWB.

For researchers interested in comparing their results with other studies, it is a good idea to consider using the taxonomy and concepts that Mintzberg (1973) proposed. Mintzberg's work is still an important and well-known reference for management research. His detailed and thorough descriptions of his research approach and of his activity categories are exemplary, especially compared to both previous and some later work activity studies. The choice of categories is important since categories form the cornerstone of the structure that the semi-structured method adds to shadowing. The structure already has some measure of abductive reasoning that shadowing tests. It is thus important to stay open to possible changes in the categories used during such research.

Mintzberg's structure of activities focuses on what is going on and what is being done in a fairly open way. His basic definition of an activity is useful in practice because it permits the researcher to note rather easily when there is a change in activity. However, other basic activity categories are conceivable, depending on the focus of the research. Based on our experiences, we offer for consideration some possible adaptations to Mintzberg's categories. Mintzberg's categories distinguish between face-to-face contacts of different kinds and those mediated by technology and conducted at a distance (telephone calls). However, Mintzberg's categories do not reflect communication activity that is temporally distanced. For example, Mintzberg's category of 'Desk work' includes written correspondence. Since today's e-mail communication complicates this category, in our studies we include both e-mails and document handling in 'Desk work'. However, e-mailing may also be categorized as a communication category of its own, like telephoning, since e-mails are often part of a dialogue, even though disrupted in time. Also, technology can be used to supplement traditional observations of computer work, for example, as Barley and Kunda (2001) propose, by printing e-mails, thus making it possible to track an entire set of exchanges. Such measures give the researcher more time to write open-ended observations, for example, of how e-mails are treated, when analysing them later in their printed form.

How a researcher defines and records 'activity' clearly has consequences for work activity studies. For example, traditionally the number of separate activities in a particular time frame has been used to determine and discuss the fragmentation of managerial work. The concept of fragmentation is complex. Fragmentation of time, place/space, as well as type of work content, tasks, or identities can all be observed (see Tengblad, 2002; Kuhn, 2006). The characteristics of tasks that demand time alone or collaboration with others, and the flow and sequencing of activities have also been usefully examined (see Perlow, 1998, 1999). Thus, in abductive reasoning about managerial work and the issue of fragmentation, the decision about when a particular 'activity' begins and the definition of its content are essential discussion points in semi-structured observation studies.

In order to achieve a balance in semi-structured shadowing, it is important to maintain the structured aspect of recording at an optimal level. The structured aspect should not crowd out the free recording of what happens during the workday. Later coding of the unstructured notes and abductive reflections may answer many questions that might be tempting to add to pre-structured recording. In the health care sector study, we found that some slight modifications of the Mintzberg method facilitated completion of the structured records with time left over that could be used to record anecdotal, ethnographic data.

Resolving challenges of recording

Once researchers have decided on an observation method, they have the challenge of recording the observed data. A major disadvantage of shadowing is that, for several reasons, it is very time-consuming as well as physically demanding (Mintzberg, 1973; Kotter, 1982; McDonald, 2005; Czarniawska, 2007). First, the quality of observation depends on the researcher's sustained attention, which may be difficult to maintain during a long workday. Second, typically shadowing generates an immense amount of empirical material, which makes data management and analysis quite challenging. These are the challenges in the abductive process where much time and energy are necessary as the researcher (metaphorically speaking) goes down many blind alleys before finding the preferred and most interesting explanations. This process involves committing to articulating anomalisms and to being aware of how the researcher's embodied abductions influence the recording.

Recording quickly and slowly, easily and with difficulties

Unsurprisingly, recording observations and taking notes while in motion requires some skill. In our studies, we found that one manager in particular was very challenging to shadow. This manager, who had been a competitive athlete, walked very quickly. Some of his colleagues even suggested that his competiveness made him increase his speed if the researcher followed closer than two steps. As our recording skills improved during the course of our research, we produced more detailed accounts of meetings, including real-time dialogues. Thus, in their planning, we recommend that researchers take the necessary time for training in shadowing.

We find it likely that our research had some observer effects. Usually, the managers' days were quite hectic, filled with many unscheduled meetings with various people. In this environment, there was evidence that the managers mostly acted automatically and habitually. Thus, in such situations, our shadowing presence did not influence them to any significant extent. However, some managers reported that because they felt somewhat self-conscious in our presence, they tried to be more efficient while being observed. However, this reaction typically occurred in situations when the managers were working undisturbed at their desks and not in meetings or in conversations. Some managers also reported that their subordinates came to see them in private somewhat less frequently when we were present.

We experienced few incidents of direct renegotiation of access with the managers or with their colleagues. Prior to the shadowing, the managers informed their units about the shadowing research, presented the researcher, and introduced the study. They repeated this procedure when we met persons who were unfamiliar with our study. We concur with McDonald (2005) that it is easier for those interacting frequently with a manager to accept our presence during shadowing. We note, however, that we did not observe meetings whenever a manager met someone who felt uncomfortable with our presence. Additionally, we did not observe managers in the health care study when they met with patients.

Even managers' slow-paced activities could be a challenge to record. One example was when a health care manager spent several essentially uninterrupted hours as she thought about and planned a development seminar for her staff. We felt somewhat like intruders into a private space when we observed this type of activity. Moreover, there was little to record that fit the work activity categories typical of faster-paced activities. Most previous studies have indicated that such slow-paced activities take place at home rather than in the workplace. However, such work may also fit Mintzberg's description (1973) of the kind of 'strategy work' that managers are criticized for not doing enough of.

We found that computerization in data recording improves the researcher's efficiency. First, typing notes on a laptop computer facilitates writing of text in the field. Second, a software database can be used to organize the text. Although handwritten notes must be transferred to a database, which takes approximately as much time as the observations, this process of rewriting handwritten field notes in digital form may offer the researcher the opportunity to develop new abductions. We believe this same opportunity exists when reading and coding field notes.

We also found that we save energy by alternating observations of the same manager between two researchers. This procedure gives us more time between observations to record our impressions and other information from the field. Florén (2005) also used this method in his study of owner-managers of small firms. The alternation of researchers improves the quality of the abductions through their articulation in better field notes used for later (developments of) coding and thus abductive reasoning.

There are also ethical explanations for the difficulties encountered in recording. These difficulties relate to the continuous negotiations about access. Because of the sensitive nature of the shadowing method, renegotiations about access may continue during the actual shadowing due to the exposure to sensitive information. The role of the researcher is indeed an important issue in shadowing studies. In her account of her experience in shadowing a finance director in Warsaw, Czarniawska (2007) writes about the researcher's problems in blending into the research context. From her narrative it is evident that the relationship with this director was quite strained and that she was excluded from many activities. Czarniawska writes: 'The main problem was that the Finance Director and I were too alike to achieve an easy distance, and yet too alien to become close' (ibid. 2007: 50).

310 The Work of Managers

We did not experience this problem, possibly because of our ages (we were younger than the managers). Our similar education backgrounds also reduced possible tensions. It is also possible that the managers saw our efforts to understand what managers do as a form of apprenticeship and a natural continuation of our studies in our professional fields. It is also likely that all these factors affected the embodied abductions rendered and judged as interesting. Since abduction rests on the importance of context, the context is seen as something positive instead of a disturbance in the inductive or deductive process, particularly if reflexively investigated (Alvesson and Kärreman, 2007).

Multiple perspectives

One major advantage as well as challenge of shadowing is that the researcher may become very sympathetic to the shadowed person's views and problems. Although McDonald (2005) warns against uncritical acceptance of a single view of the organization, her only advice is that the researcher must retain sight of the research question. This advice highlights the importance of the anthropological distinction between 'emic' and 'etic' that corresponds to the concepts used by the people being studied versus those used by the people doing the studying (Kunda, 1992). The implication is that it is good to become very sympathetic with the informants in the field as long as you are able to become more detached when you return to your desk and begin writing. In part, this detachment can be achieved by using concepts and language from theory and previous research. Also, articulated abductions revealing sympathetic/unsympathetic perspectives or explanations can contribute to creating more distance for critical reflection, including distance from the researcher's embodied abductions.

To counteract the innate danger of the single perspective in shadowing, it is also advantageous to include different types of participant perspectives. For instance, in addition to shadowing, the researcher can use interviews or interviews combined with observation. Barley and Kunda (2001) claim that while interviews are not particularly credible sources of information on what people actually do or how they do it, they are useful for understanding how people make sense of what they are doing. Furthermore, Barley and Kunda recommend the combination of field observation with real-time interviewing. However, such interviews are not always easy to conduct during certain activities because they may disturb the interviewees' work.

Another obvious research strategy used to avoid taking a single managerial perspective is to shadow non-managerial informants who may provide non-managerial perspectives, background information, and multiple perspectives on the shadowed person's work. Thus, the researcher achieves a certain distance from the shadowed manager and also acquires a greater variation in interpretation.

In qualitative studies of the relationship between work and family time, Perlow (1998, 1999) shadowed software managers and engineers and demonstrated that shadowing can be combined with other methods such as ethnographic observations, diaries, and in-depth interviews. Such mixed methodology illustrates that in case study design, the researcher may consider triangulation. For example, Yin (2002) describes this use of multiple and different sources, methods, investigators, and theories in case study research. In addition to offering the benefit of multiple perspectives, triangulation can also be accomplished by comparisons with previous studies.

In summary, the abductive approach means being committed to and staying open to new and multiple observations and explanations, no matter where or how they are found. Thus, we encourage researchers to address the potential problem of the single perspective when they develop their research designs and to consider the possibilities of multiple perspectives.

Privacy and anonymity

There is always a danger that the informants in a study may not trust the researcher. Informants may suspect the researcher is a spy for management or fear that the research may be detrimental to their best interests in some way. There is no doubt that shadowing is, to some extent, an invasion of the shadowed person's privacy. In our research, since we wished to allay these fears in the informants, we were very concerned with preserving their anonymity as well as the confidentiality of our data. We found the organizations and managers often seemed more worried about the issue of confidentiality than anonymity. Although we were not asked to conceal the corporate name in the R&D setting, we nevertheless used a pseudonym in our reporting. We also altered minor details about both organizations in our research to prevent identification of the managers. Sometimes we also changed the gender identification of the informants to ensure further anonymity.

We conducted participant validation differently in our two studies. In the R&D corporate study, we presented the managers with their field notes, timetables, and descriptions of observed events, with an invitation to comment. We included these comments in the data set and analysis. In the health care study, we presented each manager with the statistical results and asked for comments. We documented discussions of our results and used this documentation as additional data for some parts of our analysis. The health care managers had few comments on the findings, but they liked discussing the issues.

Physical resources and artefacts are among the web of complex factors that influence activities in the workplace. Information on such resources and artefacts is often readily available, even when the researcher uses purely text-based field material. However, we note that such data are underdeveloped in MWB studies, if not in organizational theory as a whole. Shadowing, for example, offers the researcher the opportunity to add images, videos, or drawings of important physical spaces. Although such complementary research methods have been little discussed in the literature or tried in practice, Mintzberg (1973) included a category that described the activity's location. Additionally, activity theory researchers have used videos, photographs, and artwork from observations of work as seen from several perspectives (Engeström et al., 1996; Kerosuo, 2006).

Thus, we recommend that researchers consider the possibilities of complementing shadowing with additional empirical materials.

Physicality

We found that the physical layout of the managers' offices affected their activities. For instance, a health care manager's office was at the entrance to the ward. As she left her door open and faced the reception area, there were many possibilities for interruptions. Another health care manager's office was behind the storage room, far from the entrance to the ward. People had to make a determined effort to find him. Despite the fact that this kind of data on physical location provides interesting information, we have rarely followed up these abductions in order to narrow the scope of the discussion we target.

Making theoretical contributions

We support Hales' conclusion (1999) that MWB studies are in search of theories that could explain their empirical evidence. Researchers trying to integrate empirical data and theory by relating them to work should pay attention to both the data and the theory (Barley and Kunda, 2001). However, particularly in the use of shadowing, few efforts have been made to link findings to the general theoretical developments in management and organizational research, and vice versa (Tengblad, 2006). Perhaps one explanation for this difficulty is that shadowing studies, such as those discussed here, relate to the wealth and complexity of the data generated. Qualitative and unstructured data require analysis that is more time-consuming than the analysis of statistics from structured observations. The selection of general patterns from the many details collected – both the unusual and the everyday – is a challenge that all qualitative researchers face. Remaining open to embodied abductions means considering many possible explanations before choosing which to apply in order to develop appropriate theoretical concepts.

In addition to the richness and complexity of its content, the study of MWB offers researchers many possible perspectives and theories since they are engaged in many areas related to managerial work: organizational theory, sociology, psychology, occupational medicine, ethics, economics, and many more. Many researchers in the MWB tradition originally viewed managers from a Tayloristic, Fayolian, or systems theoretical perspective. Their managerial expectations followed the classic POSDCORB[2] model where managers plan and make decisions, even if this model was both criticized and developed (Mintzberg, 1973). In fact, more recent studies have revealed quite a different work situation for most managers as the chapters in this book describe. While middle and lower level managers are primarily preoccupied with relationships, top managers are more involved in symbolic activities. According to Tengblad (2006), such symbolic activities signal a shift in executive work towards institutional leadership. This is one example of how other theoretical traditions and perspectives are useful for acquiring a broader understanding of managerial work.

After the researcher accepts that managerial work is a very complex issue, the question is how best to convey this complexity to the reader. Theoretical models and concepts help us to picture the terrain as we move from the specific to the abstract (this also relates to ideal types, discussed above). At the same time, the researcher must take care not to sacrifice all the details of the terrain in the quest for an overview. One way to handle the complexity of data and theory is to focus on several 'threads' or angles by using different frameworks or sections of the data individually. This approach may be especially useful in writing journal articles. However, the whole picture may fragment if sectioned into too many smaller parts. Continuing the picture metaphor, ideally the researcher needs to zoom between the larger organizational overview and the minutiae of daily life, without losing focus and resolution.

As an illustration of how empirical findings link to theory, we next describe how the 'care' concept was developed in the R&D study. The illustration depicts several steps of abductions that were followed up and developed as we organized the complex data and developed theory.

Developing the 'care' concept

After our initial coding of observed verbal exchanges, using Mintzberg's taxonomy, we developed the 'care' concept. We had encountered difficulties in coding certain informal conversational events. Such events included verbal exchanges at coffee breaks, lunches, and small talk occasions between managers and others. However, we concluded that these events could be coded under the concept of 'care' (von Krogh, 1998; von Krogh et al., 2000). Taking advantage of the flexibility in Mintzberg's original methodology (1973) formulation, we developed the category 'Care and consideration' to cover greetings, social chit-chat, and displays of concern for other people.

After our tabulation of how the managers spent their time, it took quite some time to decide how this material could be used to make a theoretical contribution. The process started after returning to the observational data. We then undertook multiple readings of our field notes and interview transcripts. In this step, we were mainly guided by the case study approach (Eisenhardt, 1989; Yin, 2002) with inspiration from aspects of the grounded-theory approach (Glaser and Strauss, 1967; Strauss and Corbin, 1990). At this point, having analysed many observations involving care, we could formulate several propositions about care. As we tested these propositions, several attempts at conceptualizations and revisions of some propositions resulted. An important step in this process of theory formulation was to present and discuss our conceptualization with our peers at conferences before beginning the journal submission process.

If researchers begin with questions, it is part of the abductive nature of a qualitative study that they will stumble on more interesting questions along the way, both related to the empirical data and to the theoretical conceptualizations (see also Stewart, 1982). The decision of whether to begin with a theoretical question or whether to search for it after the data are collected relates to the use of temporary hypotheses and hunches in the abductive approach. The researcher who uses deductive thinking exclusively – using Bacon's classic simile (1620/1960) – is like a spider that forms its web of knowledge from its own substance. This simile highlights a potential problem in MWB studies because deductive interpretations, which are more obvious, may dominate in the relationship of inductive and abductive interpretations. The main lesson from the 'care' concept example and our discussion in this chapter is that pure replication of semi-structured methods, without careful consideration of the categories used, is unwise because it reduces the abductive potential of shadowing. Based on our experiences and reading, we believe that a balance between structure and openness can be achieved using the semi-structured method that supports emerging abductive reasoning. Thus, we agree with McDonald (2005) when she states that the qualitative variant of shadowing, in contrast to the quantitative variant, has the greatest potential for extending current organizational research. However, unlike McDonald, we think that collection of data on how managers spend their time is worthwhile and can also be a part of the abductive process.

ADVICE TO RESEARCHERS USING SHADOWING

Shadowing as a research method permits the researcher to begin with the observation of a number of events for which there is no obvious and immediate explanation. Yet the researcher has a commitment to find a coherent explanation. We have described such explanations as embodied abductions. To conclude, we offer some recommendations to researchers using, or thinking about using, shadowing.

- Consider how your background affects your abductions. Begin shadowing in organizations or occupations you are familiar with. Such familiarity will reduce some of the challenges of recording and making initial abductions.
- Provide training to the person(s) conducting the shadowing. Allow time for practice shadowing sessions prior to the study.
- Use Mintzberg's concepts and taxonomy (1973), at least as a starting point, since they are established, enable comparison, and have been tested.
- Counterbalance the potential negative aspects of the active role of a priori categories and theory with a clear use of embodied abduction during the research process. Use rules of inference without absolute certainty and with sensitivity to the context.
- Follow up abductions by changing the categories or conducting multiple coding, if necessary, during the course of the study.
- Modernize the categories as needed, for instance, by including the category of e-mail as a new medium for communication in addition to telephone conversations.
- Use a computer or other modes of direct recording for data collection.
- Consider your definition of 'activity' and how that definition affects the measurement of the frequency and duration of the managerial work. The 'activity' sets the parameters for the observation's beginning, end, and interruptions.
- Include different types of participant perspectives and use multiple types of data collection, for triangulation purposes, to provide more distance and to counteract the single perspective. When possible, use real-time interviews for descriptions of the shadowed person's activities.
- Consider including abductive data on physical surroundings, bodies, and space.

- Use different angles on the data individually. However, avoid the temptation to divide the observed managerial work into meaningless parts or to construct impractical abstract models.

In general, our advice to researchers is to recognize the flexibility, openness, and possibility of developing new concepts that are inherent in the methodology of semi-structured observations and shadowing. New theoretical contributions are possible when we use interesting theoretical literature to inform our research questions and when we use empirical material as well as embodied abductions to answer these questions and/or raise others. We highly recommend the research method of semi-structured shadowing because it is the method that brings the researcher closest to everyday managerial work.

NOTES

1. Ideal types are useful abstract concepts without any strong requirement of correspondence to a specific reality (Weber, 1949). As such, they are fictions that nevertheless are not entirely fictitious because they approximate reality in different ways. In practice, both strategies (i.e. openness and structure) can be used alternately and can overlap without creating any problems.
2. POSDCORB is the acronym for Planning, Organizing, Staffing, Directing, Coordinating, Reporting, Budgeting.

REFERENCES

Alvesson, M. and Kärreman, D. (2007). Constructing mysteries: Empirical matters in theory development. *Academy of Management Review*, 32(4): 1265–81.

Bacon, F. (1620/1960). *The New Organon, and Related Writings*. New York: Liberal Arts Press.

Barley, S. R. and Kunda, G. (2001). Bringing work back in. *Organization Science*, 12(1): 76–95.

Blackler, F. (1995). Knowledge, knowledge work and organizations: An overview and interpretation. *Organization Studies*, 16(6): 1021–46.

Carlson, S. (1951/91). *Executive Behaviour: Reprinted with Contributions by Henry Mintzberg and Rosemary Stewart*. Uppsala, Sweden: Studia Oeconomiae Negotiorum.

Czarniawska, B. (1999). *Writing Management: Organization Theory as a Literary Genre*. Oxford: Oxford University Press.

—— (2007). *Shadowing and Other Techniques for Doing Fieldworkin Modern Societies*. Malmö/Copenhagen/Oslo: Liber/CBSPress/Universitetsforlaget.

Eisenhardt, K. M. (1989). Building theories from case study research. *The Academy of Management Review*, 14(4): 532–50.

Engeström, Y., Virkkunen, J., Helle, M., Pihlaja, J., and Poikela, R. (1996). Changelaboratory as a tool for transforming work. *Lifelong Learning in Europe*, 1(2): 10–17.

Florén, H. (2005). *Managerial Work and Learning in Small Firms*. Dissertation, Gothenburg: Chalmers tekniska högskola.

Gardner, W. L. (1985). Beyond structured observation: Methodological issues and new directions. *The Academy of Management Review*, 10(4): 676–95.

Glaser, B. G. and Strauss, A. L. (1967). *The Discovery of Grounded Theory: Strategies for Qualitative Research*. New York: Aldine de Gruyter.

Guest, R. H. (1956). Of time and the foreman. *Personnel*, 32(6): 478–86.

Hales, C. (1986). What do managers do? A critical review of the evidence. *Journal of Management Studies*, 23(1): 88–115.

—— (1999). Why do managers do what they do? Reconciling evidence and theory in accounts of managerial work. *British Journal of Management*, 10(4): 335–50.

Jasinski, F. J. (1956). Foremen relationships outside the work group. *Personnel*, 33: 130–6.

Kerosuo, H. (2006). Boundaries in action: An activity-theoretical study of development, learning, and change in health care organization for patients with multiple and chronic illnesses. Dissertation, University of Helsinki, Faculty of Behavioural Sciences, Department of Education, Center for Activity Theory and Developmental Work Research.

Kotter, J. P. (1982). *The General Managers*. New York: The Free Press.

Kuhn, T. (2006). A 'Demented Work Ethic' and a 'Lifestyle Firm': Discourse, identity, and workplace time commitments. *Organization Studies*, 27(9): 1339–58.

Kunda, G. (1992). *Engineering Culture: Control and Commitment in a High-Tech Corporation*. Philadelphia, PA: Temple University Press.

Kurke, L. B. and Aldrich, H. E. (1983). Mintzberg was right! A replication and extension of the nature of managerial work. *Management Science*, 29(8): 975–83.

Martinko, M. J. and Gardner, W. L. (1985). Beyond structured observation: Methodological issues and new directions. *The Academy of Management Review*, 10(4): 676–95.

McDonald, S. (2005). Studying action in context: A qualitative shadowing method for organizational research. *Qualitative Research*, 5(4): 455–73.

Mintzberg, H. (1968). *The Manager at Work-Determining his Activities, Roles and Programs by Structured Observation*. Cambridge, MA: Massachusetts Institute of Technology.

—— (1970). Structured observation as a method to study managerial work. *The Journal of Management Studies*, 7(1): 87.

—— (1973). *The Nature of Managerial Work*. New York: Harper & Row Publishers.

—— (1975). The manager's job: Folklore and fact. *Harvard Business Review*, 53(4): 49–61.

—— (1990). Retrospective commentary. *Harvard Business Review*, 68(2): 170.

—— (1991). Managerial work: Forty years later. S. Carlson, *Executive Behaviour: Reprinted with Contributions by Henry Mintzberg and Rosemary Stewart* (Vol. Studia Oeconomiae Negatiorum). Uppsala: Uppsala University.

Mullins, P. (2002). Peirce's abduction and Polanyi's tacit knowing. *The Journal of Speculative Philosophy*, 16(3): 198–224.

Noël, A. (1989). Strategic cores and magnificent obsessions: Discovering strategy formation through daily activities of CEOs. *Strategic Management Journal*, 10(SI): 33–49.

Noordegraaf, M. (2000). *Attention! Work and Behavior of Public Managers Amidst Ambiguity*. Delft: Eburon.

—— Stewart, R. (2000). Managerial behaviour research in private and public sectors: Distinctiveness, disputes and directions. *Journal of Management Studies*, 37(3): 427–43.

Peirce, C. S. (1934/60). *Collected Papers* (2nd ed.). Cambridge, MA: Harvard University Press.

Perlow, L. A. (1998). Boundary control: The social ordering of work and family time in a high-tech corporation. *Administrative Science Quarterly*, 43(2): 328–57.

—— (1999). The time famine: Toward a sociology of work time. *Administrative Science Quarterly*, 44: 57–81.

Polanyi. M. (1967). *The Tacit Dimension*. New York: Anchor Books.

—— (2002). *Personal Knowledge*. London: Routledge.

Selznick, P. (1957). *Leadership in Administration: A Sociological Interpretation*. New York: Harper & Row.

Stewart, R. (1967/88). *Managers and Their Jobs: A Study of the Similarities and Differences in the Ways Managers Spend Their Time* (2nd ed.). Basingstoke: The Macmillan Press.

—— (1982). *Choices for the Manager*. Englewood Cliffs, NJ: Prentice-Hall.

—— (2008). A tougher world: Managerial work and behaviour. In S. Dopson, M. J. Earl, and P. Snow (Eds.), *Mapping the Management Journey: Practice, Theory, and Context* (pp. 49–62). New York: Oxford University Press.

Strauss, A. L. and Corbin, J. (1990). *Basics of Qualitative Research: Grounded Theory, Procedures and Techniques*. Newbury Park, CA: Sage Publications.

Tengblad, S. (2002). Time and space in managerial work. *Scandinavian Journal of Management*, 18: 543–65.

—— (2006). Is there a 'New Managerial Work'? A comparison with Henry Mintzberg's classic study 30 years later. *The Journal of Management Studies*, 43: 1437–61.

Tourish, D. and Robson, D. (2006). Sensemaking and the distortion of critical upward communication in organizations. *Journal of Management Studies*, 43(4): 711–30.

Weber, M. (1949). 'Objectivity' in Social Science. In E. Shils and H. Finch (Eds.), *The Methodology of the Social Sciences* (pp. 49–112). New York: The Free Press.

Whyte, W. F. (1943/93). *Street Corner Society: The Social Structure of an Italian Slum* (4th ed.). Chicago: University of Chicago Press.

von Krogh, G. (1998). Care in knowledge creation. *California Management Review*, 40(3): 133–53.

—— Ichijo, K., and Nonaka, I. (2000). *Enabling Knowledge Creation: How to Unlock the Mystery of Tacit Knowledge and Release the Power of Innovation*. New York: Oxford University Press.

Yin, R. K. (2002). *Case Study Research: Design and Methods* (3rd ed.). Thousand Oaks, CA: Sage Publications.

17

Bridging the management theory and practice gap

Rob B. Briner, Lars Engwall, Tina L. Juillerat, Henry Mintzberg, Frederick P. Morgeson, Michael G. Pratt, and Stefan Tengblad

INTRODUCTION

The aim of the book is to contribute to the further development of a practice-based management theory. For this purpose, several experienced management scholars were invited to present their views on how to renew methodological approaches in management theory and on how to deal with the persistent divide between management theory and practice. The invited scholars – Rob Briner, Lars Engwall, Henry Mintzberg, Frederick P. Morgeson, and Michael G. Pratt – participated in a plenary session at the Academy of Management 2009 Annual Meeting in Chicago (Managerial Work in Modern Organizational Contexts: New Work or New Challenges). The organizer of the session, Tina Juillerat, also provides her reflections on the ideas presented in the seminar.

The chapter presents and discusses research strategies aimed at achieving a better grounding of management theory in managerial practices. For instance, the chapter focuses on areas neglected in previous research, readdresses topics from other theoretical framing and understandings, and identifies areas/aspects where empirical evidence is lacking. The chapter considers such research strategies as the more experimental research designs, the use of new research methods, the organization of research collaborations, and researchers' interactions with managers where the goal is the framing, analysis, presentation, and publication of new and/or improved research.

FINDING OUR KEYS: ON THE IMPORTANCE OF OBSERVING MANAGERS WHERE THEY WORK

Michael G. Pratt

A man approaches a second man in a parking lot. The second man is looking for something on the ground under a lamppost.

First Man: 'Can I help you?'
Second Man: 'I've lost my keys.'
First Man: 'Where did you lose them?'
Second Man: 'In the bushes.' (He points off to the distance).
First Man: 'Then why are you looking here?'
Second Man: 'Because there are no lights by the bushes.'

In thinking about how scholars study managing and managers, I am often reminded of this joke. Where do we look for insights about management? To get to the punch line, I argue we often look where it is easier to see, not necessarily where the keys are. As Combs (2010) argues, there is a trend among organizational researchers to gather increasingly large data sets; however, at the same time, the effects of sizes that come from our deductive analysis of these data are often becoming smaller. Combs reminds us not to equate statistical significance with theoretical or practical significance. I would argue further that perhaps the large data sets he describes are not where we need to be looking for managerial insights – at least in terms of understanding how managers do their jobs.

My apprehension about the utility of using large-scale quantitative data sets to study the intricacies of management and managing no doubt comes from my preference for qualitative, inductive work. I am trained to think of the people we study as 'informants' rather than as 'subjects' or 'respondents'. That is, I believe that to best understand managing and managers, one should talk to and observe managers in their element. This research approach is messy and time-consuming. It sometimes feels like looking for keys under an unlit bush; and you never know what you will find. However, I think your chances of success – of learning something worthwhile – are more likely with this approach than with a more distant, uninvolved approach.

However, I want to advocate for something more specific than 'inductive research'. I want to make a strong argument for observing, be it participant or non-participant observing. Although observation is a hallmark of 'empirical' research (even if the term, 'empirical', is often misused as a characteristic solely of quantitative, deductive research), I do not think we – as a discipline – take enough advantage of observation.

It is perhaps ironic, however, that my advocacy for observation not only comes from personal and powerful experiences with ethnographic research but it also comes from my work on intuition (Dane and Pratt, 2007, 2009): an area of research that is built on a theory very different from that of ethnography. By way of background, my interest in intuition involves understanding how managers make decisions rapidly and without conscious reflection. Such intuitive decisions may even be better than the so-called 'rational' decisions. In these situations, managers know what they have decided but cannot really explain their decision-making process; that is, they know what they want to do, but they do not know why.

In exploring the theoretical roots of intuition, I discovered a large body of research on 'automaticity', defined by Bargh and Williams (2006: 1) as 'the control of one's internal psychological processes by external stimuli and events in one's immediate environment, often without knowledge or awareness of such control'. This research argues that our lives are governed to a great extent by non-conscious processes (e.g. see Bargh and Chartrand, 1999). Claims such as this remind me of a psychology conference I attended in 2003 where a speaker said, 'I want to make the case that the conscious mind is good for something'. Whether you believe these claims in whole or in part, or in the deterministic ontology that underlies them, there is a growing body of evidence that suggests that we do not consciously think a lot about what we do. The first tests of these automaticity-related ideas involved 'relatively simple' notions, such as routinized performances and the activation of heuristics and stereotypes. However, later research suggests that automaticity is critical for higher-order functions such as goal striving, which is an activity normally attributable to managers.

If we take this research seriously, what are the implications for the study of managing and management? I suggest there are at least three implications worthy of consideration. First, and perhaps most importantly, managers themselves may not have a good idea of why they do what they do. This would seem to make survey methods problematic. Second, and in a related vein, the managers we study most in management research may be the managers least able to explain their decisions and actions. We often tend towards upper-level, experienced managers (e.g. CEOs). Such managers have built complex cognitive structures that allow them to act with great skill in relatively complex situations – yet without conscious thought (Dane and Pratt, 2007). This assertion is bolstered by the claim that situational cues can trigger even complex behaviours and that these cues may come to replace conscious thought. Therefore, watching what managers do (and maybe doing it ourselves) – rather than asking them what they do – may be a more fruitful way of exploring and understanding *managing*. A third implication, which arises from the second, is that since action triggers may be found in situations, research should expand beyond observations of managers to observations of their environments. That is, we need to take context more seriously.

The editor of this book has challenged its contributors to propose research strategies that better bridge the gap between management theory and management practice. I argue that one such strategy is to observe: to observe what managers do and to observe the environmental factors that influence their actions. Observing may be the best way to understand how experienced managers manage; and theories grounded in observations may have the best chance of being 'transferable' to management practices in a given domain. Returning to the joke that opened this essay, careful observations 'in the field' (and under bushes) may also give us the best chance of finding the keys – and if we extend this metaphor – of unlocking new insights.

BRIDGING THE GAP THROUGH THE
CONSIDERATION OF EXECUTIVE CONTEXT

Lars Engwall

The significance of context

A significant finding of the earlier research on executive behaviour (Carlson, 1951/91; Stewart, 1967; Mintzberg, 1973; Kotter, 1982) has been the fragmentation of work. However, Stefan Tengblad's findings (2002, 2006), based on new studies in the 2000s, provided other results. His data indicated that today there are fewer disruptions in executive work than earlier studies had found. A possible explanation appears to be the changes in the executive context (Engwall, 2006; Engwall et al., 2010). This in turn implies that future empirical studies should focus less on individual executives and more on the executives' organizational context. In such research, executives' working conditions could be related to (*a*) the existence of buffering, boundary-spanning units, (*b*) the corporate structure, and (*c*) corporations' external relationships.

Buffering through boundary-spanning units

Thompson (1967) pointed out that organizations tend to protect their technical core through the creation of boundary-spanning units. The task of these units is to adapt the organization to the 'constraints and contingencies' it cannot control (Thompson, 1967: 67). Similarly, executives' boundary-spanning units aim to support the leadership by their careful selection of external contacts *as well as* to produce contacts in the interest of the corporation. Among these boundary-spanning units, those for media relationships play a particularly significant role. For example, communication units today are large, strategic groups closely linked with executives that are given the task of protecting and promoting the corporate brand. Similarly, investor relations units have the important role of communicating trustworthy information about the corporation to the equity and bond markets. Government relations units have to deal with the regulatory frameworks. And so on. In this way, boundary-spanners protect executives from disturbances as well as direct their stage performance. New research should examine these changes in the micro-environment of executives that have implications for executive behaviour.

The corporate structure

However, it is not enough to look at the organizational solutions close to the executives. It is also necessary to look at the corporate structure at large. In this context, it is relevant to recall the findings and arguments of Chandler (1962, 1977, 1990), who pointed to the strong movement towards divisionalization that results from corporate growth achieved by new product introductions and geo-graphical expansion. These developments have had a significant effect on the working conditions of executives. According to Fligstein (1990), one effect is the change in the selection of executives. First, as a response to production problems, engineers made it to the top, but when markets expanded, marketing managers were promoted to executive positions. Then divisionalization allowed financial directors to advance to these positions. Given the increasing significance of the media, communications people may be promoted next to top positions. Irrespec-tive of whether this prophecy is right or wrong, the media influence may be expected to affect CEO behaviour. Therefore, future studies of executive beha-viour need to consider both the organizational set-up and the background of executives. It is of particular interest to study the interaction between CEOs and their subordinate directors as well as the working conditions of the latter. It may be that some patterns that were observed for CEOs are now found more frequent-ly among subordinate directors where the buffering support is less.

External relations

Stefan Tengblad's research also brought to our attention that today's executives participate 'more frequently in ceremonies (business dinners, inaugurations and other social gatherings)' (Tengblad, 2006: 1448). Besides managing the organiza-tion, increasingly CEOs have to act as 'ministers of foreign affairs'. Such respon-sibilities require them to work with various external intermediaries that generally fall into two groups: Consultants and Business Interest Organizations. In the first group, communication consultants and investment bankers play a particularly significant role by offering advice on communication strategies and financial solutions, respectively. Business Interest Organizations, which represent the inter-ests of their members, have, of course, always existed. However, recently they have gone in new directions owing to the integrative process termed globalization. The most significant of these organizations are no longer local chambers of commerce but rather multinational NGOs that operate on a global scale. It is evident that the interactions of CEOs with these and similar intermediaries will be of vital interest to researchers of executive behaviour.

Conclusions

This discussion suggests that future researchers should take a wider perspective in the study of executive behaviour. In part, such studies can be conducted using traditional research methods. However, these studies should be supplemented by research into organizational structures at the top and below the top as well as into the external relationships. Such supplementary research is likely to require both quantitative and qualitative data collection and data analysis. For the latter, an appropriate research method is network analysis (e.g. Burt, 1982; Burt and Minor, 1983).

We should also expect that shadowing would be a particularly useful research strategy for data collection since shadowing can identify different aspects of contemporary executive behaviour (e.g. Czarniawska, 2007). In addition, modern information technology will make it possible to more closely analyse the communication behaviour of CEOs through e-mail correspondence, blogs, home pages, etc.

In terms of analysis, a particular interest is in explaining variations in executive behaviour. It is of value to learn what effect, if any, boundary-spanning arrangements, the corporate structure, and external relationships have on executive behaviour. Clearly, we also need to make more cross-cultural comparisons. The field of management research begun by Sune Carlson in his path-breaking study some sixty years ago still has the potential for a number of interesting future research projects.

SUPPOSE WE TOOK CONTEXT SERIOUSLY WHEN STUDYING MANAGERIAL BEHAVIOUR

Frederick P. Morgeson

There have been thousands of studies on the topics of leadership and managerial behaviour.[1] This research has enhanced our understanding of the nature of leader effectiveness and the innumerable ways in which leaders can impact individual, team, and organizational performance. Despite this impressive body of theoretical and empirical research, there is a curious gap in our understanding of how context can shape managerial behaviour. This is unfortunate because context can have a profound effect on managerial behaviour as well as influence the relationship between managerial behaviour and effectiveness. Here, I explain some reasons why leadership research should begin to take context a little more seriously.

As activity studies have shown, managerial work is inherently frantic, varied, fragmented, reactive, and disorderly (Mintzberg, 1873; Sayles, 1964; Kotter, 1982). This research has shown the complexity and diversity of managerial behaviour and acknowledge that leaders are often prompted into action by a variety of different factors (variously termed problems, fires, disturbances, crises, or events). As Sayles (1964: 47) noted over forty-five years ago, the managerial job involves 'stabilizing work systems in response to recurring disturbances of one kind or another'. But with only a few exceptions (e.g. Osborn and Hunt, 1975; Stewart, 1982; Hammer and Turk, 1987), scholars have tended to ignore how elements of the context (i.e. the disturbances) shape managerial work. This is unfortunate, in part because managerial work tends to be highly reactive in nature (in response to various contextual elements). This fact led Davis and Luthans (1980: 70) to conclude: '. . . if reactive behaviors are the rule rather than the exception, it follows that theory building and research need to give more attention to the important effects of the stimulus environment around the manager'. I reiterate this call and note that some colleagues and I have begun to explore these issues by looking at how elements of the task, and social, physical, and cultural context shape the managerial work role (Morgeson and DeRue, 2006; Shin et al., 2007; Dierdorff et al., 2009). We have found that context can have far-reaching effects on managerial behaviour.

Beyond this omnibus effect of context on managerial behaviour (see Johns, 2006), context is likely to make some managerial behaviours more or less effective. In essence, certain managerial behaviours are likely to better 'fit' particular contexts. This could manifest itself in a variety of ways. For example, it might reflect matching leader behaviour to broader work climates. As Hofmann et al. (2003) found, the impact of leader–member exchange (LMX) on subordinate role definitions was greater in positive safety climates. Or it might reflect tailoring leader behaviour to very specific events in the work environment. As Morgeson (2005) found, the novelty and disruptiveness of events in a team's context have significant implications for the effectiveness of different leader behaviours. Taken together, these studies suggest that considering the contextual contingencies on leader behaviour can provide insight into the effectiveness of leader relationships and actions.

So, if context has largely been neglected in past leadership research, what can researchers do to address this gap? There are at least three specific things that could be done. First, in order to more fully incorporate context into the study of managerial behaviour, it would be helpful to study managers in situ (i.e. in their context). This has been done in the past to great effect, but seems to have fallen out of favour as a research approach. To understand the role that context might play, it is helpful to talk with managers about their specific context and how they both influence and are influenced by it. This would generally involve qualitative methods that have been used in past research, but the focus would be different. In addition to focusing on managerial behaviour, scholars should explicitly assess and explore how leaders' contexts shape their activities. This would include studying different leaders in different contexts as well as leaders as they move through different contexts in the performance of their work. Context is rarely directly examined, but attention to context can inform our understanding of leadership behaviour.

Second, scholars can begin to incorporate context as a substantive variable in their theorizing and empirical data collection efforts. There now exist models of context that can help scholars identify the particular contextual elements that might be relevant given their substantive research questions. For example, most contexts can be described in terms of discrete task, social, and physical contextual elements. Research linking these contextual elements to broad categories of leadership activities (e.g. conceptual, interpersonal, and technical) can enhance our understanding of the links between context and leadership role enactment. In addition, theory and research should begin to articulate how different aspects of context can moderate the relationship between leadership activities and outcomes. For example, are certain leadership behaviours more effective in certain contexts than other behaviours? In addition, leadership challenges arise from the different contexts in which leaders operate. These challenges arise from the team, organizational, and environmental context (Morgeson et al., 2010). Attending to these challenges and the contexts from which they arise can enhance our understanding of the interplay between leadership and performance.

Third, utilizing different event methodologies can provide insight into managerial behaviour and context. Such methodologies may include experience sampling where managers report on their behaviours over time (as they occur) and on how these behaviours vary depending upon the context they find themselves in (e.g. dealing with a problem employee; briefing upper management). Event-based methodologies may be another technique where managers recount what they did when certain kinds of events occurred. As Mintzberg (1973: 223) has noted, this technique is 'interesting and useful because it focuses on concrete examples, allowing the manager to describe what he knows best (actual events), and leaving interpretation of data and development of theory to the researcher'. Regardless of how one approaches the study of context, however, research that explores contextual factors should take a high priority given its potential to help us better understand managerial behaviour.

BRIDGING THE GAP THROUGH EVIDENCE-BASED MANAGEMENT AND MANAGEMENT-BASED EVIDENCE

Rob B. Briner

The idea that there is a gap between management research and management practice is now well established. The nature of this gap and how it can be narrowed have been described in different ways using different language. For example, Huff (2000) discusses the role of Mode 2 research that attempts to generate knowledge in the context of practice while Cummings (2007) draws on the notion of engaged scholarship. While there are subtle but sometimes-important differences in the way this gap is described and understood, it is generally seen to have two main consequences. First, what researchers study and how they choose to study it – in this case, managerial behaviour – are insufficiently informed by what managers and organizations actually do. While research produced in this way may have many qualities, relevance is unlikely to be one of them. The second consequence of this gap is that what managers and organizations do is insufficiently informed by those research findings that are of relevance. Managers do not make full use of what we know from research about the way management and organizations work.

Within management, the most recently proposed approach to closing this gap is *evidence-based management*. Although this approach represents a family of approaches rather than a single practice, evidence-based management generally involves organizations 'making decisions through the conscientious, explicit, and judicious use of four sources of information: practitioner expertise and judgment, evidence from the local context, a critical evaluation of the best available research evidence, and the perspectives of those people who might be affected by the decision' (Briner et al., 2009: 19). While managers and organizations routinely make use of at least three of these sources of information, they make relatively little if any use of research evidence.

How then can evidence-based management approaches be used to develop research on managers and managing? A useful starting point might be to conduct a systematic review and research synthesis (e.g. Rousseau et al., 2008) of what is known and, equally importantly, not known about managerial work. Systematic reviews adopt an explicit methodology and use focused review questions to identify and critically appraise relevant evidence in order to more clearly establish what is known and the basis of such knowledge. They are an essential element of evidence-based management in that they help make evidence accessible to managers who wish to use it in their decision-making. They are also extremely useful for researchers in that they help to resolve debates about what is known and not known and identify gaps for future research. While narrative reviews of managerial work do exist, there are, to my knowledge, no systematic reviews of this sort.

A second way in which evidence-based management approaches may help develop research in this field is through promoting *practice-based* or *management-based evidence*. Evidence-based practice approaches, particularly when used in medical and related fields, have been criticized for focusing exclusively on existing empirical evidence when conducing systematic reviews. As already mentioned, an important limitation of much existing research is that it often bears little or no relation to what practitioners are doing in their daily work. One solution to this problem proposed in other fields (and also by other contributors to this chapter) is to gather practice-based evidence to better understand what managers actually do as well as the consequences of such actions. Evidence gathered in this way can then be used to help inform practice. Where practices are found to be effective, the boundary conditions or contexts in which they are more or less effective can be identified. Where practices are found to be ineffective, the reasons can be further explored and alternative practices drawing on existing evidence can be developed and implemented. These practices can in turn be empirically evaluated, thus adding to the body of practice-based evidence.

A third way in which evidence-based management approaches could be used to develop research in this field is through evidence-based management interventions and experiments. Introducing evidence from systematic reviews into the managerial decision-making process will tell us much about managerial work. For example, do managers see such evidence as relevant or useful? What factors make it more or less likely that such evidence will be used? When might managers place more emphasis on other sources of information such as their experience and intuition? While, as suggested elsewhere in this chapter, close observation of managerial work is essential, interventions and experiments, whether they are evidence-based or in some other form, may also provide important insights.

Common concerns about evidence-based management approaches are that they are overly rationalistic, too closely based on evidence-based medicine where the evidence available has more in common with the physical than the social sciences, and privilege evidence from academic research over other sources of information. However, as mentioned above, evidence-based management also involves the use of three other sources of information and evidence: the manager's experience and judgement, evidence from the local context, and the views of those who may be affected by the decision. In many cases, it may be that these sources of information are much more relevant and useful than any formal research evidence. In addition, research evidence also needs to be critically evaluated for relevance and applicability. Here, too, managers' experience and judgement are vital for appraising whether the research evidence available applies to their context. Evidence-based management is about using the best available evidence. While such concerns are understandable, a more recent attempt to clarify what evidence-based management is and what it is not (Briner et al., 2009) places great emphasis on the importance of *combining* these four sources of information and evidence in the decision-making process. Ultimately, people and not evidence make decisions.

There is little doubt that a gap exists between research on managerial work and what managers do. What is far less clear is the nature of this gap, the purpose of narrowing or filling it, and how it can be done. I believe that evidence-based management approaches provide a framework for addressing each of these questions.

THAT RESEARCH ON MANAGING BE DEVELOPED

Henry Mintzberg

I have been asked to write about *how* research on managing can be developed. But first we have to be concerned *that* research on managing be developed. How extraordinary that the most fundamental subject for the field of management – namely what the job of managing is all about – has been all but ignored by researchers and by the programmes of the business schools. Sure, there is plenty on leadership – ad nauseam. But that is mostly about the grandeur of the great leader, not the nuts and bolts of the down-to-earth manager. The former may be more enticing, but that has led to an awful lot of hubris in organizations these days: heroic leadership disconnected from the requirements of plain old managing.

So we need to get back to managing. Actually researchers in the business schools need to get to managing. They have never been there.

When I published *The Nature of Managerial Work* in 1973, I could not find much research on simply what managers do – what the job is all about, based on empirical evidence. There was Sune Carlson's original study of the 1940s, Len Sayle's excellent book of 1964, and quite a lot of research by Rosemary Stewart, but not much more. (My own book gave rise to a number of studies, especially in the realm of school management, most of them replications in one form or another, but that soon died out.)

When I set out to publish *Managing*, which appeared in 2009, the situation was hardly better – in fact, worse. Stefan Tengblad was the only very active publisher of research that I found. In fact, even on such an important subject as the impact of the Internet, especially e-mail, *on the practice of management*, I could find nothing of an empirical nature.

Why? I have no idea. Do we avoid facing our own deities? (Probably) Are business schools that detached from managerial realities? (For sure – just read the titles of the articles in the journals.) Is managerial work that complicated, or at least not amiable to 'rigorous' methods of research?

Let me pick up on this last point, because it brings us back to what I was supposed to write about here – how research on managing can be developed.

'Rigorous', when used in this sense, usually means fancy, also deductive, so that statistical methods can be applied. It is too bad that the really interesting questions in our whole field, not just this one, do not lend themselves to such 'rigor'. Hence, we get so many banal studies of uninteresting topics, chopped up beyond what could possibly be of interest to even the most thoughtful managers – although the journal editors love them.

Since we have so little fundamental knowledge of the essence of managing, we have few interesting hypotheses to test (let alone the means to test them so that they produce insights, which is the real purpose of research). So research on managing has to be inductive (which is usually wrongly labelled 'qualitative' – my first book, wholly inductive, was loaded with numbers). The problem is that many journal editors are suspicious of this approach. A rigorous deductive study that proves nothing can usually be published more easily than an insightful study that is inductive.

So, how can research on managing be developed? Easy. Replace many of the journal editors with those concerned about insights. (Good luck.) Institute an 'intelligent practitioner' review of all articles, submissions to conferences, and tenure files too. (Good luck again.) Bring business schools down to earth by stopping them from pretending that they are developing leaders out of barely experienced twenty-somethings instead of working with real managers on *their own* concerns – which of course might promote a change in the nature and the interests of the faculty themselves. And then, just maybe, the latter might get interested in the most fundamental subject in the whole field of management. I wish us all a very great deal of luck.

WHAT HAPPENED AND WHAT NEXT? REFLECTIONS ON THE ACADEMY OF MANAGEMENT PANEL SESSION

Tina L. Juillerat

What happened?

As a graduate student in management (and a former practicing manager), I was surprised to discover the lack of research focusing on managerial work (Mintzberg, 1990; Morgeson and Campion, 2003; Hambrick et al., 2005). I also shared scholars' concerns about whether existing management theories and knowledge were still accurate given dramatic changes in organizational contexts (Barley and Kunda, 2001; Parker et al., 2001; Rousseau and Fried, 2001; Johns, 2006), several of which I had personally observed or experienced in the workplace.

To help address these issues, I thought it might be useful to talk with researchers who shared my concerns and interest in this gap in organizational research. To reach a broad audience, I hoped to organize a panel discussion at the Academy of Management's 2009 Annual Conference in Chicago. I was very fortunate and thrilled that several distinguished scholars agreed to contribute to the symposium and to serve as panellists: Rob Briner, Lars Engwall, Henry Mintzberg, Frederick Morgeson, Michael Pratt, and Stefan Tengblad. Our goal was to help ensure that future management research and theoretical development would be guided by an understanding of 'what managers actually do' (Mintzberg, 1990) in modern organizations. As such, the symposium was designed to both stimulate interest in studying managerial work and provide suggestions to guide future research. The session resulted in a lively and insightful exchange that spawned further collaborations, including this chapter. It has been exciting to see the symposium elicit further dialogue and efforts to connect management theory and practice.

This dialogue has generated several insights and future research directions that could substantially improve our understanding of managerial work. Clearly, we need to know more about the role of organizational contexts (Engwall and Morgeson, this chapter), as well as how managers make decisions (Pratt, this chapter). Integrating these perspectives, I also suggested that we more explicitly consider the interplay between the organizational context and managerial decision-making. In particular, before criticizing managers' decisions or practices, we need a better understanding of the interpersonal, institutional, or political goals they are trying to achieve in a particular context (Lerner and Tetlock, 1999).

What next?

Given that the symposium highlighted both significant challenges and opportunities for research on managerial work, perhaps it is not surprising that this chapter presents diverse views on the likelihood of reducing the gap between management theory and practice. The authors' assessments range from a less optimistic 'good luck' (Mintzberg, this chapter) to greater optimism driven by specific strategies believed to represent unexploited opportunities. My own view is mixed. Certainly, the challenges are not imaginary, and the next generation of management researchers needs to have a realistic view of what is possible. Moreover, unless scholars develop greater *interest* in managers and the nature of their work, a less optimistic view is warranted.

On the other hand, I remain reasonably optimistic and have been further inspired by the panellists, who have successfully pursued an array of interests in managerial work and contributed to management theory and practice. Hopefully, these role models can change attitudes about the possibilities for achieving high levels of academic career success *and* for reducing the gap between management research and practice. These authors also provide excellent guidance for current students, including research strategies and methods to learn and employ during our training and future careers. Armed with this knowledge, future generations of scholars can be better equipped to conduct management research that is both more grounded and more clearly linked to management practice. Still, the next generation of researchers is unlikely to be able to lead the way. We need more established scholars who are willing to serve as role models, provide mentoring, and pursue new research questions and new methods.

However, I believe that all scholars, not just those whose work is explicitly focused on managers or primarily qualitative research, can contribute to our understanding of managerial work. To this end, I highlight a few basic guidelines which can be applied by any researcher and that I would like to implement in my own research. First, I would like to incorporate a qualitative component into all future studies by simply asking several open-ended questions. Second, to identify influential yet underexplored contextual moderators and mechanisms, I will talk to more practitioners when both planning and interpreting future studies. Lastly, to help reduce the traditional challenges of studying managers in situ, I plan to search for innovative ways to apply newer technologies to the study of managerial work. Although researchers have discussed the challenges of technological changes for managers, we have only begun to leverage the opportunities these changes can provide in our own context.

Most organizational scholars seem to hope that our individual or collective work 'matters' (Hambrick, 1994), and we often lament our perceived lack of influence on management practice (Rynes et al., 2001; Pfeffer and Sutton, 2006; Rousseau, 2006). Is there a connection between our perceived (in)ability to influence managerial practice and our admitted lack of interest in and understanding of what managers do? Wouldn't management scholars who acquired new insights about the nature of managerial work be much more likely to influence managerial practice and 'matter more' (Hambrick, 1994)? We need to 'get back to managing' (Mintzberg, this chapter) to further develop and connect management theory and practice.

IS THE GAP BRIDGEABLE?

Stefan Tengblad

Summarizing the contributions

There are some important similarities among the contributions in this chapter. These include a call for studying micro-practice, preferably through observations and encounters with managers, and an awareness of the importance of contextual factors. Managers work in many different settings, and even if there are general traits in managerial behaviour, great variances have been identified over the years. It is also agreed that mainstream research based on large-sample surveys, using correlations between various standardized questionnaire items, cannot bridge the gap between theoretical frameworks and real-life managerial practices. This is true, not least in the sense of the so-called 'rigorous' management theory that without any evidence maintains that complexity and hard performance pressures are best handled by a greater emphasis on systematic knowledge gathering and on designing formal management routines for planning and decision-making.

These contributions also address particular topics. Mike Pratt argues effectively for the need to study non-conscious and intuitive managerial behaviour based on experience and routine. In our research, we should never take-for-granted that managers can provide accurate accounts about what they are doing and why. Managerial routines are, to a large extent, habitual and non-reflective. There is therefore a definite risk that such managerial accounts reflect more their notions of what managers are supposed to do in accordance with popular myths and beliefs. I highly support the study of non-conscious and intuitive managerial behaviour through direct observations.

Lars Engwall's contribution concerns the need to more systematically address some important contextual factors, especially the influence of external stakeholders. In particular, large organizations that are publicly owned and/or are subject to political influence need to be sensitive to external relationships. In such organizations, top leaders should devote considerable energy to those relationships in order to maintain much needed legitimacy.

Fred Morgeson continues the discussion on the importance of context. He suggests useful methods for studies of context, namely experience sampling and event-based methodologies. He advocates the development of managerial behaviour theories that integrate core contextual factors, especially the stimulus environment managers face in different settings.

Rob Briner makes an interesting advocacy for an evidence-based management theory based in management practices rather than in large-scale surveys. By systematically reviewing previous studies of managerial behaviour and engaging managers in dialogues and experiments, solid, practice-based management theories can be developed.

In his advocacy of a more holistic and practice-oriented management research, Henry Mintzberg's outlook is less optimistic. As a proponent of this approach for some three decades, Henry is critical of the general development within management research that he thinks has gone in the wrong direction. However, he pinpoints some important structural features that hamper the development of the approach: the career/tenure system that is oriented towards publication in A-journals and the associated conservative effect of the reviewing processes. Additionally, the lucrative business of promoting simplified and overly rationalistic conceptual models for popular consumption contributes to the vast divide between management theory and practice.

Finally, Tina Juillerat's contribution calls for greater attention to managerial practice that deals with the relevance problem in management science through increased interaction with practitioners and increased collaboration between young and senior researchers in our discipline.

I can only concur with the contributors' wish to deal with the gap through new and better methods and approaches for capturing the essence of management. To conclude the chapter, I expand this discussion of the need to develop a more holistic and practice-based understanding of management. The emergence of a multipolar world may provide great opportunities to suggest viable alternatives to mainstream research.

The need to establish a holistic understanding of the realities of management

In Chapter 2, Ola Vie and I wrote that acting rationally by making decisions based on objective facts is a cornerstone of the management institution and a main reason for allocating so much power and so many economic resources to managers. Highlighting the emotional, habitual, and reactive aspects of management is therefore to question the management institution as such to a fairly large degree. Thus, many managers and management educators often prefer the fairy tales of well-run administrative processes built on enlightened foresight, systematic planning, and smooth execution. As a consequence, however, individual managers may feel inadequate and therefore reluctant to subject their real behaviour to external scrutiny. Instead, they adapt to management rituals and ceremonies when needed in order to establish their legitimacy as competent managers. This requires a significant amount of effort aimed at producing various written documents and compliance with superiors' instructions.

Therefore, in the renewal of management theory, there should be a quest to find a new way to legitimize management as an institution. A suggestion is that emotions, improvisation, and reactive – or better – interactive behaviour are useful in dealing with typical management challenges such as unexpected events, open-ended work tasks, complexity, incompatible expectations, and performance pressures.

To effect such a change, we need to develop a strong alternative to the physics-inspired methodology of developing general (context-independent theory) and hypothesis testing based on simple cause–effect assumptions. If we accept that managerial processes are very complicated, with numerous important factors that interact with each other in unpredictable ways, then we need to study management in an integrated fashion. The increasing fragmentation of management research contributes to the relevancy problem since managers, unlike researchers, need to address the whole picture. It is probably impossible to integrate all relevant factors in a single piece of research, but a synthesis of various streams of research and many factors (at least) may contribute more than a purely theoretical approach focused on a single factor. Even when it is necessary to study management in small chunks, the research community still needs to understand the whole picture of management and to communicate this understanding to management practitioners. Otherwise the researcher–practitioner gap will widen into an unbridgeable divide.

The need for interactive research

The dominant research tradition tells us to ignore the impact of the field when planning a study. Empirical research is supposed to be theory-driven and context-independent without any interference from the study objects. The data should preferably be pure and untouched like an old document from the past. But our inability to develop empirically grounded theories that are context-independent is a sign that the research community alone cannot satisfactorily develop a new understanding of management. Both researchers and managers in practice suffer from the success of normative management theory that tells us management should be a well-ordered and deliberative process.

In order to deal scientifically with the high level of complexity in management, new understandings of this complexity as well as new methods of studying it are required. One such methodological approach is to invite practitioners to become 'co-researchers' who participate in the exploration of everyday management activities where reflective action, rather than orderly control, is more the ideal.

The chapter cannot describe all the implications of the interactive co-research approach. However, Ingalill Holmberg and Mats Tyrstrup (Chapter 3, this book) offer an excellent example of the approach. Another example is Kristian Kreiner and Jan Mouritsen's concept (2005) of the 'the analytical interview' that proposes that the researcher and the respondent can reach a complex and rich understanding through an in-depth conversation with each other. From this perspective, the interview becomes an opportunity that permits both researcher and respondent to learn something they had not known before. This method can be pivotal for generating scientific insights (as suggested by Mintzberg, 2009) or wisdom – both practical and scientific (as proposed by Czarniawska, 2003).

Management research in a multipolar world

Modern management is to a large degree an American innovation. American companies, educational institutions, and research institutes – as well as management gurus – have dominated for some decades although there have also been significant achievements in these areas in Great Britain, France, Japan, Canada, The Netherlands, and other countries. However, many countries have followed the American business model, with its focus on innovation, technological progress, and a consumer economy. Given the increasing economic problems in the United States with its national budget and trade deficits (and indeed in many European countries as well), combined with the rise of new economic powers, the twenty-first century business world will inevitably be more multipolar. For example, in their business practices, South Korea, China, India, and Brazil reflect a new and increasing diversity in the world of management. The expectation is that such diversity will increase the competition between different management cultures and institutional frameworks. Management educators in the future will hopefully teach case studies of corporations such as Samsung, Huawei, Hyundai, and Infosys as well as Google, General Electric, Procter & Gamble, Nokia, Toyota, or Unilever.

This increased multipolarity should also promote the development of a rich discourse in management science in which managerial experiences and behaviours worldwide are described and analysed. The American influence on management science and education will endure, but there will be other important influences from other researchers, other countries, and other models. The outcome will be the realization that management research can expand beyond a strong paradigm based on a 'Fayolism' theory of management (established in a totally different time period) to a paradigm that captures the complex and information-rich world of management. It is perhaps not possible to build a single bridge between theory and practice in our discipline, but it should not be impossible to build a strong, practice-based management theory.

NOTE

1. Although some have made distinctions between leadership and management, for the purposes of this chapter I treat them as largely equivalent.

REFERENCES

Bargh, J. A. and Chartrand, T. (1999). The unbearable automacity of being. *American Psychologist*, 54(7): 462–79.

—— Williams, E. L. (2006). The automacity of social life. *Current Directions in Psychological Science*, 15(1): 1–4.

Barley, S. R., and Kunda, G. (2001). Bringing work back in. *Organization Science*, 12(1): 76–95.

Briner, R. B., Denyer, D., and Rousseau, D. M. (2009). Evidence-based management: Construct clean-up time? *Academy of Management Perspectives*, 23(4): 19–32.

Burt, R. S. (1982). *Toward a Structural Theory of Action: Network Models of Social Structure, Perception, and Action*. New York: Academic Press.

—— Minor, M. J. (1983). *Applied Network Analysis: A Methodological Introduction*. Beverly Hills, CA: Sage.

Carlson, S. (1951/91). *Executive Behaviour: Reprinted with Contributions by Henry Mintzberg and Rosemary Stewart*. Acta Universitatis Upsaliensis, Studia Oeconomiae Negotiorum 32, Stockholm: Almqvist & Wiksell International.

Chandler, A. D., Jr. (1962). *Strategy and Structure. Chapters in the History of the American Industrial Enterprise*. Cambridge, MA: MIT Press.

—— (1977). *The Visible Hand. The Managerial Revolution in American Business*. Cambridge, MA: The Belknap Press of Harvard University Press.

—— (1990). *Scale and Scope. The Dynamics of Industrial Capitalism*. Cambridge, MA: The Belknap Press of Harvard University Press.

Combs, J. G. (2010). From the editors: Big samples, small effects – Let's not trade relevance and rigor for power. *Academy of Management Journal*, 53(1): 9–13.

Cummings, T. G. (2007). Quest for an engaged Academy. *Academy of Management Review*, 32(2): 355–60.

Czarniawska, B. (2003). Organisational learning, knowledge and wisdom. *Journal of Organizational Change Management*, 13(6): 595–618.

—— (2007). *Shadowing and Other Techniques for Doing Fieldwork in Modern Societies*. Malmö: Liber.

Dane, E. and Pratt, M. G. (2007). Intuition: Its boundaries and role in organizational decision-making. *Academy of Management Review*, 32(1): 33–54.

—— —— (2009). Conceptualizing and measuring intuition: A review of recent trends. In G. P. Hodgkinson and J. K. Ford (Eds.), *International Review of Industrial and Organizational Psychology* (Vol. 24, pp. 1–40). Chichester, UK: Wiley-Blackwell.

Davis, T. R. V. and Luthans, F. (1980). Managers in action: A new look at their behavior and operating modes. *Organizational Dynamics*, 9(Summer): 64–80.

Dierdorff, E. C., Rubin, R. S., and Morgeson, F. P. (2009). The milieu of managerial work: An integrative framework linking work context to role requirements. *Journal of Applied Psychology*, 94(4): 972–88.

Engwall, L. (2006). Global enterprises in fields of governance. In M-L. Djelic and K. Sahlin-Andersson (Eds.), *Transnational Governance: Institutional Dynamics of Regulation* (pp. 161–79). Cambridge: Cambridge University Press.

—— Associates (2010). Corporate governance in action: A field approach. Book Manuscript, Department of Business Studies, Uppsala University.

Fligstein, N. (1990). *The Transformation of Corporate Control*. Cambridge, MA: Harvard University Press.

Hambrick, D. C. (1994). What if the Academy actually mattered? *Academy of Management Review*, 19(1): 11–16.

—— Finkelstein, S., and Mooney, A. (2005). Executive job demands: New insights for explaining strategic decisions and leader behaviors. *Academy of Management Review*, 30(3): 472–91.

Hammer, T. H. and Turk, J. M. (1987). Organizational determinants of leader behavior and authority. *Journal of Applied Psychology*, 72(4): 674–82.

Hofmann, D. A., Morgeson, F. P., and Gerras, S. J. (2003). Climate as a moderator of the relationship between leader–member exchange and content specific citizenship: Safety climate as an exemplar. *Journal of Applied Psychology*, 88(1): 170–8.

Huff, A. S. (2000). Changes in organizational knowledge production. *Academy of Management Review*, 25(2): 288–93.

Johns, G. (2006). The essential impact of context on organizational behavior. *Academy of Management Review*, 31(2): 386–408.

Kotter, J. P. (1982). What effective general managers really do. *Harvard Business Review*, 60(6): 157–69.

Kreiner, K. and Mouritsen, J. (2005). The analytical interview. In S. Tengblad, R. Solli and B. Czarniawska (Eds.), *The Art of Science* (pp. 153–76). Malmö, Sweden: Liber & Copenhagen Business School Press.

Lerner, J. S. and Tetlock, P. E. (1999). Accounting for the effects of accountability. *Psychological Bulletin*, 125(2): 255–75.

Mintzberg, H. (1973). *The Nature of Managerial Work*. New York: Harper and Row.

—— (1990). The manager's job: Folklore and fact. *Harvard Business Review*, 68(2): 163–76.

—— (2009). *Managing*. San Francisco, CA: Berrett-Koehler.

Morgeson, F. P. (2005). The external leadership of self-managing teams: Intervening in the context of novel and disruptive events. *Journal of Applied Psychology*, 90: 497–508.

—— Campion, M. A. (2003). Work design. In W. Borman, R. Klimoski, and D. Ilgen (Eds.), *Handbook of Psychology, Volume Twelve: Industrial and Organizational Psychology* (pp. 423–52). New York: John Wiley.

—— DeRue, D. S. (2006). Event criticality, urgency, and duration: Understanding how events disrupt teams and influence team leader intervention. *Leadership Quarterly*, 17(3): 271–87.

—— Lindoerfer, D., and Loring, D. (2010). Developing team leadership capability. In E. Van Velsor, C. D. McCauley, and M. N. Ruderman (Eds.), *The Center for Creative Leadership Handbook of Leadership Development* (3rd ed., pp. 285–312). San Francisco, CA: Jossey-Bass.

Osborn, R. N. and Hunt, J. G. (1975). An adaptive–reactive theory of leadership: The role of macro variables in leadership research. In J. G. Hunt and L. L. Larson (Eds.), *Leadership Frontiers* (pp. 27–44). Kent, OH: Kent State University Press.

Parker, S. K., Wall, T. D., and Cordery, J. L. (2001). Future work design research and practice: Towards an elaborated model of work design. *Journal of Occupational and Organizational Psychology*, 74(4): 413–40.

Pfeffer, J. and Sutton, R. I. (2006). Evidence-based management. *Harvard Business Review*, 84(1): 62–74.

Rousseau, D. M. (2006). Is there such a thing as evidence-based management? *Academy of Management Review*, 31(2): 256–69.

—— Fried, Y. (2001). Location, location, location: Contextualizing organizational behavior. *Journal of Organizational Behavior*, 22(1): 1–15.

—— Manning, J., and Denyer, D. (2008). Evidence in management and organizational science: Assembling the field's full weight of scientific knowledge through syntheses. *The Academy of Management Annals*, 2: 475–515.

Rynes, S. L., Bartunek, J. M., and Daft, R. L. (2001). Across the great divide: Knowledge creation and transfer between practitioners and academics. *Academy of Management Journal*, 44(2): 340–55.

Sayles, L. R. (1964). *Managerial Behavior: Administration in Complex Organizations.* New York: McGraw-Hill.

Shin, S. J., Morgeson, F. P., and Campion, M. A. (2007). What you do depends on where you are: Understanding how domestic and expatriate work requirements depend upon the cultural context. *Journal of International Business Studies,* 38(1): 64–83.

Stewart, R. (1967). *Managers and their Jobs.* Maidenhead: McGraw-Hill.

—— (1982). A model for understanding managerial jobs and behavior. *Academy of Management Review,* 7(1): 7–13.

Tengblad, S. (2002). Time and space in managerial work. *Scandinavian Journal of Management,* 18(4): 543–65.

—— (2006). Is there a 'New Managerial Work'? A comparison with Henry Mintzberg's classic study 30 years later. *Journal of Management Studies,* 43(7): 1437–61.

Thompson, J. D. (1967). *Organizations in Action.* New York: McGraw-Hill.

18

Conclusions and the way forward: Towards a practice theory of management

Stefan Tengblad

Of the numerous management studies conducted over the years – particularly studies from Scandinavia, the United Kingdom, and the United States – many have reached similar conclusions. The twenty-one studies reviewed in Chapter 2 are among the most distinguished. The purpose of presenting empirical evidence of managerial work in different sectors in this book is to outline a practice theory of management. To do so, I return to the book's five themes and related researcher recommendations that were presented in Chapter 1.

Theoretical themes	Advice for researchers
1. Management as social practice	Use a different ontology and methodology than mainstream positivism/natural sciences research
2. Complex and unpredictable human/ social systems	Be attentive to the ambiguous, emergent, and unexpected. Use insights from complexity theory
3. Multiple perspectives on the complexity of human/social systems	Apply multiple and holistic perspectives
4. Professional excellence – adapting to unique contexts	Use expert knowledge way to understand complex social practices; be attentive to the improvisational character of expert knowledge
5. Research as a reflective practice	Be open to the practitioners' lifeworlds and engage them in interactions

This book presents an understanding of management practice that is substantially more grounded in empirical evidence than one typically encounters in management literature or in the classroom. The management practices described by quantitative research or promoted in textbooks are often presented in a detached and decontextualized way without acknowledgement of the complexity, uncertainty, and performance pressures managers face at work. Furthermore, the focus on reducing management knowledge to stepwise instructions that are presented as scientific findings does not recognize the intuitive and creative way in which experienced and skilful managers work (Dreyfus and Dreyfus, 1986).

338   *The Work of Managers*

The real work of managers is neither so specialized nor as delimited as management research typically presents it. While most management researchers focus on specific topics, managers, on the contrary, have to integrate many knowledge areas in their work. There is an important difference in the research that examines a particular aspect of management as a complex and varied set of work practices. A practice view of management therefore requires a more hermeneutic and holistic perspective (cf. Flyvbjerg, 2001). Work practices associated with labels such as leadership, innovation, and strategy cannot be prescribed by formula; as management phenomena, they are far too complex, context-specific, and ambiguous for one-size-fits-all rules. It is not enough that good managers possess certain, often science-based, knowledge. They must also have rather deep experience combined with a constant willingness to learn, perhaps from research findings and certainly from their actions (cf. Schön, 1983).

Measuring the statistical correlations between complex and ambiguous variables may produce rather weak or spurious correlations since cause-and-effect relationships between them are typically unclear (Sanderson, 2002; Alvesson and Svenningsson, 2003). In order to portray the complexity, contextuality, and uncertainty – inherent in the work of managers – the chapters in this book differ from the mainstream management research tradition that is more oriented towards developing abstract theories about management than with describing management as it is practiced. Paradigmatic changes occur when the gap between scientific explanations and empirical data becomes unbridgeable (Kuhn, 1970). After almost a hundred years of management research, the gap between traditional management research and management practice seems actually to have widened. It is time for the research community to question the rather naïve belief that, in management studies, a body of formal, universally applicable spheres of knowledge, modes of logical reasoning, and forecasting skills is discoverable. Indeed, we need to learn more about how managers deal with the extreme work pressure that often arises in complex and ambiguous environments where unforeseen events constantly thwart goals and interfere with plans. Instead of studying managers as unprofessional practitioners, we need to examine how experienced and skilful managers cope with the real demands of managerial work. Normative management ideas should reflect this admission. Highly competent and experienced managers prefer to be involved in joint knowledge production (Kreiner and Mourisen, 2005) in the same way that Frederick Taylor, Henri Fayol, and Chester Barnard were in past years. According to Ziliak and McCloskey (2008), management research should be grounded in empirical evidence rather than in old-fashioned, methodological rituals. Thus, the study of actual management practice should not be seen as the deviant case or the inferior approach – in research, education, or consulting.

A FOUNDATION FOR A PRACTICE-BASED THEORY OF MANAGEMENT

A practice perspective, which offers a comprehensive understanding of management as a societal and economic institution, is necessary for the understanding of how modern societies function properly. This perspective can build on the expanding field of practice theories within the social sciences.[1] While there is no single coherent theory of practice, the commonality of practice theories is that they focus on individuals' habits, routines, and (innovative) actions in their societal contexts as well as on the social rules individuals produce and reproduce. Thomas Ahrens (2009) describes practices in the field of accounting as socially embedded practices and skilful accomplishments that are influenced by the serendipity of everyday life. The actions of managers, as they deal with unexpected events, contradictory expectations, and regulations, are crucial for the maintenance of social order.

As a contribution to the practice perspective, the thirteen empirical chapters of this book plus the twenty-one seminal studies reviewed in Chapter 2 lay the foundation for a practice-based theory of management that is based on robust and recurrent findings about management behaviour in various settings and times. This foundation is built on ten theses – three theses describe the context of managerial work and seven theses depict its characteristics that, in many ways, are heavily influenced by contextual factors. Of course it is possible for researchers to expand these ten theses into various research topics that deal with management practice and theory grounded in empirical evidence.

For each of the ten theses, described in the following sections, I reference the relevant empirical chapters in this book in conjunction with some of the important studies reviewed in Chapter 2.

THESES ON THE CONTEXT OF MANAGERIAL WORK

Managerial work is subject to various expectations and high performance pressures (1)

A manager typically is exposed to pressures and expectations that may often seem overwhelming, especially if the manager has relatively little experience coping with such pressures and expectations. Many managers say they lack the time to talk with subordinates, to work with development and long-term issues, and to work with quality improvement. Therefore, since there are nearly always too many work tasks given the demands on their time and energy, managers necessarily have to prioritize their work tasks. The success of that prioritization depends on how thoughtful and thorough they are in determining which tasks are most important (i.e. examining the consequences that may arise from managerial action or inaction). This is indeed a difficult challenge almost all managers face.

Moreover, managers' work demands are often contradictory, even mutually exclusive. Shareholders and superiors in the management hierarchy expect higher financial returns, customers want better service and terms, employees want higher salaries, more personal development and better work environments, union representatives want more influence, and various stakeholders expect donations, investments, jobs, environmental action, or tax revenues. Although managers at all levels are in the crossfire of such often-contradictory demands, individual experiences vary. As Chapter 6 discusses, subordinates expect that health care managers will always be accessible, even at short notice. Chapter 12 shows the market pressure on CEOs to produce certain financial results. The construction site managers described in Chapter 7 must meet tight time schedules in order to avoid cost overruns. The municipal directors in Chapters 9 and 10 are held accountable for managing efficient administrative processes and keeping within budgets.

The studies reviewed in Chapter 2 expand the research on the external demands on managers that Carlson (1951) described in his pioneering study. In Carlson's study, the manager-directors had to spend much of their time in trade association and government committee meetings, often in negotiations on financing, supplies, energy sources, and export orders. At the same time they had to deal with disgruntled shareholders who were dissatisfied with the companies' financial returns that followed the economic destruction and burdensome governmental regulations post-World War II (see also Tengblad, 2003). Sayles (1964), Mintzberg (1973), Stewart (1976), Kanter (1977), and Kotter (1982) also report in detail on the importance of high work pressures and expectations on managers. Jackall (1988) describes how upper level managers expect subordinate managers to conceal their anxieties by always appearing positive, cheerful, and in control. Hill (1992) and Watson (1994/2001) also analyse the importance of irreconcilable expectations on managers.

Managerial work exists in complex and often ambiguous environments (2)

Working as a manager means being partially responsible for a well-functioning social system. By their very nature, social systems are complex since they consist of different value sets, economic exchange patterns and dependencies, cultural and institutional frameworks, and power relationships. Managers must both give and follow instructions as they try to meet organizational objectives and satisfy assorted (internal and external) demands – even as they try to exert their work discretion by being proactive, enterprising, and resourceful.

One explanation for the increased complexity of managerial work in recent decades is the changing role of middle managers. In the bureaucratic era, managers were mainly functional experts. Their role was that of the decision-maker who took the expert's perspective on the work. For instance, the engineering manager had a technical perspective, and the tax accountant manager had a legal perspective. Today, such middle managers, in greater degree, are more likely to be generalists with multifaceted responsibility for the economic and social as well as operational aspects of their work.

As an example, first-line managers in Sweden now help prepare economic budgets for their units, track the financial results of their units, work with development activities aimed at improving operations, and set operational priorities and targets. Concurrently, they are responsible for supervising their subordinates' employment terms and environments and for providing them with professional opportunities. They also manage compensation and staffing and settle workplace grievances. While there are support personnel available to assist managers in some of these areas, the managers are ultimately 'in charge'. Managers who are obliged to work in a 'systematic' fashion with all these tasks and responsibilities may rightly feel overwhelmed.

The ambiguity in the demands made on managers adds to the complexity of their work. Several chapters in the book describe the contradictory information and vague instructions that are characteristic of managerial work – in everyday leadership (Chapter 3), in health care management (Chapter 6), and in municipality directorship (Chapters 9 and 10). Municipal directors in particular receive ambiguous requests in politically charged environments involving legal, administrative, financial, and operational issues.

Several studies reviewed in Chapter 2 also deal with the complexity and ambiguity of managerial work – Dalton (1959), Sayles (1964), Mintzberg (1973), Kanter (1977), Hill (1992), Watson (1994/2001), and Noordegraaf (2000*a*, 2000*b*). Of these – in relation to this thesis – my favourite is the Watson study that describes managerial work as largely the effort to make sense of one's environment, of one's organization, and, not least, of one's self in a cognitively overwhelming organizational world.

Managerial work involves much uncertainty and many unforeseen events (3)

Managers experience a great deal of uncertainty in their work when they cannot predict the occurrence of external events or foresee the consequences of their own and others' actions. Much of this uncertainty stems from the complexity of their work that makes it impossible to imagine outcomes. However, chance is a factor as well. For example, unforeseen events such as personal scandals, environmental disasters, or ill-phrased public statements by executives may have a negative influence on an organization. In such situations, managers have the unenviable task of controlling results in often-uncontrollable situations.

Chapter 3 describes the high level of uncertainty in managerial work where, following unforeseen and unplanned-for events, the managers have to constantly revise their plans. Similarly, Chapter 7 deals with the uncertainty in construction site managers' work. Chapter 11 looks at how institutional changes in higher education require university leaders to act proactively by introducing new planning and control measures.

Uncertainty is also a central concept in several important studies about managerial behaviour, in particular in the managerial research stream that began in the 1970s. Kanter (1977) argues there is a direct link between the high level of uncertainty in organizational life and the behaviour conformity and marginalization of minorities and women. Jackall (1988) makes a similar claim in a study of corporate ethics. Watson (1994/2001) gives a detailed account of the unanticipated effect of a top-down change programme, intended to produce an entrepreneurial organizational culture, which instead produced chaos and confusion. Finally, Hannaway's study (1989) of managers in a US school district deserves special mention for its discussion on the importance of uncertainty and its effect.

The school managers in his study dealt with uncertainty by imitating their superiors' behaviour and by taking symbolic action. In this way, they gave the impression they understood and controlled matters that actually they barely grasped.

THESES ABOUT THE CHARACTERISTICS OF MANAGERIAL WORK

Managerial work involves a hectic work pace and long working hours (4)

As a consequence of the pressures and demands of managerial work, managers work long hours, often in hectic and chaotic circumstances. For many managers, the outcome is a poor work–life balance and symptoms of physiological and psychological stress. Mintzberg (1973) summarizes this often-observed research finding in his Proposition 1 about managerial work: 'Managerial work consists of great quantities of work conducted at an unrelenting pace'. In this book, Chapter 10 examines the demanding work hours of municipal directors who, on average, worked sixty-three hours a week, with one director working eighty-one hours in a week! Chapter 7 also looks at the problems created by long working hours and hectic working environments for construction site managers. Chapter 11 (university managers) and Chapter 12 (CEOs at large and medium-sized companies) examine similar problems.

Carlson (1951) describes executive work as physically demanding (an average workweek of fifty-seven hours with only a few, short breaks). Kanter (1977), Jackall (1988), Hill (1992), and Matthaei (2010) write about the effects of long hours on managerial performance. Matthaei concludes that office work has expanded to include work on the weekends, at home, and during travel. Among the German executives he studied, Matthaei found that such constant availability and work flexibility were job requirements for managers. In a 65.5-hour workweek, these executives spent only 10.5 hours (or 16 per cent of their time) in their own offices.

Managerial work is usually fragmented (5)

The work of managers is usually fragmented owing to both frequent interruptions and the great variety in their tasks (see also Thesis 2 on work complexity). In Chapter 6, health care managers, with almost 100 different activities each day, are shown to have some of the most fragmented managerial work situations. The entrepreneurs in Chapter 13 also experience work fragmentation (with slightly more than fifty different activities per day). This variety in work activities, with the constant interruptions and work venue changes, is an unavoidable feature of most managerial jobs and a source of frustration for many managers.

Carlson (1951) observes that the large task variation in manager-directors' work often makes it difficult for them to comprehend the entire scope of their positions. Work fragmentation is influenced, however, not only by work context but also by managerial style. Some managers are less able than others to switch frequently between tasks. And some managers, as described by Stewart (1976), are almost too responsive to disturbances, jumping between work activities like grass-hoppers, with the result that few work tasks are finished and no efforts are directed towards long-term matters.

Managers who are close to the operational level, with significant administrative responsibility and many meetings with others, normally experience more work fragmentation than managers at the executive level. Guest's classic study (1956) of supervisors in automotive assembly, where each work activity on average lasted only forty-eight seconds, supports this conclusion. By contrast, studies of top executives show that on average they spend twenty minutes per activity (Mintzberg, 1973; Tengblad, 2002, 2006). However, twenty minutes is still not much time to spend on complicated issues or problems.

Managerial work is performed in a processual and adaptive manner (6)

Most managers prefer to work proactively, following thoughtful and deliberate plans. However, they often have to spend much of their time dealing with surprise events and disruptions to administrative routines. Ambitious plans are often of little use when such situations arise. Moreover, strategies designed to handle such situations are often unsuccessful – not because they are ill conceived but because they are ineffectively implemented and insufficiently robust. The ability to manage such fuzzy work situations is probably more important for success than planning, competence, and strategic thinking.

Chapter 3 describes how middle managers in the telecom industry constantly have to respond to urgent demands by using trial and error solutions in order to deal with work complexity, time pressure, and lack of reliable information. In Chapter 7, the construction site managers also have to adjust their plans as they improvise solutions to the complex problems that are common in construction projects. For these managers, with little formal management training or education, site management is a craft that is learned through experience.

While managers are formally the decision-makers in organizations, often their main activities are unrelated to choosing among options. The statistics from several chapters make this point. The time spent on decision-making:

- health care managers, in Chapter 6: 6 per cent
- R&D managers, in Chapter 8: 7 per cent
- municipal managers in, Chapter 10: 2 per cent
- top executives, in Chapter 12: 7 per cent

Furthermore, decision-making, which is mainly rather intuitive and habitual, often does not involve a systematic evaluation of different action alternatives (see the Interview excerpt and Concluding discussion in Chapter 12). Chapter 5 describes the long process by which the decision-makers reached a tentative decision even though the significant uncertainty about market conditions, organizational capabilities, and executive support meant the decision was 'fragile'. They agreed to try the new direction although they knew they might have to reconsider if an 'error' appeared later. When no such error occurred, in hindsight the trial decision was viewed as an important strategic decision.

The processual and adaptive character of managerial work is also confirmed by several studies reviewed in Chapter 2. For example, Carlson (1951) observes that the executives of his study worked in rather chaotic conditions with many disturbances and very little time for formal and long-term planning. Mintzberg's study (1973) shows that the managers frequently have to respond to current events and situations. The studies of middle and lower managers are even clearer on this point. In sum, they conclude that formal planning and decision-making are only minor aspects of skilful managerial work. A manager's ability to reschedule, to change course, and to introduce innovations is a more important criterion for success. Indeed, skilful strategists often work in an incremental and searching way (Quinn, 1978; Mintzberg, 1994).

Managerial work is a collective accomplishment (7)

This thesis is fairly self-evident since the main purpose of management is to achieve cooperation in human activities related to organizational goals (cf. Barnard, 1938/71). Frequently, however, the focus of management research is the individual manager's cognition, values, and behaviour. Although managers normally supervise groups of people, researchers seldom examine leader–follower and intra-group interactions, and often regard followers as more or less passive recipients of visions, ideas, decisions, and instructions from superiors. In the stereotypical imagery, the manager sits in an office reading, writing memos, taking telephone calls, and making appointments. However, there is little empirical support for this image. For instance, the top executives described in Chapter 10 spent more than two-thirds of their work time outside their offices and about half their work time in meetings with more than one participant (see also Tengblad, 2002, 2006). Managers have to master the crucial skill of forming and maintaining good relationships with people (see Chapters 4, 6, and 8, this book; Hill, 1992). Perhaps Sayles (1964) best describes this aspect of managerial work when he observes that managers belong to 'systems of relationships' that are highly interdependent.

Another important aspect of managerial work as a collective effort is that managers are themselves followers, co-workers, subordinates, or group members. Chapter 13 proposes that entrepreneurs in fast-growing firms spend more of their time in interactions with employees than in control and decision-making activities. Chapter 5 uses the term 'membership work' to describe how managers cooperate, show their trust in others, and make joint contributions and commitments. Such managers are charged with the implementation of strategies and decisions that have been made collectively.

Carlson (1951) acknowledges the collective aspect of managerial work in his finding that executives' contact patterns reflect others' wishes more than their own. Burns (1955) finds that the faster the rate of change, the more time managers spend talking to each other. Luthans et al. (1988) reach similar results in their study in which managers categorized as effective interact more with their subordinates than less effective managers do. According to this study, effective managers are also less occupied with planning, decision-making, and controlling. The conclusion is that managers may be more effective by cooperating with co-workers in collective efforts than by unilaterally issuing directions.

Managerial work is emotionally intense (8)

Historically, good management has been thought of in terms of formal rationality and objectivity. This understanding of good management has been used to justify managerial prerogatives. As a consequence, emotionality in managerial work has been regarded as dysfunctional and unprofessional behaviour. Such opinions have been especially common in large American corporations where managers' ability to control their emotions by concealing them is considered a crucial skill (Kanter, 1977).

Despite this rather widespread preference for non-emotionality in management, numerous studies have described the highly emotional character of managerial work, not least due to its relational nature, its extreme work pressure, and the high stakes involved. In this book, the role and importance of emotions in managerial work are highlighted in Chapters 8 and 15 that describe, respectively, personnel responsibilities among R&D managers and strategy work among entrepreneurs.

In addition, Chapter 2 reviews several important studies that show the importance and prevalence of the emotional aspects of managerial work. Jackall (1988) describes how managers are expected to behave optimistically, as if they are in full control, even when they feel pessimistic and powerless because of the unpredictability of their work. Kanter (1977) and Hannaway (1989) also discuss the relationship between conformity in managerial work and the managers' feelings of insecurity and inadequacy. Watson (1994/2001) adds managers' feelings of doubt and anguish to the list. Hill (1992) identifies exhaustion and burnout as evidence of the high level of emotionality in managerial work.

I think the emotional aspects of managerial work have been systematically undervalued (and underresearched) compared to the so-called cognitive elements of management work. Manfred Kets de Vries (2009), a prominent management scholar, psychotherapist, and consultant, claims that managers, like everyone else, make choices influenced by complex and irrational emotions. In his extensive practice, Kets de Vries has found that managers at work are greatly influenced by emotions related to sexual desire, fear of death, and the quest for happiness, money, and material possessions. If we are to understand the full richness and complexity of managerial behaviour, these aspects of management should be examined more deeply.

Managerial work requires symbolic actions (9)

It is insufficient for managers to work only towards good financial and operational results. It is also important for managers to achieve and maintain internal and external legitimacy. Among the symbolic actions, managers need to take are the following:

- Master the contemporary business language for use in documents and policies; participate in management training; wear appropriate business dress; become proficient in the latest office technology (even if not used).
- Lead and attend public ceremonies.
- Acquire diplomas and certificates.
- Produce accounts (e.g. forecasts, calculations, and written reports) that justify decisions and actions.

The health care managers in Chapter 6 engage in many legitimating processes in their clinical work so as to avoid the perception among other health care workers that they are only bureaucrats and administrators. (Similarly, in the academic world, professors in supervisory administrative positions are often expected to continue research work in order to maintain credibility with other academics.) To influence the governing and opposition politicians, the municipal directors described in Chapters 9 and 10 use many discreet procedures and tactics to advance administrative processes. These managers, as well as university directors (Chapter 11) and CEOs at private companies (Chapter 12), participate in many public ceremonies such as inaugurations, congratulatory celebrations, organization dinners, and courtesy visits.

One reason for the importance of symbolic action in managerial work is that it is difficult to measure performance, even when managers have explicit, bottom-line responsibilities. Organization results are affected by many more factors than managerial competence and effort. While managers have no influence over business cycles and little influence over the quality of co-workers, the carryover effects from predecessors, or the competition, these factors have a crucial impact on 'their' performance. Probably, the more difficult it is to measure performance in output terms, the more important it is for managers to display their performance in input terms (e.g. their number of work hours, workplace presence, their accessibility, their physical appearance, and their compliance with value systems, rules, and requests).

Managerial work involves substantial participation in informal activities (10)

Not all important managerial work actions are suitable for public display. It is often preferable to exchange sensitive information, to evaluate other people, to socialize, to display emotions, and even to negotiate in informal arenas. Managers who participate in such informal actions often strengthen their positions in the organization, advance their careers, and acquire larger salaries/bonuses and other perquisites. There are many venues for these informal activities: restaurants, hunting lodges, golf courses, sail boats, cafeterias, staircases, airport lounges, hotel lobbies, etc. (Sjöstrand et al., 2000).

There are strong institutional norms in organizations that serve communities controlled by elected politicians. These norms require that important decisions be made in formal and open settings, for instance, in town council meetings where citizens and their representatives have the opportunity to influence the decisions. Often, however, the governing powers want to avoid such transparency; in truth, in such organizations the most important decisions are made beforehand in informal negotiations. The formal meetings, with their rituals and pretence of democratic decision-making, frequently are mere covers for the reality of the informal decision-making process.

Informal activities are often important as the support for formal management techniques and alignment processes. Employees are rarely motivated by central mandates: informal activities typically are better instruments for gaining employee commitment. Many studies highlight the importance of informal managerial work activities. Burns (1955) notes that managers are members of coalitions, cliques, and cabals in which there is intense rivalry for organizational position and rewards. Dalton's study (1959) is well known because of its identification of the importance of membership in non-work organizations for career managers in the United States (e.g. organizations such as yacht clubs, the Masons, and the Republican Party) and the engagement of managers in power struggles, resource competition, and trading of favours. Kanter (1977) also points to the significance of informal activities in a study that describes the managerial homogeneity in organizations and the exclusion of minorities. Kotter (1982) observes that 'joking, kidding and talking about non-work issues' are essential elements of managerial conversation. Luthans et al. (1988) show that successful managers spend a significant amount of time on networking and politicking. Both Jackall (1988) and Watson (1994/2001) describe informal managerial work activities in detail. Also, Munro (1999) shows how managers are constantly evaluated informally in a British insurance company.

PUTTING THE PRACTICE PERSPECTIVE INTO WORK

It is not easy to understand why management studies in business administration generally use (normative) theory rather than empirical evidence as their core foundation. Scientific orthodoxy as taught and as preferred by editors and reviewers may offer some explanation. Yet one still wonders why the practice-perspective is not more widespread if it is indeed superior in terms of empirical realism and even practical usage. The reason may be attributable to 'the consumers of management knowledge'. Although such consumers (i.e. managers) usually trust the experiences of colleagues more than they do academic research, they typically expect the academic community to provide them with new models and techniques based in formal rationality. There is a constant demand for models that seem to simplify the complex reality and hopefully make it more manageable. While such models are initially received enthusiastically, disappointment frequently follows.

Following the recognition that management is an academic discipline, an idea that has gained favour is that scientific knowledge can change the nature of managerial work in profound ways by reducing complexity and uncertainty. However, many management techniques proposed have had the opposite effect when managers in organizations employ these complex techniques for decision-making, planning, and reporting. It is assumed (and often required) that the deliberative manager will use such techniques.

Despite the often-poor results stemming from the use of such formal management techniques, managers of today use them at least as frequently as managers did in earlier years. It seems that, in spite of their shortcomings, the popularity of these techniques may be explained by the fact that they give managers a sense of security, signal their professionalism, and show them in control. For example, I have met few managers who entirely trust budgets, since they are often sceptical of the predictive value of budgets. Yet they continue to prepare budgets, imprecise as they think they are, because of tradition and because the budgeting process provides them with a sense of self-importance and control.

In many ways, formal management practices represent a better world – the ideal world of well-ordered, deliberate, and rational reality. The wish to create a better world is admirable, but the ideal management world is not the real world of managers. We need to educate students about this real world of management work practices that exists outside the theoretical textbook world.

FOUR TYPES OF MANAGEMENT WORK PRACTICES

The matrix in Table 18.1 shows how future researchers can use the practice perspective on management. This book frequently describes two dimensions of this perspective. The first dimension refers either to deliberate action that is pre-planned or to reactive action that is caused by an environmental trigger. The second dimension refers either to formal management activities (e.g. public speeches and board meetings) or to informal management activities (e.g. chatting,

Table 18.1 Four types of management work practices

	Work with intentionally driven activities (deliberate)	Work with activities that arise from unintended events (reactive)
Formalized work behaviour (systematic)	A: Classical management (Taylor and Fayol; Ansoff, 1965)	B: Disturbances and crisis management (Liker, 2004; Weick and Sutcliffe, 2007)
	Strategy formulation, planning, budgeting, forecasting, formal decision-making, leadership, Human Resource Management, etc.	Systematic work with customer complaints, deviations from economic planning, grievance handling, etc.
'Unformalized' work behaviour (habitual)	C: 'Muddling-through-management' (Lindblom, 1959; Kotter, 1982)	D: Management of ambiguity and constant disturbances (Walker et al., 1956; Watson, 1994/2001)
	Habitual decision-making, networking, politicking, dialogue-based information exchanges	Dealing with organizational problems that are urgent, complex, unforeseen, and/or ambiguous

intuitive decision-making, and habitual actions). Combined, these two dimensions generate a matrix consisting of four types of managerial activities.

The preoccupation with Type A management in textbooks and in mainstream management research is inherited from the era of Frederick Taylor, Henri Fayol, and the scientific management movement. This research tradition continued with the interest in operations research and management science, and now extends to today's popular 'computer-aided-management'. Type B management primarily developed in the area of quality management in which error reduction, statistical techniques, and formal methods of problem-solving are key concerns, and in the area of crisis management in which systematic management of risk and unexpected events is the key concern (e.g. Weick and Sutcliffe, 2007). However, this kind of 'managing the unexpected' is scarcely a key element in the curriculum of management education.

Unlike Type A and Type B managements, Type C management has not produced a popular reform movement among scientists, consultants, and practitioner-believers. Type C management is perhaps best described as 'muddling-through' (see Lindblom, 1959 and Chapter 7, this book). Kotter (1982) also writes about such management in describing 'agenda setting' that, in combination with fragmented and hectic work environments, allows managers to pursue their agendas in opportunistic and habitual ways. Informal activities related to socializing and politicking, which are often conducted in a deliberate manner, are typical of Type C management.

Although Type D management is rarely taught in formal settings, it is a very important management work practice. There are a number of studies reviewed in this book – from Walker et al.'s classic study (1956) of foremen in assembly production to Watson's study (1994/2001) of middle managers in the telecommunication industry – that show managers trying to cope with the ever-increasing complexity and pressure of work in accordance with this management work practice (see also Chapter 3, this book). Munro (1999) gives an excellent description of Type D management in a British insurance company where managers tried to maintain access to senior management in order to be seen as someone 'who delivers'. Type D management is usually learned through experience or from friendly advice offered by more seasoned managers.

There is no question that Type A management firmly dominates in management education. This strong emphasis on Type A management leaves little room for teaching Type B management and still less for Type C and Type D management. Yet, as many of the chapters in this volume indicate, there are more managerial work activities in the right columns of the matrix (reactive: Type B and Type D) than in the left columns (deliberate: Type A and Type C), and more activities in the lower columns (habitual: Type C and Type D) than in the upper columns (systematic: Type A and Type B). While Type C and Type D management work practices are often viewed negatively, these management practices can be viewed as functional responses to the typical contextual factors of managerial work – extreme work pressures, task variety, complexity, ambiguity, and uncertainty. If a manager does not know what lies ahead, careful planning is unproductive. Frequently, time spent dealing with unexpected and unimaginable events also leaves little time to plan for expected and known events. It is a very common problem that managers have to devote more of their effort to current problems than to future plans.

The disparity between how management is practiced and how management is taught is the main reason managers often find management education of little use. They rarely work 'according to the book', and when they try to apply formalized management methods, they often find them too difficult and too time-consuming. Thus, the disparity between management education and managerial work practices may also explain why many people believe the most valuable management education is on-the-job-training (Hill, 1992) and why managers so often prefer the advice of experienced and successful managers over the advice of well-known business professors/researchers who have spent their careers refining Type A management.

That said, I do not argue any of the four types of management work practices should be neglected. On the contrary, successful management likely depends on a combination of these practices – knowing what should be done, working systematically with deviations and unexpected events, and acting rapidly and opportunistically according to (sometimes rough) visions, plans, and agendas. Also, good management means being able to act quickly and energetically in unexpected and complex situations when the best course of action is unclear but inaction probably will worsen the situation. Managers should work *both* deliberately and reactively. While formal management techniques can be very useful if they are applied in a pragmatic way, managers also need to develop effective (informal) work habits so that time and energy can be saved for the more cognitively challenging tasks. Management educators can do a much better job if they balance the curriculum between the four management types by giving more attention to Type C and Type D management. Management students and practitioners need better guidance than they receive today about the real nature of managerial work.

FUTURE RESEARCH DIRECTIONS

This book presents several recent studies about actual work practices and work behaviour in everyday management. The practice perspective on management avoids the scientists' yardstick prescriptions of how managerial work should be competently performed. Instead, the practice perspective uses the behaviour and activities of successful, experienced, and skilful managers as the primary data for theorizing about good management. In this perspective, managerial work is a craft that requires experience, skill, and artistry. Instead of evaluating management techniques according to their internal logic and systematic qualities, the practice perspective is interested in how widespread certain management practices are, how they are performed in everyday work, and what their outcomes are. In viewing management as work practices, the attention often shifts from formal management techniques to rules-of-thumb and behavioural patterns.

There are numerous research implications based on the practice perspective of management. Four areas are highlighted in this section.

The importance of unanticipated consequences in management (1)

In the first volume of the *American Sociological Review*, Robert Merton (1936) published his classic analysis of the concept of unanticipated consequences that arise from purposive social action. Merton stated that it is a well-documented fact that interventions in social systems typically create unanticipated and/or unintended consequences due to the systems' complex natures. Given the validity and universality of this observation, it is therefore not surprising that managers have to spend a lot of time and effort dealing with the side effects of their own and/or others' decisions. Such side effects cannot be precisely predicted, if at all, and an additional group of side effects often arises from the first group, sometimes escalating the intensity and complexity.

As unanticipated consequences are frequently occurring phenomena in management, management researchers (and consultants) should always be attentive to those consequences and should even expect them. Such consequences may not be exceptional or extraordinary, only unexpected. And management educators, especially in the fields of strategy, planning, and leadership, should add Merton's concept to the learning outcomes of their courses. Strategies can be more or less successful, but they never develop exactly as planned.

The practice of management in the complex zone between order and chaos (2)

Modern physicists are increasingly interested in phenomena that on closer examination seem more chaotic than orderly (Wolfram, 1985; Pagels; 1988; Roetzheim, 2007). In the physical world that, increasingly, is less satisfactorily explained by immutable laws, many natural phenomena are better explained by chaos theory than by Newtonian physics. Our world has an emergent character and past 'truths' may not be valid in the future. Therefore, the scientific disciplines need to reformulate theoretical core assumptions if such assumptions are to remain viable.

Similarly, economics and management science often assume that there are stable laws that regulate human affairs (e.g. Smith's 'invisible hand', the concept of equilibrium, and Taylor's 'one-best-way'). While this assumption has enhanced the scientific prestige of these disciplines in the past, it now contributes to an increasing loss of confidence in them. For example, traditional and well-established economic theories failed not only to predict the 2008–9 financial crisis but also to explain the dynamics of the crisis escalation and containment. Theories about unintended consequences and dissipative (self-organizing) structures are more useful for this purpose. Human actors are simply unable to understand the overall functioning of their social systems, and they cannot know the consequences of certain actions. However, they can reflect on future possibilities and adapt to new circumstances. Educators should expose students to these ideas in introductory management classes.

352 The Work of Managers

Work habits and managerial practices of (extraordinary) managers (3)

Many more studies of managerial practices and work habits are needed to give us empirical evidence about the many sub-disciplines of effective management. For example, these questions need answers: How do financial managers actually make financial decisions? How are different management policies and codes-of-conduct implemented and enacted? How do facilities managers deal with various maintenance problems? How do marketing managers work? How do managers on various levels make sense of their most important problems? How do managers deal with ambiguity and irreconcilable expectations?

In order to learn more about highly efficient management practices, we should also study managers and organizations that have experienced more than ordinary success. Such studies exist, but typically they are framed in a Type A management discourse in which it is taken-for-granted that success can be explained, vision formulation is superior, and strategic plans are executed with so-called military precision. (Military theorists since the time of von Clausewitz almost 200 years ago have written extensively on the chaos and unpredictability of war where victories are determined in large degree by chance and opportunity.) Successful managers rarely object when they are portrayed as especially gifted visionaries, strategists, and decision-makers. However, in my opinion, alternative explanations of success are often more plausible. Such explanations suggest that successful managers are better than less successful managers at improvising, at learning from experience, at recognizing opportunities, and at taking advantages of serendipities. Since good luck, in its many forms, is also an important success factor, a 'guaranteed' recipe for success may fail when the tides of fortune change.

As Schön (1983) and Dreyfus and Dreyfus (1986) argue, real experts have to break free from the constraints of formal reasoning processes in problem-solving and take more intuitive and complex approaches. Such experts apply creative solutions and redefine problems instead of constructing systematic analyses of predefined problems. Management theorists should learn from experienced managers, if possible live with them (Rasche and Chia, 2009), and, even better, involve them in the joint development of management knowledge (Kreiner and Mouritsen, 2005).

An integrated understanding of management as a work practice (4)

Management is such a large and complex phenomenon that it is probably impossible to reach complete understanding of it. Nevertheless, to supplement the body of existing management theory, we need a theoretical understanding of management that is based on the actual practice of management in everyday work settings. It is very problematic that many important concepts and theories have weak empirical groundings. The managerial work research tradition has developed empirical constructs that focus on the conditions most managers face despite their significant contextual differences that vary depending on their complexity, fragmentation, ambiguity, time pressures, uncertainty, and emotional and political aspects. In such conditions, where there is a struggle to achieve legitimacy and a need to act 'professionally', linear planning approaches are rarely very useful. The analysis of such contextual differences can provide a coherent and empirically based theoretical core.

All in all, the research community – especially the individuals who evaluate papers for prestigious journals and determine the core curricula in leading educational institutions – should question the strong belief in the superiority of Type A management. Developing a practice-oriented understanding of management science means recognizing an alternative to the metaphysical belief in deliberation, stable and scientific laws, and the formal logic that the research community has cherished for the last 100 years. This alternative understanding is possible through researcher collaboration with successful managers who work in situations where competitive forces weed out bad management practices far more effectively than in the world of science where poor ideas and misconceptions can survive for long periods of time due to institutionalization.

IMPLICATIONS FOR PRACTITIONERS

Our book, which is mainly addressed to the research community, is intended to contribute to the development of a practice theory of management. However, we also think that practitioners may find some useful management ideas in these chapters. These recommendations have their source in the chapters in this book that describe managers' experiences as they cope with the complex, fuzzy, and demanding world of management.

Deal with complexity and avoid paralysis

Managers need to act practically and deliberately, even in the absence of complete information. Reliance on textbook management models in complex situations can easily lead to paralysis and inaction. Managers therefore need to embrace holistic approaches, cooperate with co-workers with complimentary competences, and recognize that actions often lead to unintended consequences. Not knowing what the consequences will be is rarely a good reason for doing nothing.

Develop an experimental and learning attitude

To avoid paralysis in complex situations, managers should know what they intend to achieve. With this knowledge, they should engage in open exchanges with co-workers and other collaborators, try solutions, and analyse outcomes. With useful feedback loops it is possible to make corrections to proposed solutions and then to develop better strategies. Messiness is not pleasant, but since management typically is messy by nature, it is better to learn to live with a certain degree of messiness. Trying to avoid messiness typically does not work.

Work with risk management issues

Managers may develop a set of functional practices that their stakeholders support. Yet caution is advised. Unintended and surprising consequences may occur since these practices cannot guarantee success in all circumstances. Sometimes there are disruptive and negative events that require immediate, corrective action. The key to good management is to recognize that while many events cannot be prepared for, a sense of the risks that pose threats and an understanding of the ways of dealing with them can be developed. Maintenance and safety work, good external and internal relationships, open flows of information, and financial reserves are examples of risk preventive measures that often are useful in dealing with, even avoiding, unexpected events.

Be aware of the hidden aspects of management

Even though most management textbooks do not write about the confusion, emotions, politicking, dubious ethics, and selfish behaviour often found in organizations, they exist, and managers have to deal with them. However, sceptical one may be of others' intentions, managers have a responsibility to act ethically. It is even possible to act from self-interest while taking a responsible attitude towards other organizational stakeholders. Although the world of management is often portrayed (in some cases, rightly) as immoral, cynical, greedy, and heartless, organizational management is, nevertheless, a cornerstone of modern society. Management is a societal institution we cannot live without.

Maintain good relationships and have fun!

The talent for developing good relationships with other people is more a factor in managerial effectiveness and success than hours and hours spent on planning, decision-making, and control. Therefore, use a Type A management style in moderation in dealing with problems and with co-workers, colleagues, and stakeholders. And not least, enjoy your work. Managers who have fun at work do a better job!

NOTE

1. Owing to space limitations, this chapter cannot present a comprehensive description of practice theories developed by Pierre Bourdieu, Michel Foucault, Anthony Giddens, Theodore Schatzki, and others. For an overview, see Schatzki et al. (2001).

REFERENCES

Ahrens, T. (2009). Everyday accounting practices and intentionality. In C. S. Chapman, D. J. Cooper, and P. B. Miller (Eds.), *Accounting, Organizations & Institutions: Essays in Honour of Anthony Hopwood* (pp. 30–47). Oxford: Oxford University Press.

Alvesson, M. and Svenningsson, S. (2003). The great disappearance act: Difficulties in doing 'leadership'. *Leadership Quarterly*, 14: 359–81.

Ansoff, H. I. (1965). *Corporate Strategy: An Analytic Approach to Business Policy for Growth and Expansion*. New York: McGraw-Hill.

Barnard, C. (1938/71). *The Functions of the Executive*. Cambridge, MA: Harvard University Press.

Burns, T. (1955). The reference of conduct in small groups: Cliques and cabals in occupational milieux. *Human Relations*, 8(4): 467–85.

Carlson, S. (1951). *Executive Behaviour*. Stockholm: Strömbergs.

Dalton, M. (1959). *Men who Manage: Fusions of Feeling and Theory in Administration*. New York: John Wiley.

Dreyfus, H. and Dreyfus, S. (1986). *Mind over Machine. The Power of Human*. New York: Free Press.

Flyvbjerg, B. (2001). *Making Social Science Matter*. Cambridge: Cambridge University Press.

Guest, R. H. (1956). Of time and the foreman. *Personnel*, 32(6): 478–86.

Hannaway, J. (1989). *Managers Managing: The Workings of an Administrative System*. New York: Oxford University Press.

Hill, L. A. (1992). *Becoming a Manager: Mastery of a New Identity*. Boston: Harvard Business School Press.

Jackall, R. (1988). *Moral Mazes: The World of Corporate Managers*. New York: Oxford University Press.

Kanter, R. M. (1977). *Men and Women of the Corporation*. New York: Basic Books.

Kets de Vries, M. (2009). *Sex, Money, Happiness and Death*. Houndmills, Basingstoke, Hampshire, UK: Palgrave Macmillan.

Kotter, J. P. (1982). What leaders really do. *Harvard Business Review*, 60(3): 156–67.

Kreiner, K. and Mouritsen, J. (2005). The analytical interview. In S. Tengblad, B. Czarniawska, and R. Solli (Eds.), *The Art of Science*. Copenhagen: Liber and Copenhagen Business Press.

Kuhn, T. S. (1970). *The Structure of Scientific Revolutions*. Chicago: University of Chicago Press.

Liker, J. K. (2004). *The Toyota Way: 14 Management Principles from the World's Greatest Manufacturer*. New York: McGraw-Hill.

Lindblom, C. E. (1959). The science of muddling through. *Public Administration Review*, 19(2): 79–88.

Luthans, F., Hodgetts, R. M., and Rosenkrantz, S. A. (1988). *Real Managers*. Cambridge, MA: Ballinger.

Matthaei, E. (2010). *The Nature of Executive Work*. Wiesbaden, Germany: Gabler.

Merton, R. K. (1936). The Unanticipated Consequences of Purposive Social Action. *American Sociological Review*, 1(6): 894–904.

Mintzberg, H. (1973). *The Nature of Managerial Work*. New York: Harper & Row, Publishers.

—— (1994). The fall and rise of strategic planning. *Harvard Business Review*, January–February: 107–14.

Munro, R. (1999). The cultural performance of control. *Organization Studies*, 20(4): 619–40.

Noordegraaf, M. (2000a). *Attention! Work and Behavior of Public Managers Amidst Ambiguity*. Delft: Eburon.

—— (2000b). Professional sense-makers: Managerial competencies amidst ambiguity. *The International Journal of Public Sector Management*, 13(4): 319–32.

Pagels, H. (1988). *The Dreams of Reason. The Computer and the Rise of the Sciences of Complexity*. New York: Bantam Books.

Quinn, J. B. (1978). Strategic change: Logical incrementalism. *Sloan Management Review*, 20(1): 7–19.

Rasche, A. and Chia, R. (2009). Researching strategy practices: A genealogical social theory perspective. *Organization Studies*, 30(7): 713–34.

Roetzheim, W. (2007). *Why Things Are. How Complexity Theory Answers Life's Toughest Questions*. Jamul, CA: Level 4 Press.

Sanderson, I. (2002). *Evaluating Complexity: Theory, Evidence and Practical Guidance*. Paper for the Symposium on 'Theory-Based Evaluation', European Evaluation Society, Seville, Spain, October 10–12, 2002.

Sayles, L. R. (1964). *Managerial Behavior: Administration in Complex Organisations*. New York: McGraw-Hill.

Schatzki, T., Knorr Cetina, K., and von Savigny, E. (Eds.) (2001). *The Practice Turn in Contemporary Theory*. London: Routledge.

Schön, D. (1983). *The Reflective Practitioner*. New York: Basic Books.

Sjöstrand, S-E., Sandberg, J., and Tyrstrup, M. (Eds.) (2000). *Invisible Management. The Social Construction of Leadership*. London: Thomson Learning.

Stewart, R. (1976). *Contrasts in Management*. Maidenhead: McGraw-Hill Book Company.

Tengblad, S. (2002). Time and space in managerial work. *Scandinavian Journal of Management*, 18: 543–65.

—— (2003). Classic, but not seminal: Revisiting the pioneering study of managerial work. *Scandinavian Journal of Management*, 19(1): 85–101.

—— (2006). Is there a 'New Managerial Work'? A comparison with Henry Mintzberg's classic study 30 years later. *Journal of Management Studies*, 43(7): 1437–61.

Walker, C. R., Guest, R. H., and Turner, A. N. (1956). *The Foreman on the Assembly Line*. Cambridge, MA: Harvard University Press.

Watson, T. J. (1994/2001). *In Search of Management: Culture, Chaos and Control in Managerial Work* (Rev. ed.). London: Thomson Learning.

Weick, K. E. and Suthcliffe, K. M. (2007). *Managing the Unexpected*. San Francisco, CA: Jossey-Bass.

Wolfram, S. (1985). Undecidability and intractability in theoretical physics. *Physical Review Letters*, 45: 735–8.

Ziliak, S. T. and McCloskey, D. N. (2008). *The Cult of Statistical Significance*. Ann Arbor, MI: University of Michigan.

Index